SYSTEMIC ECONOMIC OFFENCES AS INTERNATIONAL CRIMES

This open access book asks whether systemic economic offences can qualify as international crimes and be prosecuted as such.

Taking a four-part approach to the question, it traces the origins of the concept of international economic crime, and draws the line between ordinary economic crimes and economic offences of international significance. To this end, it examines six cases involving the commission of serious economic crimes in different regions of the world, including Europe, the Americas and Africa: the crime of grand corruption in the *Petrobras* case; the theft of natural resources in the Niger Delta region and Liberia; the international money-laundering scheme in the *Bolichicos* case; the crime of financing terrorism in the *Chiquita* case; the *Volkswagen* conspiracy case in the US and the *Haarde* case related to gross-negligence in preventing serious economic damage. It then goes on to discuss a potential sui generis category of international economic crimes, before considering the advantages and the challenges of the multilevel enforcement system of international criminal justice in prosecuting such crimes.

This book provides an innovative and original avenue for the analysis of a controversial and yet overlooked topic in international criminal law.

Volume 102 in the series Studies in International Law

Studies in International Law

Recent titles in this series

South-South Migrations and the Law from Below:
Case Studies on China and Nigeria
Oreva Olakpe

Territorial Status in International Law
Jure Vidmar

Marine Bioprospecting, Biodiversity and Novel Uses of
Ocean Resources: New Approaches in International Law
Edited by Niels Krabbe and David Langlet

The Standard of Review Before the International Court of Justice:
Between Principle and Pragmatism
Felix Fouchard

Global Lawmaking and Social Change: The Varieties of Customary
International Law
Gregor Novak

The Effectiveness of the Inter-American Court of Human Rights:
The Case of Indigenous Territorial Rights
Gabriela CB Navarro

Individuals in International Humanitarian Law: A Historical Analysis
Sarina Landefeld

The Pathology of Plenty: Natural Resources in International Law
Lys Kulamadayil

The United Nations Security Council and the Authorisation of Force:
Form, Character and Nature
Marko Svicevic

Protecting the Right to Leave in an Era of Externalised Migration Control
Emilie McDonnell

Pluralising Actors and Norms in Human Rights Treaties:
Beyond Monolithic States
Hinako Takata

Systemic Economic Offences as International Crimes:
Theorising a New Paradigm of Mass Criminality
Nicole Citeroni

For a complete list of titles in this series
see www.bloomsbury.com/uk/series/studies-in-international-law/

Systemic Economic Offences as International Crimes

Theorising a New Paradigm of Mass Criminality

Nicole Citeroni

•HART•

OXFORD • LONDON • NEW YORK • NEW DELHI • SYDNEY

HART PUBLISHING

Bloomsbury Publishing Plc

Kemp House, Chawley Park, Cumnor Hill, Oxford, OX2 9PH, UK

1385 Broadway, New York, NY 10018, USA

Bloomsbury Publishing Ireland Limited, 29 Earlsfort Terrace, Dublin 2, D02 AY28, Ireland

HART PUBLISHING, the Hart/Stag logo, BLOOMSBURY and the Diana logo are trademarks of Bloomsbury Publishing Plc

First published in Great Britain 2026

A catalogue record for this book is available from the British Library.

A catalogue record for this book is available from the Library of Congress.

ISBN: HB: 978-1-50998-659-0
ePDF: 978-1-50998-661-3
ePub: 978-1-50998-660-6

Typeset by Compuscript Ltd, Shannon

To my parents, Rosita and Giuseppe

To my brother, Roberto

Acknowledgements

THIS BOOK WOULD not have been possible without the guidance and support of many people and institutions. I am extremely grateful to my doctoral supervisor, Prof Stefan Braum, who constantly encouraged me to develop the ideas contained in the thesis that served as the basis for this book and taught me the importance of always taking a critical approach to the analysis of law.

Special thanks go to my postdoctoral supervisor, Dr Britta Sjöstedt, for her invaluable advice and trust in my research projects.

I am also deeply grateful to Prof Isabelle Riassetto, Prof Matthew Happold, and Prof Christoph Safferling, for their comments, constructive criticism and guidance during my doctoral studies and defence.

I particularly thank Prof Adán Nieto Martín for his insightful comments on the draft chapters of the thesis during my research stay at Universidad de Castilla-La Mancha and for his constant support of my research.

I would like to express my sincere gratitude to Judge Rosario Salvatore Aitala for his dedicated mentoring during my time as an intern and as a visiting professional at the International Criminal Court.

I am immensely grateful to Francesco Rossi, for his comments, meticulous revisions, and unconditional support.

I wholeheartedly thank a host of inspiring friends, colleagues and professors that I had the privilege of meeting at the University of Luxembourg, at Universidad de Castilla-La Mancha, at Lund University, and at the International Criminal Court. Each of them enriched me both professionally and personally during the drafting of this book.

I am also grateful to Lund University, Formas (Swedish Research Council for Sustainable Development), the University of Luxembourg, the Luxembourg National Research Fund (FNR), the Fondation Jacqueline NOEL, and the Fondation de Luxembourg, for financially assisting my research over the past few years.

Contents

Abbreviations

AEC	ASEAN Economic Community
ACHPR	African Charter on Human and Peoples' Rights
ACtJHR	African Court of Justice and Human Rights
ASEAN	Association of Southeast Asian Nations
BHR	Business and Human Rights
CCL	Control Council Law
COPLA	*Corte penal latinoamericana y del Caribe contra el crimen transnacional organizado*
CSO	Civil Society Organisation
ECCC	Extraordinary Chambers in the Courts of Cambodia
ECHR	European Convention on Human Rights
ECtHR	European Court of Human Rights
EPA	Environmental Protection Agency
FARC-EP	Revolutionary Armed Forces of Colombia
FIDH	*Fédération Internationale des Ligues des Droits de l'Hommes*
GDR	German Democratic Republic
HRC	Human Rights Committee
IAC	international armed conflict
ICC	International Criminal Court
ICCPR	International Covenant on Civil and Political Rights
ICD	International Crimes Division
ICESCR	International Covenant on Economic, Social and Cultural Rights
ICJ	International Court of Justice
ICL	international criminal law
ICTR	International Criminal Tribunal for Rwanda
ICTY	International Criminal Tribunal for the former Yugoslavia

ILC	International Law Commission
IMT	International Military Tribunal
IMTFE	International Military Tribunal for the Far East
JEP	*Jurisdicción Especial para la Paz*
LRA	Lord Resistance Army
MBS	mortgage-backed securities
MICT	International Residual Mechanism for Criminal Tribunals
NGOs	non-governmental organisations
NIAC	non-international armed conflict
OCCRP	Organized Crime and Corruption Reporting Project
OTP	Office of the Prosecutor
OWEC-L	Office for the War and Economic Crimes Court of Liberia
PDVSA	*Petróleos de Venezuela*
RPE	Rule of Procedure and Evidence
RTLM	*Radio Télévision Libre des Milles Collines*
RUF	Revolutionary United Front
SCSL	Special Court for Sierra Leone
SDGs	Sustainable Development Goals
SS	*Schutzstaffel*
STL	Special Tribunal for Lebanon
TRC	Truth and Reconciliation Commission
TFV	Trust Fund for Victims
UDHR	Universal Declaration of Human Rights
UN	United Nations
UNCAC	United Nations Convention against Corruption
UNODC	United Nations Office on Drugs and Crime
UNEP	United Nations Environment Programme
US	United States
UNWCC	United Nations War Crimes Commission

Table of Cases and Documents

International Criminal Court Decisions

International Criminal Tribunal for Rwanda Decisions

International Criminal Tribunal for the Former Yugoslavia Decisions

Other International and National Court Decisions

Treaties

United Nations Documents

Other International Documents

1

Introduction

OVER THE CENTURIES, human beings have witnessed countless episodes of wars, atrocities and mass violence that have been recorded in the collective memory of humanity until new unimaginable crimes were conceived and perpetrated. This 'replacement mechanism' has allowed only the most recent atrocious events to be preserved within the narrow confines of collective memory. In this sense, the advent of international criminal law (ICL) has been revolutionary, as it has helped to fill in the gaps left in the collective memory, by addressing the identification, prevention, and punishment of crimes that 'shock the conscience of humanity'[1] at any time in history.[2]

The twentieth century was indelibly marked by the tragical occurrences of the First and Second World Wars, while the beginning of the new century has given us a world in which conflicts and mass violence are systematically perpetrated in a sort of 'piecemeal Third World War', to quote Pope Francis.[3] Today, human rights are threatened and violated in new ways that may escape the paradigms of international criminality created to respond to past atrocities. To give a concrete example, one of the most significant events of the twenty-first century from a historical, economic, and social point of view was the global financial crisis of 2007–2008, which has raised awareness of the fact that economic power, systematically exacerbated by institutional and political structures, can cause international harm and have a negative impact on human rights. Nonetheless, economic crimes resulting from a system that allows such harm to occur are not yet classified as international crimes.

For a large group of scholars and civil society, the need to address this *lacuna* has become increasingly urgent, considering the complexity and interconnectedness of postmodern globalised society, which have strongly influenced the way economic crimes are perpetrated as well as their gravity. In other words, completely excluding economic crimes of international significance from the

[1] Preamble of the Rome Statute of the International Criminal Court (Rome, 17 July 1998) (also known as the ICC Statute).

[2] On the evolution of international criminal law, see TLH McCormack, 'From Sun Tzu to the Sixth Committee: The Evolution of an International Criminal Law Regime' in TLH McCormack and GJ Simpson (eds), *The Law of War Crimes: National and International Approaches* (Kluwer Law International, 1997) 31.

[3] 'Pope Francis warns on "piecemeal World War III"' (*BBC News*, 13 September 2014) https://www.bbc.com/news/world-europe-29190890.

scope of the most serious crimes of concern to the international community would mean replicating the mechanism that for centuries has made collective memory defective. This scenario would defeat the purposes of international criminal law to prevent and punish all crimes considered most serious at any given time and in any given place.

This book thus aims to draw the attention of the scientific community and public opinion to the gravity of international economic crimes in order to give them the value and space they deserve in our collective memory and in international law.

DOCTRINAL FOUNDATIONS AND SCHOLARLY DEBATES

The absence, among international crimes, of economic crimes capable of causing international harm has received critical attention. Over the past two decades, a growing number of scholars has recognised the importance of reflecting on this topic, thus contributing to a deeper understanding of a series of controversial legal issues that form the basis and the starting point of this research. These issues include the role of economic private actors in the commission of international crimes, which has been examined in several studies. Among them, Baars provided a thought-provoking and well-documented account of the Nuremberg trials and subsequent proceedings, focusing on the economic actors and the crimes they committed.[4] However, although extensive research has been carried out on these actors' involvement as accessories, limited attention has been paid to their role as principal perpetrators of international crimes.

Furthermore, a significant number of scholars, including Roksandić Vidlička and Arenal Lora, undertook a thorough and comprehensive review of the contextual elements of crimes against humanity, as defined in the Rome Statute (the 'Statute' or the 'ICC Statute'), to determine whether this category can be used to prosecute serious economic crimes.[5] Nonetheless, the concept of international economic crime as an autonomous category of international crimes has not been explored in depth in legal doctrine,[6] although similar concepts have been discussed both in the legal field, such as the notions of 'patrimonicide' and

[4] G Baars, *The Corporation, Law and Capitalism: A Radical Perspective on the Role of Law in The Global Political Economy*, Historical Materialism Book Series 188 (Brill, 2019).

[5] S Roksandić Vidlička, *Prosecuting Serious Economic Crimes as International Crimes – a New Mandate for the ICC?*, Research Series of the Max Planck Institute for Foreign and International Criminal Law Series BC: Publications of the Max Planck Partner Group for Balkan Criminology 2 (Duncker & Humblot, 2017); L Arenal Lora, *Crímenes económicos en derecho internacional: Propuesta de una nueva categoría de crímenes contra la humanidad* (Editorial Aranzadi, 2019).

[6] An exception is the proposal to recognise the crime of '*expolio de riquezas*' ('plunder of wealth') elaborated in MA Castillo-Monterrey, 'Contornos de un "modelo tipo" de expolio de las riquezas de las naciones como crimen de Derecho Internacional' (2017) 1 *Revista de derecho de la facultad de ciencias jurídicas y sociales UNAN-Léon*, 203.

'economicide' proposed by Kofele-Kale and Zaffaroni respectively,[7] and in the criminological field, such as the concepts of 'state-corporate crime' proposed by Kramer and Michalowski,[8] and of 'crime of maldevelopment' proposed by Böhm.[9]

Another issue relating to the inclusion of economic crimes in the Rome Statute that has received limited scholarly attention to date concerns the enforcement challenges that the prosecution of the most serious economic crimes before the International Criminal Court (ICC or 'the Court') could entail.[10] With a few exceptions,[11] no detailed investigation has been conducted into alternative solutions to the ICC that could enable the prosecution of the most serious economic crimes at supranational level.

Two other aspects relevant to this study have been examined in the literature but require further investigation. On the one hand, emphasis should be placed on the impunity of perpetrators of serious forms of economic crimes resulting from the inability or unwillingness of national jurisdictions to tackle such crimes. On the other hand, although scholars have long debated the impact of serious economic crimes on human rights,[12] more sustained research is needed to bring to light the overlap between these offences and gross violations of human rights.

In light of the above, although considerable progress has been made in this field of research, studies remain in their infancy. This book thus aims to build on existing knowledge and literature to provide new perspectives on the issue of including serious economic crimes that violate fundamental values and human rights in the list of crimes that 'shock the conscience of humanity'.

The book also addresses opposing views, including those arguing that economic crimes are non-violent in nature, which would make it difficult and almost artificial to link them to international crimes, as well as the sceptical view that broadening the scope of international criminal law to include serious economic crimes would mean not only distorting the concept of international crime but also pursuing a utopian project. A third concern addressed in the book relates to the normative value of classifying economic

[7] N Kofele-Kale, *The International Law of Responsibility for Economic Crimes: Holding State Officials Individually Liable for Acts of Fraudulent Enrichment* (Ashgate, 2006); N Kofele-Kale, 'Only Fools Who Send Hyenas to Roast Meat for Them: In Search of the Doctrinal Foundations of the Not-So-Ordinary Crime of Patrimonicide' (2013) 9 *Florida A&M University Law Review* 1; ER Zaffaroni, '¿Por qué no un delito de economicidio?' (*La Tecla Eñe*, 2021) https://lateclaenerevista.com/por-que-no-un-delito-de-economicidio-por-e-raul-zaffaroni/.

[8] RJ Michalowski and RC Kramer, *State-Corporate Crime: Wrongdoing at the Intersection of Business and Government* (Rutgers University Press, 2006).

[9] ML Böhm, *The Crime of Maldevelopment: Economic Deregulation and Violence in the Global South* (Routledge, 2019).

[10] N Citeroni, 'International Economic Crimes in the Rome Statute? Reflections on Multilevel Enforcement of International Criminal Law' in K Ligeti and KH Brodersen (eds), *Studies on Enforcement in Multilevel Regulatory Systems* (Nomos, 2022) 239.

[11] See Roksandić Vidlička, *Prosecuting Serious Economic Crimes.*

[12] E Schmid, *Taking Economic, Social and Cultural Rights Seriously in International Criminal Law* (Cambridge University Press, 2015).

crimes as international crimes in an area of law characterised by a crisis of over-criminalisation.

PURPOSE AND SCOPE OF THE BOOK

This book aims to determine whether and, if so, to what extent serious economic crimes committed in certain contexts can be qualified as international crimes and prosecuted as such. The central hypothesis of this book is that nowadays certain economic offences are perpetrated in contexts that make them internationally relevant, which implies the need to rethink the concept of international crime from a contemporary perspective. To answer the research question and test the validity of the hypothesis, the book addresses the following sub-questions:

(i) 'Where' does the concept of international economic crime come from?
(ii) 'Why' should serious economic crimes be included among the 'most serious crimes of international concern'?
(iii) 'What' would be the constituent elements of the concept of international economic crime?
(iv) 'How' could international economic crimes be prosecuted in the current multilevel system of international criminal justice?

In answering these questions, the book explores issues that have been addressed in the literature but that require further investigation. By analysing the genesis and evolution of the concept of international economic crime in international criminal law, both the ancillary and the principal roles of private actors in the commission of international crimes are examined. The second sub-question allows addressing the issue of the gravity of economic crimes and thus their potential to overlap with serious violations of human rights. In response to the third sub-question, the book delves into the analysis of the constituent elements of an autonomous category of international economic crime, while the problem of domestic impunity for serious economic crimes and the challenges that the Rome Statute would pose to their prosecution are scrutinised in response to the fourth sub-question.

The scope of this book is limited to examining the concept of international economic crimes within the existing framework of international criminal law and the principles governing this branch of law, including the principle of legality and that of individual criminal responsibility. This means that, despite references to the involvement of corporations in the commission of international economic crimes, this research will focus on individuals as criminal agents and will not address the issue of corporate criminal responsibility, on which much has already been said elsewhere.[13] Furthermore, this book concerns criminal

[13] Baars, *The Corporation, Law and Capitalism* 282–308, proposing to remake international criminal law by shifting the focus from individual businessmen to corporations as perpetrators of international crimes. See also, in favour of corporate criminal responsibility for international crimes,

responses to serious forms of economic crimes, leaving aside issues related to the potential of civil and administrative mechanisms to deal with them.

A FOUR-STEP METHODOLOGICAL APPROACH TO THE ANALYSIS OF ECONOMIC CRIMES AS INTERNATIONAL CRIMES

The book adopts a four-step methodological approach to answer the research question, with each step corresponding to one of the four main chapters addressing a sub-question. This is an innovative method compared to the one traditionally applied by most scholars in this field. The traditional method involves three main steps: (i) identifying one or more economic crimes; (ii) analysing the gravity of the effects of these crimes; and (iii) suggesting their inclusion in existing categories of international crimes, in particular crimes against humanity.

Despite its merits, this approach does not justify the distinction between, on the one hand, one or more economic crimes that deserve to be qualified as international crimes and, on the other hand, other equally serious economic crimes. Another flaw in the traditional approach is that it focuses on the severity of the harm caused by economic crimes, neglecting the gravity of the context in which these offences are committed. Furthermore, unlike previous studies on the subject, the four-step approach emphasises that the gravity test is necessary but not sufficient to justify the international criminalisation and prosecution of serious economic crimes, as the principle of legality also plays a crucial role when suggesting the inclusion of these offences in existing categories of international crimes or as an autonomous category.

As regards the order of the four steps, the decision to address the sub-question pertaining to the origin of the concept of international economic crime in Chapter 2 stems from the dual need to trace the evolution of this concept since the emergence of international criminal law and to provide a comprehensive historical and legal framework that lays the foundations for the key arguments developed in Chapter 3.

In replying to the sub-question of why certain economic crimes should be included among the 'most serious crimes of international concern', Chapter 3 is structured around a legal syllogism, involving de jure and de facto considerations.

J Kyriakakis, *Corporations, Accountability and International Criminal Law: Industry and Atrocity* (Edward Elgar Publishing, 2021); W Kaleck and M Saage-Maaß, 'Corporate Accountability for Human Rights Violations Amounting to International Crimes: The Status Quo and Its Challenges' (2010) 8 *Journal of International Criminal Justice* 699; Parliamentarians for Global Action, 'Modernising the International Criminal Court: Crimes against the Environment, Trafficking in Human Beings, Hybrid Justice and Corporate Accountability' (2022) https://www.pgaction.org/resources/modernising-the-international-criminal-court.html, 51–66. For a different perspective, see T Weigend, 'Societas Delinquere Non Potest? A German Perspective' (2008) 6 *Journal of International Criminal Justice* 927.

This approach is useful for clarifying the legal understanding of the concept of 'gravity', providing concrete examples of economic crimes that may reach the threshold of gravity in international criminal law, and identifying the circumstances in which this is possible. Six case studies involving the commission of serious economic crimes were selected based on four criteria, including the variety of categories of economic crimes. Therefore, the cases selected concern five different economic crimes: corruption, theft or plundering of natural resources, international money-laundering, financing terrorism, and fraud. The second criterion for case selection is linked to the fact that economic crimes are an international problem, as they affect the global community not only from an ideological view but also from a practical perspective. Consequently, the chapter focuses on economic crimes committed in different regions of the world, including Europe, the Americas and Africa.

Another selection criterion is the language and accessibility of the research material. The selected cases are those for which sufficient research material was available in one of the languages in which the research underlying this book was conducted.[14] Lastly, the decision not to limit the scope of Chapter 3 to economic crimes that have never been prosecuted at domestic level is motivated by the function of the ICC – and other potential supranational tribunals – to act as court of last resort. This choice made it possible to assess the effectiveness of the approaches adopted by domestic jurisdictions to combat systemic forms of economic crimes. Different responses were implemented in different States: in some cases, the State was consciously absent, in others national authorities took concrete action to prosecute the perpetrators, although this has not always been synonymous with fair and impartial justice.

The findings of Chapter 3 are necessary to proceed to the next step, namely the attempt to translate the circumstances in which economic crimes reach a high gravity threshold into the contextual elements of a concept of international economic crime, examined in Chapter 4. In turn, only after defining the potential constituent elements of an international economic crime within the limits of the principle of legality, does the question arise as to how such an international crime can be prosecuted. The potential avenues considered in Chapter 5 include the ICC and other national, regional, or international *fora* that may constitute an alternative to the ICC or complement it.

In terms of data collection, the primary and secondary sources used in the book are in one of the four languages in which the research was conducted. Primary sources include the most relevant laws and cases of international criminal law relating to the subject matter of this book. They have been selected from the case-law of international criminal courts, from the Nuremberg Tribunal to the ICC, with references to the ad hoc tribunals of the former Yugoslavia

[14] The languages used for research purposes in this book are the following: English, Spanish, French and Italian.

and Rwanda and to internationalised courts and tribunals. They also include other sources of international law, such as resolutions of the United Nations (UN) General Assembly (UNGA) and Security Council (UNSC), as well as international human rights law sources, in particular the European Convention on Human Rights (ECHR) and the African Charter on Human and Peoples' Rights (ACHPR).

Secondary sources mainly consist of books, book chapters and journal articles on international criminal law. However, this research also draws on insights from other disciplines, in particular criminology. In this book, primary sources are of paramount importance, as it is in them that both the legal foundations and the limits of the concept of international economic crime must be identified. Secondary sources, on the other hand, play a fundamental complementary role to primary sources, since the elements of a potential concept of international economic crime can only be derived from theoretical and doctrinal discussions.

STRUCTURE AND OVERVIEW OF THE CHAPTERS

The body of this book consists of four central chapters, preceded by an introductory chapter and followed by a concluding chapter. Chapter 2 seeks to ascertain the historical and legal genesis of the concept of international economic crime. The arguments are presented in three sections. The first section traces back the origins of international criminal law, arguing that a primordial notion of international economic crime can be inferred from an in-depth analysis of the major war criminal trials and the industrialists' proceedings held before the military tribunals set up by the Allies in Germany after the Second World War. In the second section, a parallel is drawn between the proliferation of supranational treaties harmonising the criminalisation of economic crimes, on the one hand, and the limited interest in the prosecution of economic offences by the second-generation of international criminal law tribunals, on the other. Lastly, the chapter reflects upon the 'crisis focus' of international criminal justice and its impact on the content of the categories of international crimes listed in the Rome Statute.

Chapter 3 is structured as a legal syllogism divided into three sections. The first section, corresponding to the major premise of the syllogism, examines the most important theories defining the concept of gravity in international criminal law. In the minor premise of the syllogism, six case studies are analysed, while in the last section the gravity threshold is applied to the case studies to determine whether and, if so, when economic crimes are serious enough to be considered international, thus delimiting the scope of a prospective notion of international economic crime. The potential constituent elements of this notion are elaborated in Chapter 4, which opens with a section devoted to the examination of the principle of legality in international criminal law. This principle is a benchmark for providing a comprehensive definition of international economic crimes that is not the result of an arbitrary exercise of legislative and judicial powers. The second section analyses the constituent elements of the notion of international economic crimes within the limits set by the principle of legality, while the third and last section outline a tentative definition of international economic crimes.

Chapter 5 reflects on the possibilities of prosecuting international economic crimes within the current multilevel system of international criminal law. The first section addresses the question of how such a concept could be integrated into the Rome Statute and what the positive consequences and obstacles of such an inclusion would be, while the second section sheds light on possible additional or alternative solutions to the prosecution of international economic crimes before the ICC.

Interim conclusions are presented at the end of each chapter and summarised in Chapter 6, where the main research question is answered in the positive: the concept of international economic crime can be qualified as an international crime and prosecuted as such, provided that a definition of international economic crime is formulated in accordance with the parameters of the principle of legality and that existing or emerging accountability mechanisms within the multilevel system of international criminal justice take action to investigate and prosecute these offences. Chapter 6 concludes by outlining prospects for further research on this important, increasingly debated and still controversial topic in the field of international criminal law.

FRAMING THE DISCOURSE: KEY CONCEPTS AND DEFINITIONS

The Concept of Crime

Although an exhaustive analysis of theories of crime is beyond the scope of this book, it is nevertheless important to specify how the concept of crime should be defined for the purposes of the present research and how this may help justify the creation of a new paradigm of mass criminality.

Orthodox criminologists define crimes as violations of criminal law,[15] a definition that is supported by part of the criminal law literature that embraces a normative theory of criminalisation, according to which a crime is any conduct prohibited through an authoritative act of criminalisation.[16] However, since the enactment of a law defining a behaviour as a crime implies the prosecution and trial of those who have allegedly committed that behaviour, according to other scholars the act of criminalisation is a crucial component of the criminalisation

[15] MJ Lynch, PB Stretesky, MA Long, *Defining Crime: A Critique of the Concept and Its Implication* (Palgrave Macmillan, 2015) 30.

[16] AP Simester and A von Hirsch, *Crimes, Harms and Wrongs: On the Principles of Criminalisation* (Hart Publishing, 2011) 6.

process, but it is not the only one.[17] That act is followed by other stages in which several actors – eg prosecutors, judges – act as agents of criminalisation, thus contributing to outlining the scope of substantive criminal law.[18] Therefore, a normative theory of criminal law should also address these elements, as is done in this book, where Chapter 5 will discuss the potential role played by national and international prosecutors and judges in criminalising systemic economic conduct.

As the act of criminalisation is public, coercive and censorious, in criminalising conduct the law addresses agents capable of deliberation and moral reflection, allowing them to assess ex ante the consequences threatened by non-compliance and decide whether to engage in the disapproved conduct. Therefore, in addition to a communicative and labelling effect, the act of criminalisation plays a deterrent function as it discourages the addressees from engaging in the conduct and aims to satisfy the social regulation needs.

However, not all behaviour can be defined as a crime. The creation of a crime is possible when there is good reason, ie when the behaviour is 'wrongful'. While for some scholars, wrongfulness is sufficient to justify prohibition,[19] others argue that, although the wrongfulness of a behaviour is necessary to justify the act of criminalisation due to its punitive and censorious nature – all the more so in the context of international criminal law – this is, however, insufficient and requires an additional legitimate ground.[20] The insufficiency is justified by the fact that there may be instruments other than criminal law that are better suited to deal with the wrongfulness of conduct. Should these alternative options be excluded, the criminalisation of a behaviour could not only be justified on the basis of its wrongfulness, but also on the basis of its direct or indirect impact on people's lives. As an artificial creation designed to promote the well-being of its subjects, the State is not interested in regulating conduct that does not affect people's lives.

In discussing systemic economic crimes as potential international crimes, this book argues for a theory of criminalisation according to which such crimes consist of conduct that is *mala in se*, ie whose wrongfulness is unquestioned and pre-exists the act of criminalisation.[21] However, it also acknowledges the need to complement the wrongfulness of conduct with other grounds that affect people's lives and justify coercive prohibition.

Among these grounds is the harm principle, according to which conduct that wrongfully harms or threatens to harm people's lives must be criminalised.

[17] RA Duff, *The Realm of Criminal* Law (Oxford University Press, 2018) 39.
[18] ibid 43.
[19] Simester and von Hirsch, *Crimes, Harms and Wrongs*, 4 and 21, citing MS Moore, *Placing Blame: A Theory of Criminal Law* (Oxford University Press, 1997).
[20] ibid 21.
[21] On the distinction between *mala in se* and *mala prohibita* and its relation to the choice between a strong or a weak interpretation of wrongfulness see Duff, *The Realm of Criminal* Law 20.

Feinberg famously defines harm as a 'wrongfully set-back interest'.[22] In addition to emphasising the need for wrongful conduct,[23] this definition introduces the concept of 'setback of interest'. According to Feinberg, an interest should be interpreted as a 'welfare interest', that is, any interest that allows individuals to achieve their ulterior goals and aspirations.[24] Thus, harmful conduct is conduct that harms individuals' interests and resources that are fundamental to their well-being. As for the term 'setback', this is one of the verbs used by Feinberg to describe the effect of harm on people's interests. To determine if one is harmed it is necessary to compare their current situation with their previous situation and show that their position has worsened: when harm is caused an interest is violated, invaded, impaired, set back, defeated.[25]

The harm principle will be discussed throughout Chapter 2, which raises two issues. First, it points out that the harmed person is not necessarily the victim of crime. When international crimes are perpetrated, it is not only the direct victims who suffer harm, but also humanity as a whole. Moreover, harm can be caused without the victim being identified, as is the case with most systemic economic crimes. Secondly, Chapter 2 addresses the peculiarity of harm in property offences, namely the fact that their harmful nature may not stem from the conduct itself, but rather from its widespread implications for individuals' lives and rights. In their book, Simister and von Hirsch cite the example of a company's collapse resulting from massive corporate fraud, which is harmful because of its consequences for the company's employees, who lose their jobs, and for shareholders, who lose their savings.[26]

Some thoughts on the harm principle will also be provided in Chapter 3, which reflects on the adaptation of the harm principle to the legal framework of international criminal law through the so-called 'international harm principle', which makes it possible to justify the criminalisation of conduct that, by causing a 'group-based harm', wrongfully harms the whole humanity.

The harm principle will be discussed in relation to the cases cited throughout the book, which include not only offences that generate direct harm – eg corruption, fraud, looting of natural resources – but also offences that generate remote primary harm, ie conduct that indirectly harm the resources underlying individuals' well-being. This category of offences includes cases of mediating interventions, that is, conduct that is not inherently wrongful but that induces or

[22] J Feinberg, *The Moral Limits of the Criminal Law Volume 1: Harm to Others* (Oxford University Press, 1987) 106. This definition is also embraced by Simester and von Hirsch, *Crimes, Harms and Wrongs* 37, according to whom 'harm occurs through the impairment of some resource (physical, proprietary, or otherwise) over which the harmed person has a legitimate claim'.

[23] Feinberg, *The Moral Limits of the Criminal Law* 36.

[24] ibid 37. Welfare interests are the most vital interests an individual can have, including the individual's security and material resources, see Feinberg, *The Moral Limits of the Criminal Law* 62.

[25] ibid 51: 'The acts […] that harm people have been said (alternatively) to be those that (1) violate, (2) invade, (3) impair, (4) set back, (5) defeat, (6) thwart, (7) impede, and (8) doom their interests.'

[26] Simester and von Hirsch, *Crimes, Harms and Wrongs* 40.

leads to wrongful conduct that generates or presents a risk of harm. Mediating interventions raise a number of concerns, starting with the question of whether the denial of individual liberties can be justified to prevent remote harms. On the other hand, the legitimacy of these offences is also contested on the ground that conduct that generates remote harm is not a wrong per se, which may raise an issue of fair imputation and over-criminalisation.

To overcome these obstacles, it has been suggested that the harm principle should include imputation doctrines capable of providing individuals with important liberty safeguards.[27] These doctrines make it possible to avoid criminalising prophylactic or preventive conduct that is not inherently wrongful or harmful,[28] while allowing liability to be attributed to perpetrators who are normatively involved in the commission of wrongful conduct that directly generates harm. Such normative involvement can take many forms, including assistance, encouragement, and endorsement of a wrongdoing committed by others. These forms will be mentioned throughout the book with reference to cases relating to the supply of dual-use products used to commit international crimes.

In addition to the harm principle, another theory that may complement the wrongfulness of conduct and legitimise coercive prohibition is the *Rechtsgüter* principle, according to which wrongful conduct that violates or threatens a *Rechtsgut*, that is, an individual or collective legal interest, must be criminalised. There are other principles of criminalisation that could be discussed,[29] but this book will mainly rely on the harm principle and the *Rechtsgüter* principle. In Duff's words, both principles can be described as 'thin' principles as it is necessary to further elaborate which interests or *Güter* are protected by the act of criminalisation.[30] This discussion, as well as reflections on how these principles can be used for the purposes of this book, namely to theorise a new paradigm of international economic crimes, will be addressed in Chapter 3.

It follows from the above that this book supports the theory that the criminalisation of conduct must be justified by its wrongfulness but acknowledges that this is not sufficient. It must be demonstrated that the wrongful conduct cause harm to individual or collective legal goods, and that criminal law is the most appropriate regulatory tool to deal with that conduct. Regarding the latter condition, since criminalisation is only one of the responses to wrongdoings, the book sheds light on the added value of resorting to international criminal law as a regulatory tool to prevent and punish the most serious economic conduct. Although a study of regulatory instruments alternative to criminal law is beyond

[27] ibid 64.

[28] Duff, *The Realm of Criminal Law* 246, according to whom criminalising a conduct that prevents the commission of wrongful harm 'does not make that conduct itself wrongful or harmful'.

[29] ibid 232, describing Duff's master principle of criminalisation which criminalises a type of conduct if, and only if, it constitutes a public wrong, and if and only if, such a public wrong violates the polity's civil order.

[30] ibid 254.

the scope of this book, reference is made throughout the chapters to civil law instruments, which are used in many countries to hold corporations accountable for their illegal activities. Among the alternatives to criminal law are also regulatory agencies, which are entitled to impose sanctions or financial penalties for behaviours that do not comply with norms. Despite their merits, these regulatory tools lack the condemnatory character of criminal law, which is the harshest instrument for regulating individuals' behaviours and, for this reason, should be used when there is a social justification for it. In such cases, criminal law can be more effective than other tools in communicating to individuals that a certain behaviour is wrongful and that its commission implies consequences that may infringe the perpetrator's liberty.

In order to be coercive and condemnatory, criminal law must be clear and predictable. Thus, Chapter 4 explores how the definition of international economic crime can comply with the principle of legality in international criminal law, including its corollaries of non-retroactivity, foreseeability, fair labelling and the principle of fair warning for crimes involving gross negligence. Unambiguous offences also contribute to better implementation of criminal law by enforcement authorities. Therefore, when proposing criminal law as a regulatory tool, practical and enforcement obstacles must also be considered. In addition to discussing the advantages of prosecuting serious economic offences as international crimes, Chapter 5 examines potential enforcement challenges.

Systemic Economic Offences as International Crimes

The concept of crime provides only a partial understanding of the term 'systemic economic crime', which thus needs further clarification. Like the concept of 'white-collar crime' coined by Edwin Sutherland in 1940,[31] the concept of 'systemic economic crime' refers to offences committed by respectable individuals of high social standing, who have been entrusted power that they abuse in the course of their occupation. However, while Sutherland's category includes not only crimes but also deviant acts,[32] systemic economic offences are limited to 'crimes' in the strict sense of the term, ie any wrongful conduct that harms individual and collective legal goods. Another difference is that white-collar crimes are primarily committed in the private sector, while economic crimes include illicit financial activities carried out by individuals who hold power in both the private and public sectors.

The latter feature of systemic economic crimes is typical of the social science construct of 'corruption', which, as a fluid concept, is a category that has been used to encompass a wide range of economic offences.[33] However, what clearly

[31] EH Sutherland, 'White-Collar Criminality' (1940) 5 *American Sociological Review* 1.

[32] M Button, B Hock and D Shepherd, *Economic Crime: From Conception to Response* (Routledge, 2022) 6.

[33] ibid 5.

distinguishes corruption crimes from the systemic economic crimes discussed in this book is that the former also cover offences committed by lower status public officials in modest positions of power. This is not the case for systemic economic crimes that are committed by high-ranking individuals capable of causing significant damage to a country's natural or economic public wealth.

The concept of economic crime developed by Button to compensate for the uncertainties arising from other theories of economic crimes, also deserves consideration. It helps identify and define other characteristics of systemic economic crimes, such as their purpose, which is to obtain a financial advantage, ie, to gain economic benefit or cause economic loss.[34] Another element that emerges from Button's theory and applies to systemic economic crimes is that the planning and execution of economic crimes are shrouded in deception and secrecy.[35]

Nonetheless, the main features of systemic economic crimes that distinguish them from other economic crimes are the offenders' status and the contextual circumstances in which the crimes are committed, which will be discussed in Chapter 4 with respect to the elements of the notion of international economic crimes. These two salient features are taken from the criminological concept of 'state-corporate crime', defined by Kramer and Michalowski as any illegal or socially injurious behaviour that is committed within a specific context characterised by the interconnection between political and economic institutions.[36] Different variants of this notion have been developed over the years and will be discussed in Chapter 2.

To sum up, despite the merits of the various definitions of economic crimes that have been developed by institutions and academics, there is still no consensus on what falls within the scope of 'economic crime'.[37] Therefore, based on the literature mentioned, this book provides its own understanding of the concept of systemic economic crimes, which include i) any wrongful conduct that cause harm to individual or collective legal goods, ii) planned or executed in deception and secrecy and iii) committed to obtain a financial advantage iv) by a person who holds a position of power in the private or public sector, which is abused in the course of their occupation. These elements are examined in detail with reference to the case studies discussed in Chapter 3 and lay the foundations for defining the category of 'international economic crimes' discussed in Chapter 4.

[34] ibid 14.

[35] ibid, arguing that 'economic criminals can operate deep in the shadows and can do so for many years'.

[36] Michalowski and Kramer, *State-Corporate Crime* 15.

[37] Button, Hock and Shepherd, *Economic Crime* 11.

2

Origin and Evolution of the Concept of International Economic Crime

INTERNATIONAL ECONOMIC CRIMINALITY is a timeless and ubiquitous criminal phenomenon. Over the centuries, a considerable number of serious economic offences have been committed in peacetime and wartime. Nevertheless, the international criminal justice system, created as a legal response to the wide range of atrocities perpetrated during the Second World War, has remained blind and deaf to both the economic crimes committed since then and the criminal responsibility of the public and private actors involved.

This chapter reflects on the genesis and evolution of the concept of international economic crime in four sections, corresponding to the most relevant stages in the evolutionary process of international criminal law. The first section traces the origins of this branch of law, arguing that a primordial notion of international economic crime can be deduced from a thorough analysis of the trials of major war criminals, held before the International Military Tribunal (IMT) at Nuremberg, and the industrialists' proceedings, held before the military tribunals established by the Allies in their German zones of occupation. During these trials, both politicians and industrialists were accused of committing crimes with an economic dimension. After outlining the historical and legal framework that gave rise to the concept of international economic crime, the second section of this chapter discusses its content as it emerged from post-war trials.

The third section examines the involution of the concept of international economic crime before the 'second generation' of international criminal law courts and tribunals. Since the 1980s, the criminalisation and prosecution of ordinary economic crimes have been prompted by a gradual proliferation of supranational instruments aimed at harmonising domestic responses. However, during the same period, ad hoc and internationalised courts and tribunals have not been as attentive as domestic courts to the gravity of economic crimes allegedly committed during the humanitarian tragedies they were called upon to investigate.

The last section reflects on the approach adopted so far by the ICC, symbol of the 'third generation' of international criminal courts. The drafters' choice not to include any economic offence among the acts potentially falling within the three categories of international crimes recognised during the Rome negotiations is scrutinised along with the position endorsed in this respect by the Office of the Prosecutor (OTP) and the judges. Their approach is challenged on the ground that, during the twenty-first century, systemic economic crimes have proven to be among the main causes of serious violations of human rights and international law, suggesting that their international criminalisation should be reconsidered. The main findings of this chapter are summarised in the concluding remarks, which foreshadow the issues addressed in the subsequent chapters.

GENESIS OF THE CONCEPT OF INTERNATIONAL ECONOMIC CRIME

During the Second World War, public and private actors who held economic power played a key role in the commission of international crimes.[1] They were involved in a system designed to denigrate and exterminate specific categories of individuals on several grounds, including race, ethnicity, religion, and economic prestige.[2] Some of the offences perpetrated under this system were of economic significance, although only a few were prosecuted as international crimes.

The Nuremberg trials, named after the German city, where the IMT was established, focused on the prosecution of 'major war criminals', ie high-ranking politicians and military commanders of the Third Reich. Public representatives of economic power, including bankers and Hitler's economic advisers, were also tried before the IMT for illicit business activities related to the war. Shortly afterwards, influential German industrialists were tried during the so-called 'subsequent Nuremberg proceedings', the American trial that took place in Nuremberg in 1946. Other economic actors were prosecuted by the French, British and Soviets in their German zones of occupation. In contrast, more lenient treatment was meted out to industrialists from Allied countries, who had taken part in illegal activities in Germany during the war.

The 'Economic Case' in the Major War Criminals' Trials

In *The Nomos of the Earth*, Carl Schmitt used the term 'amity lines' to refer to those boundaries that run along the equator in the South and the Azores in the West, and that have artificially divided the world in two since 1559, when they first

[1] For a comprehensive description of the role that private economic actors played during the Second World War, see FR Nicosia and J Huener, *Business and Industry in Nazi Germany* (Berghahn Books, 2004).

[2] Public and private actors were the 'two principal concentrations of power in Germany', see JA Bush, 'The Prehistory of Corporations and Conspiracy in International Criminal Law: What Nuremberg Really Said' (2009) 109 *Columbia Law Review* 1094, 1202. See also US Military Tribunal, 'The Flick case', Vol VI, Trials of War Criminals before the Nuremberg Military Tribunals under Control Council Law No. 10 (October 1946–April 1949) 32.

appeared in a clause contained in the Treaty of Cateau-Cambrésis.[3] On this side of the 'amity lines' was the Old World, where lawful forms of violence were allowed and regulated; beyond the lines was the New World, depicted as an area of unbridled freedom, where men confronted each other as wild animals. Nonetheless, during the Second World War, power and selfishness removed every trace of justice, freedom, and security on the European continent. Outrageous crimes were perpetrated in violation of the laws of war, thus replacing the Schmittian idea of an organised Old World with a scenario more akin to the Hobbes' state of nature.[4] The only difference between the latter scenario and Europe in 1939 is that the reason that triggered the outbreak of the Second World War was not the human instinct for survival. On the contrary, Germany's quest for economic and political hegemony and the spread of theories of Aryan supremacy were among the main causes of the rise of Nazism and the subsequent outbreak of war.

It is generally agreed that the German banking crisis, caused by the bankruptcy of the Danatbank, led by the Jewish banker Jakob Goldschmidt, boosted the electoral success of the Nazi movement.[5] Unemployment, misery, frustration, and desire for revenge against the Jews, who had been chosen as the common enemy on whom to discharge responsibility for the crisis, 'opened the ears of the masses […] to demagogic whispers'.[6]

As for the consequences of the war, the peaceful aspirations of the international community, enshrined in the Moscow Declaration, were translated into concrete action with the creation of the first international military tribunal in Nuremberg.[7] The trials opened on 20 November 1945 and were held on the basis of the London Agreement[8] and the annexed Charter,[9] signed on 8 August 1945 by the Four Allies. The latter instrument was the felicitous outcome of complex negotiations, in which the drafters sought to ensure that international criminal justice would not fail again, as it had after the First World War.[10] The tribunal was created to prosecute the 'major war criminals

[3] C Schmitt, *The Nomos of the Earth in the International Law of the Jus Publicum Europaeum* (Telos Press, 2006) 92.

[4] L May, *Crimes against Humanity: A Normative Account* (Cambridge University Press, 2004) 15. Cesare Beccaria emphasised the power of the laws, which are the tools by which human beings, born independent and isolated, decided to unite in society to counteract the state of war, in which they would live in constant fear of losing their freedom, see C Beccaria, *Dei delitti e delle pene* (Mondadori, 2019) 11.

[5] S Doerr et al, 'Financial Crises and Political Radicalization: How Failing Banks Paved Hitler's Path to Power' (*BIS Working Papers*, 2021) www.bis.org/publ/work978.htm.

[6] Office of the United States Chief of Counsel for the Prosecution of Axis Criminality, *Nazi Conspiracy and Aggression ('Red Series'): Supplement B* (1945) https://www.loc.gov/item/2011525363_NT_Nazi-Suppl-B/, 508.

[7] Moscow Declaration on Atrocities (Moscow, 30 October 1943).

[8] Agreement for the Prosecution and Punishment of the Major War Criminals of the European Axis (London, 8 August 1945).

[9] Charter of the International Military Tribunal – Annex to the Agreement for the Prosecution and Punishment of the Major War Criminals of the European Axis (London, 8 August 1945).

[10] GA Finch, 'The Nuremberg Trial and International Law' (1947) 41 *American Journal of International Law* 20, 20.

of the European Axis', ie those responsible for committing crimes that had no geographical localisation and whose punishment depended on a joint decision of the Allied governments.[11] By focusing on this category of defendants, emphasis was put on the connection between their power and the ravaging effects of their acts. Willis Smith, an observer of the American Bar Association, while standing in the courtroom on 14 March 1946, wondered whether he was really 'looking on the physical features of the men [...] whose activity in the destruction of human life and physical property, to say nothing of spiritual values, caused them to *become the most hated and feared of humans*?'[12]

Smith had the chance to attend in person a trial that constituted several firsts. It was the first time that an international tribunal had been established by a joint decision of different governments. Moreover, the Charter was an unprecedented example of an international penal code, in which the wording of each provision was the result of a compromise reached to balance extremely heterogeneous legal cultures and systems.

Against this background, the United States (US) Chief Prosecutor Robert H. Jackson decided to inquire into the responsibilities of political and military authorities, without neglecting those involved in the industrial and financial life of Germany.[13] For this purpose, a team of ten lawyers, led by the American Frank Shea, was set up to deal with the 'economic case', ie that part of the prosecution case relating to the economic aspects of the war and the criminal liability of economic actors. As a result of the prosecution team's work on the economic case, a provisional list of defendants having 'given Hitler the material means to rearm Germany, with full knowledge'[14] of his military plan, was drawn up. However, the election of Truman – a more 'business-oriented' leader – as President of the United States led to a significant decline in the importance of the Nuremberg 'economic case'. In 1946, the Allies' strategy towards Germany shifted from punishment to rehabilitation of the country, including from an economic point of view.[15] Hence, the list of defendants suggested by Shea was drastically reduced, while the idea of organising subsequent proceedings against industrialists was gradually gaining credibility.[16]

[11] Moscow Declaration, para 5.

[12] W Smith, 'The Nuremberg Trials' (1946) 32 *American Bar Association Journal* 390, 390 (emphasis added).

[13] Bush, 'The Prehistory of Corporations' 1110. See also F Jessberger, 'On the Origins of Individual Criminal Responsibility under International Law for Business Activity: IG Farben on Trial' (2010) 8 *Journal of International Criminal Justice* 783, 797 and G Baars, 'Capitalism's Victor's Justice? The Hidden Stories Behind the Prosecution of Industrialists Post-WWII' in KJ Heller and G Simpson (eds), *The Hidden Histories of War Crimes Trials* (Oxford University Press, 2013) 163, 165.

[14] Baars, 'Capitalism's Victor's Justice?' 170.

[15] G Baars, *The Corporation, Law and Capitalism: A Radical Perspective on the Role of Law in The Global Political Economy*, Historical Materialism Book Series 188 (Brill, 2019) 155.

[16] M Lippman, 'War Crimes Trials of German Industrialists: The Other Schindlers' (1995) 9 *Temple International and Comparative Law Journal* 173, 178.

Among the economic actors indicted as major criminals before the IMT was Gustav Krupp von Bohlen und Halbach.[17] He had played a leading role in the industrial reorganisation and rearmament of Germany, complementing Hitler's political and military projects. Although he was diagnosed with dementia and declared unable to stand trial before the IMT,[18] Krupp's involvement in the planning and execution of the war was so significant that it was mentioned on several occasions during the trial[19] and in the judgment of the IMT,[20] while his son Alfried could not escape the 'subsequent proceedings' held before the US Military Tribunal. Gustav Krupp was the first and only industrialist to be indicted before the IMT,[21] but three politicians who had held important economic positions in Germany were also indicted by the prosecution: Schacht, Funk, and Speer.

Hjalmar Schacht was considered the 'financial genius' behind Germany's rearmament.[22] Actively involved in the economic reorganisation of Germany,[23] Schacht held relevant political and economic mandates in the years before and during the war. A controversial personality and a man of great intelligence,[24] the banker and economist born in current-day Denmark gained prestige and authority when he succeeded in adopting economic policies to overcome the hyperinflation of the German mark caused by Germany's defeat in the First World War. In the decade from 1930 to 1940, he cooperated with Hitler as Reich's Minister of Economics and President of the Reichsbank,[25] two positions that, according to the prosecution, he had constantly abused. He was charged with 'participation in a common plan or conspiracy to commit crimes against peace, war crimes or crimes against humanity' (Count One) and with crimes against peace (Count Two).[26]

At trial, Schacht was depicted by his counsel, Herbert Kraus, as a man whose only fault was that he had failed to recognise Hitler's criminal intentions and

[17] He was the President of the Reich Union of German Industry and the Head of the Group for Mining and Production of Iron and Metals under the Reich Ministry of Economics. See KR Jacobson, 'Doing Business with the Devil: The Challenges of Prosecuting Corporate Officials Whose Business Transactions Facilitate War Crimes and Crimes against Humanity' (2005) 56 *Air Force Law Review* 167, 174.

[18] Bush, 'The Prehistory of Corporations' 1112.

[19] Baars, 'Capitalism's Victor's Justice?' 171–173.

[20] ibid 173. See also IMT, *Trial of the Major War Criminals before the International Military Tribunal*, Vol I (Judgment, 1 October 1946) 183, 246.

[21] Lippman, 'War Crimes Trials of German Industrialists' 178.

[22] L Goldensohn, *The Nuremberg Interviews: An American Psychiatrist's Conversations with the Defendants and Witnesses* (Alfred A Knopf, 2004) 220.

[23] Jacobson, 'Doing Business with the Devil' 175. See also IMT, *Trial of the Major War Criminals* 307.

[24] Gustav Gilbert, an American Army psychologist, examined the Nazi leaders who were tried at Nuremberg and to whom he administered a German version of the Wechsler-Bellevue IQ test. Schacht scored 143, the highest score among the tested leaders, after an upward adjustment to take due account of his age. See GM Gilbert, *Nuremberg Diary* (Da Capo Press, 1995) 34.

[25] Office of the United States, *Nazi Conspiracy and Aggression* 504.

[26] IMT, *Trial of the Major War Criminals* 74.

plans at an early stage. He was also described as a vigorous protector of the Jews, not so different from Schindler.[27] According to the defence, the most challenging incriminating arguments against Schacht concerned his choice to finance Germany's rearmament and his decision to remain minister without portfolio during Hitler's regime until 1943.

On the rearmament argument, the defence counsel compared Schacht's contribution to the war to the activity of a car manufacturer: when a drunk driver causes an accident, the car manufacturer cannot be held liable.[28] Similarly, Schacht could not be held liable for Hitler's choice to use weapons and ammunitions – which Schacht had financed – to commit international crimes. Schacht's decision, as President of the Reichsbank, to grant loans and finance Germany's rearmament program was eventually perceived by the judges as a legal and not criminal act, in particular considering that this practice was slowed down in 1936 and discontinued in 1938.[29] According to the majority of the judges, had the policies carried out by the defendant not been part of the Nazi plan to wage aggressive war, but had they aimed to strengthen the German arsenal of weapons – as the defendant contended[30] – then he could not have been held responsible for crimes against peace or war crimes since he had not contributed to their commission.[31] Schacht himself stated that 'all [he] wanted was to build up Germany industrially [...]. The only thing they [could] accuse [him] of [was] breaking the Versailles Treaty'.[32]

However, it should be noted that the IMT judges analysed the interplay between Schacht's economic policies and the Nazi aggressive plan without giving weight to his initial and undisputed financial and ideological support to the Nazi party but focusing almost exclusively on the last few years of the defendant's activity. While it is true that on the eve of the Second World War Schacht lost power and credibility, it is equally correct to assume that the Nazi war of aggression was the result of a plan elaborated over several years. Along the lines of this observation was the argument raised by the Soviet judge of the IMT in his dissenting opinion, according to which the acquittal of Schacht was unfounded since he 'consciously and deliberately supported the Nazi Party'[33] and his knowledge of Hitler's plans could be inferred from a number

[27] Office of the United States, *Nazi Conspiracy and Aggression* 517. See also Lippman, 'War Crimes Trials of German Industrialists' 174.

[28] Office of the United States, *Nazi Conspiracy and Aggression* 505.

[29] IMT, *Trial of the Major War Criminals* 308–309. See also Baars, *The Corporation, Law and Capitalism* 154.

[30] Goldensohn, *The Nuremberg Interviews* 220.

[31] IMT, *Trial of the Major War Criminals* 310: 'He was clearly not one of the inner circles around Hitler which was most closely involved with this Common Plan. He was regarded by this group with undisguised hostility'.

[32] F Megret, 'Bring Forth the Accused: Defendant Attitudes and the Intimate Legitimacy of the International Criminal Trial' (2019) 36 *Arizona Journal of International and Comparative Law* 397, 435.

[33] IMT, *Trial of the Major War Criminals* 343.

of elements, including the type of weapons planned for the rearmament of Germany and the scale of the rearmament policy.[34] Irrespective of the different interpretations and conclusions reached by the IMT judges as to the evidence submitted by the parties, the Schacht's trial set the standard for the prosecution of economic actors involved in the commission of international crimes: not only their *mens rea*, but also the type of economic activities accomplished by them, were relevant factors in establishing their criminal liability.

Another authoritative banker involved in business dealings with Nazi political leaders was Walter Funk. He replaced Schacht in his mandates and became Hitler's Economic Adviser. He was accused of abusing his power to commit not only crimes against peace but also war crimes and crimes against humanity. During the trial, Funk acted as a repented defendant, showing empathy for the victims of the atrocities committed by his government.[35] Nonetheless, the defendant's moral condemnation of his own conduct was not followed by a guilty plea.[36]

The majority of the IMT judges acquitted him of the conspiracy charge, as it was proven that he had not taken part in planning the war of aggression.[37] On the contrary, Funk was convicted of crimes against humanity since, as Minister of Economics (1937–1945), he had signed the 'Aryanisation' laws that led to the exclusion of Jews from economic life in Germany. In addition, he was convicted of war crimes because he had plundered occupied territories[38] and, as the President of the Reichsbank, he had stored and laundered gold and precious materials belonging to concentration camps inmates. In agreement with Himmler, he had devised a system whereby these materials were delivered to the Reichsbank, then processed into bars at Degussa, and finally purchased by the Deutsche and Dresdner banks.[39] On several occasions, Funk denied any involvement in such a perverse scheme,[40] to the point that when asked where he thought such goods might have come from, he replied that he was aware of the existence of some SS deposits, but not of their nature.[41] The naïve presentation of the facts by the defence did not convince the judges and resulted in Funk being sentenced to life imprisonment.[42]

[34] ibid 345.

[35] Megret, 'Bring Forth the Accused' 457: '[…] some of the accused, such as Funk at Nuremberg or Erdemovic at the ICTY, have occasionally been seen weeping following victim testimony, a powerful signal of empathy with witnesses'.

[36] ibid 460.

[37] Lippman, 'War Crimes Trials of German Industrialists' 180. See also IMT, *Trial of the Major War Criminals* 305–307.

[38] ibid 306–307: '[H]e was eventually convicted on these grounds. These activities also included the seizure of vast amounts of gold reserves, funds, oil and other products from the territories occupied by the Nazis'.

[39] GD Feldman, 'Financial Institutions in Nazi Germany. Reluctant or Willing Collaborators?' in FR Nicosia and J Huener (eds) *Business and Industry* 15, 36.

[40] Goldensohn, *The Nuremberg Interviews* 82.

[41] ibid 90–91.

[42] IMT, *Trial of the Major War Criminals* 365.

Unlike Schacht and Funk, Albert Speer was not a banker. As Minister for Armaments and Munitions, he was found guilty of war crimes and crimes against humanity for aiding Germany to strengthen its arsenal in view of the approaching war 'in the same way that other productive enterprises aid'.[43] Not only he repented but also admitted his guilt, acknowledging the merits of the international trial he was attending by arguing that it 'must contribute towards preventing such degenerate wars in the future and towards establishing rules whereby human beings can live together'.[44]

In the three cases mentioned so far, the potential harmful nature of certain business activities did not go unnoticed. However, the IMT was a 'war crimes-oriented' tribunal, meaning that its material scope of jurisdiction was limited to war-related offences.[45] Inevitably, the peculiar nature of this tribunal had an impact on the selection of defendants and the crimes for which they could be charged.

Other tribunals shared the 'war crimes-oriented' nature of the IMT, such as the International Military Tribunal for the Far East (IMTFE) established in Japan in 1946. Along the lines of its Nuremberg sibling, the IMTFE dealt with cases involving politicians in charge of reorganising the Manchukuo's economy with the purpose of preparing aggressive wars in China.[46] Although the IMTFE trials showed that economic policies had a huge impact on the commission of international crimes,[47] the Nuremberg 'economic case' had no counterpart in Tokyo, where no leader of the Japanese *zaibatsu* – a Japanese term used to indicate large enterprise combines, usually organised around a single family, which were active in Japan until the end of the Second World War and could operate in different economic sectors – was brought to trial.[48]

Some Japanese businessmen were tried by the Allied governments before their military tribunals. Among the main cases cited in the literature is the Japanese Nippon Mining Company, whose managers and employees were indicted and tried before the British War Crimes Court in Hong Kong, for using prisoners of war as forced labourers in their mines during the Second World War.[49]

[43] ibid 330.

[44] ibid 406. See also Megret, 'Bring Forth the Accused' 448.

[45] The link to war was also evident from the provision defining crimes against humanity in the Nuremberg Charter, according to which the listed acts could constitute crimes against humanity if they were committed 'before or during the war'.

[46] Jacobson, 'Doing Business with the Devil' 196.

[47] ibid 197.

[48] Baars, 'Capitalism's Victor's Justice?' 187. See also Baars, *The Corporation, Law and Capitalism* 217–223.

[49] A Ramasastry, 'Corporate Complicity: From Nuremberg to Rangoon-an Examination of Forced Labor Cases and Their Impact on the Liability of Multinational Corporations' (2002) 20 *Berkeley Journal of International Law* 91, 112. This case is also discussed in K Ambos, 'International Economic Criminal Law. The Foundations of Companies' Criminal Responsibility under International Law' (2018) 29 *Criminal Law Forum* 499, 506. Other Japanese businessmen were tried before the Dutch, US and Soviet military tribunals for a series of war crimes perpetrated during or because of their businesses, including enforced prostitution, abuse of prisoners of war, preparation and use of bacterialogical weapons, see Baars, *The Corporation, Law and Capitalism* 225–232.

The decision to prosecute private individuals and punish human rights abuses perpetrated in the context of their business activities is what most closely links the trials before the British Court in Hong Kong and those before the military tribunals set up in Germany shortly after the end of the IMT trial.

The Industrialists' Trials as a Relevant Part of the 'Subsequent Nuremberg Proceedings'

The Allies adopted Control Council Law (CCL) no 10 to 'establish a uniform legal basis in Germany for the prosecution of war criminals [...] other than those dealt with by the IMT'[50] before the military tribunals set up in the Allies' German zones of occupation. Twelve trials, known as 'subsequent Nuremberg proceedings', took place from December 1946 to April 1949 before the US Military Tribunal at the Palace of Justice in Nuremberg.[51] The accused were prominent figures in Nazi Germany, including jurists, physicians, doctors, and industrialists. The latter were German citizens who had run private-owned enterprises in strategic economic sectors, such as the production of iron, steel, chemicals, and metals used to manufacture weapons.

During the war, many of these businessmen abandoned their position as passive spectators to become active and, in some cases, willing collaborators of the *Führer*.[52] They were 'representatives of one of the two principal concentrations of power in Germany',[53] ie the State – including the army – on the one hand, and the industry, on the other. It is rightly argued that Hitler's expansionist ambitions could not have been pursued without the support of a strong military and industrial apparatus: the State and the army benefited from the services and materials provided by German companies, while the profits and prestige of the latter increased considerably due to their contributions to the military economy and the slave labour programs.[54]

At the 'subsequent Nuremberg proceedings', Telford Taylor led the prosecution against these 'men of profit',[55] whom he considered to be 'those who [had] made the war possible'.[56] Among the most difficult challenges for the prosecution team was the selection of potential defendants. The three companies considered

[50] Article II(1) of the Control Council Law no 10, Punishment of Persons Guilty of War Crimes, Crimes Against Peace and Against Humanity (20 December 1945) (the 'CCL no 10'), lists four crimes of international concern, namely crimes against peace (a), war crimes (b), crimes against humanity (c) and membership in criminal groups recognised as such by the IMT (d). The CCL no 10 was considered international law applied by international tribunals, as stated in 'The Flick case' 1188.

[51] Baars, *The Corporation, Law and Capitalism* 161.

[52] Feldman, 'Financial Institutions in Nazi Germany' 15.

[53] 'The Flick case' 1191.

[54] Lippman, 'War Crimes Trials of German Industrialists' 176, 185.

[55] ibid 261.

[56] JE Du Bois, *Generals in Grey Suits: The Directors of the International 'IG Farben' Cartel, Their Conspiracy and Trial at Nuremberg* (Bodley Head, 1953) 75.

the most suitable targets – Flick, IG Farben and Krupp – were not the only ones with blood on their hands. They had been selected on the basis of the gravity of their misdeeds and the key role they had played during the war, although it was widely believed that many other industrialists were involved in international crimes.[57] The reasons why the latter were spared trial before the US Military Tribunal included the aforementioned new lenient policy of the Allied towards the representatives of the German economy, the limited human and financial resources the Americans had at their disposal and the lack of cooperation from the other Allied powers. The French were the most active in the attempt to complement the Nuremberg 'economic case' with subsequent proceedings, but the Soviets and the British were much more reluctant to cooperate.[58]

With respect to the *Flick* case, Friedrich Flick was the head of a company bearing his family name and specialised in the production of iron and steel.[59] Flick's flair for business enabled him to build an economic empire in Germany. At the beginning of the war, in 1932, he had managed to overcome economic hardships by relying on the policies adopted by Adolf Hitler and his party. The fifty thousand *Reichsmarks* paid to the *Führer* as a sign of gratitude marked the beginning of a long-lasting collaboration, during which Flick and other industrialists became officially known as the 'Military Economy Leaders'.[60]

However, the plans did not go as expected. At the end of the Second World War, Friedrich Flick and five other defendants were charged with war crimes and crimes against humanity for participating in slave labour programs and the looting of public and private properties;[61] crimes against humanity for persecuting Jews through the 'Aryanisation' of their properties;[62] and membership to a criminal organisation for contributing to the commission of offences perpetrated by the *Schutzstaffel* (SS).[63] Three of six defendants were convicted by the US Military Tribunal IV, while the decision to acquit the others was due to their passive role in enforcing German government programs.[64]

The conviction of the four defendants was based on the first and last counts, with the exclusion of the second count concerning the 'Aryanisation' policies. These policies had been implemented before the outbreak of the Second World

[57] For instance, the top executives of the Daimler-Benz, Degussa and Siemens companies were not tried before the courts created after the war, despite their alleged large contributions to it. See Bush 'The Prehistory of Corporations' 1196; see also Ramasastry, 'Corporate Complicity' 126.

[58] The reason why the French were more inclined to prosecute German industrialists relates to their desire to prosecute French businessmen who had collaborated with the enemy, in order to bring justice to all French people who had worked as slave labourers. See Bush, 'The Prehistory of Corporations' 1134 and 1188; Baars, *The Corporation, Law and Capitalism* 189.

[59] Bush, 'The Prehistory of Corporations' 1173.

[60] Lippman, 'War Crimes Trials of German Industrialists' 187.

[61] 'The Flick Case' 13 and 17.

[62] ibid 21.

[63] The latter count implies a distinction between, on the one hand, a 'material support charge', which relates to the fact of facilitating or accepting to take part in activities carried out by criminal organisations or groups, and on the other hand, a 'membership charge', which concerns the very fact of being members of such an organisation or group. See Bush, 'The Prehistory of Corporations' 1175.

[64] ibid 1218.

War, meaning that they were not related to the war and could not fall within the jurisdiction of the Tribunal.[65] Moreover, the judges emphasised that the expropriation of Jewish property was a crime committed against 'property' and not against 'persons', which prevented it from being qualified as a crime against humanity.[66] This approach departs significantly from the interpretation adopted by Prosecutor Jackson in the *Funk* case before the IMT, where he had included in the concept of crimes against humanity both crimes against persons and crimes against property.[67] As for the third count on 'membership to a criminal organisation', only Flick and Otto Steinbrinck were found guilty as accessories. It was proven that they had been members of the Himmler's Circle of Friends – named after the Head of the SS, Heinrich Himmler – and they had financially contributed to this circle with full knowledge of its illegal activities.

Turning to the *IG Farben* case, twenty-three officials of the leading German manufacturer of carbon-based chemicals and main supplier of *Zyklon* B, the chemical used in the gas chambers, were indicted.[68] The *Interessen-Gemeinschaft Farbenindustrie Aktiengesellschaft* (IG Farben) was one of Germany's most important companies not only within national borders, but also worldwide.[69] The company had significantly contributed to scientific progress by inventing and producing medicines for the treatment of epilepsy, malaria and other diseases.[70] Despite these merits, the company was involved in serious criminal activities during the Second World War. In addition to the charges of enslavement and plunder of public and private property as war crimes and crimes against humanity, IG Farben officials were indicted on Count Five concerning their participation in a common plan or conspiracy to commit war crimes and crimes against humanity, and on Count One relating to the charge of conspiracy to commit crimes against peace.[71]

The judges acquitted the defendants of the latter charge on the grounds that it was not proven that they were aware that their actions were part of a plan to

[65] 'The Flick Case' 1212. It was necessary for crimes against humanity to be committed 'in execution of or in connection with any crime within the jurisdiction of the Tribunal'.

[66] ibid 1215: 'The 'atrocities and offenses' listed therein [...] are all offenses against the person. Property is not mentioned. Under the doctrine of *eiusdem generis* the catch-all words 'other persecutions' must be deemed to include only such as affect the life and liberty of the oppressed peoples. Compulsory taking of industrial property, however reprehensible, is not in that category'.

[67] IMT, *Trial of the Major War Criminals* 74.

[68] See US Military Tribunal, 'The IG Farben case', Vol VII and VIII, Trials of War Criminals before the Nuremberg Military Tribunals under Control Council Law No. 10 (October 1946–April 1949). Under the third count concerning participation in slave labour, Farben officials were indicted for the supply of *Zyklon* B, their engagement in medical experiments on concentration camps' prisoners, and the use of forced labour. See Jessberger, 'On the Origins of Individual Criminal Responsibility' 791. See also P Hayes, 'The Chemistry of Business-State Relations in the Third Reich' in FR Nicosia and J Huener (eds), *Business and Industry*, 66, 67.

[69] Du Bois, *Generals in Grey Suits*, 11.

[70] ibid 3.

[71] Baars emphasises that the IG Farben case was the only industrialist case where the defendants were charged with aggressive war (Count one), see Baars, *The Corporation, Law and Capitalism* 170.

wage aggressive war, an offence qualified as 'leadership crime'.[72] The lack of knowledge was presumed from the fact that they were 'men of industry' and not 'makers of policy'[73] as well as from the lack of sufficient evidence proving their access to Hitler's inner circles and Nazi governmental plans.[74] To reach this conclusion, the US Military Tribunal adopted the 'conspiracy test' elaborated by the IMT, which required proof of an agreement to wage aggressive war that was not far from 'the time of decision and of action'.[75]

With regard to the other counts, the tribunal qualified Farben's appropriation of private properties as plunder since it took place 'against the will and consent of (their) owners'.[76] A significant amount of evidence also showed the German company's involvement in 'work-to-death labour', especially in its Auschwitz factory.[77] The defendants were not forced to follow any governmental order in this respect, but they were willing to profit from the exploitation of the workers, thus being responsible for their treatment.[78] Regarding the production and sale to the SS of lethal gas and substances used for medical experiments, the tribunal concluded that none of Farben's executives and employees could have been aware of the actual use of these products, since their supply was reasonably justified by the demand for large amounts of insecticides in concentration camps. Hence, with respect to this count, Farben's officials were found to be innocent businessmen who carried out their usual economic activities 'under unusual circumstances'.[79]

Lastly, twelve defendants were tried before the US Military Tribunal IIIA in Nuremberg as officials of the Krupp company, a German enterprise that produced metals and processed them into war materials.[80] The Krupp firm had been the most relevant and active German company in the field of weaponry since the First World War, when the father of the above-mentioned Gustav Krupp had pledged his support to Kaiser Wilhelm II. Some years later, Gustav Krupp's son, Alfried, became known as the '*Führer* of industry'.[81] During the industrialists' trial, Alfried Krupp, eight members of the *Vorstand* (board of directors) and three executives were charged with the same counts on which Farben

[72] Jessberger, 'On the Origins of Individual Criminal Responsibility' 795.

[73] 'The IG Farben Case' Vol VIII 1125–1126. The principle whereby industrialists could not be held criminally liable for crimes against peace as they were not political leaders was established for the first time by the IMT. See Jacobson, 'Doing Business with the Devil' 180; Jessberger, 'On the Origins of Individual Criminal Responsibility' 790.

[74] Jacobson, 'Doing Business with the Devil' 179–180.

[75] 'The IG Farben Case' Vol VIII 1127. See also Lippman, 'War Crimes Trials of German Industrialists' 223.

[76] ibid 224.

[77] Baars, 'Capitalism's Victor's Justice?' 183.

[78] 'The IG Farben Case' Vol VIII 1180–1187.

[79] Baars, 'Capitalism's Victor's Justice?' 184.

[80] US Military Tribunal, 'The Krupp case', Vol IX, Trials of War Criminals before the Nuremberg Military Tribunals under Control Council Law No. 10 (October 1946–April 1949).

[81] SA Goldman, 'A Fuhrer of Industry: Krupp before, during and after Nuremberg' (2017) 39 *Loyola of Los Angeles International and Comparative Law Review* 187.

officials were indicted.[82] With regard to crimes against peace and conspiracy, the judges eventually acquitted the defendants by applying the 'beyond any reasonable doubt' standard.[83] On the contrary, the tribunal found a significant involvement of Krupp's officials in war crimes and crimes against humanity.[84] It is well known that Alfried Krupp suggested that Hitler implement the theory of 'extermination through work' (*Vernichtung durch Arbeit*)[85] in its eighty-one factories, where in five years (1940–1945) '69,898 foreign civilian workers; 4,978 concentration camp inmates; and 23,076 prisoners of war'[86] were employed.

Despite the heterogeneity of the factual backgrounds and procedural circumstances underlying the proceedings described above, it is possible to identify some common features, which will be discussed in more detail below. First, the defendants were criminal masterminds involved in the commission of international crimes of an economic nature – such as slave labour and plunder – or in business activities closely linked to the commission of international crimes – eg the sale and purchase of commodities. Secondly, most of the defendants were motivated by economic gain. German industrialists profited from forced labour to such an extent that this widespread practice was described as a 'business of genocide'.[87] An illustrative example is the slave labour policy implemented at the IG Farben synthetic rubber factory in Auschwitz, where high mortality rates were reached.[88] With regard to the crime of plunder of public and private properties, the judges adopted a broad interpretation of this offence to criminalise the systematic seizure and exploitation of properties in occupied territories for economic purposes.[89] Thirdly, in the three industrialists' cases, offences involving dual-use goods made it difficult to determine the criminal nature of the defendants' conduct.[90]

[82] Crimes against peace and conspiracy or common plan to commit such crimes (Count One); war crimes and crimes against humanity for participating in slave labour (Count Two) and plunder and spoliation (Count Three).

[83] 'The Krupp Case' 1329.

[84] ibid 1370, 1374–1375.

[85] Goldman, 'A Fuhrer of Industry' 189.

[86] Lippman, 'War Crimes Trials of German Industrialists' 244.

[87] See MT Allen, *The Business of Genocide: The SS, Slave Labor, and the Concentration Camps* (The University of North Carolina Press, 2005). See also D Bloxham, 'A Survey of Jewish Slave Labour in the Nazi System' (2001) 10 *Journal of Holocaust Education* 25, 32. For further information on different categories of slave labourers, see Goldman, 'A Fuhrer of Industry' 190.

[88] Hayes, 'The Chemistry' 74. For a comprehensive overview of Jewish forced labour practices, see also BB Ferencz, *Less Than Slaves: Jewish Forced Labor and the Quest for Compensation* (Indiana University Press, 2002).

[89] See L van den Herik and D Dam-de Jong, 'Revitalizing the Antique War Crime of Pillage: The Potential and Pitfalls of Using International Criminal Law to Address Illegal Resource Exploitation' (2011) 22 *Criminal Law Forum* 237, 265.

[90] For a definition of dual-use commodities, see C Burchard, 'Ancillary and Neutral Business Contributions to "Corporate–Political Core Crime": Initial Enquiries Concerning the Rome Statute' (2010) 8 *Journal of International Criminal Justice* 919, 926. For instance, the sums of money paid by Flick to the Himmler's Circle of Friends could have been used for illegal purposes as much as for cultural purposes, see 'The Flick Case' 1219 and 1221. Another example is the *Zyklon* B sold by IG Farben to the SS, which could have been used as an insecticide, see 'The IG Farben Case'

For the sake of completeness, the *Rasche* case deserves to be mentioned in this section. Karl Rasche was one of the twenty-one defendants tried in 'The Ministries Case' before the US Military Tribunal IV. Although he had held prominent positions in the Nazi government, he was prosecuted for his activities as an executive officer of the Dresdner Bank.[91] These activities included donations to the Himmler's Circle of Friends, loans to the SS and 'Aryanisation transactions'.[92] He was acquitted of all charges as, according to the judges, it would have been difficult to argue that his business conduct had turned him into a 'partner of a criminal enterprise'.[93] This remark raised controversial issues that will be discussed below.

The Industrialists' Proceedings in the French, British and Soviets' German Zones of Occupation

As a subsidiary of IG Farben, the German company known as Tesch and Stabenow supplied *Zyklon* B to SS officials, who used it in the Auschwitz/Birkenau concentration camp to exterminate over four million people.[94] In 1946, the owner of the company, Dr. Bruno Tesch, together with his second-in-command, Karl Weinbacher, and the firm's gas technician, Joachim Drosihn, were charged with war crimes before the British Military Court set up in Hamburg.[95] The conduct alleged against the defendants fell into three categories: supplying gas and gassing equipment, providing technicians for field operations and, lastly, instructing SS officials on how to use the gas supplied.[96]

Considering that these acts were part of the company's daily business activities, only proof of the defendants' knowledge of the actual use of the gas

Vol VIII 1168. In the Krupp case, it is stated that the sale of weapons is not a crime per se, see 'The Krupp Case' 309. On the definition of weapons as a multi-use product see also Jacobson, 'Doing Business with the Devil' 211.

[91] He was an officer in the SS, a member of the Nazi party and the Himmler's Circle of Friends. However, he was a member of the Vorstand of the Dresdner bank and also worked in other banks and firms, see US Military Tribunal, 'The Ministries case', Vol XII, Trials of War Criminals before the Nuremberg Military Tribunals under Control Council Law No. 10 (October 1946-April 1949) 18. For this reason, he was defined as a 'banker by profession' see US Military Tribunal, 'The Ministries case', Vol XIV, Trials of War Criminals before the Nuremberg Military Tribunals under Control Council Law No. 10 (October 1946–April 1949) 621.

[92] Vol XII, 'The Ministries Case' 43.

[93] Vol XIV, 'The Ministries Case' 622. For additional information on the *Rasche* case and on the *Pohl* case, see Baars, *The Corporation, Law and Capitalism* 182–185.

[94] United Nations War Crimes Commission (UNWCC), Case No. 9 (The Zyklon B. Case: Trial of Bruno Tesch and Two Others) www.legal-tools.org/doc/297178/, 'The *Zyklon* B Case' 94. See also Baars, *The Corporation, Law and Capitalism* 186–188.

[95] Unlike the other military tribunals that applied the CCL no 10, the British Military Courts' jurisdiction was limited to war crimes as defined in Regulation 1 of the Royal Warrant and 'did not cover crimes against humanity or crimes against the peace', see Baars, *The Corporation, Law and Capitalism* 186.

[96] 'The *Zyklon* B Case' 94.

supplied would have made it possible to hold them criminally liable for war crimes. Had the British judges' analysis of the accused's *mens rea* focused on determining their purpose rather than their knowledge, it is likely that none of the defendants would have been convicted. In this scenario, their defence counsels could easily have shown that a lawful purpose – making profit – was being pursued by individuals carrying out lawful business activities.[97] Therefore, the choice of 'knowledge' as the most appropriate *mens rea* standard was decisive for the court's findings: the two company executives were convicted as war criminals, since they knew that the death and illness of concentration camps inmates had been the inevitable consequence of the use of the lethal gasses and pharmaceutical substances supplied. In contrast, the gas technician was acquitted because of his subordinate position and, thus, his lack of knowledge.[98]

Similarly, officials of the Roechling Enterprises, a company located in Saarland and specialised in the production of coal and metal,[99] were tried before the General Tribunal of the Military Government of the French Zone of Occupation in Germany. At the time of Hitler's rise, Hermann Roechling was running the company. He became a member of the Nazi Party and, for his loyal support to the *Führer*, was appointed by Hitler as President of the 'Reich Association Iron'.[100] Despite the existence of a relationship of mutual esteem between Hitler and Roechling, the judges acquitted the latter of crimes against peace, as he had not played any leading role in waging an aggressive war. The argument, already put forward by the American judges in the *Farben* case, that crime against peace was a 'leadership crime' planned by policymakers and not by 'men of industry' was reiterated by the French Military Tribunal.[101]

Nonetheless, Roechling was convicted of contributing to the continuation of the war of aggression.[102] As to the other charges, the French judges acknowledged that political leaders of the Third Reich could not have committed atrocities of such a large scale and gravity without the 'conscious assistance of certain great German industrialists and financiers'.[103] In particular, Hermann and Ernst Roechling were convicted of profiting from economic plunder and spoliation of factories situated in the Alsace-Lorraine region.[104]

Finally, among the German companies that contributed substantially to the implementation of Third Reich policies was Töpf & Sohne, founded in 1878

[97] S Michalowski, 'Doing Business with a Bad Actor: How to Draw the Line between Legitimate Commercial Activities and Those That Trigger Corporate Complicity Liability' (2015) 50 *Texas International Law Journal* 403, 458.

[98] 'The *Zyklon* B Case' 102.

[99] Trials of War Criminals before the Nuremberg Military Tribunals under Control Council Law No. 10, Vol XIV, Appendix B, 'The Roechling Case' (October 1946–April 1949) 1064.

[100] Lippman, 'War Crimes Trials of German Industrialists' 182.

[101] ibid.

[102] 'The Roechling Case' 1072; Jacobson, 'Doing Business with the Devil' 191; Baars, *The Corporation, Law and Capitalism* 190.

[103] 'The Roechling Case' 1062.

[104] ibid 1072–1073; Lippman, 'War Crimes Trials of German Industrialists' 183.

and based in Erfurt. The company specialised in the production of several types of equipment, including ovens and ventilation systems, which were sold to the SS for the most notorious and infamous purposes. The two Töpf brothers who headed the company became members of the Nazi Party and went into business with Adolf Hitler shortly before the outbreak of war. Several concentration camps, including Dachau, Mathausen and Auschwitz were supplied with machinery manufactured and patented by Töpf & Sohne. It is worth noting that the company's engineers, in particular Kurt Prüfer, designed and supplied ovens capable of holding multiple bodies at the same time, which could raise suspicions about the company's executives' knowledge of what was happening in the camps. Not only the company supplied materials to commit international crimes, but also provided services, including the installation of the equipment, which was supervised directly by the company's employees.

The Soviets tried Prüfer together with four other employees, who were all found guilty and sentenced to twenty-five years imprisonment.[105] Compared to the sentences issued by other military tribunals, those delivered by the Soviets were certainly the harshest. This was in line with the strict policy the Soviet Union had suggested during the London Charter negotiations, according to which those accused of international crimes were to be presumed guilty.[106] As for the Töpf brothers, one of them committed suicide, while the other spent the rest of his life claiming to be innocent and blaming the SS for the misuse of the equipment legally supplied by his company.

What about the Industrialists of the Allied Countries?

The *Schacht* case raised several issues related to the '*tu quoque* defence'.[107] During the trial, a weak parallel was drawn between Schacht's involvement in the implementation of Nazi policies and the involvement of companies headquartered in the Allied countries. Schacht's defence counsel argued that 'the *outside world* knew the existence of this rearmament and held it as endurable in any case for the preservation of world peace longer than *Schacht* did'.[108] In other words, it was held that the prosecution of German industrialists for allegedly assisting Germany in its rearmament efforts should go hand in hand with the prosecution of businessmen who ran companies based in the Allied countries, which traded with Germany or had subsidiaries there.[109]

[105] Baars, 'Capitalism's Victor's Justice?' 189. See also Holocaust Encyclopedia, 'Topf and Sons: An 'Ordinary Company'' https://encyclopedia.ushmm.org/content/en/article/topf-and-sons-an-ordinary-company; Baars, *The Corporation, Law and Capitalism* 193–194.

[106] R Cryer et al, *An Introduction to International Criminal Law and Procedure*, 3rd edn (Cambridge University Press, 2014) 117.

[107] ibid 119, for a definition of the '*tu quoque defence*'.

[108] Office of the United States, *Nazi Conspiracy and Aggression* 529 (emphasis added).

[109] Jacobson, 'Doing Business with the Devil' 167.

With regard to US companies, the second version of Edwin Sutherland's book 'White Collar Crime'[110] listed those corporations – and their leading officers – that had played a significant role in the commission of white-collar crimes during the Second World War – many of which overlapped with war crimes.[111] For instance, Krupp and General Electric Co. signed an agreement to control the production of steel during the war.[112] It is also known that IBM sold punch card sorting machines to the Germans. Hermann Hollerith had invented IBM machines to help the Census Bureau in Washington DC produce a detailed portrait of the population.[113] He could never have imagined that a product that he had patented at the age of nineteen would have facilitated the identification of the Jews and, ultimately, the concrete realisation of the Holocaust.[114]

From a legal perspective little was done. Although empirical data called for the prosecution of serious economic offences linked to the perpetration of international crimes, no tribunal was set up to prosecute the US industrialists involved, and none of them was tried before the tribunals established under CCL no 10. Some corporations and their officials were sanctioned before national courts, although there are controversial examples of justice in this regard. For instance, the directors of the Ford plant in Cologne, where slave labourers were employed, were tried and sentenced to mild sanctions, before being reinstated as managers of the same company.[115]

The reasons behind the neutral approach adopted towards the business leaders who worked for companies headquartered in the Allied countries were primarily political. Since its inception, the international criminal justice system has been the result of legal and political considerations. In the aftermath of the Second World War, the selection of cases and charges was heavily influenced by politics: it is well known that the US War Department had expressly instructed Du Bois, as prosecutor in the *Farben* case, not to charge the defendants with aggressive war, for fear of retaliation by US companies that had done business

[110] EH Sutherland, G Geis and C Goff, *White Collar Crime: The Uncut Version* (Yale University Press, 1983).

[111] JF Galliher and TJ Guess, 'Two Generations of Sutherland's White-Collar War Crime Data and Beyond' (2009) 51 *Crime, Law and Social Change* 163, 164. For further information on the involvement of American industrialists in business dealings with the Nazis, see also AC Sutton, *Wall Street and the Rise of Hitler: The Astonishing True Story of the American Financiers Who Bankrolled the Nazis* (Clairview Books, 2010).

[112] Galliher and Guess, 'Two Generations' 169.

[113] E Black, *IBM and the Holocaust: The Strategic Alliance between Nazi Germany and America's Most Powerful Corporation* (Time Warner Paperbacks, 2002) 32.

[114] S Roksandić Vidlička, *Prosecuting Serious Economic Crimes as International Crimes – a New Mandate for the ICC?*, Research Series of the Max Planck Institute for Foreign and International Criminal Law Series BC: Publications of the Max Planck Partner Group for Balkan Criminology 2 (Duncker & Humblot, 2017) 95.

[115] Ramasastry, 'Corporate Complicity' 123. M Dobbs, 'Ford and GM Scrutinized for Alleged Nazi Collaboration: Firms Deny Researchers' Claims on Aiding German War Effort' (*The Washington Post*, 1998) www.washingtonpost.com/wp-srv/national/daily/nov98/nazicars30.htm.

with Farben's officials.[116] In this respect, one of Farben's most important executives, Carl Krauch, stated

> When I heard the final plea of the prosecution yesterday, I often thought of my colleagues in the United States and in England and tried to imagine what these men would think, when they heard and read these attacks hurled at us by the prosecution. For after all, they, too, are scientists and engineers; they had similar problems [...].[117]

Despite the positive results achieved by the industrialists' trials, something more could have been done in addition to bringing non-German business officials to justice. For instance, the number of economic actors prosecuted under CCL no 10 was lower than expected, considering the scale and gravity of the atrocities committed within and through their companies.[118] Furthermore, the sentences imposed on the defendants were objectively lenient and non-restorative,[119] which gave the victims the impression that international criminal justice was merely 'symbolic justice'.[120]

On the other hand, the doctrinal and jurisprudential contribution of post-Second World War proceedings to the development of international criminal law is indisputable. In particular, the industrialists' proceedings can be seen as a first step towards the recognition of the criminal responsibility of businessmen for international crimes and the potential qualification of some economic offences as crimes of international significance.[121]

A PRIMORDIAL CONCEPT OF INTERNATIONAL ECONOMIC CRIME

The historical vicissitudes and legal developments outlined above provide the framework in which a primordial notion of international economic crime could emerge. Three observations relating to the cases discussed help to grasp the essence of the concept of international economic crime and will be examined in detail below. First, in the Nuremberg trial and the subsequent proceedings,

[116] Baars, 'Capitalism's Victor's Justice?' 181.
[117] ibid.
[118] Burchard, 'Ancillary and Neutral Business' 920.
[119] ibid. See also Jessberger, 'On the Origins of Individual Criminal Responsibility' 788. Unlike the IMT, which sentenced Funk and Speer to life imprisonment and to twenty years' imprisonment, respectively, the sentences issued by CCL no 10 tribunals were more lenient. For instance, Frederic Flick and Hermann Roechling were sentenced to seven years' imprisonment; Carl Krauch in the *Farben* case was sentenced to six years' imprisonment; Alfried Krupp was sentenced to twelve years' imprisonment and confiscation of his property. The British Court was the harshest as it sentenced Bruno Tesch and his second-in-command to death by hanging. The Soviets sentenced Kurt Prufer to twenty-five years' imprisonment.
[120] The limited value of the IMT trial and subsequent proceedings for the victims of crimes committed during the Second World War has been much criticised in the literature, see Baars, *The Corporation, Law and Capitalism* 197, 236–238.
[121] Jessberger, 'On the Origins of Individual Criminal Responsibility' 783, 801. See also Roksandić Vidlička, *Prosecuting Serious Economic Crimes* 97.

public and private actors were held criminally responsible for two categories of offences of economic significance. Secondly, the perpetration of these two categories of crimes entailed the application of different modes of liability. Lastly, the Nuremberg tribunals were pioneers in recognising that crimes of an economic nature can reach a high threshold of gravity when committed in a certain context.

Categories of Crimes of Economic Significance

In post-war trials, public and private economic actors were charged with offences belonging to one or more of the three categories of international crimes envisaged by the drafters of the Nuremberg Charter: crimes against peace, war crimes and crimes against humanity. Among the acts falling into these categories were offences with an economic dimension, namely slave labour and plunder. Both involved the production of an economic advantage for the offender, although the former was a crime against persons, whereas the latter a crime against property. Nonetheless, the gravity of crimes against property was explicitly recognised by the Nuremberg judges, and their perpetrators were usually convicted as war criminals. In particular, the harm caused by these offences was greater than that perceived 'in terms of francs or marks or acres or tons',[122] since the act of plundering or seizing properties could have a huge detrimental effect on the economic resources of the occupied and victimised countries, causing 'famine, inflation, and an active black market'.[123]

These were not the only acts of economic significance in which public and private actors were involved during the Second World War. Some defendants contributed to the perpetration of international crimes through the commission of economic offences that did not fall within the subject-matter jurisdiction of the tribunals[124] and included the laundering of the proceeds of international crimes, the sale of commodities and services knowing that they would be used to commit international crimes, and the financing of international crimes.

Walter Funk's trial is illustrative of the first type of economic offence. Had the defendant not been aware of the unlawful nature of the materials sent by the SS to the Reichsbank, he could have considered their conversion into gold bars as a neutral banking activity. However, the IMT found that 'he either knew what was being received or was deliberately closing his eyes to what was being done'.[125] His mental element – knowledge or wilful blindness, according to the judges – was deduced from the fact that he was President of the Reichsbank and

[122] 'The Flick Case' 985–986.
[123] ibid.
[124] Vest H, 'Business Leaders and the Modes of Individual Criminal Responsibility under International Law' (2010) 8 *Journal of International Criminal Justice* 851, 852.
[125] IMT, *Trial of the Major War Criminals* 306.

this made the conversion of stolen materials into gold bars a criminal conduct equivalent to money-laundering. Consequently, he was convicted of war crimes and crimes against humanity for laundering the proceeds of international crimes.

A similar reasoning applies to the sale of commodities and services to the SS. A sale contract is, by definition, an agreement between a seller and a customer, whereby the former transfers the ownership of a commodity or a service to the latter in exchange for payment. To simplify, it is a neutral and profitable activity, provided that the seller has no knowledge of the purpose of the commodities or services supplied; instead, it becomes a criminal activity as soon as the seller becomes aware that the buyer will use them to commit criminal conduct. It is not easy to draw a line between neutral business activities and corporate crimes for several reasons, which have been extensively explored in case law and literature.[126] These reasons include, on the one hand, the multi-use nature of the products and services supplied and, on the other hand, the need to prove the *mens rea* of the supplier. These challenging issues were largely discussed in some of the industrialists' cases (eg the *Farben* case, the *Tesch and Stanebow* case, and the *Töpf and Sohne* case), in which the defendants were charged with the commission of war crimes and/or crimes against humanity for supplying chemicals, ovens, and services to the SS.

Financing criminal activities is the third type of business conduct in which economic actors engaged during the Second World War. In the *Flick* case, defendants Flick and Steinbrinck were charged with membership in the SS for largely financing this organisation with knowledge of its criminal purposes. The two accused had paid a significant amount of money to the Himmler's Circle of Friends, knowing that the founder of the group was the Reich Leader of the SS – a paramilitary organisation under Hitler and Himmler's control, in charge of the implementation of Nazi racial policies and the management of concentration camps – and that his person 'could be hardly separated from his organisation'.[127] The US Military Tribunal admitted that the connection between the financial contributions and the perpetration of international crimes could not be inferred from the nature of the Circle, which had been founded as a group of bankers, industrialists, government officials and SS officers with the main purpose of debating economic issues.[128] Himmler himself was 'a man of dual personality; on the one hand a gentleman with cultural interests and on the other an inhumane monster'.[129] Despite the existence of evidence militating

[126] Vol XIV, 'The Ministries Case' 382: 'The demarcation of what is permissible or unauthorized within the scope of an activity directed towards earnings and profits, will always be more or less fluctuating'. The difficulty of tracing the line between lawful and unlawful business activities is also highlighted in Feldman, 'Financial Institutions in Nazi Germany' 32 and in Roksandić Vidlička, *Prosecuting Serious Economic Crimes* 103.

[127] 'The Flick Case' 1218.

[128] ibid 1219 and 1164: '[the Circle of Himmler] consisted of a circle of people who were invited to pleasant social gatherings'. See also Sutton, *Wall Street* 123–132.

[129] 'The Flick Case' 1218.

in favour of a mitigation of the sentence, the judges ultimately found both defendants guilty, as they were aware of Himmler's criminal activities and, nonetheless, decided to contribute to his Circle without being compelled to do so.

On the contrary, in the *Rasche* case, the judges acquitted the German banker on the grounds that Himmler's Circle of Friends, which the defendant had also financed, could not be considered a 'policy-making institution'.[130] Had the judges been more attentive to the fact that the ultimate beneficiaries of Rasche's financial contributions were the SS, the outcome of the trial might have been different.

In the cases mentioned so far, the defendants were either charged with or convicted of one or more international crimes, in particular war crimes or crimes against humanity, through the perpetration of economic offences. However, none of the three types of economic conduct described above was ever considered an act potentially falling within one of the categories of international crimes for two main reasons. On the one hand, one of the main defensive strategies adopted to spare defendants the burden of a trial and the consequences of a potential conviction was to emphasise the neutral character of their economic activities and the low level of social harm they caused.[131] On the other hand, despite their inevitable link to war, none of these economic crimes were explicitly listed as violations of the laws and customs of war or as acts directed against civilians.

Instead of exploring the possibility of broadly interpreting the concept of war crimes and crimes against humanity to include certain economic offences, the IMT and CCL no 10 tribunals relied on modes of liability other than direct perpetration to convict public and private actors for contributing to the commission of international crimes by laundering criminal proceeds, supplying materials necessary to exterminate thousands of innocent individuals or financially supporting the Nazi system.

Individual Criminal Liability of Economic Actors: Principals and Accomplices

The Nuremberg Charter contains no provision listing modes of liability. The only indirect reference to the different roles played by the offenders during the war is found in the third paragraph of Article 6, concerning the concept of common plan or conspiracy, according to which: '*Leaders*, *organisers*, *instigators* and *accomplices* participating in the formulation or execution of a common

[130] Vol XIV, 'The Ministries Case' 622.

[131] W Coleman, 'Toward an Integrated Theory of White-Collar Crime' (1987) 93 *American Journal of Sociology* 406, 411–414. Coleman analyses several techniques of neutralisation used by white-collar criminals as defensive strategies. Among them is the 'denial of harm', to which defence counsels frequently resorted at Nuremberg.

plan or conspiracy to commit any of the foregoing crimes are responsible for all acts performed by any persons in execution of such plan'.[132] Several modes of liability, including instigation, complicity, direct and indirect perpetration, are thus mentioned, without being accurately defined. The drafters of the CCL no 10 were more cautious and provided a list of six modes of liability under Article II(2), including direct perpetration and accessory participation.

Based on this legal framework, the IMT and the Allied military tribunals adopted a two-pronged approach in choosing the most appropriate mode of liability for economic actors, depending on the nature of the crimes committed. Those who had perpetrated international crimes with an economic dimension were convicted as 'principal perpetrators' who had taken relevant steps in the execution of Nazi slave labour policies or programs involving the plunder of public or private properties. On the contrary, those who had committed economic offences that did not constitute international crimes – laundering of criminal proceeds, supplying commodities or services for criminal purposes, financing criminal activities – were convicted as 'accomplices' of high-level politicians and military commanders. In the *Flick* case, the US Tribunal held that 'one who knowingly by his influence and money contributes to the support thereof must, under settled legal principles, be deemed to be, if not a principal, certainly an *accessory* to such crimes'.[133]

Similarly, the British judges found Bruno Tesch and Karl Weinbacher guilty of war crimes as accessories for placing the means to commit war crimes in the hands of the SS. The judges acted on the principle that 'any civilian who is an accessory to a violation of the laws and customs of war is himself also liable as a war criminal',[134] where the alleged war crime in that case was a violation of Article 46 of The Hague Convention of 1907.

The analysis of the *mens rea* element was decisive in finding whether the defendants were guilty of international crimes as accessories. In the *Rasche* judgment, the act of financing the SS was not considered criminal conduct and the defendant was not convicted, despite evidence showing that he was aware of the consequences of his behaviour.[135] On the contrary, in the *Funk* case the IMT adopted a broader interpretation of the *mens rea* element, concluding that the defendant's wilful blindness would suffice to meet the subjective element required to be held criminally liable as an accessory for war crimes and crimes against humanity.[136] This is in line with the principle that when the principal perpetrator is 'visibly inclined' to commit a crime, the risk undertaken by

[132] Emphasis added.
[133] 'The Flick Case' 1217.
[134] 'The *Zyklon* B Case' 103.
[135] Burchard, 'Ancillary and Neutral Business' 930, arguing that the judgment in the *Rasche* case 'drew a thin red line between ordinary (neutral and non-criminal) and exceptional (criminal) business affiliations'.
[136] 'The Funk Case' 306: 'The Tribunal is of the opinion that he either knew what was being received or was deliberately closing his eyes to what was being done'.

businessmen is no longer permissible, as this would give a criminal connotation to the business activity related to the predicate crime.[137]

In the *Farben* case, the judges were more lenient. They required that the executives' knowledge – excluding *dolus eventualis* – of the actual use of *Zyklon* B in the concentration camps be proven beyond any reasonable doubt, which was not done.[138] The US judges believed that 'knowledge' could not be inferred from the position held and the authority exercised by the accused within the company – eg from the fact that Farben defendants were members of the supervisory council of DEGESH – or from the fact that extraordinarily huge quantities of poison had been delivered to the SS. On the contrary, in the so-called *Zyklon* B case, the British judges convicted Tesch and Weinbacher to death on the grounds that, given their high-ranking positions, they perfectly knew how the SS would have used the chemical.[139] In this case, it was recognised that the position held by the defendants within the company was an important element from which to infer a guilty state of mind.[140]

In conclusion, while the IMT and the Allied military tribunals adopted divergent approaches in determining the mental element required to be considered as an accomplice, they unanimously recognised economic actors not responsible for international crimes as material perpetrators, ie as those who filled the gas chambers with chemicals or took care of the functioning of the furnace system. Rather, they were 'desk murderers',[141] criminals behind the scenes of the Holocaust.

Elements of a Primordial Concept of International Economic Crime

One of the greatest merits of the post-war military trials was their decision not to overlook the gravity of economic offences committed in the unprecedented context of the Second World War. Albeit in a vague and rudimentary manner, the above cases depicted a primordial concept of 'international economic crime', which seems to include any economic crime (1) chronologically and significantly connected to international crimes and war (2), perpetrated by high-ranking public or private individuals (3) involved in a deviant state-corporate system (4). Although these factors reflect the seriousness of the crimes in question, in the aftermath of the war such crimes were not considered a threat to the fundamental values of the international community (5) and, as a result, the concept of international economic crime was never coined.

[137] M Cupido, 'Causation in International Crimes Cases:(Re)Concenptualizing the Causal Linkage' (2021) 32 *Criminal Law Forum* 1, 29.
[138] 'The IG Farben Case' Vol VIII 1169. See also Baars, *The Corporation, Law and Capitalism* 175.
[139] 'The *Zyklon* B Case' 102.
[140] ibid 101.
[141] See Holocaust Encyclopedia, 'Topf and Sons'.

Economic Crimes

Public and private economic actors have been convicted by international military tribunals for committing 'criminal' acts. However, the uncertainty underlying the distinction between unlawful and lawful business activities has raised considerable difficulties for the judges. In the *Ministries* case, the American judges recognised the criminal nature of the acts of slave labour in which the companies to which defendants Puhl and Rasche had granted loans were involved.[142] Nonetheless, the US Tribunal failed to acknowledge the criminal character of the act of financing those criminal activities, on the questionable ground that a transaction does not make a banker a criminal even if he or she knows or has good reason to believe that the transaction will finance criminal activities.[143] The tribunal justified its position by referring to the need to keep morals and law separate and to consider the purely economic nature of the acts committed by the two businessmen in those circumstances.[144] The US judges adopted a more reasonable stance on this issue in the industrialists' proceedings. In the *Flick* case, the tribunal did not hesitate to recognise the criminal character of the financing activities carried out by Flick and Steinbrinck in support of the SS. Therefore, according to some scholars, the reasoning elaborated in the *Rasche* case must be regarded as an interlude, which was dismissed by subsequent case law.[145]

The second common denominator of the acts for which economic actors were convicted at the end of the war is their 'economic' character. It is said that 'every degree of business has its invitation of evil: necessity tempts the poor man; avarice tempts the rich'.[146] Most of the accused were motivated by avarice,[147] with the exception of Alfried Krupp, who was not only encouraged by the idea of maximising his earnings, but also by Nazi racist doctrines.[148] Besides this exceptional case, the typical perpetrator of economic crimes during the Second World War corresponded to the degeneration of the *homo economicus*:[149] an

[142] Vol XII, 'The Ministries Case' 61–62.

[143] Vol XIV, 'The Ministries Case' 622.

[144] ibid.

[145] Roksandić Vidlička, *Prosecuting Serious Economic Crimes* 99, citing Burchard, 'Ancillary and Neutral Business' 929–930.

[146] Defoe is cited in H Berghoff and U Spiekermann, 'Shady Business: On the History of White-Collar Crime' (2018) 60 *Business History* 289, 289.

[147] In the *Roechling* case the French Tribunal highlighted Hermann Roechling's dissatisfaction with the properties he had been given, which he called a 'slice of cake', see 'The Roechling Case' 1113. See also Jessberger, 'On the Origins of Individual Criminal Responsibility' 785, who describes the collaboration between IG Farben and the Nazi regime as a 'marriage of convenience'. Industrialists who worked for companies in the Allied countries (eg Coca Cola, Ford, IBM) also aimed to maximise their profits, see Galliher and Guess, 'Two Generations' 169 and 171–172.

[148] Goldman, 'A Fuhrer of Industry' 189.

[149] Burchard, 'Ancillary and Neutral Business' 928. See also S Starr, 'Extraordinary Crimes at Ordinary Times: International Justice Beyond Crisis Situations' (2007) 101 *Northwestern University Law Review* 1257, 1301.

individual who followed the logic of profit to the detriment of non-measurable values, such as human dignity.

Chronological and Significant Connection to International Crimes and War

International criminal law scholars have extensively explored the link between economic crimes committed during the Second World War and traditional categories of international crimes, in order to identify the most appropriate modes of criminal liability under which economic actors could be convicted.[150] It was commonly acknowledged that international crimes and economic crimes were primarily connected through a 'causation continuum' link,[151] meaning that there was a chronological factual connection between them. For instance, the gas supply took place before the extermination of concentration camp inmates in the gas chambers. On the contrary, the storage of gold and personal belongings of concentration camp inmates in the Reichsbank and their conversion into gold bars was carried out to launder the proceeds of international crimes and to profit from their sale. In both scenarios, economic acts and international crimes were linked by a relationship of proximity, as the economic criminal activity was committed immediately before or after the perpetration of international crimes.[152]

This connection was not only chronological but also significant. As noted by the defendants Funk and Speer,[153] and by the IMT itself,[154] the activities of the Nazi State and army depended heavily on German industry for the supply of materials and services, to the extent that German industrialists were qualified as 'magicians who made the fantasies of 'Mein Kampf' come true'.[155] However, this should be interpreted to mean that economic criminal activities were not a *condicio sine qua non* for the commission of international crimes, but a significant contribution to them. In the *Zyklon B* case and in the *Farben* case, the use of the chemical sold to the SS was defined as one of 'different methods of extermination'.[156] In other words, had the gas not been sold, the killing of thousands of human beings would still have been possible, but in a different manner and to a different extent.

[150] See, inter alia, Burchard, 'Ancillary and Neutral Business'; Jacobson, 'Doing Business with the Devil'; Vest, 'Business Leaders'. See also S Manacorda, A Marletta and G Vanacore (eds), 'Individual Liability for Business Involvement in International Crimes' (2017) 1 *Revue Internationale de Droit Pénal* and J Kyriakakis, 'Developments in International Criminal Law and the Case of Business Involvement in International Crimes' (2012) 94 *International Review of the Red Cross* 981.

[151] Burchard, 'Ancillary and Neutral Business' 923.

[152] ibid. See also Cupido, 'Causation in International Crimes Cases' 47, stating that '[…] criminal liability "is more likely when a corporate actor provides more direct assistance or is more closely involved in the commission of the criminal act, for example by specifically tailoring products to assist perpetrators of crime"'.

[153] Lippman, 'War Crimes Trials of German Industrialists' 207.

[154] 'The Roechling Case' 1062.

[155] Jessberger, 'On the Origins of Individual Criminal Responsibility' 787.

[156] 'The IG Farben Case' Vol VIII 1169.

High-Ranking Public and Private Individuals as Economic Criminals

Both public and private economic actors were tried before the international military tribunals as individuals allegedly responsible for international crimes. The principle of individual criminal responsibility was expressly provided for in Article 6 of the Nuremberg Charter and in Article II(2) and (3) of the CCL no 10, where the term 'person' referred exclusively to natural persons, thus excluding legal persons from the scope of personal jurisdiction of the post-war military tribunals. The importance of the principle of individual criminal responsibility also emerges from the IMT's well-known statement that '[c]rimes against international law are committed by men, not abstract entities, and only by punishing individuals who commit such crimes can the provisions of international law be enforced.'[157]

The decision to prosecute individuals and not 'abstract entities' was justified on two main grounds: on the one hand, the need to prevent natural persons from hiding behind artificial entities,[158] and on the other, the choice not to deviate from fundamental principles of criminal law recognised in most legal systems, including the principle of individual criminal responsibility. Although it is beyond the scope of this investigation, at the time of the Nuremberg trials, a long-standing debate was initiated on the advantages and disadvantages of prosecuting corporations for their involvement in the perpetration of international crimes.[159]

Another relevant observation regarding the perpetrators of economic crimes during the Second World War is that these individuals held important positions both within the State or within private companies, which means that international criminal liability also applied to private individuals. In this respect, it is necessary to mention the *Flick* case, where the judges held that:

> The distinction [between public officials and individuals holding no public offices] is unsound. International law, as such, binds every citizen just as does ordinary municipal law. Acts adjudged criminal when done by an officer of the government are criminal also when done by a private individual. The guilt differs only in magnitude, not in quality. The offender in either case is charged with personal wrong and punishment falls on the offender in propria persona.[160]

[157] IMT, *Trial of the Major War Criminals* 223. This principle had already been anticipated in the Nuremberg Charter under Article 6 and in the indictment before the IMT, stating on several occasions that defendants 'are individually responsible for their own acts'.

[158] Bush, 'The Prehistory of Corporations' 1162. On the distinction 'individuals-abstract entities' see B Fisse and J Braithwaite, *Corporations, Crime, and Accountability* (Cambridge University Press, 1993) 17–58.

[159] For a comprehensive analysis of this debate see Bush, 'The Prehistory of Corporations' 1130–1159.

[160] 'The Flick Case' 1192.

Lastly, it should be noted that despite the indictment of industrialists who held subordinate positions,[161] most of the defendants who were eventually convicted held senior and institutional positions.[162] The military tribunals considered that high-level individuals were the only ones with sufficient power and influence to make important decisions and interact with their public or private counterparts.[163]

The Nazi State-Corporate System

Neither the Nuremberg Charter nor the CCL no 10 provided an explicit and exhaustive definition of conspiracy, which both legal instruments mentioned as a constituent element of crimes against peace and as a mode of liability.[164] The concept was first investigated in the indictment submitted to the IMT, according to which members of the Nazi Party and those who became accessories to its aims could be qualified as 'conspirators' if they knew the purposes fulfilled by the Party.[165] The Nuremberg Tribunal introduced relevant guidelines for the interpretation of the notion of conspiracy, stating that it cannot consist of mere declarations but must involve, on the one hand, a concrete plan 'not too far removed from the time of decision and of action',[166] and on the other, two or more participants who have knowledge of the criminal purpose of the plan.[167]

With the sole exception of Hermann Roechling, none of the defendants involved in the commission of criminal economic activities was convicted of 'conspiracy' to commit international crimes. However, the creation of the 'Hitler Fund', the '*Wehrwirtschaftsführer*' (Military Economic Leaders), and the 'Himmler's Circle of Friends' were indicia of the existence of a system in which the role of industry in Nazi Germany was preponderant.

In her groundbreaking book on the possibility to prosecute serious economic crimes before the ICC, Roksandić Vidlička refers to the existence of an '*interconnection* of businessmen and state officials'[168] during the Second World War,

[161] For instance, in the *Zyklon* B case, the Prosecutor charged Joachim Drosihn, who was the firm's gassing technician. In the *Prufer* case before the Soviet Tribunal, Prufer was not the owner of the Töpf and Sohne company, nor did he hold managerial powers; nonetheless, as the company's most important engineer, he was convicted for doing business with the SS.

[162] See 'The IG Farben Case' Vol VIII 1095–1096.

[163] Vol XII, 'The Ministries Case' 43: '[...] through his position and influence in the Dresdner Bank [...].'

[164] Nuremberg Charter, Art 6(2)(a) and (3). In the CCL no 10 the concept of conspiracy appears under Art II(1)(a), while it is implicitly mentioned as a mode of liability under para (2).

[165] IMT, *Trial of the Major War Criminals* 29–30.

[166] ibid 225.

[167] The American judges reiterated this definition of conspiracy in the *Farben* case, emphasising the need to prove the accused's knowledge of the plan. See 'The IG Farben Case' Vol VIII 1127.

[168] Roksandić Vidlička, *Prosecuting Serious Economic Crimes*, 93 (emphasis added).

a concept close to Jessberger's '*web* of personal and institutional connections between companies, the party and the state [...]'.[169] An even more powerful word was used in Du Bois' book published in 1953, where the American attorney and Nuremberg prosecutor said that Farben was involved in a *cartel*.[170] In other words, although there was no conspiracy – in the legal sense of the term described above – behind the commission of economic crimes, it can be legitimately argued that these offences would not have been so serious and would not have attracted so much attention had they not occurred within the Nazi state-corporate system active in those years.[171]

Threat to the Fundamental Values of the International Community

Post-war tribunals did not question the effects caused by the commission of international crimes or the intensity of their harm. These were violations of international law that infringed both collective and individual fundamental values, such as international peace and security and human dignity.[172] In the *Flick* case, the prosecution defined human freedom, dignity and life as the three pillars on which the concept of human decency is based, and concluded that by undermining these values, slave labour as a war crime and a crime against humanity ranks among the most serious and harmful crimes.[173]

However, the judges did not overtly address the question of whether economic crimes committed within and because of the Nazi state-corporate system could cause similar damage or undermine similar values as those undermined by international crimes. This was the case for two main reasons. On the one hand, apart from plunder and slave labour, no other crime of economic significance was considered at the time to be a violation of the laws and customs of war, nor a violation of the laws of humanity – a notion that the drafters of the Nuremberg Charter used to elaborate the concept of crimes against humanity.[174] On the other hand, economic offences were perceived as 'victimless' crimes when compared to other acts that involved violence and that were committed against persons. Contrary to this presumption, the economic crimes perpetrated

[169] Jessberger, 'On the Origins of Individual Criminal Responsibility' 785 (emphasis added).

[170] He used this term in the title of his book on the *IG Farben* case, see Du Bois, *Generals in Grey Suits*.

[171] Roksandić Vidlička, *Prosecuting Serious Economic Crimes*, 100 citing RJ Michalowski and RC Kramer, *State-Corporate Crime: Wrongdoing at the Intersection of Business and Government* (Rutgers University Press, 2006).

[172] Vol XIV, 'The Ministries Case' 622.

[173] 'The Flick Case' 69.

[174] The Martens Clause appeared for the first time in the Preamble of the Convention (II) with Respect to the Laws and Customs of War on Land' (The Hague, 29 July 1899) (The Hague Convention (II)). According to this clause: 'Until a more complete code of the laws of war is issued, the High Contracting Parties think it right to declare that [...] populations and belligerents remain under the protection and empire of the principles of international law, as they result from the usages established between civilized nations, from the *laws of humanity* and the requirements of public conscience' (emphasis added).

in connection to international crimes during the Second World War and as a result of a deviant state-corporate system, caused extremely serious harm, which was not always their immediate consequence but rather their by-product.[175] With the benefit of hindsight, it would be reasonable to acknowledge that Funk's decision to launder objects stolen from the Jews in the context set up by the Nazi state-corporate system, resulted in a gross violation of the victims' human dignity, equivalent to that caused by other crimes against humanity.

In sum, the Nuremberg trial and the subsequent industrialists' proceedings drew attention to the need to prosecute economic crimes committed in a context characterised by war, international crimes, and the existence of a deviant state-corporate system. This context meant that ordinary economic crimes could go so far as to threaten international values such as human dignity, thus reaching a high gravity threshold. Nonetheless, the time was not yet ripe to give the concept of international economic crime a place in international criminal law.

DIVERGING PATHS: 'ORDINARY' VS. 'INTERNATIONAL' ECONOMIC CRIMES

Primo Levi, Italian writer and Holocaust victim, used these words to describe the arrival of deportees in the Auschwitz camp: '[T]his is hell. Today, in our times, hell must be like this. A huge, empty room [...] What can one think about? One cannot think anymore, it is like being already dead'.[176] The chapter to which this excerpt belongs is significantly titled 'On the bottom'. During the Second World War, humanity hit the bottom and the only way to rise again was to acknowledge and vehemently prohibit the atrocities that had been committed until then. This became the major commitment of the international community, and to this end, States decided to supplement ex post facto and ad hoc proscriptive measures – including the creation of international military tribunals – with prescriptive solutions.[177]

International human rights law thus developed as a reaction to the need to identify human rights to which everyone is entitled and to establish obligations for governments to 'protect, respect and fulfil' those rights.[178] In accordance with these commitments, a series of human rights instruments were adopted.

[175] See Coleman, 'Toward an Integrated Theory' 408, pointing out that white-collar crimes cause 'far more deaths and injuries than other types of crime', but that 'this violence is always a by-product of the offense not the immediate goal, as it is in assault or murder'. See also M Button, B Hock and D Shepherd, *Economic Crime: From Conception to Response* (Routledge, 2022) 18–19, emphasising that financial losses are only a limited result of economic crimes, since the harm caused by these crimes may also include physical and mental health issues for individual victims and, in the most serious cases, can undermine institutions and infrastructures of a country, thereby compromising collective interests.

[176] P Levi, *If This Is a Man* (The Orion Press, 1959) 15.

[177] MC Bassiouni, 'International Crimes: Ratione Materiae' in MC Bassiouni (ed), *Introduction to International Criminal Law*, 2nd edn (Brill, 2012) 137, 217.

[178] Starr, 'Extraordinary Crimes' 1308.

The Universal Declaration of Human Rights (UDHR) was symbolically proclaimed the day after the adoption of the Genocide Convention, on 10 December 1948.[179] Five years later, the ECHR entered into force after being ratified by forty-seven Member States of the Council of Europe, the most notable human rights organisation in the Old Continent.[180] The Convention contributed to the spread of a human rights-oriented culture and was supplemented by a series of protocols.

However, the merits of these instruments were severely impaired by the Cold War, which triggered a latent conflict between two opposing spheres of the globe, East and West, emphasising the economic and political differences between the States involved.[181] The rivalry between Eastern and Western countries resulted in the entry into force of two Covenants adopted in 1966, the International Covenant on Civil and Political Rights (ICCPR) and the International Covenant on Economic, Social and Cultural Rights (ICESCR).[182]

While this complex system of norms related to the protection of human rights was taking shape, the international community began to address other relevant social issues. Between the eighties and the nineties, the criminalisation and prosecution of ordinary economic crimes became the subject of an increasing wave of harmonisation at international and regional level. The same decades witnessed a slow but significant evolution in the orientation of international criminal law tribunals, which shifted from being tribunals focused on the prosecution of war-related crimes to tribunals capable of exercising jurisdiction over offences not necessarily related to armed conflict. Despite this leap forward, no economic crime has been included in the categories of international crimes and the 'second generation' of international criminal law tribunals has only partially contributed to developing the elements of a potential concept of international economic crime.

From Fragmentation to Alignment: Efforts to Harmonise Economic Crimes Enforcement

In the second half of the twentieth century, several international and regional treaties were adopted with the two-fold purpose of defining economic crimes

[179] Universal Declaration of Human Rights (Paris, 10 December 1948).

[180] Convention for the Protection of Human Rights and Fundamental Freedoms (Rome, 4 November 1950) (also known as European Convention on Human Rights or ECHR).

[181] PS Morris, 'Economic Genocide under International Law' (2018) 82 *The Journal of Criminal Law* 18, 23.

[182] N Schrijver, 'Fifty Years International Human Rights Covenants: Improving the Global Protection of Human Rights by Bridging the Gap between the Two Covenants' (2016) 41 *Nederlands Tijdschrift voor de Mensenrechten* 457, 457. See International Covenant on Civil and Political Rights (New York, 19 December 1966) and the International Covenant on Economic, Social and Cultural Rights (New York, 19 December 1966).

and harmonising their criminalisation and prosecution at domestic level.[183] Regarding the first purpose, as anticipated in Chapter 1, a consensus definition of economic crime has never been accepted, although there have been several attempts to determine its content.[184] An economic crime is generally defined as any prohibited act or omission committed for the purpose of generating an economic or professional gain.[185] The breadth of this definition is reflected in the heterogenous nature of the offences that fall into this category.[186]

The second purpose of these regional and international instruments was to draw attention to the fact that economic criminal phenomena, which had hitherto concerned individual States and been dealt with by them individually, were beginning to transcend national borders, raising increasingly serious transnational issues that required harmonised action. The advent of post-modern society, based on the idea of a single globalised world, combined with the development of technologies, has been among the factors that drastically influenced the transnational character of economic crimes and their gravity.[187]

As a result, States had to find a single, coherent answer to problems that had become common. To this end, various regional[188] and international[189] instruments were adopted, although they have not been implemented effectively and equally in all signatory countries.[190] By way of example, despite the entry into force of conventions aimed to harmonise States' reactions to the crime of corruption,[191] there are still some discrepancies in the legislation of States that have ratified those instruments. A report issued in 2020 by the Implementation

[183] S Wharton, 'Redrawing the Line? Serious Crimes of Concern to the International Community Beyond the Rome Statute' (2015) 52 *Canadian Yearbook of International Law/Annuaire canadien de droit international* 129, 139.

[184] Roksandić Vidlička, *Prosecuting Serious Economic Crimes* 51.

[185] ibid. See also L Kohalmi and K Mezei, 'The Concept and Typical Forms of Economic Crime' (2015) 2 *Journal of Eastern-European Criminal Law* 33, 33.

[186] Button, Hock and Shepherd, *Economic Crime*, 9–15. See also a comprehensive classification of economic crimes was proposed by Peter Gottschalk, cited in Roksandić Vidlička, *Prosecuting Serious Economic Crimes* 60–61.

[187] RM Amjad et al, 'Non-Linear Impact of Globalization on Financial Crimes: A Case of Developing Economies' (2021) 25 *Journal of Money Laundering Control* 360, 360: 'One of the reasons why illicit financial flows have increased is globalization, making these criminal activities hard to detect'.

[188] See Inter-American Convention against Corruption (Caracas, 29 March 1996); Council of Europe Criminal Law Convention on Corruption (Strasbourg, 27 January 1999); African Union Convention on Preventing and Combating Corruption (Maputo, 1 July 2003).

[189] See UN Convention against Illicit Traffic in Narcotic Drugs and Psychotropic Substances (Vienna, 19 December 1988); UN Declaration Against Corruption and Bribery in International Commercial Transactions (New York, 16 December 1996); UN Convention for the Suppression of Financing of Terrorism (New York, 9 December 1999); UN Convention against Corruption (New York, 9 December 2003) (UNCAC).

[190] Amjad et al, 'Non-Linear Impact of Globalization' 361.

[191] See n 188 and 189. Kofele-Kale talks about an 'international regime against corruption', see N Kofele-Kale, 'Only Fools Who Send Hyenas to Roast Meat for Them: In Search of the Doctrinal Foundations of the Not-So-Ordinary Crime of Patrimonicide' (2013) 9 *Florida A&M University Law Review* 1, 5.

Review Group on the effects of the UN Convention against Corruption (UNCAC) notes that '[t]he criminalization and enforcement of national and transnational bribery offences under the United Nations Convention against Corruption has presented States Parties with a number of challenges'.[192] Among these challenges is the failure of some States to criminalize certain economic offences.[193] Thus, the system based on suppression treaties is far from being perfect and complete. Nonetheless, it has provided States with preventive and cooperative tools necessary to curb domestic and transnational economic criminality.

Erasing the Economics of War: How Second-Generation ICL Tribunals Overlooked the Economic Drivers of Conflict

Economic crimes continued to be perpetrated in contexts of international significance even after the end of the Second World War, during conflicts that caught the attention of the international community and called for a global reaction. Torn by wars and appalled by precarious financial and political conditions, Sierra Leone, Cambodia, Yugoslavia, and Rwanda have witnessed the most outrageous and inhumane offences since 1945. Nevertheless, the tribunals established to dispense justice in those contexts have generally disregarded economic crimes and activities that contributed to triggering conflicts or that were committed during conflicts,[194] with a few exceptions, including some cases before the ad hoc criminal tribunals and the *Charles Taylor* case before the Special Court for Sierra Leone (SCSL).

The Prosecution of Economic Crimes before the Ad Hoc Criminal Tribunals

In the early nineties, two large-scale conflicts took place in different parts of the world. The Balkans were hit by a series of wars that devastated the political and socio-economic stability of the countries involved, leaving an indelible mark on the lives of their citizens and their national histories. At the same time,

[192] See UNCAC Implementation Review Group, 'Effective Action against Bribery: Criminalization and Enforcement of National and Transnational Bribery Offences under the United Nations Convention against Corruption' (13 November 2020) CAC/COSP/IRG/2020/CRP.16 para 1.

[193] ibid, it is noted that '[w]hile the majority of States parties had criminalized the active and passive bribery of domestic public officials, at least to some degree, the active bribery of foreign public officials and officials of public international organizations was found to be not, or not sufficiently criminalized in many States'. This was confirmed in later reports of the UNCAC Implementation Review Group, 'Implementation of chapter V (Asset recovery) of the United Nations Convention against Corruption' (9 October 2023) CAC/COSP/2023/5, para 44. When discussing issues of dual criminality requirements, it asserts that these mainly arise in States that have not criminalised basic economic offences, such as bribery.

[194] Baars, *The Corporation, Law and Capitalism* 238, arguing that, after the subsequent proceedings against the industrialists, the focus on the 'economic causes of conflict' was removed from international criminal law.

the inhabitants of a small African country, Rwanda, became perpetrators and victims – according to the ethnicity to which they belonged – of acts of genocide. The international community's response to the gruesomeness of the crimes perpetrated in these geographically and culturally distant countries was the same: two Security Council resolutions were adopted to set up an ad hoc tribunal for each country with the goal of establishing truth and justice and avoiding impunity for international criminal offenders.[195]

The International Criminal Tribunal for the former Yugoslavia (ICTY) and the International Criminal Tribunal for Rwanda (ICTR) were created in The Hague and Arusha, respectively. The drafters of their statutes adapted the legacy of the international military tribunals to a new set of factual and legal circumstances. To begin with, the ICTY and ICTR's jurisdiction was limited in time and space, which made them ad hoc and not permanent international criminal tribunals.[196] Their limited territorial and temporal jurisdiction had a significant impact on the selection of crimes falling within their scope of jurisdiction: priority was given to prosecuting those most responsible for the most serious crimes.[197]

A remarkable novelty was the introduction of the 'crime of crimes' within the tribunals' material jurisdiction.[198] Fifty years before the ad hoc tribunals came into operation, Raphaël Lemkin had come to the conclusion that a specific international crime had been committed during the Nazi regime that did not yet have a name: the crime of genocide.[199] Lemkin's work had the merit to lay down the foundations of the so-called Genocide Convention, which defines the elements of the crime of genocide in Article II. The same definition was reiterated verbatim in the Statutes of the ICTY and ICTR tribunals.[200]

Another significant deviation from the post-war international criminal justice system was the gradual detachment from the *nexus* requirement. This marked the beginning of a new phase in international criminal law, characterised by a progressive tendency for ad hoc tribunals to focus on the prosecution of the most serious crimes related to mass violence rather than war.[201]

[195] UNSC Res 827 (25 May 1993) S/RES/827 for the ICTY; UNSC Res 955 (8 November 1994) S/RES/955 for the ICTR.

[196] According to Art 8 of the ICTY St, the jurisdiction of this ad hoc criminal tribunal could be exercised over crimes committed on the territory of the former Yugoslavia from 1 January 1991; while according to Art 7 of the ICTR St., this tribunal could exercise its jurisdiction over crimes perpetrated in Rwanda or by Rwandan nationals on the territory of neighbouring countries, from 1 January 1994 to 31 December 1994.

[197] C Del Ponte, 'Prosecuting the Individuals Bearing the Highest Level of Responsibility' (2004) 2 *Journal of International Criminal Justice* 516, 518.

[198] Schabas defines genocide as the 'crime of crimes', see WA Schabas, *Genocide in International Law: The Crime of Crimes*, 2nd edn (Cambridge University Press, 2009).

[199] R Lemkin, *Axis Rule in Occupied Europe: Laws of Occupation, Analysis of Government, Proposals for Redress* (Carnegie Endowment for International Peace, 1944) 79.

[200] Art 4 of the ICTY Statute; Art 2 of the ICTR Statute.

[201] Starr, 'Extraordinary Crimes' 1310.

In this evolving legal framework, economic crimes have found no place. The sheer volume of evidence and the complexity of the cases prevented the judges from filling this *lacuna* and prompted them to focus on other offences considered more serious based on the factual circumstances of the selected cases and on the limited resources available to them.[202] Despite this strategic choice, both ad hoc tribunals have contributed to addressing the economic dimension of international crimes in at least two different respects: on the one hand, they prosecuted certain international crimes of an economic nature and qualified any other economic crime connected to international crimes as an act of complicity; on the other hand, they clarified how economic actors, including private ones, can be held criminally liable under international criminal law for engaging in unlawful business activities.[203]

International crimes with a clear economic dimension were committed during the conflict in the former Yugoslavia. These included the crime of pillage, prosecuted as a war crime and defined as a form of 'fraudulent appropriation of public or private funds',[204] ie an act committed in violation of the right to property of the legitimate owner.[205] Furthermore, the ICTY went one step further by prosecuting the destruction and looting of cultural property as a war crime. This crime had a huge impact on the economy of the countries involved in the war.[206] Many artefacts that fell under the category of 'cultural property' were stolen during the war and are still being sold and bought on the black market.[207]

As regards any other economic crime connected to international crimes, they were prosecuted as acts of complicity. The *Tadić* case examined in depth the supply of arms and other goods intended for use in international crimes. The judges referred on several occasions to post-war military trials in which industrialists had been convicted of international crimes as accomplices. In the Opinion and Judgment issued on 7 May 1997, the majority of the Trial

[202] For instance, both tribunals were pioneers in prosecuting rape and sexual violence as acts of genocide and crimes against humanity. The first conviction for rape as a crime against humanity dates to 1998, when ICTR convicted Jean-Paul Akayesu; see M Ellis, 'Breaking the Silence: Rape as an International Crime' (2006) 38 *Case Western Reserve Journal of International Law* 225. However, the qualification of rape as a crime against humanity is mainly associated with the *Foca* case; see J McHenry, 'Justice for Foca: The International Criminal Tribunal for Yugoslavia's Prosecution of Rape and Enslavement as Crimes against Humanity' (2002) 10 *Tulsa Journal of Comparative and International Law* 183.

[203] The relevance of the ad hoc tribunals' decisions on the individual criminal responsibility of business actors for assistance is emphasised in Jacobson, 'Doing Business with the Devil' 200–201.

[204] *Prosecutor v Jelisić* (Trial Judgment) IT-95-10-T (14 December 1999) para 48. See also *Prosecutor v Kunarac et al* (Trial Judgment) IT-96-23-T & IT-96-23/1-T (22 February 2001) para 916.

[205] See *Prosecutor v Kordić and Čerkez* (Appeals Judgment) IT-95-1472-A (17 December 2004) para 79.

[206] Morris, 'Economic Genocide' 29.

[207] H Walasek, *Bosnia and the Destruction of Cultural Heritage* (Routledge, 2016) 75: 'In Sarajevo, the studios of non-Serbs artists in Serb-held parts of the city were looted, their paintings later appearing for sale on the black market in Belgrade'. The same had happened during the Second World War, see KD Alford, *Hermann Goring and the Nazi Art Collection: The Looting of Europe's Art Treasures and Their Dispersal After World War II* (McFarland & Co, 2014).

Chamber (Judge McDonald dissenting) relied on the *Zyklon B* case to determine the type of contribution made by Bruno Tesch and his second-in-command in the perpetration of war crimes. More precisely, the Trial Chamber noted that by supplying lethal gas 'the accused put the means of committing the crime of extermination in the hands of the concentration camp officials'.[208] On the basis of this precedent, the ad hoc tribunal concluded that it was possible to hold someone criminally liable for contributing directly, without physical presence, to the perpetration of international crimes. As a result, Tadić was held criminally liable as an aider and abettor for any offence in which he participated, knowing that his conduct would directly and substantially affect the commission of international crimes before, during or after their perpetration.[209]

The ICTR also referred to the *Zyklon B* case in the *Akayesu* case with respect to aiding and abetting crimes against humanity and war crimes. The judges took a strict approach, stating that this mode of liability implies the commission of acts and not omissions, and that it includes forms of participation such as procuring weapons, instruments or 'any other means' to be used to commit the principal's offence, knowing that they will be used for such a purpose.[210] It was further clarified that the concept of 'any other means' includes any good that is directly useful in committing a crime, for instance the *Zyklon* B gas. However, the judges did not specify whether money or any other item used to commit an international crime could be included in that concept.[211]

Ad hoc criminal tribunals have also helped to address the economic causes of the conflict in the former Yugoslavia by prosecuting public and private economic actors. Along the lines of the *Streicher* and *Fritzsche* cases before the IMT,[212] in the *Nahimana et al* case – also known as the *Media* case – the role played by the media in spreading ethnic hatred came once again under the spotlight of international criminal law.[213] The discriminatory policies adopted by public officials in Rwanda were intensified by the widespread use of stereotypical expressions in newspapers and on the radio, which were not censored by the managers of the *Radio Télévision Libre des Milles Collines* (RTLM) or the directors of local newspapers.[214] These were private individuals holding high-level positions in telecommunication companies, who were prosecuted and convicted for

[208] *Prosecutor v Tadić* (Trial Opinion and Judgment) IT-94-1-T (7 May 1997) para 680.

[209] ibid, para 692.

[210] *Prosecutor v Akayesu* (Trial Judgment) ICTR-96-4-T (2 September 1998) para 536.

[211] Jacobson, 'Doing Business with the Devil' 206.

[212] These trials are known as the 'hate speech' prosecutions in Nuremberg, as the defendants were leaders of anti-Semitic radio stations and newspapers. See IMT, *Trial of the Major War Criminals* 301, 336. See also GS Gordon, 'The Propaganda Prosecutions at Nuremberg: The Origin of Atrocity Speech Law and the Touchstone for Normative Evolution' (2017) 39 *Loyola of Los Angeles International and Comparative Law Review* 209.

[213] *Prosecutor v Nahimana et al* (Trial Judgment and Sentence) ICTR-99-52 (3 December 2003) ('The Media Case').

[214] Nahimana was the head of RTLM, Barayagwiza was one of the members of the committee founding the radio, and Ngeze was editor-in-chief of the *Kangura* newspaper.

participating in the commission of international crimes.[215] For instance, in an article titled 'Appeal to the Conscience of the Hutu', published in the 'Kangura' newspaper, members of the Tutsi ethnic group were unfairly discriminated against for having access to financial resources. This episode is reminiscent of the accusations made against the Jews at the dawn of the Second World War, on the ground that they held and managed a large part of Germany's wealth.

In the *Félicien Kabuga* case the criminal responsibility for international crimes of a Rwandan businessman was also called into question. When the alleged crimes were committed, Kabuga was the President of the *Comité Provisoire* of the *Fond de Défense National* and the President of the *Comité d'Initiative* of the RTLM and one of its founders.[216] In 2011, a first indictment was issued charging the suspect with genocide and crimes against humanity, whereby Kabuga had allegedly conspired to commit genocide with several groups of individuals, not only private actors,[217] but also public officials[218] and members of the military.[219] The term 'conspiracy' was not defined in the indictment, but was used as a synonym for 'in agreement with'.[220] In 2021, a second indictment was issued by the Office of the Prosecutor of the International Residual Mechanism for Criminal Tribunals (MICT), charging the accused with three counts related to genocide – including conspiracy to commit genocide – and three counts related to crimes against humanity.[221] Kabuga was not tried as he was found unable to stand trial and, on 8 September 2023, the Trial Chamber issued a decision imposing an indefinite stay of proceedings.[222]

In light of the above, it can be said that the 'ICTY and ICTR have flirted with various composites of economic value, such as plundering of property and the looting and destruction of cultural heritage',[223] but both advocated a cautious approach, avoiding excessive focus on the economic aspects of the respective conflicts. Nonetheless, the jurisprudence of the ICTY and the ICTR has confirmed the validity of many findings reached by international military tribunals. On the one hand, they prosecuted criminal economic activities as acts of complicity that had substantially facilitated the perpetration of international crimes. On the other one, they reinforced the idea that not only public officials,

[215] These individuals were also involved in politics, but in the *Media* case they were indicted either as members of the *Comité d'initiative* of the RTLM, or as founders of the *Kangura* newspaper. See *Prosecutor v Nahimana et al* (Trial Judgment and Sentence) paras 5–7.

[216] *Prosecutor v Kabuga* (Amended Indictment) ICTR-98-44B-I (17 March 2011) para 9.

[217] ibid paras 41–42.

[218] ibid paras 63–64.

[219] ibid para79.

[220] ibid paras 41–42, 63–64 and 79.

[221] *Prosecutor v Kabuga* (Prosecution's Second Amended Indictment) MICT-13-38-PT (1 March 2021) para 20.

[222] *Prosecutor v Kabuga* (Trial Chamber's Decision Imposing an Indefinite Stay of Proceedings) MICT-13-38-T (8 September 2023).

[223] Morris, 'Economic Genocide' 33.

but also private citizens, especially businessmen, can be held individually responsible for international crimes.

The Prosecution of Illicit Trade in 'Blood Diamonds' before the SCSL

Nobody could have predicted the outcome of the Nuremberg military trials, let alone the functioning of the ad hoc tribunals and their influence on the future of international criminal justice. Likewise, the decision to establish special criminal tribunals and courts was an unprecedented experiment, born out of a joint initiative of the international community, on the one hand, and countries affected by the commission of international crimes, on the other. As a result of this initiative, in the early 2000s, the Special Court for Sierra Leone, the Extraordinary Chambers in the Courts of Cambodia (ECCC), and the Special Panels for Serious Crimes – known as East Timor Tribunal – were established in their respective countries, while the Special Tribunal for Lebanon (STL) was set up in The Hague.

The first 'hybrid' criminal court was created in 2002 in Sierra Leone, a country torn apart by civil war, with the specific mandate to exercise jurisdiction over crimes committed since November 1996. The SCSL was the first court to try and convict a sitting Head of State, Charles Taylor, then President of Liberia. To date, the *Taylor* case is one of the most relevant international criminal law cases concerning the prosecution of high-ranking individuals involved in the financing of international crimes and the illicit trade of natural resources.[224]

He was convicted by the Trial Chamber to fifty years of imprisonment for providing weapons, financial means and moral support to the Revolutionary United Front (RUF) and other rebel forces, in exchange for natural resources – mainly diamonds – from Sierra Leone. The Chamber found that with Taylor's material and moral support, the RUF had committed a series of international crimes, including crimes against humanity – including killings,[225] sexual violence and rape,[226] and slave labour in diamond mines[227] – and war crimes – including acts of terrorism,[228] pillage,[229] and conscripting or enlisting child soldiers into armed forces or groups.[230]

Taylor's conviction as an aider and abettor of war crimes and crimes against humanity was appealed, but the Appeals Chamber upheld the Trial Chamber's judgment and sentence.[231] The Chamber rejected the interpretation of the *actus*

[224] As Starr pointed out, the head prosecutors of the ICC and the SCSL have publicly referred to the international criminal responsibility of participants in the diamonds trade, see Starr, 'Extraordinary Crimes' 1312.

[225] *Prosecutor v Taylor* (Trial Judgment) SCSL-03-01-T (18 May 2012) paras 212–345.

[226] ibid paras 346–392.

[227] ibid paras 583–664.

[228] ibid paras 691–755.

[229] ibid paras 665–690.

[230] ibid paras 496–582.

[231] SCSL, *Prosecutor v Taylor* (Appeals Judgment) SCSL-03-01-A (26 September 2013).

reus of aiding and abetting elaborated in the *Perišić* judgment,[232] arguing that the conduct of an aider and abettor ought to have a substantial effect on the crime, while it is not required for that conduct to be specifically directed at providing assistance to the physical perpetrator of the crime.[233]

The financing of the RUF consisted of a lucrative activity substantially related to war crimes and crimes against humanity and was committed with the requisite *mens rea* by a high-ranking public individual for the main purpose of maximising his own profits.[234] However, unlike the economic crimes perpetrated during the Second World War, Taylor's criminal economic activities were not committed in a context characterised by the existence of a deviant state-corporate system. There was insufficient evidence to prove a joint criminal enterprise involving both Taylor and the rebels, which prompted the judges to resort to 'aiding and abetting' instead of 'direct perpetration' as a mode of liability to convict the then President of Liberia.[235]

It follows from the above that the growing interest of the international community in tackling the phenomenon of economic crimes through cooperation mechanisms and the harmonisation of national laws has been matched by a limited interest on the part of ad hoc and internationalised tribunals in dealing with economic crimes and prosecuting economic criminals. This lack of interest was justified not only by prosecutorial strategies and restrained resources, but also by the nature of the conflicts in Yugoslavia, Rwanda and Sierra Leone. The economic offences committed to facilitate the perpetration of international crimes in such conflicts were not 'systemic' as they played an ancillary role and did not reach the point of threatening values of concern to the international community.

REVITALISING THE CONCEPT OF INTERNATIONAL ECONOMIC CRIME IN THE CURRENT SYSTEM OF INTERNATIONAL CRIMINAL JUSTICE

Over the years, several strategies have been developed to prosecute international crimes before international criminal law tribunals. Most of them have focused

[232] Momčilo Perišić was Chief of the General Staff of the Yugoslav Army from 1993 until 1998 and was charged with aiding and abetting crimes against humanity and war crimes, including by providing military equipment and supplies. In *Prosecutor v Perišić* (Appeals Judgment) IT-04-81-A (28 February 2013) paras 25–36, the Appeals Chamber referred to the Appeals Judgment in *Tadić* to conclude that it is necessary, but not sufficient, that the aider and abettor's act is directly and substantially linked to a core crime. On the contrary, it is sufficient to prove that this act is 'specifically directed to assist, encourage or lend moral support' to a core crime and this has a substantial effect upon its perpetration.

[233] Regarding the subjective element, the Chamber confirmed that the *mens rea* standard for aiding and abetting is knowledge of the principal's conduct. See *Prosecutor v Taylor* (Appeals Judgment) para 483.

[234] *Prosecutor v Taylor* (Trial Judgment) paras 6947–6952.

[235] Kyriakakis, 'Developments in International Criminal Law' 999.

on prosecuting crimes perpetrated by high-level public officials, due to limited resources and the resulting need to select the most serious cases.[236] However, Robert Jackson's strategy to target the three main pillars of Nazi Germany, namely the State, the military and the industry, has recently been taken as a model to reaffirm the need to prosecute individuals who hold important positions within private entities as instigators or accomplices of international crimes.[237]

In 2003, the ICC's first prosecutor, Luis Moreno Ocampo, stated that the involvement of private economic actors in armed conflicts and international crimes would not be overlooked.[238] This statement left no room for interpretation: Prosecutor Ocampo admitted that it was necessary not to underestimate the seriousness of money laundering, illegal exploitation of oil, trade of weapons and illicit gold mining.[239] When she took office in 2012, Prosecutor Fatou Bensouda also recognised the role that corporations play in fuelling international crimes and the role they could play in preventing them.[240] The Rome Statute itself provides for modes of liability that would allow economic actors to be prosecuted as co-perpetrators, aiders and abettors, contributors of international crimes.[241]

The current prosecutor, Karim Khan, was the Lead Defence Counsel in the *Charles Taylor* case, where, as seen above, the defendant was charged with aiding and abetting war crimes and crimes against humanity for engaging in illegal economic activities. The current Office of the Prosecutor has taken concrete action by launching a new policy initiative aimed at promoting accountability

[236] See ICC-OTP, 'Paper on Some Policy Issues before the Office of the Prosecutor' (5 September 2003) www.legal-tools.org/doc/f53870/, 3: 'The Court is an institution with limited resources [...] On the one hand, it will *initiate prosecutions of the leaders who bear most responsibility* for the crimes. On the other hand, it will *encourage national prosecutions, where possible, for the lower-ranking perpetrators*, or work with the international community to ensure that the offenders are brought to justice by some other means' (emphasis added). See also Y McDermott, *The Ashgate Research Companion to International Criminal Law: Critical Perspectives* (Routledge, 2013) 469, arguing that the requirement of 'gravity' in article 17(1)(d) of the Rome Statute relating to the admissibility of a case before the ICC 'demands that the ICC Prosecutor adopt a policy of focussing only on those few individuals who he believes bear the greatest responsibility for the most serious crimes that have been committed in each situation'.

[237] Bush, 'The Prehistory of Corporations' 1110.

[238] ICC-OTP, 'Communications Received by the Office of the Prosecutor of the ICC' (16 July 2003) https://legal-tools.org/doc/df602e/, 3.

[239] ibid 3–4. See also ICC-OTP, 'Second Assembly of States Parties to the Rome Statute of the International Criminal Court Report of the Prosecutor of the ICC, Mr Luis Moreno-Ocampo' (8 September 2003) www.legal-tools.org/doc/8873bd/.

[240] International Criminal Justice Today, 'International Corporate Liability in Conflict Zones' (21 March 2013) www.international-criminal-justice-today.org/events/international-corporate-liability-in-conflict-zones/. See also L Enneking et al, *Accountability, International Business Operations and the Law: Providing Justice for Corporate Human Rights Violations in Global Value Chains* (Routledge, 2019) 126.

[241] Baars, *The Corporation, Law and Capitalism* 270–282, providing an overview and critical analysis of the application of the Rome Statute's modes of liability to the businessmen.

for crimes within the Court's jurisdiction that are committed by means of or that result in environmental damage.[242] Although this initiative does not specifically target economic crimes, it would allow the Office of the Prosecutor to consider crimes of an economic nature, such as illegal exploitation of natural resources, committed not only in times of war but also in times of peace, and to assess the criminal responsibility of economic actors.

Despite this recent policy being developed, it is clear that Robert Jackson's vision to target the State, the army and the industry '[…] has yet to become a reality in modern international criminal justice'.[243] No serious economic crimes have found their way into the Rome Statute, nor has any private individual allegedly involved in such crimes been prosecuted before the ICC to date.[244]

This inaction is even more worrying when one considers, on the one hand, the current scope of international criminal law and, on the other hand, the recent events that have shaped modern society. Among the various crises that the global community has had to face, the 2008 financial crisis clearly demonstrated that new threats to security, peace, and the global values of the international community exist. Economic power, further strengthened by institutional and political structures, caused a global financial catastrophe that resulted in serious violations of collective and individual rights, to the point that some have spoken of 'economic crimes against humanity'.[245] The following sections focus on the question of whether traditional categories of international crimes should be supplemented by the concept of 'international economic crime' in order to better define the spectrum of the most serious contemporary crimes.

Beyond the Scope of International Crimes

Since the Nuremberg trials, the international community has strived to establish peace and justice in those parts of the world that are prey to wars and uncontrollable races for power and profit. The need to ensure a just and peaceful society led to the creation of the first permanent international criminal court in 1998, when the Statute of the International Criminal Court was adopted in Rome before entering into force in 2002. The Preamble of the Rome Statute explicitly

[242] ICC-OTP, 'Policy on Addressing Environmental Damage Through the Rome Statute' (4 December 2025) https://www.icc-cpi.int/news/policy-addressing-environmental-damage-through-rome-statute.

[243] Jessberger, 'On the Origins of Individual Criminal Responsibility' 920.

[244] ibid 801. See also Burchard, 'Ancillary and Neutral Business' 920, arguing that 'modern international criminal justice […] had focused on political and military, but not business figure heads'. See also Ambos, 'International Economic Criminal Law' 564, acknowledging that 'the relevance of corporate conduct for the commission of Nazi crimes [is a] lesson [that] seems to have been almost completely forgotten in "Den Haag ICL".'

[245] The term 'economic crime against humanity' was coined by S Zuboff, 'Wall Street's Economic Crimes against Humanity' (*Bloomberg*, 20 March 2009) https://www.bloomberg.com/news/articles/2009-03-20/wall-streets-economic-crimes-against-humanity.

delimits the material scope of jurisdiction of the ICC to 'the most serious crimes of concern to the international community as a whole', namely genocide, crimes against humanity, war crimes and the crime of aggression.[246] However, the negotiations of the statutory provisions reveal that although the drafters had considered some 'treaty-crimes' – ie offences regulated by supranational treaties – they expressly excluded them from the Court's jurisdiction *ratione materiae*. It is plausible to imagine that they feared that extending the Court's material jurisdiction would entail a limitation of their sovereignty in criminal matters. Moreover, the ICC's alleged difficulties in investigating transnational crimes were among the reasons that militated against their inclusion in the macro category of international crimes.[247] These reasons prevented any economic 'treaty crime' from being considered a potential international crime, regardless of the context of international significance in which it might be committed.

Nonetheless, since the entry into force of the Rome Statute, some States Parties have proposed to look beyond the traditional categories of international crimes. In 2009, Trinidad and Tobago and Belize suggested amending Article 5 of the Statute to incorporate international drug trafficking as a separate category of international crimes.[248] The proposal defined the constituent elements of this new offence and listed its underlying acts.[249] The rationale behind this request for amendment was two-fold: first, the fact that international drug trafficking is a 'major challenge to the international community [that has] transboundary impacts [calling for] international legal sanctions';[250] and secondly, the idea that the introduction of this crime into the ICC Statute would facilitate its prosecution in the countries most affected by the scourge of drugs, where access to impartial justice is not always guaranteed. The parallel proposal to bring international terrorism within the material scope of the Rome Statute was based on similar reasons.[251]

In response to these proposals, the Assembly of States Parties drew a clear line between international crimes, on the one hand, and other offences – implicitly less serious than the former – on the other.[252] The Assembly reiterated the main concerns expressed by the drafters of the Rome Statute about the political sensitivities that international drug trafficking and terrorism could raise.[253] Moreover, the Assembly noted that delegations of the States Parties had raised

[246] Art 5 of the Rome Statute of the International Criminal Court (Rome, 17 July 1998) (also known as the ICC Statute).

[247] Starr, 'Extraordinary Crimes' 1270.

[248] Trinidad and Tobago, 'Proposal for the inclusion of the Crime of International Drug Trafficking in the Rome Statute of the International Criminal Court' (30 September 2009) C.N.737.2009. See also ICC-ASP, 'Informal Compilation of Proposals to Amend the Rome Statute' (23 January 2015).

[249] ICC-ASP, 'Informal Compilation' 7.

[250] ibid 8.

[251] See P Robinson, 'The Missing Crimes' in A Cassese, P Gaeta and JRWD Jones (eds), *The Rome Statute of the International Criminal Court: A Commentary*, Vol 1 (Oxford University Press, 2002).

[252] ICC-ASP, 'Report of the Bureau on the Review Conference' (15 November 2009) ICC-ASP/8/43, para 16.

[253] ibid para 17.

the issue of the lack of an agreed definition of international terrorism, which could have made negotiations difficult.[254]

In addition to international drug trafficking and terrorism,[255] other crimes had been discussed as potential candidates for inclusion in the Statute by the delegations of the States Parties attending the Rome Conference.[256] Among them, 'apartheid'[257] and 'attacks against UN and associated personnel',[258] which were included into the Statute as crimes against humanity and war crimes, respectively. The crime of aggression was introduced in 2018 after lengthy negotiations,[259] while the crime of 'wilful and severe damage to the environment' was discussed by the International Law Commission (ILC) in relation to Article 26 of the 1991 Draft Code of Crimes against Peace and Security of Mankind.[260] This proposal was further developed and recently revived when the Working Group on Amendments of the Assembly of States Parties considered the proposal by the Republic of Vanuatu to formally introduce 'ecocide' into the Rome Statute as a fifth international crime.[261]

This partial extension of the subject-matter jurisdiction of the ICC has been relevant in two respects. On the one hand, the direction taken by this extension has made it clear that the umbilical cord linking international crimes – and international criminal justice in general – to armed conflicts and situations of mass violence has not been severed. The idea that fundamental global values can only be threatened by crimes perpetrated under 'exceptional' violent circumstances still permeates international criminal law. On the other hand, the partial extension of the boundaries of the concept of international crime has shown that 'the content of the Rome Statute is not set in stone'[262] but can and should evolve according to the needs of society to ensure that justice is done for all serious crimes.

Nonetheless, the lack of discussion during the Statute preparatory works regarding the possibility of introducing economic crimes as international crimes

[254] ibid paras 20–22.

[255] See UN Diplomatic Conference of Plenipotentiaries on the Establishment of an International Criminal Court, Official Records, (15 June-17 July 1998) A/CONF.183/13 (Vol II), eg 72 para 5, 73 para18, 77 paras 71, 74.

[256] ibid, eg 102, para 82.

[257] ibid eg 154, para 178; 172, para 125.

[258] ibid, eg 68 para 60; 77, paras 71, 74; 85 para 36; 111 para 86.

[259] In 2010, at the Rome Statute Review Conference in Kampala, a statutory provision was agreed upon defining the crime of aggression as a manifest violation of the UN Charter.

[260] See 'Report of the Commission to the General Assembly on the Work of its Forty-third Session' (1991) II(2) Yearbook of the International Law Commission A/CN.4/SER.A/1991/Add.l (Part 2) 79, 107.

[261] ICC-ASP, 'Report of the Working Group on Amendments' (1 December 2024) ICC-ASP/23/26. The proposal defines 'ecocide' as 'unlawful or wanton acts committed with knowledge that there is a substantial likelihood of severe and either widespread or long-term damage to the environment being caused by those acts'.

[262] HL Kiefer, 'Just Say No: The Case against Expanding the International Criminal Court's Jurisdiction to Include Drug Trafficking' (2009) 31 *Loyola of Los Angeles International and Comparative Law Review* 157, 157.

has not been remedied either by the OTP or by the judges. The ICC's blindness to the risk of leaving the perpetrators of these crimes unpunished cannot be attributed to the strategies of the OTP or to the choice to focus the Court's limited resources – time and personnel – on international crimes of a violent nature.[263] These are only outward manifestations of deeper structural problems concerning the system of international criminal justice itself. The main flaw of this system lies in the artificial distinction between 'extraordinary' and 'systemic' crimes and in the exclusion of the latter from the macro category of international extraordinary crimes.[264] This fictitious distinction is being challenged in several ways, both by States Parties' proposals to qualify crimes committed outside situations of conflicts and mass violence as international crimes,[265] and by scholars who have begun to question whether contemporary international crimes also include 'entrenched, long-term abuses'[266] of power, such as institutionalised large-scale economic offences.[267]

International Economic Crimes as a New Paradigm of International Crimes?

The 2008 financial crisis is frequently cited as a salient example when considering cases of serious economic crimes, given its scale and far-reaching consequences. It is in light of this historic event that the following section rethinks the traditional definition of the concept of 'extraordinary crisis' in international criminal law and questions its exclusive association with war and mass violence. The section argues that the extraordinary character of the context in which serious economic crimes are committed in peacetime derives from their 'systemic' or 'structural' nature. In this respect, concepts such as 'political white-collar crime', 'state-corporate crime', 'crime of maldevelopment', which have been used to shed light on the dangerous effects of systemic interactions between politics and business, provide a criminological and legal basis for shaping the concept of international economic crime.

[263] Starr correctly points out that 'there is no reason to believe that exclusively trying crisis crimes is the best use of tribunals' resources', where 'crisis crimes' is meant to indicate crimes committed during wars or mass violence, see Starr, 'Extraordinary Crimes' 1273.

[264] H Cullen, P Kastner and S Richmond, 'Introduction: The Politics of International Criminal Law' (2018) 18 *International Criminal Law Review* 907, 919, pointing out that 'the current structure of ICL privileges physical manifestations of violence, such as incidents of physical targeting or persecution of civil populations, whereas collective and structural dimensions of violence, power differentials, economic crimes and poverty are given less attention'.

[265] For instance, the above proposal to include 'ecocide' among international crimes.

[266] Starr, 'Extraordinary Crimes' 1257. Starr considers that 'to date, international criminal tribunals have (…) wholly ignored entrenched, longer-term abuses of the sort that cause everyday suffering far out of proportion'.

[267] On the ongoing doctrinal debate on the gravity of economic crimes, see also V Oosterveld, 'ICC Assembly of States Parties Symposium: Economic Acts as Criminal Acts' (*INTLAWGRRLS*, 4 December 2019) https://ilg2.blog/2019/12/04/icc-assembly-of-states-parties-symposium/.

International Economic Crimes as 'Extraordinary' Offences

One of the reasons why the drafters of the Rome Statute decided to stick to traditional categories of international crimes without broadening their scope is the existence of an invisible thread that connects them. Since the post-World War II trials, the concept of international crime has been used to describe the most serious offences committed during armed conflicts and extraordinary contexts of mass violence. Although the most recent definitions of international crimes other than war crimes omit any reference to the '*nexus* requirement',[268] the idea that fundamental global values are threatened by acts perpetrated under violent circumstances has remained alive.

As a result, 'massive systemic crimes committed during peacetime'[269] have been consistently neglected by international criminal law. The rationale behind this lies in the 'crisis focus' inherent in the current system of international criminal justice, namely the overriding interest in addressing 'crises that threaten international security – specifically, mass atrocity and war'.[270] The ICC might be considered an exception to this trend, as some crimes against humanity listed in Article 7 of the Rome Statute are systemic in nature.[271] However, this shift towards a more far-reaching international criminal law has not been reflected in the Court's practice, where crimes committed in 'extraordinary situations' – in the traditional sense of the term – have predominantly been prosecuted.

Therefore, if serious economic crimes are to be considered international crimes, a more contemporary reading of the 'crisis focus' of international criminal justice is needed, one that encompasses both mass atrocities related to wars and systemic abuses of power in peacetime.[272] It is the unique and exceptional context in which an offence is committed that makes it an international crime, and today the extraordinariness of a context of international significance extends beyond violent disruptions of peace. Over the past few years, the term 'crisis' has been used to define a wide range of criminal, sociological and political phenomena, not always related to conflict and mass violence, including the 'migration crisis', the 'climate change crisis', the 'Covid-19 crisis' and the 2008 'financial crisis'.[273] The term 'crisis' should thus refer not only to instances of 'direct violence', but also to those of 'structural violence', ie violence that 'is

[268] The 'nexus requirement' is the term used to define the link between war crimes and armed conflicts.

[269] Starr, 'Extraordinary Crimes' 1258.

[270] ibid 1260.

[271] For instance, the crime of persecution Art 7(1)(h) and apartheid 7(1)(j) of the Rome Statute.

[272] These systemic long-term abuses of power are harbingers of 'silent deaths', see E Davidsson, 'Economic Oppression as an International Wrong or as Crime against Humanity' (2005) 23 *Netherlands Quarterly of Human Rights* 173, 173. See also S Jodoin and Y Saito, 'Crimes Against Future Generations: Harnessing the Potential of Individual Criminal Accountability for Global Sustainability' (2012) 7 *McGill International Journal of Sustainable Development Law & Policy* 115, 122.

[273] N Citeroni, 'International Economic Crimes in the Rome Statute? Reflections on Multilevel Enforcement of International Criminal Law' in K Ligeti and KH Brodersen (eds), *Studies on Enforcement in Multilevel Regulatory Systems* (Nomos, 2022) 250.

done in terms not only of directly damaging another, but also generating conditions that may damage him or her' and 'prevent people from meeting their basic needs'.[274]

The 2008 financial crisis was the biggest 'economic catastrophe since the Great Depression'.[275] It was a man-made crisis, as its outbreak and management can be attributed to a group of high-level individuals operating within a deviant state-corporate system,[276] who failed to prevent a crisis that could have been avoided.[277] The 2008 financial crisis was also a crisis of confidence in the economic and financial system, because members of private and public élites betrayed the relationship of trust with their clients by committing heinous economic crimes.[278] The main consequences of this crisis were axiomatic. Those who had trusted the system were the ones who suffered the most. Thousands of families lost their savings and homes, while many workers faced the hardships of unemployment and poverty. Far from being 'victimless' or 'invisible' crimes,[279] economic offences committed in such an 'extraordinary' circumstance caused severe damage to the extent that,

[274] ML Böhm, *The Crime of Maldevelopment: Economic Deregulation and Violence in the Global South* (Routledge, 2019) 43.

[275] J Eisinger, 'Why Only One Top Banker Went to Jail for the Financial Crisis' (*New York Times Magazine*, 30 April 2014) www.nytimes.com/2014/05/04/magazine/only-one-top-banker-jail-financial-crisis.html.

[276] M Max-Neef, 'The Good Is the Bad That We Don't Do: Economic Crimes against Humanity: A Proposal' (2014) 104 *Ecological Economics* 152, 153, arguing that the 'markets' and the economic and financial system are not responsible for the 2008 financial crisis, as those responsible are individuals operating in that system. The same argument is upheld by Zuboff, 'Wall Street's Economic Crimes', and by L Benería and C Sarasúa, 'Crímenes económicos contra la humanidad' (*El País*, 29 March 2011) https://elpais.com/diario/2011/03/29/opinion/1301349604_850215.html.

[277] See Benería and Sarasúa 'Crímenes económicos'.

[278] On the definition of the 2008 financial crisis as a 'systemic' crisis see S Braum, 'Droit pénal des risques et risques du droit pénal' in C Bourin and JL Putz, *Le risque pénal du banquier* (Anthemis, 2020) 13, 18–19. See also M Max-Neef (2014) 'The Good Is the Bad That We Don't Do: Economic Crimes against Humanity: A Proposal' 104 *Ecological Economics* 152, 153, who provides examples of individuals responsible for the crisis. A major role in the collapse of the US housing market was played by the banks, which encouraged an extension of consumer credit at a lower prime rate and suggested low-risk customers to lend to sub-primers at higher rates. Customers seized the opportunity to buy durable goods, especially houses, at favourable rates. As a result of such speculation, home prices increased to levels beyond their intrinsic value, causing a 'housing bubble'. At that point, many banks found the unique opportunity to invest and make profits by offering customers mortgage loans with 'balloon payments'. This operation was particularly risky for those customers having few assets or low credit, as they would not have been able to repay the loans. Perfectly aware of these risks, banks decided to sell mortgages in capital markets as mortgage-backed securities (MBS). When the housing market reached a saturation point, house prices fell, thus triggering a domino effect: sub-primers who were not able to pay the loans defaulted and MBS lost value with dire consequences for credit institutions. But it was only when the Lehman Brothers investment bank filed for bankruptcy that the crisis escalated. See Simmons & Simmons, 'The Legacy of Lehman: Economic Crime and the Global Financial Crisis' (11 September 2018) https://www.simmons-simmons.com/en/publications/ck0b2aamseaji0b59h2cv4p50/07092018-crime-and-punishment-economic-crime-andthe-global-financial-crisis.

[279] M Krambia-Kapardis, *Corporate Fraud and Corruption: A Holistic Approach to Preventing Financial Crises* (Springer, 2016) 12, listing physical (eg work injuries, illnesses, death) and psychological (eg anxiety, depression) damages suffered from the victims. For a detailed overview of the consequences of the 2008 economic and financial crisis, see L Arenal Lora, *Crímenes económicos en derecho internacional: Propuesta de una nueva categoría de crímenes contra la humanidad* (Editorial Aranzadi, 2019) 99; Coleman, 'Toward an Integrated Theory' 408.

in 2009, Shoshana Zuboff qualified these acts as 'economic crimes against humanity' committed by 'institutionalised narcissists' who had taken part in a 'full-scale administrative economic massacre'.[280]

Nevertheless, justice turned a blind eye to these crimes. After the Great Depression in 1929, the Head of the New York Stock Exchange was sentenced to prison.[281] Likewise,

> [t]he 1980s savings product scandals in the US led to 1,100 prosecutions including those of top executives at failed banks. Following the Nasdaq bubble bursting in the late 1990s and early 2000s, corporate accounting scandals led to top executives at WorldCom, Enron, Qwest and Tyco being imprisoned.[282]

This is not what happened in the aftermath of the 2008 financial crisis, when impunity allowed those involved in state-corporate crimes to get away with it. During the crisis, most high-level executives lost their jobs but got bonuses – 'golden parachutes' – to compensate for their departure. One of the few exceptions was Kareem Serageldin, a leading banker of Egyptian origin at Credit Suisse, who had concealed millions of losses in the bank's mortgage-backed securities (MBS) portfolio.[283] This same criminal conduct had been carried out by many other bankers, but only Serageldin paid the 'debt he owed to society'.[284] The lack of reaction from US courts was not an isolated case, as only a few senior executives were prosecuted in Europe for crimes related to the 2008 financial crisis.[285] One of the few attempts to prevent impunity for these crimes was made in Iceland, as will be further explained in Chapter 3.

In light of the above, a twofold conclusion can be reached. On the one hand, the 'crisis focus' inherent in the system of international criminal justice is not in itself wrong, as it allows a clear line to be drawn between ordinary offences addressed at national level and the most serious crimes in need of international adjudication, provided that national courts are unable or unwilling to intervene.[286] On the other hand, in the twenty-first century, 'extraordinary' crises do not exclusively coincide with armed conflicts or mass violence. Acknowledging this could help prevent and promptly respond to the increasingly frequent systemic threats to fundamental values that occur in times of peace.[287]

[280] Zuboff, 'Wall Street's Economic Crimes'.
[281] Simmons & Simmons, 'The Legacy of Lehman'.
[282] ibid.
[283] A Plateroti, 'Quelle partite di giro sulle multe che salvarono le banche USA' (*IlSole24ore*, 29 September 2018) www.ilsole24ore.com/art/quelle-partite-giro-multe-che-salvarono-banche-usa-AECJYe9F.
[284] Eisinger, 'Why Only One Top Banker'.
[285] Impunity has been the general approach adopted towards those most responsible for the consequences of the economic crisis; see Simmons & Simmons, 'The Legacy of Lehman'; Benería and Sarasúa 'Crímenes económicos'.
[286] Citeroni, 'International Economic Crimes in the Rome Statute?' 250.
[287] These systemic threats to fundamental values are defined by Starr as 'massive suffering [...] inflicted on a daily basis under circumstances too often taken for granted (...)', see Starr, 'Extraordinary Crimes' 1277.

If the purpose of international criminal justice is to ensure peace, security and stability throughout the world, any serious threats to these pillars of civil society must be addressed.

A general reluctance toward this theory would be understandable, since it directly affects the very essence of international criminal law, or rather a well-established interpretation of what its essence should be. Therefore, the only way to understand the need to open international criminal justice to crimes that have hitherto been outside its scope is to look at today's reality through new lenses.[288]

International Economic Crimes as 'Systemic' Offences

The extraordinary character of the economic crimes committed during the Second World War and during the 2008 financial crisis stems from their 'systemic' nature, that is, the fact that they were both part and result of a deviant state-corporate system. Over the years, several theories have been elaborated with the aim of defining offences committed under these circumstances. These theories are discussed below according to the extent of their scope, from the criminological theories of 'state-corporate crimes' and 'crime of maldevelopment' to the narrower legal concept of 'political white-collar crimes', passing through the intermediate notion of 'corporate-political core crimes'.

The concept of 'state-corporate crime' first appeared in a series of papers presented by Ronald Kramer and Raymond Michalowski at the meeting of the North Central Sociological Association and the Southern Sociological Association in 1990. As the name suggests, 'state-corporate crime' is a macro category that encompasses criminal behaviour that is committed within a specific context characterised by the interconnectedness of political and economic institutions.[289] More specifically, this notion consists of three layers: (i) the individual actor who commits the conduct – act or omission; (ii) the institutional context – a state or corporate entity – in which the individual operates; (iii) the existence of a 'network of economic-political forces' in which the above-mentioned institutional contexts are situated.[290] In other words, the concept of 'state-corporate crime' recognises the risks related to the existence of an interdependent structure in which governmental and business practices may degenerate into abuses of power. As a result, the gravity of any conduct committed within this context is increased.

The concept of 'state-corporate crime' has proven particularly useful to define a number of events, including the space shuttle 'Challenger' tragedy

[288] Kofele-Kale, 'Only Fools' 2.

[289] The original definition of this concept is provided in Michalowski and Kramer, *State-Corporate Crime*, 15: '[I]llegal or socially injurious actions that occur when one or more institutions of political governance pursue a goal in direct cooperation with one or more institutions of economic production and distribution'.

[290] ibid 18.

in 1986,[291] the fire at the Imperial Food Products plant in Hamlet that took place five years later,[292] and the business activities carried out during the Second World War by industrialists and bankers in support of Nazi policies.[293] Despite their differences, all these events represent 'forms of organisational deviance created or facilitated by the intersection of political and economic institutions'.[294]

The degree of involvement of the institutional context in the network of economic-political forces may differ in time and nature. Based on these two parameters, four subcategories of state-corporate crimes can be identified. A crime may be committed at the corporate level, but it may have been initiated (state-initiated corporate crime) or facilitated (state-facilitated corporate crime) by state policies or practices. On the contrary, a criminal conduct can be attributed to state actors who could not have perpetrated it without the initial boost (corporate-initiated state crime) or support (corporate-facilitated state-crime) from corporations. Any of these forms of state-corporate interaction can underlie the perpetration of any international crime. This means that the interdependence between political and economic institutions is not sufficient to characterise the context in which international economic crimes can be committed, but is one of the key elements in defining it.

Another interesting criminological concept for the purposes of this book is the 'crime of maldevelopment', the essential elements of which have been identified by María Laura Böhm. These include the fact that the crime of maldevelopment is the 'cause and result of violence', which should be intended in an inclusive manner, as encompassing not only physical violence but also cultural and structural (or invisible) violence.[295] The crime of maldevelopment is also defined as an 'aggravated form of white-collar crime'.[296] As mentioned in Chapter 1, in his article 'White-collar criminality',[297] Sutherland resorted to the concept of 'white-collar crime' to define any 'crime committed by a person of respectability and high social status in the course of his occupation'.[298] The aggravating factor in the crime of maldevelopment would arise from the seriousness of the harm caused, which is social harm at national and international level of a kind that results in serious violations of human rights and democracy, as well as from the opacity of today's economic structures.[299] As such, the crime of maldevelopment is an 'aggravating form of criminality

[291] ibid 27 et seq.
[292] ibid 45 et seq.
[293] ibid 116 et seq.
[294] ibid 18.
[295] Böhm, *The Crime of Maldevelopment* 208.
[296] ibid.
[297] See EH Sutherland, 'White-Collar Criminality' (1940) 5 *American Sociological Review* 1.
[298] ibid 2.
[299] Böhm, *The Crime of Maldevelopment* 208-209.

by [...] powerful'[300] economic and political actors and may coincide with an aggravated form of state-corporate crime.

These criminological concepts have had a significant impact on international criminal law. For instance, the notion of 'corporate-political core crimes' was forged by Christoph Burchard to define international crimes that are facilitated by economic and business activities. This theory stems from one of the subcategories of the concept of state-corporate crime, namely the 'corporate-facilitated state crime'. However, unlike the latter, Burchard's theory was specifically designed to clarify the interconnection between politics and business involved in the commission of international crimes. The German scholar defines 'corporate-political core crimes' as 'any core criminal activities of one or more actors of political governance that are also (and thus not exclusively) enabled, exacerbated or facilitated by (arguably socially injurious but not yet necessarily criminalised) policies or practices of a corporate actor in pursuit of its own economic, political and other interests'.[301]

If one compares this definition with the notion of state-corporate crime, it is evident that there are some differences due to the adaptation of the latter to the field of international criminal law. First, the three layers conceived by Kramer and Michalowski are replaced by two layers, one pertaining to the individual actors involved, and the second one related to the institutional context in which these actors operate, namely 'political governance' and 'corporate institutions'. The third layer, which for Kramer and Michalowski is the 'mutual interaction' between economics and politics, is superseded by the unidirectional support of corporate actors to their political counterparts.

Secondly, corporate-political core crimes encompass international crimes perpetrated at the state/government level and enabled, exacerbated, or facilitated by corporate actors' policies or practices, which do not need to be necessarily criminal.[302] In other words, the notion of corporate-political core crime defines those international crimes that are perpetrated through ancillary activities carried out by economic actors.

The most recent concept that has been developed to define economic crimes of international significance resulting from systemic abuses of power is the

[300] ibid 208.

[301] Burchard, 'Ancillary and Neutral Business' 925–6.

[302] The three verbs chosen to define the corporate support to States reflect the different nature of business contributions to international crimes. Economic actors can enable the perpetration of core crimes when their contribution represents one 'crucial ingredient – a necessary though usually not the only'. By contrast, business contributions may exacerbate the commission of international crimes when the harm provoked would have been less serious, had the corporate actors refrained from any contribution. Lastly, business' involvement in the perpetration of core crimes may have an impact on the way in which the latter are carried out, by making their perpetration easier or by facilitating it. See International Commission of Jurists, 'Corporate Complicity & Legal Accountability – Report of the International Commission of Jurists Expert Legal Panel on Corporate Complicity in International Crimes' (2008) Vol I, 11–12.

notion of 'political white-collar crime'. This concept takes inspiration from Sutherland's concept of 'white-collar crime', which has been further developed in the literature,[303] and Roksandić Vidlička has recently taken it up again to qualify as international crimes those acts of economic significance that are committed at the intersection of business and politics and that blatantly violate human rights.[304]

This notion significantly differs in scope and nature from 'state-corporate crimes' and 'corporate-political core crimes'. Like these concepts, Roksandić Vidlička's notion encompasses offences resulting from systemic abuses of power by economic and political actors; however, it excludes from its scope neutral business practices and potentially injurious but not criminal business activities. Corruption, money-laundering, fraud are paradigmatic examples of 'political white-collar crimes' that may reach a high level of gravity and overlap with serious violations of human rights because of the context in which they are committed. In other words, the concept of 'political white-collar crime' is the most recent attempt to adapt the theory of 'state-corporate crimes' to international criminal law. This concept is thus the starting point for the in-depth study contained in this book on the circumstances in which certain economic offences can reach a high level of gravity and be assimilated into the traditional categories of international crimes.

CONCLUDING REMARKS

It emerges from the present chapter that the premises for a primordial concept of international economic crime were already present at the post-World War II international military trials. Most of the military tribunals did not hesitate to prosecute high-level public and private economic actors for their involvement, as perpetrators or accomplices, in the commission of international crimes with an economic dimension.

However, the attention that the military tribunals paid to the prosecution of certain economic crimes has not been followed up by second-generation international criminal courts and tribunals. Since the eighties, the international community has gradually recognised the need to tackle ordinary economic offences, which were becoming increasingly transnational in nature, by harmonising national legislation through the adoption of international and regional treaties. In contrast to this progressive trend towards the criminalisation and prosecution of ordinary economic crimes, the focus of ad hoc and

[303] See Coleman, 'Toward an Integrated Theory' 407; G Geis, 'Toward a Delineation of White-Collar Offenses' (1962) 32 *Sociological Inquiry* 160, 171, criticising the lack of a definition of 'white-collar crimes' as offences committed by individuals working within a corporation and not as offences perpetrated by the corporate structure itself.

[304] Roksandić Vidlička, *Prosecuting Serious Economic Crimes* 21.

internationalised criminal tribunals has been almost exclusively on other types of offences, particularly crimes against persons committed during armed conflicts and mass violence. The main exception to this trend was the trial of the former president of Liberia, prosecuted by the SCSL for his involvement in the illicit trade of 'blood diamonds'.

With respect to the ICC, the initial commitments of the OTP on the need to address serious economic crimes linked to international crimes have been disappointed by the facts. Although in theory the material scope of jurisdiction of the ICC has been expanded, in practice its focus has remained on international crimes related to armed conflicts.

The analysis conducted in the present chapter suggests that two conditions are necessary for the current system of international criminal law to be open to the possibility of considering other categories of offences as international crimes. First, the 'crisis focus' of international criminal law should not be abandoned but revisited. The 2008 financial crisis made it clear that, in addition to crimes committed in extraordinary situations of armed conflicts and mass violence, offences perpetrated in peacetime can also seriously jeopardise fundamental collective and individual rights. Secondly, the extraordinary nature of the context in which economic crimes are perpetrated today stems from their 'systemic' nature, ie the fact that they are committed as part of a deviant state-corporate system.

In conclusion, this chapter has demonstrated that economic crimes committed in deviant state-corporate systems are not a novelty in international criminal law, but rather a neglected concept that needs to be revitalised. The current multilevel system of international criminal justice would thus have the potential to make visible the gravity of crimes that have remained invisible for too long. Finally, this chapter has provided the basis for an in-depth study of 'why' and 'how' of defining the concept of international economic crime, which will be addressed in the following chapters.

3

The Gravity of International Economic Crimes

ALTHOUGH THE RUDIMENTARY elements of a concept of international economic crime have emerged from the post-war international military trials, this is not in itself sufficient to prove that crimes falling under this concept can legitimately qualify as international crimes. For this to be possible, a dual threshold must be met. First, it is necessary to assess whether certain economic crimes are grave enough to fall under the umbrella of 'the most serious crimes of international concern'.[1] Secondly, it is crucial to establish whether there is room to develop a potential notion of international economic crimes that meets the requirements of the principle of legality in international criminal law.

While considerations of compliance with the legality principle will be discussed at a later stage (see Chapter 4), the present chapter focuses on the research sub-question of whether certain economic crimes are serious enough to be considered international crimes. To answer this question, the chapter is structured around a legal syllogism involving de jure and de facto considerations. The first section, which corresponds to the legal premise, discusses the concept of gravity in international criminal law, considering the interpretative theories of this criterion that have been developed over the years. The minor factual premise of the syllogism corresponds to the second section in which six potential forms of systemic economic crimes are analysed. Lastly, the gravity threshold in international criminal law is applied to the six selected systemic economic crimes to critically assess whether and, if so, when the latter are sufficiently serious to be considered international. The key findings of this chapter will be identified in the concluding remarks and will serve as the basis for constructing the concept of international economic crime.

THE CONCEPT OF GRAVITY IN INTERNATIONAL CRIMINAL LAW

The 'gravity' element justifies the essence of international criminal law and the authority of international criminal law tribunals to adjudicate the most

[1] Preamble of the Rome Statute of the International Criminal Court (Rome, 17 July 1998) (also known as the ICC Statute) para 4.

serious crimes. At the ICC, this element is assessed at different stages of the proceedings,[2] depending on whether it is necessary to establish the existence of the Court's jurisdiction over certain crimes, due to their 'intrinsic gravity',[3] or the exercise of the Court's jurisdiction over a situation or a case in which serious crimes that meet the 'legal gravity' threshold are allegedly committed.[4]

As regards the inherent gravity of a crime, it is the global community that evaluates it. This assessment is relevant to delimit the scope of the 'global prescriptive authority'[5] of an international criminal law tribunal and its subject-matter jurisdiction. On the contrary, at the ICC, the assessment of the 'legal gravity' threshold is made by the judges at several stages of the proceedings.[6] For instance, during the preliminary examination phase, it is necessary to establish whether certain crimes are serious enough to initiate an investigation into the situation in which they were allegedly committed.[7] Likewise, gravity is an important criterion to ascertain the admissibility of a case under Article 17 of the Rome Statute,[8] as well as to determine a sentence.[9] In each of these scenarios, the concept of gravity is assessed by taking into account several factors, identified and defined by the OTP's policies[10] and the Court's jurisprudence.[11]

This section focuses primarily on the 'intrinsic gravity' threshold that a potential notion of international economic crime must meet, should the global community consider its international prohibition in the Rome Statute or in any other treaty. Two considerations should be made regarding this threshold. First,

[2] MM deGuzman, *Shocking the Conscience of Humanity: Gravity and the Legitimacy of International Criminal Law* (Oxford University Press, 2020) 14.

[3] M Roscini, 'Gravity in the Statute of the International Criminal Court and Cyber Conduct That Constitutes, Instigates or Facilitates International Crimes' (2019) 30 *Criminal Law Forum* 247, 252.

[4] ibid 253. See also G Paraschiv, 'On the Gravity of the Offence in International Criminal Law' (2013) 5 *Geopolitics, History, and International Relations* 136, 139.

[5] deGuzman, *Shocking the Conscience*, 7.

[6] *Prosecutor v Lubanga Dyilo* (Decision on the Prosecutor's Application for a Warrant of Arrest. Article 58) ICC-01/04-01/06-1-Corr-Red (10 February 2006) para 41: '[The] gravity threshold is *in addition to* the drafters' careful selection of crimes included in articles 6 to 8 of the Statute [...]. Hence, the fact that a case addresses one of the most serious crimes for the international community as a whole is not sufficient for it to be admissible before the Court' (emphasis added).

[7] Art 53 of the Rome Statute.

[8] See P Urs, *Gravity at the International Criminal Court: Admissibility and Prosecutorial Discretion* (Oxford University Press, 2024).

[9] Arts 77(1)(b) and 78(1) of the Rome Statute.

[10] See, inter alia, ICC-OTP, 'Policy Paper on Preliminary Examinations' (1 November 2013) www.legal-tools.org/doc/acb906/; ICC-OTP, 'Policy Paper on Sexual and Gender-Based Crimes' (5 June 2014) www.legal-tools.org/doc/7ede6c/. See also F Guariglia, 'The Selection of Cases by the Office of the Prosecutor of the International Criminal Court' in C Stahn and G Sluiter (eds), *The Emerging Practice of the International Criminal Court* (Brill, 2009) 209.

[11] The first relevant decision on gravity as part of the admissibility test was the *Prosecutor v Lubanga Dyilo* (Decision on the Prosecutor's Application for a Warrant of Arrest). See also SE Smith, 'Inventing the Laws of Gravity: The ICC's Initial Lubanga Decision and Its Regressive Consequences' (2008) 8 *International Criminal Law Review* 331, 336–338. Regarding gravity as a factor in determining sentences, see *Prosecutor v Lubanga Dyilo* (Decision on Sentence pursuant to Article 76 of the Statute) ICC-01/04-01/06-2901 (10 July 2012) and *Prosecutor v Ongwen* (Sentence) ICC-02/04-01/15-1819-Red (6 May 2021).

the legitimacy of the current system of international criminal justice is based on the concept of gravity, as it allows international crimes to be distinguished from ordinary crimes. Secondly, although there is still no consensus on the meaning of 'gravity',[12] which has given rise to numerous interpretations over the years,[13] some indicators of the inherent gravity of international crimes have been established.

The Function of Gravity

In domestic criminal law, the gravity of a crime is a relevant factor at the sentencing stage.[14] On the contrary, at international level, gravity represents not only a crucial factor in determining the most appropriate sanction for international crimes, but also a fundamental rationale of international criminality.[15] The *ratio* behind this difference lies in philosophical, historical, and legal considerations. From a philosophical point of view, in his masterpiece *De Jure Belli ac Pacis*, Hugo Grotius stated that:

> [K]ings and those who possess rights equal to those kings, have the right of demanding punishments [...] on account of *injuries which do not directly affect them but excessively violate the law of nature or of nations in regard to any persons whatsoever.*[16]

The Dutch jurist identified a category of offences that are considered more serious than others because they offend the 'law of nature or of nations'.[17] Although the concept of natural law dates back to the Greek[18] and Roman[19] philosophy, Grotius' theory represents an innovative departure from previous theories. According to Grotius, a conduct excessively violates the law of nature or of nations when it is incompatible with the 'rational and social aspects of human nature',[20] ie when it goes beyond what is permitted by human intellect

[12] MM El Zeidy, 'The Gravity Threshold under the Statute of the International Criminal Court' (2008) 19 *Criminal Law Forum* 35, 41.

[13] MM deGuzman, 'How Serious Are International Crimes-the Gravity Problem in International Criminal Law' (2012) 51 *Columbia Journal of Transnational Law* 18, 22.

[14] AP Simester and A von Hirsch, *Crimes, Harms and Wrongs: On the Principles of Criminalisation* (Hart Publishing, 2011) 5.

[15] K Ambos, 'Bien jurídico y harm principle: bases teóricas para determinar la "función global" del derecho penal internacional: una segunda contribución para una teoría coherente del derecho penal internacional' (2013) 10 *Revista de derecho penal y criminología* 343, 371–2.

[16] Emphasis added. See H Grotius, *De Jure Belli ac Pacis*, Book II, Ch XX. XL. i., cited in H Lauterpacht, 'The Law of Nations, the Law of Nature and the Rights of Man' (1943) 29 *Transactions Grotius Society* 1, 24.

[17] For a clear and concise description of the 'natural law' theory of Hugo Grotius, see Stanford Encyclopedia of Philosophy, 'Grotius, Hugo' (8 January 2021) https://plato.stanford.edu/entries/grotius/#NatuLaw.

[18] See T Burns, 'Aristotle and Natural Law' (1998) 19 *History of Political Thought* 142.

[19] See FH Llano Alonso, 'Cicero and Natural Law' (2012) 98 *Archives for Philosophy of Law and Social Philosophy* 157. See also Stanford Encyclopedia of Philosophy, 'Cicero' (14 January 2022) https://plato.stanford.edu/entries/cicero/.

[20] Stanford Encyclopedia of Philosophy, 'Grotius, Hugo'.

and society. International crimes fall into this category of 'injustices' that exceed the limits dictated by human nature and social conventions.

From a historical perspective, international criminal law arose from the need to provide a tailored response to a limited number of crimes committed in an unprecedented historical situation. On several occasions, international military tribunals highlighted the extreme gravity of the offences perpetrated during the Second World War.[21] Likewise, national judges in charge of the prosecution of criminals who were accused of committing international crimes during the war, emphasised the gravity of the crimes under their scrutiny. In the *Eichmann* case before the Supreme Court of Israel, Adolf Eichmann was indicted for international crimes of a universal character.[22] The French *Cour de cassation* expressly stated that the offence with which Klaus Barbie was charged was '*considerée par l'opinion publique comme plus grave*' compared to other crimes.[23]

From a legal perspective, the concept of gravity has served to justify the creation of the international criminal justice system and to delimit the circumstances in which recourse to that system is possible without infringing the sovereignty of States. Gravity was the perfect tool to draw a line between what should fall under domestic criminal law and what should fall under international criminal law.[24] The drafters of the Rome Statute expressly limited the Court's material jurisdiction to 'the most serious international crimes', thus enhancing the perception and acceptance of the ICC as a legitimate institution.[25] Gravity in international criminal law has been defined as a 'sacral barrier [delimiting a] narrow but increasingly contested catalogue of international crimes'.[26] This

[21] See eg IMT, *Trial of the Major War Criminals before the International Military Tribunal*, Vol I (Judgment, 1 October 1946) 229: 'The treatment of Soviet prisoners of war was characterized by particular *inhumanity*'; 231: 'Soviet prisoners of war were also made the subject of medical experiments of *the most cruel and inhuman kind*'; 247: 'The persecution of the Jews at the hands of the Nazi Government has been proved in the greatest detail before the Tribunal. It is a record of *consistent and systematic inhumanity on the greatest scale*' (emphasis added).

[22] Supreme Court of Israel, *Adolf Eichmann v The Attorney General* (Judgment) Criminal Appeal No 336/61 (29 May 1962) para 10: 'The crimes created by the Law and of which the Appellant was convicted must be deemed today to have always borne the stamp of international crimes, banned by international law and entailing individual criminal liability'.

[23] Cour de Cassation, Chambre criminelle, 85-95.166 (20 December 1985) https://www.legifrance.gouv.fr/juri/id/JURITEXT000007064048. See also deGuzman, 'How Serious Are International Crimes' 61.

[24] JL Corsi, 'An Argument for Strict Legality in International Criminal Law' (2018) 49 *Georgetown Journal of International Law* 1321, 1367. Corsi refers to the distinction elaborated by Schabas between crimes that are *mala in se* and those that are *mala prohibita*. The former group of offences includes international crimes that 'shock the conscience of humanity', while other crimes, although of a transnational character, belong to the latter category. However, this classification does not exclude grey areas in need for clarification. See WA Schabas, 'International Crimes' in JD Armstrong and J Brunée (eds), *Routledge Handbook of International Law* (Routledge, 2009) 268, 273.

[25] MM deGuzman, 'Gravity and the Legitimacy of the International Criminal Court' (2009) 32 *Fordham International Law Journal* 1400, 1404. On the concept of moral legitimacy see L May, *Crimes against Humanity: A Normative Account* (Cambridge University Press, 2004) 64–65 and Paraschiv, 'On the Gravity' 139.

[26] NM Rajkovic, 'What Is a "Grave" International Crime? The Rome Statute, Durkheim and the Sociology of Ruling Outrages' (2020) 16 *Loyola University Chicago International Law Review* 65, 68.

metaphor provides a fair description of gravity as a fictitious filter that allows the international criminal justice system to focus exclusively on a limited number of offences.[27] However, while the fundamental role played by gravity in international criminal law is unequivocal, shadows still remain over its definition.[28]

The Definition of Gravity

The extermination of people that took place during the Second World War and the acts that facilitated that massacre represented a tragedy of unquestionable gravity, which made it superfluous for the military tribunals to dwell on the general characteristics of international crimes, their gravity being axiomatic.[29] Likewise, the crimes adjudicated by the ad hoc tribunals were 'mass atrocities', which made it redundant for the judges to specify what the gravity of these offences consisted of.[30] Thus, for many years, the question of how to define the gravity of international crimes remained open and rather neglected.

At the end of the nineties, a lengthy debate involving various actors led to the drafting of a list of international offences seen as a 'sacral class of crimes',[31] whose gravity was eventually confirmed by their inclusion in the Rome Statute.[32] However, it was extremely difficult to draw a comprehensive list of offences that could meet the expectations of the countries involved in the drafting process. Shortly after the end of the post-war criminal trials, the International Law Commission was mandated by the General Assembly to prepare a Draft Code of Offences against the Peace and Security of Mankind.[33] Over the years, the Draft Code has been revised several times and the catalogue of offences included in the 1991 Draft Code was still three times longer than the one ultimately adopted in Rome, as it also included some 'treaty crimes'.[34] These were subsequently excluded as they constituted an amorphous category that did not fall within the standards of the 'Nuremberg categories of international crimes'. Yet, at the time of the drafting of the Code, there was no agreed definition of the gravity of the Nuremberg categories of international crimes.

[27] ibid 67.

[28] deGuzman, *Shocking the Conscience* 87.

[29] deGuzman, 'Gravity and the Legitimacy' 1402, arguing that '[t]he undertheorization of gravity is also due to the historical evolution of international criminal law as a response to atrocities that were undeniably grave'.

[30] E Kontorovich, 'When Gravity Fails: Israeli Settlements and Admissibility at the ICC' (2014) 47 *Israel Law Review* 379, 392.

[31] Rajkovic, 'What Is a "Grave" International Crime?' 78.

[32] ibid 86.

[33] UNGA Res 177(II) (21 November 1947) UN Doc A/RES/177(II): 'The General Assembly […] directs the Commission to […] (b) Prepare a draft code of offences against the peace and security of mankind […]'.

[34] Rajkovic, 'What Is a "Grave" International Crime?' 80 and 83.

The lack of a clear definition of the gravity element was mainly due to the absence of a set of predetermined criteria for international criminalisation. Some scholars contributed to filling in this gap as international criminal law was emerging. Among them, Bassiouni identified five criteria considered to be the most reliable for international criminalisation.[35] According to him, a conduct amounts to an international crime when: (i) it affects a significant international interest, such as international peace and security; (ii) it offends values shared by the global community, for instance a behaviour that shocks the 'conscience of humanity'; (iii) it has transnational implications, meaning that its 'planning, preparation, or commission' involves or takes place in more than one State; (iv)it is harmful to an internationally protected person or interest; (v) it violates an internationally protected interest but it does not rise to the level of conduct that meets the criteria (i) and (ii).[36]

Based on these criteria, Bassiouni identified a list of twenty-seven international crimes,[37] which was not limited to the four core crimes of the Rome Statute but also included some treaty crimes, such as 'financing of terrorism', 'counterfeiting', 'corruption and bribery of foreign public officials'. The twenty-seven international crimes were grouped under three headings, depending on whether their international criminalisation was aimed at protecting international peace and security (i); human interests (ii); or social and cultural interests (iii).[38] Therefore, based on Bassiouni's parameters, the qualification of a crime as 'international' does not necessarily imply its inclusion among 'the most serious crimes'. Only offences that harm certain values, including international peace and security, rise to the level of crimes of exceptional gravity, also known as international crimes *stricto sensu*. This reflects Kai Ambos' theory that international criminal law serves two purposes: on the one hand, it protects collective and individual fundamental values,[39] and on the other, it prevents international harm by ensuring security.[40] These two sides of the same coin will be further analysed in the following subsections as key indicators of the gravity of international crimes *stricto sensu*.

First Indicator of Gravity: Violation of Collective and Individual Legal Goods

At domestic level, the violation of certain legal goods or interests – *Rechtsgut* in Germany, *bien juridique* in France, *bien jurídico* in Spain, *bene giuridico* in

[35] MC Bassiouni, 'International Crimes: Ratione Materiae' in MC Bassiouni (ed), *Introduction to International Criminal Law*, 2nd edn (Brill, 2012) 137, 142–143. The need for criteria for international criminalisation has been also emphasised by S Wharton, 'Redrawing the Line? Serious Crimes of Concern to the International Community Beyond the Rome Statute' (2015) 52 *Canadian Yearbook of International Law/Annuaire canadien de droit international* 129, 132.

[36] Bassiouni, 'International Crimes' 143.

[37] ibid 144.

[38] ibid 150.

[39] Ambos, 'Bien jurídico' 371–372.

[40] ibid 371–374.

Italy, to name but a few – is an essential prerequisite for the criminalisation of a conduct. Hence, delimiting the concept of legal good is paramount to determine which conduct should be criminalised and punished. In this respect, the German *Rechtsgüter* theory of crime is paradigmatic.[41] Some German scholars have adopted a positivist approach, inferring the essence of the concept of legal good from a list of legal goods,[42] while others have attempted to outline a definition of the concept of legal good, thus adopting a normative approach. Among the latter is Karl Binding, according to whom a legal good is 'anything that the legislature considers valuable and the undisturbed retention of which it therefore must ensure through norms'.[43] Similarly, Claus Roxin has elaborated a definition of legal good that refers to both collective and individual legal goods. According to his definition '[l]egal goods are conditions or chosen ends, which are useful either to the *individual and his free development* within the context of an overall social system based on this objective, or to *the functioning of this system itself*'.[44]

Another definition was provided by Franz Von Liszt, according to whom legal goods correspond to 'the life conditions' of a community and crimes are 'those acts that *this people at this time* perceives as *disturbances of its life conditions*'.[45]

The need to define what legal goods are and what conduct violates these goods and should be criminalised, also permeates international criminal law.[46] In light of the narrower scope of application of this body of law, the identification of legal goods deserving of international protection makes it possible to select those behaviours that, by violating such legal interests, are sufficiently grave to be considered international crimes. Unlike domestic criminal law, international criminal law aims at protecting the most relevant global legal goods, ie 'interests, values and goals [...] in a global space of legal interaction'.[47] The protection of global legal goods can benefit both the global community (collective legal goods) and individuals (individual legal goods). There is no hierarchy between these categories, as both refer to values of primary importance; moreover, some legal goods, such as human dignity, fall into both categories.

[41] The idea that criminal law serves to protect legal goods goes back to German scholars, such as Franz Birnbaum, Karl Binding and Franz Von Liszt. See Ambos, 'Bien jurídico' 348.

[42] MD Dubber, 'Theories of Crime and Punishment in German Criminal Law' (2005) 53 *The American Journal of Comparative Law* 679, 684 citing H Jescheck and T Weigend, *Lehrbuch des Strafrechts: Allgemeiner Teil*, 5th edn (Duncker & Humblot, 1996) 6.

[43] ibid 688 citing K Binding, *Handbuch Des Strafrechts*, Vol 1 (Duncker & Humblot, 1885) 169.

[44] ibid 685 citing C Roxin, *Strafrecht Allgemeiner Teil* Vol 1, 3rd edn (CH Beck, 1997) 15 (emphasis added).

[45] ibid 698 citing F Von Liszt, 'Der Zweckgedanke Im Strafrecht' (1883) 3 *Zeitschrift für die gesamte Strafrechtswissenschaft* 1, 23.

[46] Ambos, 'Bien jurídico' 371.

[47] N Carrillo Santarelli, 'The Protection of Global Legal Goods' (2013) 13 *Anuario mexicano de derecho internacional* 405, 408.

Collective Legal Goods

In a report submitted in 1950 to the ILC, the then Special Rapporteur on the Question of International Jurisdiction, Ricardo J. Alfaro, stated that 'the community of States is entitled to prevent *crimes against peace and security* and *crimes against the dictates of the human conscience*'.[48] Alfaro identified the two most important collective legal goods to be protected by international criminal law: on the one hand, international peace and security, and on the other hand, the 'conscience of humanity'. The use of the conjunction 'and' seems to imply that in principle the first category of crimes does not necessarily offend the dictates of human conscience, nor vice versa. This sharp distinction is unrealistic since international crimes that threaten peace and security are likely to offend the conscience of humanity at the same time. However, for the sake of clarity, the two categories of collective legal goods will be examined separately.

The third paragraph of the preamble to the Rome Statute expressly states that crimes committed against millions of children, women and men during the twentieth century are 'grave crimes [that] threaten the *peace, security and well-being* of the world'.[49] The prevention of these crimes is indeed one of the main objectives pursued by the system of international criminal justice set up with the entry into force of the Rome Statute.[50] The reference in the preambular paragraph to crimes against the 'peace and security of the world' is the result of a concept of international crime *stricto sensu* that has evolved since the Nuremberg trials. The Nuremberg Charter and the IMTFE Charter expressly included in the list of international crimes acts that consisted of planning, preparing, initiating, or waging a war of aggression, thereby endangering the peace of the world. However, none of these instruments made explicit reference to the protection of the security and well-being of the world, which could nonetheless be inferred from the criminalisation of war crimes and crimes against humanity.[51]

The term 'crimes against peace and security of mankind' was first adopted by the General Assembly on 21 November 1947 in Resolution 177(II), in which the ILC was instructed to '[formulate] the principles of international law recognised in the Nuremberg Charter of the Nuremberg Tribunal and in the judgment'.[52] However, the purpose of collecting and systematising those principles was to prevent the outbreak of another war, rather than reflecting on the intrinsic gravity of international crimes.[53]

[48] ILC, 'Question of International Criminal Jurisdiction; Report by Ricardo J Alfaro, Special Rapporteur' (3 March 1950) A/CN.4/15, para 136. See also S Starr, 'Extraordinary Crimes at Ordinary Times: International Justice Beyond Crisis Situations' (2007) 101 *Northwestern University Law Review* 1257, 1268.

[49] Emphasis added.

[50] P Kirsch, 'The International Criminal Court: From Rome to Kampala' (2010) 43 *The John Marshall Law Review* 515, 515.

[51] deGuzman, *Shocking the Conscience*, 64.

[52] UNGA Res 177(II), letter a).

[53] deGuzman, 'Gravity and the Legitimacy' 1416.

It was only in 1980 that Special Rapporteur Doudou Thiam provided a detailed definition of 'crimes against the peace and security of mankind', stating that a crime can be considered international if 'its seriousness and scope are such as to impair fundamental interests of the international community'.[54] Thiam acknowledged that the exceptional gravity of international crimes stems from the fact that they involve a violation of fundamental collective legal goods, first and foremost international peace and security. A few years later, Thiam's position was reiterated in the Commentary on Article 1 of the 1987 Draft Code of Crimes against Peace and Security, in which the ILC identified the characteristics of a crime against the peace and security of mankind, including its gravity.[55]

Efforts to delimit the scope of the category of 'the most serious crimes' to offences that threaten the peace and security of the world have not diminished over time. In 1989, the General Assembly instructed the ILC to focus its work on the creation of an international criminal court.[56] As explained above, significant disagreement over whether 'treaty crimes', such as drug trafficking, should be considered as offences that threaten the peace and security of the world prevented them from being included in the 1996 final Draft Code of Crimes Against Peace and Security.[57] The circle of the 'most serious crimes' was thus tightened around four core crimes, ie crimes against peace, war crimes, crimes against humanity and genocide.

The criminalisation of war crimes perpetrated during international armed conflicts (IACs) could easily be justified by the potential of these offences to threaten international peace and security.[58] Similarly, the international character of the crime of aggression was confirmed on the basis of its ability to disrupt international peace and security.[59] On the contrary, it was more difficult to justify crimes committed during non-international armed conflicts (NIACs) as 'crimes against the peace and security of the world'.[60] The reason lies in the fact that these crimes involve both non-state actors and state armed forces, creating internal tensions within a country. It has even been argued that some violations of fundamental

[54] ILC, 'First report on the draft Code of Offences against the Peace and Security of Mankind by Mr. Doudou Thiam, Special Rapporteur' (18 March 1983) A/CN.4/364, para 35. See also deGuzman, *Shocking the Conscience*, 46.

[55] N Kofele-Kale, 'Only Fools Who Send Hyenas to Roast Meat for Them: In Search of the Doctrinal Foundations of the Not-So-Ordinary Crime of Patrimonicide' (2013) 9 *Florida A&M University Law Review* 1, 9.

[56] UNGA Res 44/39 (4 December 1989) A/RES/44/39. See also N Boister, 'The Exclusion of Treaty Crimes from the Jurisdiction of the Proposed International Criminal Court: Law, Pragmatism, Politics' (1998) 3 *Journal of Armed Conflict Law* 27, 27.

[57] ILC, Draft Code of Offences against the Peace and Security of Mankind with commentaries (5 July 1996) www.legal-tools.org/doc/5e4532/.

[58] deGuzman, *Shocking the Conscience*, 66, referring to May, *Crimes against Humanity* 8.

[59] Art 8bis of the Rome Statute defines the crime of aggression as the 'planning, preparation, initiation or execution' of an act of aggression, which is a violation of the UN Charter, the main purpose of which is to maintain international peace and security. See Art 1 of the Charter of the United Nations (San Francisco, 26 June 1945) (the 'UN Charter').

[60] deGuzman, *Shocking the Conscience* 67.

human rights in peacetime may threaten international peace and security more than small-scale abuses in armed conflict within a single country.[61] However, in order to be considered non-international armed conflicts, internal conflicts must meet high requirements in terms of intensity of the conflict and organisation of the parties involved. These characteristics are indicative of the capacity of crimes committed in these contexts to undermine international peace and security.

Lastly, the decision to expand the category of crimes against humanity to include offences not necessarily related to armed conflict has made it more difficult to argue that these crimes are against the 'peace and security of the world'. A similar argument can be made for the crime of genocide.[62] However, it is indisputable that both crimes against humanity and genocide disrupt the normal course of daily life of their victims in such a brutal and inhuman manner that their effects are perceived as a breach of peace in the world and not only in the country where the criminal conduct takes place.

Although the 'traditional basis of international criminalisation'[63] is the capacity of international crimes to undermine international peace and security, other fundamental values or 'collective legal goods' must also be protected by criminalising their violations as international crimes. The second paragraph of the preamble to the Rome Statute defines the crimes committed against millions of people during the twentieth century as 'unimaginable atrocities that deeply shock the conscience of humanity'. However, no further explanation is given as to how certain acts can shock the conscience of humanity[64] and, most importantly, what parameters the drafters had in mind when assessing the inhumane character of international crimes.

This rationale of international criminality dates back to the very origin of international criminal law. In the preamble to the 1899 Hague Convention, the contracting parties referred to the concept of 'public conscience' in the so-called Martens clause.[65] Named after Professor von Martens, the Russian representative at the 1899 Hague Peace Conference, the clause became an integral part of the laws on armed conflicts.[66] The purpose of this clause was to provide a clear reminder that circumstances unregulated by treaties were not automatically lawful but that, on the contrary, they had to comply with principles of international law derived from three sources of law, including the dictates or requirements of 'public conscience'.[67]

[61] ibid.

[62] deGuzman, *Shocking the Conscience* 66.

[63] Starr, 'Extraordinary Crimes' 1269.

[64] ibid. See also deGuzman, *Shocking the Conscience* 70; R Murphy, 'Gravity Issues and the International Criminal Court' (2006) 17 *Criminal Law Forum* 281, 289.

[65] deGuzman, *Shocking the Conscience* 69.

[66] R Ticehurst, 'The Martens Clause and the Laws of Armed Conflict' (*International Review of the Red Cross*, 15 April 1997) https://international-review.icrc.org/articles/martens-clause-and-laws-armed-conflict.

[67] Preamble of The Hague Convention (II).

This concept has stood the test of time to the present day. The IMT judges were the first to reaffirm the existence of a 'conscience of the world', whose dictates had been translated into positive law – 'pacts and treaties' – and among which was the prohibition of aggressive war.[68] A few years later, a reference to 'barbarous acts which have outraged [during the Second World War] the *conscience of mankind*' was included in the preamble to the Universal Declaration of Human Rights. Furthermore, in the above-mentioned report submitted to the ILC by Ricardo Alfaro, 'crimes against the dictates of human conscience' were mentioned as one of two categories of international crimes, together with crimes against world peace and security.[69] Nonetheless, none of these references to the concept of 'public conscience' clarified its meaning.

This gap has attracted the attention of international criminal law scholars, who began to explore this concept further. May defined 'public conscience' as a 'shorthand for what would shock many humans'.[70] Likewise, referring to Durkheim's interpretation of collective consciousness as a 'set of feelings common to the average members of the society', Rajkovic pointed out that a crime should be repressed as an international offence when it infringes on those sacral sentiments that compose our collective consciousness.[71] Although both these definitions indicate the existence of a consciousness common to all human beings, they confirm the difficulty of identifying the true essence of 'public conscience'.

In her book on the concept of gravity, Margaret deGuzman offers an interesting and compelling reflection, arguing that there are global values that represent the 'conscience' of a global community.[72] She deliberately uses the adjective 'global' instead of 'international' because the global community is 'the community of all persons in the world – humanity' who share global values and should be distinguished from the international community, which is composed of States.[73] This distinction is reminiscent of Habermas' distinction between subjects of international law, on the one hand, and 'world citizens', on the other. On this specific point, Habermas argues that 'each individual is simultaneously a world citizen (in the full juridical sense of the word) and a citizen of a State'.[74] In other words, every member of the global community – or in Habermas' words,

[68] IMT, *Trial of the Major War Criminals* 222.

[69] Emphasis added. See also deGuzman, 'Gravity and the Legitimacy' 1417.

[70] May, *Crimes against Humanity* 84.

[71] Rajkovic, 'What Is a "Grave" International Crime?' 72–74. See also MJ Lynch, PB Stretesky, MA Long, *Defining Crime: A Critique of the Concept and Its Implication* (Palgrave Macmillan, 2015) 41.

[72] deGuzman, *Shocking the Conscience* 22, 94.

[73] ibid 19–20.

[74] World citizens are members of the association of 'free and equal citizens of the world', see J Habermas, *The Inclusion of the Other: Studies in Political Theory* (The MIT Press, 2018) 181. On the significance that the recognition of every individual as a 'free and equal citizen of the world' had on the development of international criminal law see CJM Safferling, 'Can Criminal Prosecution be the Answer to Massive Human Rights Violations' (2004) 5 *German Law Journal* 1469, 1473.

every 'world citizen' – is entitled to rights '*qua* human being', which make them equally free under universal or cosmopolitan laws that go beyond the boundaries of the laws of the international community.[75]

Human dignity is a paradigmatic example of a global value embodied in the conscience of the global community and to which every 'world citizen' is entitled.[76] However, according to deGuzman, it is not possible to draw a list of global values whose violation is worthy of international criminalisation, as these values need to be identified through a discursive process involving as many actors of the global community as possible.[77] To reach this conclusion, deGuzman relied on Habermas' theory whereby the global value of peace is a deliberative and dialogical process rather than a permanent state of play.[78] Therefore, the difficulty of defining the concept of 'public conscience' stems from the arduous attempt to provide a single, permanent definition of what global values are.

A last remark should be made regarding the 'shocking the conscience of humanity' rationale of international criminality. According to the second paragraph of the preamble to the Rome Statute, international crimes that shock the conscience of humanity are 'unimaginable atrocities'. The restriction of the scope of international crimes to 'atrocities' occurred only after the Second World War.[79] Among the first acts classified as international crimes was piracy, which was not considered an atrocity but was qualified as an international crime for pragmatic reasons, as it occurred outside national waters, thus threatening international peace and security.[80]

Already in the above-mentioned Moscow Declaration, known as the 'Declaration on German Atrocities', the term 'atrocity' was used as a synonym

[75] J Habermas, 'The Concept of Human Dignity and the Realistic Utopia of Human Rights' (2010) 41 *Metaphilosophy* 464, 475, arguing that '[h]uman rights are connected with a universalistic claim to validity, which points beyond all national boundaries'.

[76] deGuzman, *Shocking the Conscience* 26, referring to Habermas' argument whereby 'human dignity is the moral "source" from which all the basic rights derive their meaning'; see Habermas, 'The Concept of Human Dignity' 466. The definition of human dignity as a global value can also be derived from international legal instruments and jurisprudence. See inter alia, para 2 of the Preamble and Art 10(1) of the International Covenant on Civil and Political Rights (New York, 19 December 1966). See also *Prosecutor v Furundzija* (Trial Judgment) IT-95-17/1-T (10 December 1998), para 183, highlighting the importance of 'human dignity' with respect to the practice of forced oral penetration and the crimes of rape and sexual assault: 'The general principle of respect for human dignity is the basic underpinning and indeed the very *raison d'être* of international humanitarian law and human rights law; indeed, in modern times it has become of such paramount importance as to permeate the whole body of international law.' This principle was recalled in *Prosecutor v Musema* (Trial Judgment and Sentence) ICTR-96-13-T (27 January 2000) para 225.

[77] deGuzman, *Shocking the Conscience* 25, 88 arguing that discovering global values implies a 'dialogic process that takes into account as many divergent views as possible.'

[78] Habermas, *The Inclusion of the Other* 185, arguing that '[the] complexity of the causes of war calls for a *conception of peace as a process* which unfolds in a nonviolent manner and which aims not merely to prevent violence but to satisfy the real preconditions for a peaceful coexistence of groups and peoples' (emphasis added).

[79] deGuzman, *Shocking the Conscience* 37.

[80] ibid 34, 36; Starr, 'Extraordinary Crimes'1268.

for international crime. The same term was reiterated in the London Agreement[81] and in CCL no 10[82] to define war crimes and crimes against humanity. The IMT and the military tribunals established in the Allied zones of occupation in Germany also used the word 'atrocity' as a synonym for international crime.[83] Even the most recent international criminal law tribunals have not missed the opportunity to emphasise the atrocious character of international offences.[84]

The atrocity rationale perpetuates the idea that a crime is international when it is 'extremely cruel, violent, or shocking',[85] inflicts physical or mental suffering, and takes place in extraordinary circumstances characterised by mass violence or war. However, in light of what has been argued above regarding the 'extraordinary' nature of the context in which international crimes are committed, the atrocity rationale of international criminality appears to be obsolete.[86] Nowadays, international crimes must be qualified as such because they violate global values 'of paramount importance to international society, such as peace and security, order and stability, equality, justice and human dignity',[87] regardless of their cruel and violent nature.

Individual Legal Goods

Human rights are among the global values that guide the global community in the process of identification of the most serious crimes. These are rights that every individual, of whatever gender, religion, ethnicity, and nation, is entitled to. However, not every human rights violation constitutes an international crime. A violation of human rights occurs when the act or omission of a state actor fails to comply with human rights obligations,[88] thus entailing the responsibility of that State.[89] Conversely, the commission of international crimes implies the criminal responsibility of individual perpetrators.

[81] Preamble: '(...) those German officers and men and members of the Nazi Party who have been responsible for (...) atrocities and crimes (...)' (emphasis added).

[82] Art I: 'The Moscow Declaration of 30 October 1943 'Concerning Responsibility of Hitlerites for Committed *Atrocities*''; Art II(1)(b): 'War Crimes. *Atrocities* or offenses against persons or property [...]'; Art II(1)(c): 'Crimes against Humanity. *Atrocities* and offenses [...]' (emphasis added).

[83] For instance, see IMT, *Trial of the Major War Criminals* 254, referring to the 'revolting and horrible nature' of the crimes. See also US Military Tribunal, 'The Flick Case', Vol VI, Trials of War Criminals before the Nuremberg Military Tribunals under Control Council Law No. 10 (October 1946–April 1949) 1214: '(...) the outcry by the other nations was against the personal *atrocities*' (emphasis added).

[84] See inter alia, *Prosecutor v Tadić* (Appeals Judgment) IT-94-1-A (15 July 1999) para 302; *Prosecutor v Akayesu* (Trial Judgment) ICTR-96-4-T (2 September 1998) para 478; *Prosecutor v Ongwen* (Trial Judgment) ICC-02/04-01/15-1762-Red (4 February 2021) para 2718 (referring to the atrocities committed during the Bosnian conflict).

[85] Cambridge Dictionary, 'Atrocity' https://dictionary.cambridge.org/dictionary/english/atrocity.

[86] deGuzman, *Shocking the Conscience* 91.

[87] N Kofele-Kale, *The International Law of Responsibility for Economic Crimes: Holding State Officials Individually Liable for Acts of Fraudulent Enrichment* (Ashgate, 2006) 69.

[88] E Schmid, *Taking Economic, Social and Cultural Rights Seriously in International Criminal Law* (Cambridge University Press, 2015) 45.

[89] ibid. See UNGA Res 56/83 (28 January 2001) A/RES/56/83. See also S Leckie, 'Another Step Towards Indivisibility: Identifying the Key Features of Violations of Economic, Social and Cultural Rights' (1998) 20 *Human Rights Quarterly* 81, 96.

Nonetheless, violations of human rights can overlap with the most serious international crimes.[90] Bassiouni listed genocide and crimes against humanity under the category of international crimes that are prohibited in order to 'protect fundamental human rights'.[91] For instance, the act of deportation ordered or allowed by a state actor would be a violation of human rights[92] – including economic, social and cultural rights[93] – which would entail the international responsibility of the State concerned. However, the same act of deportation could overlap with a crime against humanity – should the contextual elements of the latter be met – which would entail the individual criminal responsibility of the state officials involved in the act of deportation.[94] Therefore, the international criminalisation of certain conduct also aims to protect fundamental human rights as individual legal goods.[95]

The term 'fundamental human rights' refers to a specific category of human rights of the utmost importance, whose violation may constitute an international crime. The question arises as to what the concept of 'fundamental human rights' encompasses. It has been argued that civil and political rights should be considered fundamental human rights. This can be inferred from the frequent association between violations of civil and political rights, on the one hand, and international crimes, on the other. For instance, in the 2008 Report on the Reparation Programmes in Post-conflict States, the Office of the High Commissioner for Human Rights argued that the tendency to focus reparation programmes on violations of civil and political rights 'is not entirely unjustified' since 'it makes sense to concentrate on the most serious crimes'.[96] Likewise, in the *Ntaganda* case, the statement of the Trial Chamber VI that 'it is possible to identify a set of fundamental rights pertaining to any human being, the gross infringement of which may amount […] to a crime against humanity' was followed by a list of civil and political human rights.[97] Nevertheless, in international criminal law there has never been room for the supremacy of civil and political rights over economic, social, and cultural rights. International military tribunals have also implicitly acknowledged that violations of both categories of rights could overlap with war crimes and crimes against humanity perpetrated by Nazi officials, such as deprivation of food and slave labour practices.[98]

[90] Bassiouni, 'International Crimes' 217.

[91] ibid 230.

[92] Schmid, *Taking Economic* 94.

[93] Art 11 of the International Covenant on Economic, Social and Cultural Rights (New York, 19 December 1966).

[94] See Art 7(1)(d) of the Rome Statute.

[95] The idea of a combined action of international criminal law and international human rights law to protect fundamental human rights can be inferred from the well-known metaphor of the 'shield and the sword' used by Bassiouni, 'International Crimes' 217.

[96] Office of the UN High Commissioner for Human Rights, *Rule of Law Tools for Post-conflict States: Reparations Programmes* (2008) 19, 21, cited in Schmid, *Taking Economic* 10.

[97] *Prosecutor v Ntaganda* (Trial Judgment) ICC-01/04-02/06-2359 (8 July 2019) para 991.

[98] Schmid, *Taking Economic* 1.

According to a second, more plausible, school of thought, what makes it possible to distinguish a fundamental human right from other human rights is not whether it belongs to the category of civil and political rights or that of economic, social, and cultural rights. Rather, it may be the importance attributed to a human right in the field of international criminal justice that makes the difference. In this respect, May pointed out that the list of human rights in the UDHR includes several rights whose violation would not generally be considered an international crime.[99] As an example, he cites the right to periodic holidays with pay.[100] Although this is an important right for every worker, it is not justifiably relevant for the purposes of international criminal law, when compared to other human rights, such as the right to liberty or health.[101] Consequently, only the deprivation of the most fundamental human rights can constitute an international crime since the interference of international criminal law in the sovereignty of states can only be justified by such high standards.[102] Nonetheless, the rationale of international criminality based on the need to protect fundamental human rights is not exhaustive and must be accompanied by other grounds, including the capacity of wrongful conduct to cause international harm.

Second Indicator of Gravity: The Principles of International Harm and Security

Protecting collective and individual legal goods from the most serious international crimes helps prevent international harm and ensure security. The 'international harm principle' and the 'security principle' fulfil different purposes. The latter justifies the creation of categories of international crimes that can be adjudicated by international courts in order to ensure the security of individuals,[103] while the former justifies the restriction of fundamental human rights during international proceedings: the harm caused by the defendants' conduct should be so severe as to justify a potential restriction of their freedom.[104]

May argues that the attribution of jurisdiction over international crimes to the ICC is based on the security principle since the sovereignty of States 'can be legitimately abrogated when a person's security is jeopardized'.[105] The idea that

[99] May, *Crimes against Humanity* 71.
[100] ibid. See also Art 24 of the Universal Declaration of Human Rights (Paris, 10 December 1948).
[101] See respectively Art 9(1) of the ICCPR and Art 12(1) of the ICESCR. See also May, *Crimes against Humanity* 13.
[102] May, *Crimes against* Humanity 75. See also Habermas, *The Inclusion of the Other* 181, arguing that: '[...] the most important implication of a form of law that bypasses the sovereignty of states is the personal liability of individuals for crimes committed in the course of government and military service'.
[103] May, *Crimes against Humanity* 21 and 63.
[104] ibid 21.
[105] ibid 14.

the power of the sovereign ends when it fails to ensure the security of the people not only recalls Hobbes' theory of the duties of sovereigns and the rights of citizens,[106] but also legitimises supranational interference in domestic criminal justice to guarantee that the most serious crimes are effectively tried and their victims obtain justice and truth.[107]

It is worth noting that for the purposes of this book, the term 'security' refers not only to the physical security of individuals but also to their subsistence.[108] The latter term derives from the Latin word *subsistentia* and can be interpreted as the very fact of 'existing'.[109] Therefore, the security principle is violated when a State (actively) undermines the physical security and the subsistence of individuals, or (passively) fails to protect them against such a deprivation.

In other words, for a crime to jeopardise the principle of security and be considered international, the active or passive intervention of a State is required. However, there are divergent views in the literature on the relevance of state intervention. According to the 'state action' theory, the involvement of a State in the commission of international crimes is one of the main factors from which the gravity of international offences should be inferred.[110] Another doctrinal position argues in favour of a restriction of international crimes to those committed by a State towards its own citizens, due to the alleged inability and unwillingness of the State involved to prosecute its own officials.[111] In addition to being too much restrictive,[112] this theory does not adequately take into account the ability for many States to dispense justice without the need for a supranational criminal court to intervene. The last theory, which is less widely accepted but more plausible, does not reject the relevance of state involvement in the commission of international crimes, but considers it an element of certain crimes, such as the crime of aggression and crimes against humanity, rather than a rationale of international criminality.[113]

[106] ibid 14, 72–74.

[107] ibid 21, 70.

[108] ibid 68.

[109] This interpretation of 'subsistence' does not align with the one suggested by Hobbes, which also encompasses the security of welfare ('contentment and happiness'). Nonetheless, it is in line with May's argument that 'subsistence' only corresponds to the security of the existence as this is the only thing that can justify the loss of liberty that results from the potential incarceration of the defendant upon completion of an international criminal trial. See May, *Crimes against Humanity* 73.

[110] Bassiouni, 'International Crimes' 147; MJ Osiel, 'Why Prosecute? Critics of Punishment for Mass Atrocity' (2000) 22 *Human Rights Quarterly* 118, 118, cited in deGuzman, *Shocking the Conscience* 74. See also *Situation in the Republic of Kenya* (Decision Pursuant to Article 15 of the Rome Statute on the Authorization of an Investigation into the Situation in the Republic of Kenya – Dissenting Opinion of Judge Hans-Peter Kaul) ICC-01/09-19-Corr (31 March 2010) para 60.

[111] deGuzman, *Shocking the Conscience* 77.

[112] In this case, the crime of aggression should presumably be excluded by the list of international crimes as, by definition, it is committed against another State and its citizens.

[113] See B Broomhall, *International Justice and the International Criminal Court: Between Sovereignty and the Rule of Law*, Vol 1 (Oxford University Press, 2003), cited in deGuzman, *Shocking the Conscience* 79.

Although, according to May's theory, the violation of the physical security and subsistence of individuals legitimately justifies the interference of international criminal justice in matters that traditionally fall within the sovereignty of States,[114] this principle is not sufficient to justify the existence of a category of serious crimes and to delimit their scope. To this end, an additional requirement is necessary, namely the creation of international harm.

The international harm principle is not new to legal theory. It stems from a long-standing philosophical discourse centred on the need to provide reasonable explanations for society's demands to criminalise harmful conduct.[115] In this respect, John Mill's work proved to be pioneering.[116] His concept of 'harm to others' provided a solid justification for the use of coercive power by a State, arguing that '[…] the only purpose for which power can be rightfully exercised over any member of a civilised community, against his will, is to prevent harm to others'.[117] The harm principle was further developed by Joel Feinberg,[118] who defined harmful conduct as conduct that harms a person's 'welfare interests', ie those interests and resources that are vital to their well-being, such as their physical or mental health, their security and their material resources.[119]

May translated these principles into international criminal law with some adjustments. His concept of 'harm' encompasses Mill's 'harm to others' but does not coincide with it, since any conduct that harms humanity is not only harmful to others but also to oneself.[120]

The rationale behind the need to prove that a conduct causes international harm lies in the need to compensate for the significant harm – ie a potential deprivation of the right to liberty – that a defendant is likely to suffer during and at the end of the criminal proceedings.[121] It may be argued that defendants run a similar risk for a wide variety of crimes, which do not necessarily cause international harm but equally violate fundamental human rights. May anticipated this objection and emphasised that the only crimes that cause international harm to the global community – to quote deGuzman again – and justify international criminal proceedings are those directed at individuals for being part of a group[122] and those committed by individuals who are part of a

[114] May, *Crimes against Humanity* 75.

[115] ibid 66; see also Ambos, 'Bien jurídico' 354–365.

[116] E Mayr, 'International Criminal Law, Causation, and Responsibility' (2014) 14 *International Criminal Law Review* 855, 857. Mayr describes the theory of harm developed by Mill as one in which the legitimacy of a restriction on an individual's freedom depends on whether 'his or her conduct is harmful to other or to important community interests, or risks being so'.

[117] JS Mill, *On Liberty* (Cambridge University Press, 2011) 22. See also Ambos, 'Bien jurídico' 355; Dubber, 'Theories of Crime' 682.

[118] See above, 'The Concept of Crime' in ch 1, J Feinberg, *The Moral Limits of the Criminal Law Volume 1: Harm to Others* (Oxford University Press, 1987) 106. See also Ambos, 'Bien jurídico' 358–361.

[119] Feinberg, *The Moral Limits* 62.

[120] May, *Crimes against Humanity* 6.

[121] ibid 82.

[122] ibid 84–87.

group or system.[123] In other words, international harm is a group harm, where the group element can be identified in the collective character of the victims (group victimisation) or the perpetrators (group perpetration), or ideally in both of them.[124]

With respect to group perpetration, this may overlap with the 'state-intervention rationale' mentioned above, according to which the principle of security is undermined when acts are systematically carried out by state or state-like entities.[125] However, group-based perpetration of serious crimes extends beyond state collective entities, to include non-state groups.

The second component of the international harm principle is equally worthy of attention. The global community is harmed when crimes are perpetrated against individuals because of characteristics that are inherent to their 'human being'. May provided some criteria for defining these characteristics, namely that they are '[...] *out of that person's control*' or '[...] things that are *beyond their autonomous agency*'.[126] Ethnicity is a feature that an individual shares with others and cannot deliberately choose.[127] However, it can be debated whether the grounds on which acts of genocide can be committed are characteristics that are out of a person's control. The answer is controversial if one considers 'national' and 'religious' grounds, as well as 'political' and 'economic' grounds – which were suggested by Lemkin but were not eventually included in Article II of the Genocide Convention.[128] The same can be said of the grounds on which persecutions may be carried out as crimes against humanity. Therefore, it might be appropriate to revise the standard of 'group-victimisation' to include not only characteristics that are intrinsic to human beings and over which they have no control, but also features that they have consciously and voluntarily assumed as their own and that significantly contribute to determining their identity.

MONEY, POWER AND CRIME: EXPLORING SYSTEMIC ECONOMIC OFFENCES

The rationales of international criminality analysed in the previous sections provide guidelines as to where the line of 'gravity' should be drawn between international and ordinary crimes. In contrast, this section presents an overview of six cases in which systemic economic crimes were committed, that can

[123] ibid 87-90.
[124] ibid 89.
[125] ibid 88.
[126] ibid 85 (emphasis added).
[127] ibid.
[128] On the definition of the different grounds for genocide, see H Abthai and P Webb, *The Genocide Convention: The Travaux Préparatoires*, The Travaux Préparatoires of Multilateral Treaties Vol 2 (Brill, 2008).

help understand whether and under what conditions these offences can reach the 'gravity' threshold discussed above.

Applying the criteria mentioned in Chapter 1, six case studies were selected for analysis in the present chapter. First, the criminal scheme enacted in the *Petrobras* case provides relevant insights into the concept of systemic or grand corruption. Secondly, the theft or plunder of natural resources is examined as a form of systemic economic crime as it constitutes a scourge for many countries in times of peace, as well as being an international crime when committed during armed conflict. Thirdly, it is also discussed whether the laundering of illegally obtained public funds should be considered a systemic economic offence that can reach a high level of gravity if committed under specific circumstances. With respect to the crimes of terrorist financing and conspiracy to commit fraud, the difficulties in classifying them as economic crimes that reach a high threshold of gravity are critically assessed below. Lastly, the gross negligence of public economic actors in preventing the economic collapse of a country is examined, as this scenario allows not only acts but also omissions to be considered as potential candidates for the concept of international economic crime.

The Petrobras Scandal and the Crime of Grand Corruption

Brazil is one of the countries that has suffered most from the effects of systemic corruption, particularly in the field of large-scale energy projects.[129] The Petrobras scandal is in fact the most emblematic and known case of grand corruption that occurred in Brazil.[130] The case is named after *Petróleo Brasileiro SA* (Petrobras), a Brazilian state-owned enterprise founded in 1953 and based in Rio de Janeiro, whose activities range from oil extraction to refining, distribution, and sales.[131] The company was considered one of the most important in its sector, both in terms of efficiency and management practices.[132] Nonetheless, in 2014, the *Operaçao Lava Jato* (Operation Car Wash) – named after the car wash connected to the service station used by black market dealers to launder money – uncovered a vast corruption scheme involving high-level private and public individuals.[133] Under this scheme, private companies bribed Petrobras

[129] DM Goldstein, 'Already Innocent: Radioactive Bribes, White-Collar Corruption and Nuclear Expertise in Brazil' (2018) 59 *Culture, Theory and Critique* 354, 363.

[130] E Valarini and M Pohlmann, 'Organizational Crime and Corruption in Brazil a Case Study of the "Operation Carwash" Court Records' (2019) 59 *International Journal of Law, Crime and Justice* 1, 1.

[131] H Consciência Silvestre et al, 'Implementation of Brazil's Energy Policy through the National Oil Company: From Institutional Chaos to Strategic Order' (2018) 119 *Energy policy* 87, 89.

[132] RS Juaçaba, 'The Contingency Effect of National Culture on Corruption: A Comparative Case Study of Petrobras and Statoil' (*Norwegian University of Science and Technology*, March 2018) para 3.1.

[133] M Arruda de Almeida and B Zagaris, 'Political Capture in the Petrobras Corruption Scandal: The Sad Tale of an Oil Giant' (2015) 39 *Fletcher Forum of World Affairs* 87, 87.

executives in exchange for contracts at inflated prices.[134] Some of the bribes were then used to finance the activities and campaigns of political parties,[135] while the remainder was retained by senior Petrobras executives in charge of three business areas, namely the refining and supply service, the corporate service, and the international relations area.[136]

Without going into the factual details of the case, it is worth noting that three categories of economic crimes were mainly committed under this scheme:[137] several forms of corruption, money-laundering offences and cartel practices.[138] High-level economic and political actors were charged, including fifty-eight executives from Brazil's leading private construction companies,[139] senior Petrobras executives,[140] and prominent politicians.[141]

As to the consequences of the Petrobras criminal scheme, this corruption scandal drastically worsened the budgetary situation and market value of the Petrobras company, to the point that a significant number of workers lost their jobs, finding themselves forced to face poverty and indecent living conditions,[142] while the shares held by the company's shareholders lost up to 50% of their value.[143] This scandal also had an impact on the country's growth as a whole. As Petrobras is a state-owned enterprise, its debt would have been repaid by Brazilian taxpayers, thus diverting public funds intended for other purposes. The *Petrobras* case has had negative repercussions not only within Brazil,

[134] See BBC Editorial, 'Brazil Corruption Scandals: All You Need to Know' (*BBC*, 8 April 2018) www.bbc.com/news/world-latin-america-35810578.

[135] Valarini and Pohlmann, 'Organizational Crime' 2.

[136] ibid 3.

[137] Arruda de Almeida and Zagaris, 'Political Capture' 93.

[138] ibid. According to the defendants, in the *Petrobras* case, bid-rigging practices were implemented by competing private companies, forming a cartel.

[139] Eleven of them were eventually acquitted, see Valarini and Pohlmann, 'Organizational Crime' 10.

[140] Arruda de Almeida and Zagaris, 'Political Capture' 98.

[141] Luis Inácio Lula da Silva was found guilty of 'accepting a bribe from a construction cartel' and was sentenced to nine years' imprisonment in 2017, which was increased to twelve years' imprisonment by the Federal Regional Court in 2018; see Goldstein, 'Already Innocent' 358. However, in 2021, Judge Fachin of the Supreme Federal Court annulled Lula's corruption conviction, on the ground that the court that had convicted him lacked jurisdiction to do so and that the case must be re-initiated by competent judges; see T Bustamante and E Peluso Neder Meyer, 'Operation Car Wash on Trial: What to Expect from Brazilian Federal Supreme Court's Rulings on Lula da Silva (*Verfassungsblog*, 10 March 2021) https://verfassungsblog.de/operation-car-wash-on-trial/; 'Lula: Brazil Ex-president's Corruption Convictions Annulled' (*BBC*, 2021) https://www.bbc.com/news/world-latin-america-56326389. Lula ran in the elections of 2022 and was elected President of Brazil, assuming office from 1 January 2023. Furthermore, allegations were made that President Dilma Vana Rousseff had been involved in the *Petrobras* case as, during Lula's first presidency (2003–2010), she was the chair of the Petrobras board of directors, before serving as the 36th president of Brazil. See Goldstein, 'Already Innocent' 359; Arruda de Almeida and Zagaris, 'Political Capture' 92; 'Brazilian ex-Presidents Charged in Corruption Case' (*BBC*, 6 September 2017) https://www.bbc.com/news/world-latin-america-41170460.

[142] Arruda de Almeida and Zagaris, 'Political Capture' 96.

[143] ibid 88.

but also beyond its borders, due to the alleged involvement of multinational corporations and international banks in laundering the illicit proceeds of this grand corruption scheme.[144]

The economic crimes committed in the *Petrobras* case have been described as an 'endemic and institutionalised'[145] phenomenon. In fact, these were not offences committed occasionally, but orchestrated and systemic forms of economic crime.[146] The terms used to define the Petrobras criminal system – 'corruption *network*';[147] 'complex *web* of bribes, money laundering and political play […]'[148] – are reminiscent of those used by the military tribunals in the aftermath of the Second World War to define the systemic collusion between industrialists and politicians.

In the wake of similar scandals,[149] the *Petrobras* case therefore demonstrates that systemic crimes committed by public and private actors are difficult to eradicate.[150] While the case demonstrates that such conduct is criminalised by norms that are enforceable at domestic level,[151] it also shows that national investigations and prosecutions are not always synonymous with impartial and fair justice. This is what emerges from a report submitted by the UN Human Rights Committee (HRC) in March 2022, according to the majority of which a series of civil and political rights had been violated during the investigation and trial of President Lula da Silva in relation to the *Petrobras* case.[152]

The criminal scheme enacted in the *Petrobras* case is thus a paradigmatic example of economic crimes of international significance, whose gravity stems from three elements: first, the involvement of high-level public and political actors abusing their power; secondly, the systemic nature of the crimes, defined as an endemic and institutionalised problem; and thirdly, the harm caused both to individuals and to the country. This three-tiered definition encompasses the

[144] ibid 94.

[145] ibid 91.

[146] Valarini and Pohlmann, 'Organizational Crime' 2. MC Pinotti, 'The Case of Lava Jato and Grand Corruption in Latin America' (*ISPI*, 2020) www.ispionline.it/en/pubblicazione/case-lava-jato-and-grand-corruption-latin-america-25510, talking about 'systemic corruption in Brazil, with ramifications in other [countries]'.

[147] Consciência Silvestre et al, 'Implementation of Brazil's Energy Policy' 92 (emphasis added).

[148] Goldstein, 'Already Innocent' 365 (emphasis added).

[149] For a comparison between the Petrobras scandal in Brazil and the *Mani Pulite* case in Italy, see MC Pinotti, 'Lava Jato, Mani Pulite, and the Role of Institutions' in A Spilimbergo and K Srinivasan (eds), *Brazil: Boom, Bust, and the Road to Recovery* (International Monetary Fund 2019) 325, 335.

[150] Valarini and Pohlmann, 'Organizational Crime' 10, arguing that this subculture has developed through three mechanisms, namely the institutionalisation of corrupt practices which are *systemically* used; the rationalisation of the use of these practices; the socialisation of unwritten rules and informal interpretations.

[151] Arruda de Almeida and Zagaris, 'Political Capture' 97. See also Valarini and Pohlmann, 'Organizational Crime' 12.

[152] See UNHRC, 'Views Adopted by the Committee under Article 5 (4) of the Optional Protocol, Concerning Communication No. 2841/2016' (24 May 2022) CCPR/C/134/D/2841/2016, para 9.

main elements of the crime of grand corruption, which must be clearly distinguished from petty or ordinary corruption, regulated by international and regional instruments.[153]

The term 'grand corruption' is used as a synonym for 'kleptocracy'[154] – from the Greek words *kléptō*, meaning stealing, and *krátos*, meaning power – or 'patrimonicide'[155] – from the Latin *patrimonium*, meaning estate or property, and the verb *caedo, -is, cecidi, caesum, caedĕre*, meaning killing.[156] Both terms can be used interchangeably to define the act of appropriating large sums of public funds or assets by high-ranking actors who abuse the power entrusted to them.[157]

In 2016, Transparency International formulated a legal definition of this criminal phenomenon, according to which grand corruption occurs when

> A *public official or other person* deprives a particular *social group or substantial part of the population of a State* of a fundamental right; or causes *the State or any of its people* a loss greater than 100 times the annual minimum subsistence income of its people; as a result of bribery, embezzlement or other corruption offence.[158]

The definition provided by Transparency International contains the three elements that characterise the gravity of the economic crimes committed in the *Petrobras* case, namely the involvement of public and private actors,[159] the systemic and institutionalised nature of the crimes, and, most importantly, the gravity of the damage corresponding to the deprivation of fundamental rights or significant economic loss for a State and its population.[160] The goal behind

[153] On this distinction, see MJ Nystrand, 'Petty and Grand Corruption and the Conflict Dynamics in Northern Uganda' (2014) 35 *Third World Quarterly* 821. Examples of *grand* corruption are provided in Kofele-Kale, *The International Law of Responsibility for Economic Crimes* 162–3.

[154] The term 'kleptocracy' was coined by S Andreski, 'Kleptocracy or Corruption as a System of Government' in S Andreski (ed), *The African Predicament: A Study in the Pathology of Modernisation* (Atherton Press, 1968) 92, cited in S Rose-Ackerman, 'Democracy and "Grand" Corruption' (1996) 48 *International Social Science Journal* 365, 367.

[155] The term 'patrimonicide' was coined in 1995 by Kofele-Kale, see Kofele-Kale, *The International Law of Responsibility for Economic Crimes* 12–13.

[156] ibid 12 and 260, arguing that 'heads of states as well as high-ranking state officials openly and fraudulently divert national wealth and resources into their private accounts'. On the concept of patrimonicide see also N Kofele-Kale, 'Patrimonicide: The International Economic Crime of Indigenous Spoliation' (1995) 28 *Vanderbilt Journal of Transnational Law* 45.

[157] On the concepts of patrimonicide and kleptocracy see, inter alia, Starr, 'Extraordinary Crimes' 1259, 1283; Kofele-Kale, *The International Law of Responsibility for Economic Crimes* 9-30; B Bloom, 'Criminalizing Kleptocracy: The ICC as a Viable Tool in the Fight against Grand Corruption' (2014) 29 *American University International Law Review* 627; JM Hartman, 'Government by Thieves: Revealing the Monsters Behind the Kleptocratic Masks' (1997) 24 *Syracuse Journal of International Law and Commerce* 157.

[158] Emphasis added. See 'What Is Grand Corruption and How Can We Stop It?' (*Transparency International*,2016) www.transparency.org/en/news/what-is-grand-corruption-and-how-can-we-stop-it.

[159] Rose-Ackerman, 'Democracy' 365. See also Kofele-Kale, *The International Law of Responsibility for Economic Crimes* 15.

[160] Bloom, 'Criminalizing Kleptocracy' 634, identifying two main features of grand corruption, namely, on the one hand, the involvement of high-level public officials, and on the other, the significance of its impact and effects.

Transparency International's definition of grand corruption is to incentivise the international community to build consensus around it in order to prevent and put an end to this injustice.[161]

Theft of Natural Resources in Niger Delta and Liberia

Another form of economic crime that can be dangerously pervasive is the theft of natural resources.[162] These include resources that can be found in nature and '[have] an economic value to a country':[163] water, minerals, forests, animals are part of the natural wealth of a country. Like Brazil, the Federal Republic of Nigeria is known for being a 'petrostate', that is a State where oil is one of the main natural resources and sources of wealth.[164] Although Nigeria has ownership and control over its natural resources,[165] oil resources are largely exploited by private companies – usually multinational corporations – in line with the economic policies of privatisation implemented by the African country over the years.[166]

The Niger Delta is the most relevant oil-producing region in Nigeria.[167] This area has been particularly damaged by the perpetration of bunkering activities, a form of oil theft characterised by refuelling vessels or drums with stolen oil,[168] and pipeline vandalisation, ie the intentional destruction of pipelines to steal oil.[169] These illegal activities are often linked to the legal process of oil extraction: the upper world, in which legal oil lifters operate, is contaminated by the underworld of organised crime through corruption.

[161] See Transparency International 'Grand Corruption' https://www.transparency.org/en/our-priorities/grand-corruption. On the concept of grand corruption see also N Kofele-Kale, 'The Right to a Corruption-Free Society as an Individual and Collective Human Right: Elevating Official Corruption to a Crime under International Law' (2000) 34 *The International Lawyer* 149, 172.

[162] Kofele-Kale includes grand corruption and theft of natural resources under the same concept, namely 'patrimonicide' or 'indigenous spoliation'. However, for the purposes of the present chapter, the two crimes are distinguished.

[163] For a definition of natural resources see Cambridge Dictionary, 'Natural Resource' https://dictionary.cambridge.org/dictionary/english/natural-resources.

[164] For the past four decades, the dominant revenue base in Nigeria has come from oil exploratory or mining activities, see E Akpomera, 'International Crude Oil Theft: Elite Predatory Tendencies in Nigeria' (2015) 42 *Review of African Political Economy* 156, 156.

[165] OB Oluwakayode, 'Analysing Economic Crimes in Nigeria: The Political Economy Approach' (2017) 5 *Journal of Law and Criminal Justice* 65, 69.

[166] ibid.

[167] A Ajodo-Adebanjoko, 'Towards Ending Conflict and Insecurity in the Niger Delta Region: A Collective Non-Violent Approach' (*Accord*, 12 September 2017) https://www.accord.org.za/ajcr-issues/towards-ending-conflict-insecurity-niger-delta-region/.

[168] PE Igbinovia, *Oil Thefts and Pipeline Vandalization in Nigeria* (Safari Books, 2014) 27. See also OK Ufuoma and O Omoruyi, 'Political Economy Diagnosis of Crude Oil Theft in Nigeria: The Way Forward' (2014) 5 *Mediterranean Journal of Social Sciences* 297, 300.

[169] Igbinovia, *Oil Thefts*, 27. See also Bloom, 'Criminalizing Kleptocracy' 640, arguing that Nigeria as one of the most corrupt countries in the world, suffers from systemic corruption and significant daily losses of oil due to illegal bunkering.

Several political and business actors are involved in this vicious circle of theft and corruption. It has been found that while a public-private oligarchy benefits from the proceeds of crude oil illegally stolen to the detriment of Nigerians,[170] it also fuels local groups of unemployed youths willing to profit from oil revenues.[171] However, many inhabitants of the Niger Delta involved in oil theft do not consider their actions illegal, but rather a legal reappropriation of what belongs to them and what has been illegally taken from them by multinational companies.[172] Therefore, it would not be unreasonable to qualify the crimes committed in Niger Delta as 'indigenous spoliation'. According to the definition elaborated by Ndiva Kofele-Kale, 'indigenous spoliation' is a breach of fundamental human rights, in particular the right of people to freely dispose of their wealth and natural resources,[173] which stems from the principle of sovereignty over natural resources.[174]

The economic crimes allegedly committed in the Niger Delta have other features that should encourage reflection on their gravity. To begin with, the theft of natural resources has become an institutionalised practice in Nigeria,[175] which is committed at the intersection of politics and business.[176] Furthermore, this criminal phenomenon is of transnational significance. Although the acts of bunkering and pipelines vandalisation take place on Nigerian territory, their perpetration is also largely dependent on the sale of illegal oil on the international market.[177]

As for the consequences of the theft of natural resources in Nigeria, it has had a negative impact on national revenues,[178] contributing to the deepening economic crisis in Africa.[179] A second set of negative consequences concerns the environment. In 2009, Amnesty International published a report highlighting that oil spills had caused severe environmental damages and ecosystem degradation in the Niger Delta.[180] These illegal economic activities have also a negative impact on the communities living in the Niger Delta area, thus seriously violating their human rights, in particular economic, social, and cultural rights. Illegal oil refineries release smoke into the atmosphere and chemical pollutants into fishing waters, with serious implications for the health of people living in those areas.[181]

[170] Ufuoma and Omoruyi, 'Political Economy' 298 and 299.
[171] Oluwakayode, 'Analysing Economic Crimes in Nigeria' 69.
[172] Ufuoma and Omoruyi, 'Political Economy' 297; Akpomera, 'International Crude Oil Theft' 163; Kofele-Kale, *The International Law of Responsibility for Economic Crimes* 108.
[173] Kofele-Kale, *The International Law of Responsibility for Economic Crimes* 79.
[174] ibid 80 et seq.
[175] Akpomera, 'International Crude Oil Theft' 164.
[176] ibid 162.
[177] Igbinovia, *Oil Thefts* 22.
[178] Akpomera, 'International Crude Oil Theft' 160.
[179] ibid 163. In 2013, the International Energy Agency estimated the number of crude oil theft in Nigeria at US$7 billion annually, see Akpomera, 'International Crude Oil Theft' 159.
[180] See 'Petroleum, Pollution and Poverty in the Niger Delta' (*Amnesty International*, 30 June 2009), www.amnesty.org/en/documents/afr44/018/2009/en/. See also Ufuoma and Omoruyi, 'Political Economy' 298.
[181] Igbinovia, *Oil Thefts* 24.

Criminal law enforcement agencies – the police, the Nigerian Security and Civil Defence Corps, and the Economic and Financial Crimes Commission – have intervened on several occasions to prevent the perpetration of these offences.[182] Nevertheless, a general laissez faire attitude on the part of the Nigerian government, largely due to the alleged involvement of some senior public officials in the corruption-theft scheme, has been the subject of criticism.[183]

At international level, following the completion of the preliminary examination of the situation in Nigeria in 2020,[184] the OTP of the ICC has engaged in dialogue with the Nigerian authorities, thus providing them with the possibility of conducting effective and genuine national investigations and prosecutions with respect to the conduct identified by the OTP, which include crimes against humanity and war crimes allegedly committed by Boko Haram – a non-state criminal group operating in the north of Nigeria – and by Nigerian Security Forces.[185] None of the crimes committed because of the economic exploitation of natural resources in the Niger Delta area falls within the list of offences identified by the OTP.

Thus, large-scale theft of natural resources would probably have gone unpunished for a long time, had it not been for the intervention of the Dutch courts in the *Four Nigerian Farmers and Milieudefensie v Shell* case. In 2013, the District Court of The Hague had rejected the liability of Shell Nigeria and its parent company, Royal Dutch Shell, for negligent maintenance of the pipelines, arguing that the oil spills had been caused by sabotage.[186] On 29 January 2021, the Court of Appeals of The Hague, on the one hand, found Shell's Nigerian subsidiary responsible for four out of six pipeline leaks, and on the other hand, it held the parent company liable for breach of the duty of care it owed to the farmers who claimed that the oil spills had affected their farmlands and fishing grounds.[187] Indeed, it was found that the parent company had been negligent as to the installation of a leak detection system in one pipeline.[188] In 2022, Shell accepted to pay 15 million euros to the Oruma, Goi and Ikot Ada Udo villages that were affected by the oil pipeline leaks in the Niger Delta.[189] Although with the necessary caveats, it can be said that this ruling undeniably represented a step

[182] Akpomera, 'International Crude Oil Theft' 163. See also Igbinovia, *Oil Thefts* 16 and 69.

[183] Akpomera, 'International Crude Oil Theft' 163.

[184] ICC-CPI, 'Statement of the Prosecutor, Fatou Bensouda, on the Conclusion of the Preliminary Examination of the Situation in Nigeria' (11 December 2020) www.icc-cpi.int/news/statement-prosecutor-fatou-bensouda-conclusion-preliminary-examination-situation-nigeria.

[185] ICC-OTP, 'Statement of The ICC Office of The Prosecutor at The Conclusion of Deputy Prosecutor Mame Mandiaye Niang's Official Visit To Abuja, Nigeria' (27 March 2024) https://www.icc-cpi.int/news/statement-icc-office-prosecutor-conclusion-deputy-prosecutor-mame-mandiaye-niangs-official.

[186] L Roorda, 'Wading Through the (Polluted) Mud: The Hague Court of Appeals Rules on Shell in Nigeria' (*Rights as Usual*, 2 February 2021) https://rightsasusual.com/2021/02/02/wading-through-the-polluted-mud-the-hague-court-of-appeals-rules-on-shell-in-nigeria/.

[187] ibid, for a detailed analysis of the verdict.

[188] ibid.

[189] 'Shell to Pay 15 mln Euros in Settlement Over Nigerian Oil Spills' (*Reuters*, 23 December 2022) www.reuters.com/business/energy/shell-pay-15-mln-euros-settlement-over-nigerian-oil-spills-2022-12-23/.

forward for the victims of human rights and environmental violations committed by corporations in third countries.

Nigeria is not the only African State to suffer from the perpetration of systemic economic and environmental crimes that affect its natural resources and act as triggers or aggravating factors for conflict and poverty. Another State facing a similar situation is Liberia. Since economic actors have always contributed significantly to armed conflict in Liberia and benefited from it, the final report of the Truth and Reconciliation Commission of Liberia (TRC) contains a section devoted entirely to the analysis of the relation between economic crimes and conflict.[190] The report explicitly refers to the mining sector, particularly diamonds, describing it as an 'attractive sector for money laundering' and arguing that criminal instrumentalities are often traded for rough diamonds, which are illegally stolen, exported and sold.[191]

The report highlights the endemic nature of economic crimes affecting natural resources in Liberia,[192] thus confirming that these were not the result of occasional business contracts but stemmed from a criminal subculture or network involving both public and private individuals.[193] Furthermore, in addition to encouraging national jurisdictions to actively intervene to fight impunity for economic actors, the TRC suggested creating an *ad hoc* tribunal to prosecute individuals responsible for international crimes in Liberia, which should also include in its mandate 'the prosecution of grave economic crimes'.[194] Following the TRC proposal, the Office for the War and Economic Crimes Court of Liberia (OWEC-L) was established on 2 May 2024 through Executive Order 131, with the objective of studying the mechanisms and the processes for the creation of a Special War Crimes Court for Liberia as well as for the establishment of a National Anti-Corruption Court for Liberia.[195] The mandate of the OWEC-L was renewed on 1 April 2025, in the hope that the two courts will soon be established to bring justice to the victims of war crimes, crimes against humanity and corruption.[196]

[190] TRC, 'Final Report, Vol III: Appendices, Title III: Economic Crimes and the Conflict, Exploitation and Abuse' (1 December 2009). According to the report, economic actors are involved in a wide range of activities: timber, which is one of the most important natural resources (at 10–22), and mining activities (at 27–29).

[191] ibid 30, para 93.

[192] ibid 13, para 29.

[193] ibid 27, para 81.

[194] ibid 44, para 163. It is also worth noting that the report acknowledges the lack of a definition of economic crime by the international community (3, para 9) and qualifies indigenous spoliation as 'example of an international economic crime that is a breach of international law' (3, para 10).

[195] Office of the President of the Republic of Liberia, Executive Order No. 131 'Establishing the Office of a War and Economic Crimes Court for Liberia' (2 May 2024) https://www.emansion.gov.lr/publications/document-type/executive-orders.

[196] JC Brooks, 'President Boakai Renews Executive Order No. 131 to Advance War and Economic Crimes Accountability in Liberia' (*GNN Nigeria*, 1 May 2025) https://gnnliberia.com/president-boakai-renews-executive-order-no-131-to-advance-war-and-economic-crimes-accountability-in-liberia/.

Money Laundering in the *Bolichicos* Case

Like Brazil and Nigeria, Venezuela fulfils the conditions of a 'petrostate', since oil production plays an important role in the national economy and accounts for a substantial percentage of the State's GDP.[197] However, despite its natural wealth in oil, this South-American country has been constantly and systematically affected by political, economic, and humanitarian crises that have undermined its potential for prosperity. Among the various episodes worth mentioning is a major financial scandal known as the *Bolochicos* case.

Under the long presidency of Hugo Chávez, blackouts occurred regularly in several cities.[198] To tackle the problem, the government decided to contract young industrialists, known since then as *bolichicos*, who were closely tied to the Venezuelan government.[199] Alejandro Betancourt and Pedro Trebbau, who had recently started their own electricity company, the 'Derwick Associates', were awarded a significant amount of contracts in two years without participating in a competitive bidding process, which had been suspended due to the electricity emergency.[200]

Over the years, domestic authorities have uncovered a complex international money-laundering scheme linked to the management of the national electricity emergency.[201] In 2017, nine senior executives of the state oil company *Petróleos de Venezuela* (PDVSA) were arrested and accused of inflating contract prices, a practice that caused the loss of several millions barrels of oil.[202] It was claimed that the eleven projects built by the Derwick company should have cost $2.1 billion, instead of the $5 billion that the Venezuelan government paid due to the overcharges.[203] In

[197] D Roy and A Cheatham, 'Venezuela: The Rise and Fall of a Petrostate' (*Council of Foreign Relations*, 31 July 2024) www.cfr.org/backgrounder/venezuela-crisis.

[198] See Organized Crime and Corruption Reporting Project (OCCRP), 'Plunging Venezuela into the Dark' (*OCCRP*, 12 June 2019) www.occrp.org/en/investigations/plunging-venezuela-into-the-dark.

[199] The term 'bolichicos' was created in 2010 by the Venezuelan journalist Juan Carlos Zapata to define 'la nueva camada de ricos en los tiempos chavistas' ('the new breed of rich people in the Chávez era'), see T Arango M, '¿Quiénes son los 'bolichicos' y cuáles son sus tentáculos?' (*La República*, 27 April 2016) www.larepublica.co/empresas/quienes-son-los-bolichicos-y-cuales-son-sus-tentaculos-2373476.

[200] See OCCRP, 'Plunging Venezuela into the Dark'.

[201] ibid.

[202] ibid. See also A Ulmer, 'Venezuela Arrests Top Oil Executive, Eight Other PDVSA Employees: Sources' (*Reuters*, 6 September 2017) https://www.reuters.com/article/us-venezuela-oil/venezuela-arrests-top-oil-executive-eight-other-pdvsa-employees-sources-idUSKCN1BG2TZ/.

[203] See OCCRP, 'Plunging Venezuela into the Dark'. See J Weaver and AM Delgado, 'Venezuela's Business Elite Face Scrutiny in $1.2 Billion Money Laundering Case' (*Miami Herald*, 29 January 2019) www.miamiherald.com/news/local/article236793383.html, arguing that '(I)n Miami, Houston and New York, several corruption cases have been pursued by the Justice Department alleging bribery, embezzlement and money laundering activities in Venezuela and the United States'. See also US Department of Justice, 'Two Financial Assets Managers Charged in Alleged $1.2 Billion Venezuelan Money Laundering Scheme' (12 June 2022) https://www.justice.gov/usao-sdfl/pr/two-financial-asset-managers-charged-alleged-12-billion-venezuelan-money-laundering#:~:text=According%20; US Department of Justice 'Venezuelan Television News Network Owner Charged in Alleged $1.2B Money Laundering Scheme' (23 October 2024) https://www.justice.gov/usao-sdfl/pr/venezuelan-television-news-network-owner-charged-alleged-12b-money-laundering-scheme.

other words, public funds from oil production and sales were allegedly stolen on a large scale and ultimately used for private purposes. Aware of the risks associated with US investigations, Betancourt avoided reinvesting his money in the US market and allegedly diverted his assets to European shell companies, including companies registered in the Luxembourg corporate registry.[204]

Two aspects of the economic crimes committed in the *Bolichicos* case are worthy of attention. On the one hand, their perpetration was neither occasional nor limited to a short period of time; on the contrary, it has lasted more than a decade and has not slowed down despite political changes in the Venezuelan government. This means that these practices were deeply rooted in the social, political, and economic life, and particularly difficult to eradicate. A second feature of these offences relates to their nature as political-economic crimes: it was the interaction between high-level representatives of political and business entities that made the criminal plan and its actual implementation possible.

Despite the almost unlimited availability of oil and the enormous amount of money spent over the years to improve energy systems and infrastructure, Venezuela continues to suffer the serious economic and human consequences of grand corruption and the laundering of public funds. During the nationwide blackouts that occurred in March 2019, vital equipment stopped working in hospitals, causing the deaths of at least twenty-six people, including premature babies.[205] Due to the blackouts, not only was the right to life and health violated, but also the right to food. Refrigerators stopped working, and people had difficulty in storing food and, in some cases, accessing it.[206]

This dire scenario, characterised by human rights violations, deterioration of oil production, hyperinflation, and pervasive poverty is systemically linked to economic crimes committed in the country. In a report issued in 2019, the High Commissioner for Human Rights stated that 'misallocation of resources, corruption, lack of maintenance of public infrastructure' were the main causes of these human rights violations, including the right to an adequate standard of living and the right to access electricity, water, and natural gas.[207] Between September and August 2024, Venezuela was hit by a new nationwide power outage, which

[204] N Jaccard et al, 'Jet-Setting Venezuelan Businessman in Corruption Probe Linked to Luxembourg Firms' (*OCCRP*, 11 February 2021) www.occrp.org/en/openlux/jet-setting-venezuelan-businessman-in-corruption-probe-linked-to-luxembourg-firms. On the mechanisms underlying money-laundering, see M Anderson, 'International Money Laundering: The Need for ICC Investigative and Adjudicative Jurisdiction' (2013) 53 *Virginia Journal of International Law* 762, 772.

[205] S Jones, 'Venezuela Blackout: What Caused It and What Happens Next?' (*The Guardian*, 13 March 2019) www.theguardian.com/world/2019/mar/13/venezuela-blackout-what-caused-it-and-what-happens-next. See also R Dube and M Castro, 'Venezuela Blackout Plunges Millions into Darkness' (*The Wall Street Journal*, 8 March 2019) www.wsj.com/articles/venezuela-blackout-stretches-across-country-closing-schools-and-businesses-11552053011.

[206] See Jones, 'Venezuela Blackout'.

[207] UNHRC, 'Human Rights in the Bolivarian Republic of Venezuela: Report of the United Nations High Commissioner for Human Rights' (9 October 2019) A/HRC/41/18, para 12.

President Maduro blamed on a conspiracy by the political opposition and the US to overthrow his government.[208] On the contrary, the opposition blamed corruption and lack of investment in expertise as the main causes of the outages.[209]

Financing Paramilitary Violence: The *Chiquita* Case in Colombia

Located in the north-western part of South America, Colombia boasts a perfect climate for coffee production, making the country one of the world's leading producers and exporters. On the other hand, Colombia is also known for the cultivation of coca plants, from which cocaine has been extracted over the years. The growing global demand for drugs has boosted both coca cultivation and the creation of criminal groups ready to profit from this lucrative business. This has gone hand in hand with the spread of violence in Colombia, which has escalated into a long-standing armed conflict between multiple factions.

Among the parties involved in the conflict were paramilitary groups that set up the *Autodefensas Unidas de Colombia* (AUC) in 1997, with the stated aim of protecting the economic and social conditions of Colombians. These goals were pursued with violence and systematic violations of human rights.[210] The paramilitaries were able to carry out their activities with the funds and support they regularly received from politicians and multinational corporations. Indeed, Colombian society has been largely influenced over the years by two criminal and social phenomena known as 'parapolitics' and 'paraeconomics'. 'Parapolitics' refers to alleged agreements and links between Colombian paramilitaries and politicians, whereby military control of large areas of the country was granted to the former in exchange for money and economic support for elections of the latter.[211] As for the phenomenon of 'paraeconomics', the name refers to illegal cooperation between businesses and paramilitary groups in Colombia, which usually consisted of multinational companies paying large sums of money to paramilitary groups in order to obtain protection and maximise profits, knowing that the funds would be used to buy weapons and commit mass crimes.[212]

One of the multinational companies involved in this scheme was Chiquita Brands International and its fully owned subsidiary in Colombia, C.I. Bananos

[208] 'Venezuela hit by nationwide power outage, Maduro blames "criminal attack"' (*Le Monde*, 30 August 2024) www.lemonde.fr/en/international/article/2024/08/30/venezuela-hit-by-nationwide-power-outage-maduro-blames-criminal-attack_6723905_4.html.

[209] ibid.

[210] See ICC-OTP, 'ICC Interim Report: Situation in Colombia' (1 November 2012) para 25.

[211] ibid paras 174–179.

[212] The term '*paraeconomía*' ('paraeconomics') is used at the international level, see 'Financiación de grupos paramilitares es un crimen de lesa humanidad' (*Office of the High Commissioner for Human Rights in Colombia*, 2 February 2017) https://www.hchr.org.co/noticias/financiacion-de-grupos-paramilitares-es-un-crimen-de-lesa-humanidad/.

de Exportación, S.A. (also known as 'Banadex'). In 2006, Chiquita pleaded guilty to making $1.7 million in payments to the AUC between 1997 and 2004,[213] despite being aware of the paramilitaries' criminal activities in Colombia and their designation by the US as a foreign terrorist group.[214] As a result of the plea agreement in 2007, Chiquita paid a $25 million fine and that same year, a civil lawsuit on behalf of the victims whose family members were murdered by the AUC was filed against Chiquita.[215] On 10 June 2024, Chiquita was found responsible by a jury in Florida, and ordered to pay $38.3 million compensation for the victims.[216]

The crimes committed by Chiquita include trafficking of weapons and financing terrorist groups, which used the weapons and money to commit international crimes, such as murder and forced displacement.[217] The payments increased Chiquita's profits in two ways: on the one hand, the AUC relied on their death squads to kill union workers, who caused economic losses to the company by organizing strikes;[218] on the other hand, the forced displacements allowed Chiquita to expand its banana plantations.[219] In both cases, the US-Colombian company sought to illegally maximise its profits at the expense of civilians.

As Colombia is a State Party to the Rome Statute, in 2017 a group of human rights organisations and lawyers sent an Article 15 Communication to the OTP of the ICC, requesting that Chiquita's officials be investigated as contributors to the commission of international crimes, under Article 25(3)(d)(ii) of the Rome Statute.[220] According to the Article 15 communication, Colombia had not demonstrated that it was able to proceed with the investigation against fourteen Chiquita suspects.[221] Moreover, the communication contended that, although the suspects were not Colombian nationals, their alleged acts contributed to the commission of international crimes on Colombian territory by the paramilitary, which would pose no difficulty for the establishment of the ICC's territorial jurisdiction.[222] In October 2021, the OTP announced its decision to close the preliminary

[213] See Colectivo de Abogados José Alvear Restrepo, Fédération Internationale des Ligues des Droits de l'Hommes (FIDH), and International Human Rights Clinic at Harvard Law School, 'The Contribution of Chiquita Corporate Officials to Crimes against Humanity in Colombia – Article 15 Communication to the International Criminal Court' (18 May 2017) https://www.refworld.org/reference/countryrep/ifhr/2017/en/116811, 5.

[214] ibid 13, arguing that '[T]he UN High Commissioner for Human Rights released several reports on the situation in Colombia while Chiquita was operating there'; moreover, the US designed the AUC as a foreign terrorist organisation in 2001, para 17.

[215] See *Doe v Chiquita Brands International* (Earth Rights International) https://earthrights.org/case/doe-v-chiquita-brands-international-en/.

[216] ibid.

[217] 'What Are the Links between the Executives of the Multinational Chiquita and the Paramilitaries in Colombia?' (*FIDH*, 18 May 2017) https://www.fidh.org/en/region/americas/colombia/what-are-the-links-between-the-executives-of-the-multinational.

[218] Colectivo de Abogados José Alvear Restrepo et al, 'The Contribution of Chiquita' 44–46.

[219] ibid 42.

[220] ibid 5.

[221] ibid 48–55.

[222] ibid 3.

examinations on the situation in Colombia, considering the ability and willingness of national authorities to genuinely investigate and prosecute international crimes.[223] Meanwhile, in 2018, Colombia had charged thirteen former senior managers and officers from Banadex and legal representatives and executives from Chiquita-related holdings with '*concierto para delinquir agrevado*' (ie, 'aggravated conspiracy to commit a crime'), for allegedly conspiring to financing the crimes against humanity committed by paramilitary groups.[224] The list of accused was reduced to ten in 2019,[225] but no verdict has yet been handed down.[226]

Defrauding the US: Volkswagen's Conspiracy and the Emissions Scandal

A federal law that entered into force in 1970, the Clean Air Act, regulates sources of air emissions in the US. In accordance with this Act, the US Environmental Protection Agency (EPA) established emissions standards for new motor vehicles in order to protect the environment and public health.[227] Following the promulgation of these standards, car manufacturers were required to submit applications to the EPA for each group of vehicles they intended to sell in the US.[228] The standards became stricter after 1998, with the adoption of new measures that manufacturers had to comply with by 2007.

Since then, the Volkswagen Group has submitted several applications to the EPA for light diesel vehicles, declaring in a signed statement that:

> [A]ny element of design, system, or emission control device installed on or incorporated in the Volkswagen Group's new motor vehicles […] will not, to the best of the Volkswagen Group's information and belief, cause the emission into the ambient air of pollutants in the operation of its motor vehicles or motor vehicle engines which cause or contribute to *an* unreasonable risk to public health or welfare […] [and to public safety]'.[229]

[223] See below, 'National Solutions' in ch 5.

[224] 'Acusan a directivos de Chiquita Brands de financiar grupos paramilitares en Urabá' (*Verdadabierta.com*, 31 August 2018) https://verdadabierta.com/acusan-a-directivos-de-chiquita-brands-de-financiar-guerrillas-y-paras-en-uraba/.

[225] Redacción Judicial, 'En firme acusación contra exdirectivos de Chiquita Brands por presuntos pagos a AUC' (*El Espectador*, 20 September 2019) www.elespectador.com/judicial/en-firme-acusacion-contra-exdirectivos-de-chiquita-brands-por-presuntos-pagos-a-auc-article-881967/.

[226] Redacción Judicial, 'El juicio contra directivos de Chiquita Brands que está congelado en Colombia' (*El Espectador*, 11 June 2024) www.elespectador.com/judicial/el-juicio-contra-directivos-de-chiquita-brands-que-esta-congelado-en-colombia/.

[227] US EPA, 'EPA Emission Standards for Light-Duty Vehicles and Trucks and Motorcycles' https://www.epa.gov/emission-standards-reference-guide/epa-emission-standards-light-duty-vehicles-and-trucks-and.

[228] US District Court, *United States of America v Richard Dorenkamp, Heinz-Jakob Neusser, Jens Hadler, Bernd Gottweis, Jürgen Peter and Martin Winterkorn* (Second Superseding Indictment) No 2:16-cr-20394 (14 March 2018) 2 para 3.

[229] ibid 7 para 20 (emphasis added).

Therefore, from a formal point of view, the German manufacturer's vehicles, marketed as 'clean diesel' vehicles,[230] complied with the EPA standards. However, US authorities found out that the Volkswagen Group had installed a defeat device in all its diesel vehicles, designed to adapt vehicle performance to external circumstances.[231] When the vehicle was tested in the laboratory, the device ensured that its performance remained within the required emission standards; outside the laboratory, the device allowed the vehicle to release higher NOx emissions into the air.[232]

Volkswagen's diesel scandal provoked a strong reaction from national authorities, with domestic proceedings being initiated in the US and abroad.[233] In January 2017, the Volkswagen Group was charged in the US with three counts, to which it pleaded guilty and for which it agreed to pay $2.8 billion.[234] In addition to the company, six directors and senior executives were indicted for their involvement in the fraud scheme.[235] All were charged with conspiracy to defraud the US, while only some of them were charged with violating the Clean Air Act and with wire fraud offences.[236]

The consequences of the fraudulent scheme implemented by Volkswagen were so serious that they resulted in severe violations of fundamental collective and individual legal goods. First, the pollutants released by modified vehicles

[230] ibid. 8 para 22.

[231] ibid 14 para 34.

[232] ibid 15 para 35.

[233] Volkswagen was fined €1 billion by German authorities for the diesel scandal, and fifteen executives were charged in 2021, see 'VW fined €1bn by German Prosecutors over Diesel Scandal' (*The Guardian*, 13 June 2018) www.theguardian.com/business/2018/jun/13/vw-fined-1bn-german-court-diesel-scandal; 'German Prosecutors Charge More VW Managers in Emissions Scandal' (*Reuters*, 24 April 2021) www.reuters.com/business/autos-transportation/german-prosecutors-charge-more-vw-managers-emissions-scandal-dpa-2021-04-24/. A class action against Volkswagen group for the diesel scandal, has been declared admissible in France, see 'Dieselgate: une action de groupe contre Volkswagen en France jugée recevable (*Le Parisien*, 27 March 2025) www.leparisien.fr/economie/dieselgate-une-action-de-groupe-contre-volkswagen-en-france-jugee-recevable-27-03-2025-HIRRCWVD3FGMTCVO3JS3HXZ7DI.php.

[234] US District Court, *United States of America v Volkswagen AG* (Plea Agreement) No. 16-cr-20394 (10 March 2017).

[235] The accused initially included Richard Dorenkamp, Heinz-Jakob Neusser, Jens Hadler, Bernd Gottweis, Oliver Schmidt and Jürgen Peter. In 2017, Oliver Schmidt pleaded guilty to one count and was sentenced to 84 months of incarceration and to the payment of a criminal penalty of $400,000. In 2018, a fifth superseding indictment included charges against Martin Winterknorn, see US Department of Justice, *United States v Volkswagen* https://www.justice.gov/criminal/criminal-vns/case/united-states-v-volkswagen.

[236] Para 371 of Title 18 of the US Code defines 'conspiracy to commit an offence or to defraud United States' as a crime per se and not as a mode of liability. Volkswagen executives were charged with the crime of conspiracy to defraud the US, by evading the EPA standards, and to commit other offences, such as wire fraud (defined under para 1343 of Title 18 of the US Code) and violation of the Clean Air Act (defined under para 7413 (c)(2)(A) of the same Code). Wire fraud is defined as the act of transmitting by means of wire, radio, or television communication any writings, signs, promises in order to carry out a plan or artifice that the perpetrator intends to conceal. By marketing its diesel vehicles as environmentally friendly, Volkswagen intended to conceal the high emissions caused by the defeat device.

have had a negative impact on people's health.[237] A significant number of studies have linked the release of these chemicals to respiratory and cardiovascular diseases and premature mortality.[238] In addition to highlighting the harmful consequences for human beings, the World Health Organisation has declared that the offences committed by Volkswagen constitute crimes against the environment.[239]

The *Haarde* Case: Failing to Prevent Iceland's Economic Collapse

Following the outbreak of the global financial crisis in 2007–2008, Iceland was hit by a severe economic crisis. The economic collapse of this European country was the direct result of the bankruptcy of three major banks and of the government's failure to act and prevent a crisis that could have been avoided or at least mitigated in its consequences.[240] When the crisis erupted in 2008, Iceland's Prime Minister was Geir Hilmar Haarde, the first global leader to be charged with crimes related to the financial crisis.[241]

The Office of the Special Prosecutor was established with the main task of investigating any conduct that could be related to the economic crisis, such as fraud and market abuse, while a Special Investigative Commission was tasked with finding those primarily responsible for Iceland's economic collapse.[242] As a result of the investigations, Haarde was charged with gross negligence, along with three other ministers in his government. A few months later, the Icelandic Parliament, the *Althingi*, voted in favour of the decision to indict only Haarde and a special tribunal, the *Landsdómur*, was set up for his trial.[243]

Unlike the cases examined so far, Haarde was charged with gross negligence, meaning that he did not commit or participate in the perpetration of economic

[237] JR Krall and RD Peng, 'The Volkswagen Scandal: Deception, Driving and Deaths' (2015) 12 *Significance* 12, 13.

[238] M Sanger-Katz and J Schwartz, 'How Many Deaths Did Volkswagen Deception Cause in the U.S.?' (*The New York Times*, 28 September 2015) https://www.nytimes.com/2015/09/29/upshot/how-many-deaths-did-volkswagens-deception-cause-in-us.html. See also SESA-SESPAS, 'La salud pública ante el caso Volkswagen' (2015) 15 *Revista de salud ambiental* 148, 148; JC Jung and SB 'Alison' Park, 'Volkswagen's Diesel Emissions Scandal' (2017) 59 *Thunderbird International Business Review* 127, 128; L Bovens, 'The Ethics of Dieselgate' (2016) 40 *Midwest Studies in Philosophy* 262, 265–266, 272; Krall and Peng, 'The Volkswagen Scandal' 13; N Mansouri, 'A Case Study of Volkswagen Unethical Practice in Diesel Emission Test' (2016) 5 *International Journal of Science and Engineering Applications* 211, 211–212.

[239] SESA-SESPAS, 'La salud pública' 148.

[240] R Bragadóttir, 'Criminal Law and the Financial Crisis: The Proceedings against Iceland's Former Prime Minister Geir H. Haarde' in F Zimmermann (ed), *Criminal Liability of Political Decision-Makers. A Comparative Perspective* (Springer 2017) 357, 357.

[241] See 'Iceland Ex-PM Haarde 'Partly' Guilty over 2008 Crisis' (*BBC*, 23 April 2012) https://www.bbc.com/news/world-europe-17817174.

[242] Bragadóttir, 'Criminal Law and the Financial Crisis' 358.

[243] R Neate, 'Iceland Ex-Pm Geir Haarde Cleared of Bank Negligence' (*The Guardian*, 2012) www.theguardian.com/world/2012/apr/23/iceland-geir-haarde-found-guilty.

crimes, but allegedly allowed other actors to commit them by failing to prevent his country's economic collapse, which he should have been aware of due to his position.[244] The gravity of a similar act of gross negligence would derive directly from the consequences of the failure to act: a significant number of Icelanders lost their savings, jobs and homes, while the country's economy suffered severe damage.[245]

The judgment issued by the majority of the *Landsdómur* on 23 April 2012 found that the Prime Minister of Iceland had a duty to discuss the economic situation of his country during government meetings, which he had failed to do from February until September 2008, and this failure had to be considered gross negligence.[246] Thus, the special tribunal convicted the defendant for gross-negligence under Article 8(c), cf. Art 11, of Act no. 4/1963 on Ministerial Responsibility.[247] Nonetheless, on 17 October 2022, Mr Geir Hilmar Haarde lodged an application against the Republic of Iceland before the European Court of Human Rights (ECtHR), alleging that the impeachment proceedings against him and his conviction had violated his rights under Articles 6 and 7 of the ECHR.[248] On 23 February 2018, the Strasbourg judges held unanimously that there had been no violation of Article 6 and, by majority, that there had been no violation of Article 7 of the ECHR.[249]

The *Haarde* case sparked a debate on a controversial and crucial issue, namely whether and how senior public officials can be held accountable in times of economic crisis. Crosby correctly noted that accusing a Prime Minister of gross negligence in relation to the economic crisis set an important precedent that could have a deterrent effect:

> In a future case the person or persons ultimately responsible – the captains and officers of the ship of state and the former in particular – may be punished. [This case] does have a deterrent effect. A criminal sanction is possible for incompetence causing serious economic damage.[250]

THE GRAVITY OF INTERNATIONAL ECONOMIC CRIMES

Despite the significant contextual differences, the economic crimes committed in the six cases mentioned above have some points in common. The purpose

[244] ibid.

[245] BBC On the consequences of Iceland's economic collapse, see S Crosby, 'Brexit: Lessons from Different Quarters' (2019) 10 *New Journal of European Criminal Law* 205, 207.

[246] Bragadóttir, 'Criminal Law and the Financial Crisis' 368.

[247] ibid 368.

[248] Convention for the Protection of Human Rights and Fundamental Freedoms (Rome, 4 November 1950) (also known as European Convention on Human Rights or ECHR).

[249] ECtHR, *Haarde v Iceland* (First Section Judgment) Application no 66847/12 (23 February 2018) para 120 and 132.

[250] Crosby, 'Brexit' 208. On the significant effect of the *Haarde* case, see also M Max-Neef (2014) 'The Good Is the Bad That We Don't Do: Economic Crimes against Humanity: A Proposal' 104 *Ecological Economics* 152, 154, pointing out the lack of attention given to the *Haarde* case in the media, due to the fact that 'had it generated contagion, it would have been catastrophic for the power groups'.

of this section is to identify and discuss these points and establish how they enable economic crimes to reach the threshold of gravity described above, which consists, on the one hand, of the violation of collective and individual legal goods and, on the other, of the creation of international harm.

Although it is one of the oldest theories justifying the gravity of international crimes, the 'atrocity rationale' will not be applied as a yardstick to prove the gravity of certain economic crimes. The reason lies in the difficulty of reconciling the traditional interpretation of this rationale with the nature of serious economic crimes, which are non-violent offences committed not only in situations of mass violence and war, but also, and more frequently, in times of peace.[251] As a result, two paths lie open: recognising the obsolescence of a rigid interpretation of the 'atrocity rationale' and avoiding its application, or adopting a broader interpretation of this rationale, more in line with an evolutionary conception of international criminal law. Only in the latter case would certain economic crimes be considered a heinous criminal phenomenon capable of having a 'shocking' impact on the values underlying the conscience of the global community.[252] Nonetheless, this shift in perspective is difficult to implement. Kofele-Kale noted that comparing economic crimes, such as indigenous spoliation, to crimes traditionally considered barbaric and outrageous, such as genocide 'requires a mental leap that most people find hard to make'.[253] This is because a conception of international criminal law anchored on 'violent' crimes still prevails, which does not allow the nuances of contemporary serious crimes to be grasped.

International Economic Crimes Violate Collective and Individual Legal Goods

The first element common to most of the economic crimes committed in the cases mentioned above is their capacity to seriously undermine one or more of the following fundamental global values and purposes of the UN: international peace and security, the principle of sovereignty over natural resources, and the promotion and respect of fundamental human rights.[254]

International Economic Crimes Threaten International Peace and Security

The historical period in which the United Nations was created explains the choice of the objectives pursued by this international organisation, in particular its commitment to maintain international peace and security as a necessary

[251] Starr, 'Extraordinary Crimes'1259, 1312.
[252] ibid 1285.
[253] Kofele-Kale, 'Only Fools' 2.
[254] Bassiouni, 'International Crimes' 142–143, included the potential of a crime to violate an international fundamental value among the main features of the macro concept of international crime.

response to the 'scourge of war'.[255] Since the UN Charter does not provide an exact definition of what constitutes a threat to international peace and security, the Security Council has determined on a case-by-case basis what falls under this term.[256]

In 1950, the General Assembly resolution 'Uniting for Peace' linked the UN's function of maintaining peace and security to the need to overcome 'international tensions'.[257] Although international armed conflicts have always been regarded as the main threat to international peace and security, it is now widely accepted that this traditional conception of 'threat' has become too restrictive and needs to be reconsidered.[258] This position is supported by the practice of the Security Council, which has increasingly regarded phenomena other than international armed conflicts as disruptions of peace and security, including intrastate armed conflicts,[259] massive human rights violations,[260] terrorist acts,[261] weapons of

[255] See preamble and Art 1 of the Charter of the United Nations.

[256] According to Art 39 of the Charter of the United Nations, the Security Council needs to determine what a 'threat to peace and security' is. Happold defined 'threat to peace and security' as an empty concept that is given content by the Security Council, see M Happold, 'Security Council Resolution 1373 and the Constitution of the United Nations' (2003) 16 *Leiden Journal of International Law* 593, 599–600. See also CK Penny, 'Greening the Security Council: Climate Change as an Emerging "Threat to International Peace and Security"' (2007) 7 *International Environmental Agreements: Politics, Law and Economics* 35, 58.

[257] UNGA Res 337(V) (3 November 1950) A/RES/377(V).

[258] The increasing extension of this concept is emphasised by Happold, 'Security Council Resolution' 600 and Penny, 'Greening the Security Council' 68. See also S Roksandić Vidlička, *Prosecuting Serious Economic Crimes as International Crimes – a New Mandate for the ICC?*, Research Series of the Max Planck Institute for Foreign and International Criminal Law Series BC: Publications of the Max Planck Partner Group for Balkan Criminology 2 (Duncker & Humblot, 2017) 328 citing R Hernham and M Findlay (eds), *Exploring the Boundaries of International Criminal Justice* (Ashgate Publishing, 2011).

[259] See, inter alia, UNSC Res 1034 (21 December 1995) S/RES/1034. It was especially after the conflict in the former Yugoslavia and Rwanda that the Security Council focused its activity on internal armed conflicts as a threat to international peace and security. On Security Council resolutions related to NIACs, see GH Fox et al, 'The Contributions of United Nations Security Council Resolutions to the Law of Non-International Armed Conflict: New Evidence of Customary International Law' (2018) 67 *American University Law Review* 649.

[260] See, inter alia, UNSC Res 1653 (27 January 2006) S/RES/1653, concerning the situation in the Democratic Republic of the Congo and in Burundi, or the more recent UNSC Res 2564 (25 February 2021) S/RES/2564, concerning the situation in Yemen. Both resolutions condemn violations of human rights as disruptions of peace and stability in the two geographical areas concerned. It should be noted that until the adoption of the two Covenants (ICCPR and ICESCR), the concept of threat to international peace and security was strictly state-centric and human rights issues were 'absent from the Council's radar at its inception'. On this point, see HS Puri, 'Human Rights, Mass Atrocity Prevention and the United Nations Security Council: The Long Road Ahead' (*UN Chronicle*, 31 December 2016) https://www.un.org/en/chronicle/article/human-rights-mass-atrocity-prevention-and-united-nations-security-council-long-road-ahead.

[261] See, inter alia, UNSC Res 1373 (28 September 2001) S/RES/1373, which explicitly states that terrorist acts are a serious challenge and a threat to international peace and security. For a critical analysis of Res 1373, see F Rossi, *Il contrasto al terrorismo internazionale nelle fonti penali multilivello* (Jovene Editore, 2022) 110–124. An interesting critical approach to Res 1373 is presented by Happold, who points out that in this resolution the Security Council acted beyond its powers and qualified as a threat to peace and security not a specific situation, but a general conduct, namely 'terrorist acts', see Happold, 'Security Council Resolution' 598.

mass destruction[262] and pandemics – the Ebola crisis in 2014 and the most recent Covid-19 pandemic are illustrative examples.[263] Climate change is expected to be added to this list in the near future, despite the veto posed by Russia on the Security Council's draft resolution on climate and security in 2021.[264]

This raises the question of whether specific situations involving systemic economic crimes that seriously affect the public wealth of countries can give rise to threats to peace and security. The case studies examined above show that systemic economic crimes that dispossess people of its economic and natural wealth can threaten international peace and security in at least three ways: by sparking conflicts and mass violence and fuelling existing ones (*i*); by weakening the social, economic, and political development of a country, thus worsening the living standards of its population and undermining human rights (*ii*); and by endangering the environment (*iii*).

First, systemic economic crimes are among the root causes of conflicts in the world, as they act as triggers or aggravating factors in wars.[265] As Roksandić Vidlička noted, 'international criminal law should seriously deal with economic actors and atrocities, also because economic agendas may contribute significantly to the outbreak and the perpetuation of war'.[266]

This clearly emerges from some of the cases mentioned above. The systemic plundering of natural resources carried out by the *élites* in the Niger Delta has fuelled rebellions and conflicts. Similarly, the financing of paramilitary terrorist groups in Colombia and of terrorist rebels in exchange for illegal diamonds and timber in Liberia has contributed significantly to exacerbating armed

[262] See, inter alia, UNSC Res 1977 (20 April 2011) S/RES/1977.

[263] On the Ebola crisis see, inter alia, UNSC Res 2177 (18 September 2014) S/RES/2177; see also Penny, 'Greening the Security Council' 50. On the Covid-19 pandemic, see UNSC Res 2532 (1 July 2020) S/RES/2532, whereby 'the unprecedented extent of the COVID-19 pandemic is likely to endanger the maintenance of international peace and security'. See also E Pobjie, 'Covid-19 as a Threat to International Peace and Security: The Role of the UN Security Council in Addressing the Pandemic' (*EJIL Talk!*, 27 July 2020) www.ejiltalk.org/covid-19-as-a-threat-to-international-peace-and-security-the-role-of-the-un-security-council-in-addressing-the-pandemic/.

[264] See UNSC Res 990 (13 December 2021) S/2021/990. See also J Burke, 'Climate Change, a Threat to International Peace and Security?' (*Universal Rights Group*, 15 February 2022) www.universal-rights.org/blog/climate-change-a-threat-to-international-peace-and-security/; Penny, 'Greening the Security Council' 36. See also M Nevitt, 'Is Climate Change a Threat to International Peace & Security?' (2021) 42 *Michigan Journal of International Law* 527. Habermas qualifies these new 'international peace and security' threats as global dangers that have 'united the world into an involuntary community of shared risks', see Habermas, *The Inclusion of the Other* 186.

[265] On the link between economic crimes and conflict, see WA Schabas, 'War Economies, Economic Actors, and International Criminal Law' in K Ballentine and H Nitzschke (eds), *Profiting from Peace: Managing the Resource Dimensions of Civil War* (Lynne Rienner Publishers, 2005) 425; M Kersten, 'The Price of War – Economic Crimes and Justice in the Central African Republic' (*Justice in Conflict*, 16 October 2015) https://justiceinconflict.org/2015/10/16/the-price-of-war-economic-crimes-and-justice-in-central-african-republic/; MB Taylor, *War Economies and International Law: Regulating the Economic Activities of Violent Conflict* (Cambridge University Press, 2021).

[266] Roksandić Vidlička, *Prosecuting Serious Economic Crimes* 331 (emphasis added).

conflict, international crimes and terrorist activities in both countries.[267] The Preamble of the International Convention for the Suppression of the Financing of Terrorism acknowledges that terrorist financing is 'a matter of grave concern to the international community as a whole', referring to the purposes and principles of the UN Charter.[268] It is worth noting that the Preparatory Committee on the establishment of an International Criminal Court included in its report of 14 April 1998 a provisional definition of an international crime of terrorism financing, which was eventually rejected.[269] Nevertheless, it is widely recognised that terrorist financing has the potential to destabilise the economies of States by depriving them of large sums of money that could be used for legitimate purposes and are instead diverted to criminal activities.

With respect to the second way in which economic crimes can threaten international peace and security, some of the cases mentioned above show that economic crimes committed in certain contexts can weaken the social, economic, and political stability of a country, seriously jeopardising its development.[270] Article 55 of the UN Charter explicitly links the maintenance of peace and well-being in the world to the creation of economic and social progress and development. This is also confirmed by Article 2(3) of the Declaration on the Right to Development, adopted by the General Assembly Resolution 41/128 of 4 December 1986, which explicitly recognises the right and duty of States to 'formulate appropriate national development policies that aim at the constant improvement of the well-being of the entire population and of all individuals, on the basis of their active, free and meaningful participation in development and in the fair distribution of the benefits resulting therefrom'.[271]

The grand corruption system that was put in place in the *Petrobras* case and the criminal scheme of corruption and international money laundering enacted in the *Bolichicos* case had a negative impact on the social, economic, and political stability and development of Brazil and Venezuela, respectively.[272] Both Petrobras and the PDVSA were state-owned companies and the money

[267] Schabas, 'War Economies' 426, emphasising the existing invisible thread linking economic activities and conflicts, where private-sector actors, including corporations, operate 'deep within the shadows'.

[268] See Preamble of the UN Convention for the Suppression of the Financing of Terrorism (New York, 9 December 1999).

[269] According to the provisional definition, '(F)inancing […] acts of violence against another state directed at persons or property and of such a nature as to create terror, fear or insecurity in the minds of public figures, groups of persons, the general public or populations, for whatever considerations and purposes of a political, philosophical, ideological, racial, ethnic, religious or such other nature that may be invoked to justify them; […] is a terrorism offence'. See UN Diplomatic Conference of Plenipotentiaries on the Establishment of an International Criminal Court, Official Records, (15 June–17 July 1998) A/CONF.183/13 (Vol III) 21.

[270] Starr, 'Extraordinary Crimes' 1259; Bloom, 'Criminalizing Kleptocracy' 654–655.

[271] On the need for active and democratic participation in the development of a country, see Bloom, 'Criminalizing Kleptocracy' 628–9; Pinotti, 'Lava Jato, Mani Pulite' 325.

[272] L Arenal Lora, *Crímenes económicos en derecho internacional: Propuesta de una nueva categoría de crímenes contra la humanidad* (Editorial Aranzadi, 2019) 176.

embezzled and laundered by high-level politicians and private executives was public. In the *Petrobras* case, the losses incurred by shareholders and taxpayers amounted to 42 billion *reais* – corresponding to almost $12.6 billion,[273] while in the *Bolichicos* case, it is alleged that the energy projects carried out by the Derwick company should have cost $2.1 billion, instead of the $5 billion that the Venezuelan government paid as a result of the overpricing practices carried out by the PDVSA executives.[274] The remaining $2.9 billion was allegedly stolen and laundered around the world, making it unavailable to its true owner, the Venezuelan population.

Similarly, the inaction of high-level public officials, such as heads of State and prime ministers, who have a duty to ensure the economic development of their countries but fail to do so, undermines the stability and development of those countries. This happens when the grossly negligent behaviour of high-level economic actors allows their country's economic system to engage in illegal practices that ultimately bring the country to the brink of ruin. Kofele-Kale has developed the concept of a 'conspiracy of silence' to describe the attitude of those *élites* who turn a blind eye and adopt a 'studied silence' approach to the economic problems of their countries.[275]

As a consequence of the negative impact that systemic economic crimes have on the development of countries, the living standards and security of the population affected deteriorate, where 'security' refers not only the physical safety of individuals but also their subsistence.[276] Furthermore, considering the interconnected nature of our globalised world and economy, the security of individuals living in other States can also be jeopardised.[277] A paradigmatic example is the 2008 financial crisis, which undermined the security of Americans before spreading to other countries around the world. In Europe, Haarde's allegedly negligent attitude towards the 'state of health' of his country's economy in the aftermath of the global financial crisis significantly impaired the subsistence and security of Icelanders.

Lastly, the third way in which international economic crimes can threaten international peace and security stems from their potential to cause widespread and permanent harm to the environment.[278] UN agencies and non-governmental organisations (NGOs) have repeatedly acknowledged and reported that ordinary

[273] S Spagnuolo, 'Brazil's Lula Charged as 'Top Boss' of Petrobras Graft Scheme' (*Reuters*, 15 September 2016) www.reuters.com/article/us-brazil-corruption-idUSKCN11K2C6.

[274] OCCRP, 'Plunging Venezuela into the Dark'.

[275] Kofele-Kale, 'Patrimonicide' 102.

[276] See May, *Crimes against Humanity* 68. See also ML Wolf, 'The Case for an International Anti-Corruption Court' (*Brookings*, 23 July 2014) www.brookings.edu/research/the-case-for-an-international-anti-corruption-court/, cited in Roksandić Vidlička, *Prosecuting Serious Economic Crimes* 412, pointing out that individuals 'rely on the rule of law for their safety and survival'.

[277] Habermas, *The Inclusion of the Other* 174.

[278] A Nieto Martín, 'Bases para un futuro derecho penal internacional del medio ambiente' (2011) 82 *Revue internationale de droit pénal* 477, 479.

economic offences may have devastating effects on the environment and can be among the main causes of pollution.[279] In 2015, the UN members adopted the 2030 Agenda for Sustainable Development, which set out 17 Sustainable Development Goals (SDGs) aimed at ensuring that the development of States does not compromise life and peace on planet Earth. SDG 16, which focuses on promoting just, peaceful and inclusive societies, establishes an explicit link between corruption and sustainable development.[280]

A fortiori, economic crimes committed as part of a systemic attack against the natural wealth of a country can seriously endanger environmental resources. Systemic corruption and plundering of natural resources have been included among the major causes of pollution of the environment surrounding oil extraction companies and refineries in the Niger Delta.[281]

In light of the above, it can be concluded that the concept of 'international peace and security' goes beyond the mere absence of war.[282] On the contrary, it can be defined as an 'evolutionary development in the state of international relations which is meant to lead to the diminution' of social causes of war.[283] Although the economic crimes committed in the cases described above have so far never been classified as a 'threat to international peace and security', they do in fact seriously erode these international values.

International Economic Crimes Violate the Principle of Sovereignty Over Natural Resources and its Corollaries

In addition to undermining international peace and security, economic crimes committed in a systemic manner can potentially violate other fundamental values, such as the right of peoples to self-determination. This is the second objective pursued by the UN, to ensure respect for self-determination in order to 'develop friendly relations among nations'.[284] The right to self-determination

[279] See inter alia United Nations Office on Drugs and Crime (UNODC) and World Bank, 'Addressing Corruption Risks to Safeguard the Response to Climate Change; Discussion Draft II' (2024) and UNODC and World Bank, 'Addressing the Links Between Corruption and the Response to Climate Change; Discussion Draft' (2023), available at https://www.unodc.org/corruption/en/learn/thematic-areas/climate-change.html. See also UNCAC Coalition, 'Tackling Corruption Linked to Environmental Crimes to Achieve the UN Sustainable Development Goals' (13 May 2022) and UNCAC Coalition, 'Open letter to UNCAC States Parties Calling for a Strong Resolution at CoSP10 to Prevent and Combat Environmental Crime and Corruption' (3 November 2023) available at https://uncaccoalition.org/environmental-crime-and-corruption/.

[280] See UN 'Sustainable Development Goals' at https://www.un.org/sustainabledevelopment/peace-justice/.

[281] Oluwakayode, 'Analysing Economic Crimes in Nigeria' 69.

[282] Habermas, *The Inclusion of the Other* 185, whereby international peace is a deliberative evolutionary process. On the influence of positive definitions of peace on the practice of the Security Council, see Happold, 'Security Council Resolution' 600.

[283] B Simma et al, *The Charter of the UN – A Commentary*, Vol I, 3rd edn (Oxford University Press, 2012) 110.

[284] Article 1(2) of the Charter of the United Nations.

is also explicitly included in Article 1 of ICCPR and ICESCR, as well as in Article 21 of the ACHPR. On the one hand, it provides States with the 'right to *exercise control* over their national wealth and resources',[285] and on the other, it provides peoples with the right to freely '*use, exploit and dispose* of their natural wealth and resources'.[286]

Two fundamental principles of international law help define the scope of the right to self-determination: the principle of sovereignty over natural resources and the right to development.[287] With respect to the former, although the UN Charter does not explicitly mention it, Article 2(1) and Article 78 refer to the principle of sovereign equality of all UN Member States. The International Court of Justice (ICJ) recognised the principle of permanent sovereignty over natural resources in a judgment delivered on 19 December 2005 in the *Case concerning armed activities on the territory of the Congo*, in which the Court addressed the issue of Uganda's alleged violation of Congo's sovereignty over its natural resources.[288] After recalling the importance of the principle of sovereignty over natural resources as a customary international law principle, the ICJ found that it does not apply to situations of 'looting, pillage and exploitation of certain natural resources by members of the army of a State militarily intervening in another State', as it was the case in Congo.[289] However, to reach this conclusion, the ICJ referred to the General Assembly Resolution 1803(XVII), which states that any violation of the principle of sovereignty over natural resources in peacetime would be '*contrary to the spirit and principles of the Charter of the United Nations* and the *development* of international cooperation and the maintenance of peace'.[290]

Regarding the right to development, Article 55 of the UN Charter makes the promotion of the economic and social development of nations contingent, inter alia, on respect for the right to self-determination. Along the same lines, the Declaration on the Right to Development, adopted by the General Assembly Resolution 41/128,[291] acknowledges that this right is an inalienable

[285] Kofele-Kale, *The International Law of Responsibility for Economic Crimes* 107 (emphasis added).

[286] ibid (emphasis added).

[287] The connection between these three concepts has been emphasised on several occasions, for instance in UNGA Res 626(VII) (21 December 1952) A/RES/626(VII) and UNGA Res 1314(XIII) (12 December 1958) A/RES/1314(XIII). On the evolution of the interrelation between these concepts see Kofele-Kale, *The International Law of Responsibility for Economic Crimes* 80–111.

[288] ICJ, *Armed Activities on the Territory of the Congo (Democratic Republic of the Congo v Uganda)* (Judgment) ICJ Reports (19 December 2005) 168. N Schrijver, 'Self-Determination of Peoples and Sovereignty over Natural Wealth and Resources' in UN Office of the High Commissioner for Human Rights (ed) *Realizing the Right to Development: Essays in Commemoration of 25 Years of the United Nations Declaration on the Right to Development* (2013) 95, 95, referring to the ICJ Judgment in *Democratic Republic of the Congo v Uganda* where permanent sovereignty over natural resources was mentioned.

[289] ICJ, *Armed Activities on the Territory of the Congo*, para 244.

[290] UNGA Res 1803(XVII) (14 December 1962) A/RES/1803(XVII) (emphasis added).

[291] UNGA Res 41/128 (4 December 1986) A/RES/41/128. In the same year, the African Charter on Human and People's Rights (Nairobi, 27 June 1981) (the 'Banjul Charter') entered into force, referring to the right to development in Art 22.

human right and reiterates the connection existing between this right, the right to self-determination and the principle of sovereignty over natural wealth and resources.[292]

Since these rights and principles were originally created to protect indigenous peoples in developing countries, some scholars have questioned whether their relevance remains intact to this day. It has correctly been argued that they remain relevant 'if one interprets them dynamically',[293] which implies their broader interpretation as sources of rights and duties for all States and all peoples.

To date, scholars have invoked the right to self-determination to justify the international significance of two crimes that have not yet been classified as international crimes, namely 'ecocide' and 'patrimonicide'. However, relying on this right can be risky, as it is a double-edged sword.[294] On the one hand, it can be claimed that offences committed in violation of the right to self-determination and the principle of sovereignty over natural resources are international crimes because they violate a fundamental human right and a customary international law principle. On the other hand, self-determination could be invoked to shield state actors involved in ecocide and patrimonicide on the grounds that the acts allegedly committed by them are in line with their legitimate right to exercise control over national wealth and resources. In this respect, it is worth mentioning that the exercise of the right to self-determination is not without limits. In Resolution 1803(XVII) on 'Permanent sovereignty over natural resources', the General Assembly stated that free disposal of natural wealth and resources by States is limited by 'the interests of their national development and the well-being of the people of the State concerned'.[295] Furthermore, the ICCPR, ICESCR and the ACHPR recognise that self-determination is not an absolute human right, because 'in no case may a people be deprived of its own means of subsistence'.[296] As some of the cases mentioned above show, people are deprived of their own means of subsistence when their country's public wealth is damaged by the perpetration of systemic economic crimes that in no way correspond to a legitimate exercise of control over national wealth and resources by state actors.

International Economic Crimes do not Promote or Respect Fundamental Human Rights

Among the purposes of the United Nations, Article 1(3) of the UN Charter lists international cooperation to solve global problems of various

[292] Art 1(1) and (2) of the Declaration on the Right to Development, UNGA Res 41/128.

[293] Schrijver, 'Self-Determination' 101.

[294] Nieto Martín, 'Bases para un futuro' 479.

[295] UNGA Res 1803(XVII) para 1. This limit to the free disposal of natural resources is also mentioned in Art 21 of the ACHPR.

[296] Art 1(2) of the ICCPR and ICESCR; Art 21(1) of the ACHPR. See also M Saul, 'The Normative Status of Self-Determination in International Law: A Formula for Uncertainty in the Scope and Content of the Right?' (2011) 11 *Human Rights Law Review* 609, 627.

character – economic, social, cultural, and humanitarian – and to promote and encourage respect for human rights and fundamental freedoms. Article 55 of the UN Charter also reiterates the importance of promoting respect for and observance of human rights and fundamental freedoms as a prerequisite for ensuring the stability and well-being of the international community. The text of the UN Charter refers generically to 'human rights', which encompass both civil and political rights and economic, social, and cultural rights, in compliance with the principles of universality, indivisibility, interdependence, interrelatedness, and inalienability of all human rights.[297]

As mentioned above, international crimes do not always coincide with human rights violations. This occurs when criminal conduct is committed by state actors and is incompatible with the State's obligation to respect, protect or fulfil human rights.[298] However, the question arises whether an international crime can overlap with a human rights violation when criminal conduct is attributed to non-state actors.[299] This question becomes relevant in light of the current drafting of a treaty on Business and Human Rights (BHR) by the United Nations Human Rights Council.[300]

This Treaty is intended to be a legally binding international instrument regulating the activities of transnational corporations and enterprises. Its most recent draft, adopted in August 2021 and updated in 2023, refers to the purposes of the UN Charter and Article 55, reaffirms fundamental human rights and dignity of the human beings, as well as the indivisibility and universality of all human rights, and recalls that any State has the primary obligation to respect, protect, fulfill and promote human rights and fundamental freedoms.[301] Additionally, the Treaty emphasises the relevant role that businesses play in the world, namely their ability to 'foster sustainable development through an increased productivity, inclusive economic growth and job creation that respect internationally recognized human rights, labour rights, health and safety standards, the environment and climate'.[302] This implies that businesses are obliged to respect human rights, prevent any human rights abuse during or due to their business activities, and address any abuse that is threatened or committed.[303]

[297] Arenal Lora, *Crímenes económicos* 154. See also Habermas, 'The Concept of Human Dignity' 468, whereby human dignity 'grounds the indivisibility of all categories of human rights' (emphasis added).

[298] Schmid, *Taking Economic* 45.

[299] On domestic responses to human rights abuses committed by non-state actors, see Nieto Martín, 'Bases para un futuro' 487, citing the *Doe v Unocal* case and other cases concerning multinational companies, including Exxon, Pfizer and Coca Cola.

[300] For an overview of the steps taken so far in drafting the treaty, see 'UN Binding Treaty' (*Business & Human Rights Resource Centre*) https://www.business-humanrights.org/en/big-issues/governing-business-human-rights/un-binding-treaty/.

[301] See paras 4, 5, 7, 8 of the Preamble of the Third Revised Draft of the BHR Treaty (July 2023), available at https://www.business-humanrights.org/en/big-issues/governing-business-human-rights/un-binding-treaty/.

[302] See para 10 of the Preamble of the Third Revised Draft of the BHR Treaty (July 2023).

[303] The term 'human rights abuse' is defined under Art 1(2) of the Third Revised Draft of the BHR Treaty (July 2023) as 'any direct or indirect harm in the context of business activities, through acts or

Thus, a 'human rights violation' includes not only violations committed directly by state actors, but also those resulting from the activities of non-state actors, which stem from the States' failure to protect human rights from the interference of private actors. This broad interpretation of human rights violations is in line with the increasing process of privatisation of functions that once belonged to the State and can have a huge impact, both positive and negative, on human rights.[304]

The right to health is part of the broad set of interrelated economic, social and cultural human rights that States may fail to protect and that may be systemically abused by private actors as a result of their business activities.[305] In the debate on the crime of ecocide, it has been emphasised that the activities of multinational corporations that have a serious and permanent impact on the environment compromise people's right to health.[306] Similarly, systemic economic crimes committed by public or private actors may violate the right to health. In the *Volkswagen* case, the conspiracy to defraud the US by intentionally providing vehicles with a defeat device that circumvented emissions standards set by the EPA, overlapped with an abuse of the right to health by non-state actors. In the Niger Delta situation, bunkering activities have released fumes into the atmosphere and pollutants into the waters, causing a massive and systematic violation of the right to health of the inhabitants of those areas.

Another economic, social, and cultural human right that may be abused by business actors is the right to an adequate standard of living – which includes food, clothing, and housing – and to the continuous improvement of living conditions. As demonstrated by the *Bolichicos* case, Venezuelans have endured nearly a decade of blackouts and malfunctioning infrastructures that should have guaranteed adequate access to electricity, water, and food. This was allegedly the result of the large-scale and systematic theft and laundering of Venezuela's public wealth, which had a significant impact not only on the country's economy but also on the human rights of its civilian population.[307]

omissions, against any person or group of persons, that impedes the full enjoyment of internationally recognized human rights and fundamental freedoms, including the right to a safe, clean, healthy and sustainable environment'.

[304] F Raday, 'Privatising Human Rights and the Abuse of Power' (2000) 13 *Canadian Journal of Law and Jurisprudence* 103, 106.

[305] Art 12 of the ICESCR. For an extensive list of human rights abused by actors involved in economic crimes, see Arenal Lora, *Crímenes económicos* 99 and 114, referring to the HRC, 'Report of the Office of the United Nations High Commissioner for Human Rights on the Impact of the Global Economic and Financial Crises on the Realization of All Human Rights and on Possible Actions to Alleviate It' (18 February 2010) A/HRC/13/38.

[306] Nieto Martín, 'Bases para un futuro' 479.

[307] Starr, 'Extraordinary Crimes' 1301, on systemic economic crimes as gross violations of fundamental human rights.

Serious economic crimes can also overlap with violations of the right to self-determination, which, as a non-absolute human right, must be balanced with other human rights and with the principle of international economic cooperation.[308] Some of the case studies discussed above illustrate that systemic economic crimes can severely deprive people of its most vital means of subsistence, thus undermining their right to self-determination: water, food, electricity, employment, natural resources. Moreover, violations of the right to self-determination entail violations of the right to development and to a corruption-free society. Kofele-Kale described the latter as an individual and collective human right, which can be considered an integral part of the right to economic self-determination and the right to development, or as an autonomous right.[309] When grand-corruption takes place, the right to a corruption-free society is violated in the first place, and as a result other human rights – life, dignity, health, education, work, property and development – are violated.[310]

Lastly, in 2021, the UN Human Rights Council has recognised the right to a clean, healthy, and sustainable environment in Resolution 48/13.[311] Although this right is already enshrined in the constitutional legal frameworks of many States and its importance has been acknowledged at regional level,[312] Resolution 48/13 represents the first attempt to recognise this right at international level. This is a step forward that reinforces the 'ecocentric' approach to environmental protection, whereby our environment deserves to be protected as such and not only as an essential prerequisite for the protection of human life and integrity.[313] Serious forms of economic crimes, notably the systemic theft of natural resources, may overlap with abuses of the right to a clean, healthy, and sustainable environment perpetrated in the business activities of non-state actors and because of the inability of States to protect this human right.

[308] Saul, 'The Normative Status' 627.

[309] Kofele-Kale, 'The Right to a Corruption-Free Society' 153.

[310] ibid 163, 165; Roksandić Vidlička, *Prosecuting Serious Economic Crimes* 412, citing Wolf, 'The Case'. See also A Peters, 'Corruption as a Violation of International Human Rights' (2018) 29 *European Journal of International Law* 1251. The need to guarantee the right to a corruption-free society as a condition for the enjoyment of other human rights has also been recognised by the Human Rights Council. See, inter alia, HRC Res 47/7 (12 July 2021) A/HRC/RES/47/7, entitled 'The Negative Impact of Corruption on the Enjoyment of Human Rights'.

[311] HRC Res 48/13 (8 October 2021) A/HRC/RES/48/13.

[312] Y Aguila, 'The Right to a Healthy Environment' (*IUCN*, 8 October 2021) https://iucn.org/news/world-commission-environmental-law/202110/right-a-healthy-environment.

[313] From a Western law perspective, the protection of the environment can be approached through either an anthropocentric or an ecocentric lens. See A Nieto Martín, 'Cambio climático y derecho penal internacional del medio ambiente' (2020) 98 *Jueces para la democracia* 61, 61. See also D Hotz, 'Ecocide as the Missing Fifth Crime under International Criminal Law?' (2021) 133 *Zeitschrift für die gesamte Strafrechtswissenschaft* 861, 867 and 885; KJ Heller, 'Ecocide and Anthropocentric Cost-Benefit Analysis' (*OpinioJuris*, 26 June 2021) http://opiniojuris.org/2021/06/26/ecocide-and-anthropocentric-cost-benefit-analysis/.

International Economic Crimes Create International Harm

To be of international significance, an economic crime must create international harm, ie it must cause harm to individuals for the mere fact that they belong to a group, or it must be committed by individuals who are part of a group or system. The harm caused by the economic crimes committed in most of the six cases mentioned above is 'group based', meaning that the victims are part of a group that is targeted on the basis of certain grounds. The victims are usually nationals of the State whose public money or natural resources are stolen, laundered, or exploited. One might wonder whether nationality is a characteristic of the individual that is 'out of that person's control', to quote May.[314] Although this is not the case, the question should be answered in the affirmative because nationality significantly affects each person's identity, rights, and duties.[315]

In the *Petrobras* and *Bolichicos* cases, the grand-corruption and money-laundering schemes were aimed to deprive Brazilians and Venezuelan nationals of their money to satisfy private oligarchical ends. Since these crimes usually involve a 'great mobility of wealth'[316] it is likely that the stolen money cannot be easily traced and returned to its owners, meaning that the harm caused is de facto permanent. The total amount of public resources stolen and the purposes from which they were diverted – covering public debt or providing nationals with basic services[317] – provide an accurate picture of the extent of the harm suffered by the victims in these two cases. Similar international harm was caused to Icelanders by the gross negligence of state representatives, and to Nigeria and Liberia nationals by the plundering of natural resources.

It is more difficult to argue that the conspiracy to defraud the US in the *Volkswagen* case generated an international group-based harm. The victims defrauded were both US nationals and Volkswagen's customers, regardless of their nationality. The same can be said of the crime of financing terrorism. One of the main features of terrorist crimes is the 'dehumanisation' of their victims, who become a tool to pursue the political-ideological goal of their perpetrators. However, it is possible to identify a common trait among victims of terrorism that affects their identity, namely their 'being other' than the perpetrators. Victims of terrorism share values, such as democracy and the rule of law, which terrorists ignore, but which allow members of the victimised group to perceive the harm done to direct victims as indirect harm to themselves.[318]

[314] May, *Crimes against Humanity* 85.

[315] Art 15 of the UDHR. See also W Alonso, 'Citizenship, Nationality and Other Identities' (1995) 48 *Journal of International Affairs* 585.

[316] Kofele-Kale, 'Patrimonicide' 58.

[317] ibid 59.

[318] G Fourez, 'Victimes et terrorisme au XXIe siècle: une production spécifique' (2018) 4 *Revue de droit pénal et de criminologie* 414, 439–443.

In the six cases examined, the crimes were committed by individuals belonging to a group. The existence of a group of perpetrators increases the gravity of the crimes and gives the harm caused an international character. For instance, the existence of a system of high-level individuals who have access to power and abuse it is a crucial element for grand corruption and international laundering of public funds.[319] Likewise, due to the complexity of looting operations and the large number of natural resources stolen, the plundering of natural resources requires the involvement of a group of people.

Although Haarde was the only member of the government to be tried before the *Landsdómur*, other ministers were indicted along with him. Offences as serious as the one he was charged with cannot be attributed to a single individual but imply the agreement, if not at least the acquiescence, of other actors. Not to mention the conspiracy to defraud the US, which, by definition, is a crime that requires the involvement of two or more people. Even in the *Chiquita* case, the existence of a solid network between paramilitaries and businessmen was an important contextual factor.

It should be noted that in most of the cases discussed in this chapter, the perpetration of offences involves high-level public officials for practical reasons. Even when state officials are not actively involved, the commission of grand corruption, laundering of public money, and plundering of natural resources presupposes their implicit approval.[320] It would be unrealistic to think that large amounts of public funds or natural resources could be illegally misappropriated or put into circulation without the knowledge of public officials.

At the same time, the involvement of state actors does not preclude the intervention of high-level private individuals. The latter often collaborate with the former in the perpetration of economic crimes. However, in the *Chiquita* case, the executives of the multinational corporation entered into agreements with the AUC, without involving any public official in this paraeconomic criminal scheme. No public official was involved either in the conspiracy to defraud the US, set up by Volkswagen's executives. In these cases, economic crimes did not directly affect the public wealth of the respective States.

CONCLUDING REMARKS

The concept of gravity is the central pivot of international criminal justice, a system born out from the ashes of one of the darkest periods in human history. This concept has made it possible to draw a line between the most serious crimes, on the one hand, and ordinary crimes, on the other, justifying the existence and

[319] Kofele-Kale, 'Patrimonicide' 60–61.
[320] ibid.

legitimacy of the international criminal justice system to try the former category of crimes. Over the years, several theories have been developed to explain the main rationales of international criminality, shedding a light on the concept of gravity. In this chapter, some of these theories have been examined on the basis of their aims, which are to prevent violations of collective and individual legal goods, ensure the security of individuals, and prevent international harm.

In light of the concept of gravity that emerges from these theories, this chapter has addressed the question of whether it is still possible and reasonable to exclude systemic economic crimes from the most serious crimes committed in the world. The analysis of six cases has allowed identifying a number of common elements that provide useful guidance for drawing a line between ordinary economic crimes and those that could justifiably be considered crimes that violate collective and individual legal goods, jeopardise the security of individuals, and cause international harm.

Among the elements that make an economic crime a serious offence is its 'systemic' nature. This occurs when the offence is not committed occasionally, but erodes the political, social, and economic system of a State from within, which in most cases implies the involvement of high-level public and private actors who abuse the power entrusted to them. Another common feature concerns the legal goods violated by serious economic offences. These crimes threaten international peace and security by endangering public funds and natural resources. Furthermore, they may overlap with gross violations of fundamental human rights, including the right of people to freely dispose of their wealth, the right to a corruption-free society, and the right to adequate living conditions.

In light of the above, the six cases can be divided into two groups: on the one hand, there are cases where the gravity of the crimes is justified on the basis of all the rationales of international criminality – grand corruption, laundering of public money, plundering of natural resources, gross negligence in preventing the economic collapse of a country – and, on the other hand, there are cases where economic offences, however serious, do not satisfy some of the grounds for international criminality – the *Chiquita* case and the *Volkswagen* case.

The first group of cases shows that when committed under certain circumstances, which will be explored below, economic crimes can rise to the status of international crimes. On the contrary, it is difficult to justify the international gravity of terrorist financing in the *Chiquita* case and conspiracy to defraud the US in the *Volkswagen* case, based on the rationales of international criminality. First, the lack of involvement of state actors in the commission of crimes makes it difficult to justify their gravity on the basis of the theory of 'state action'.

Likewise, it is difficult to argue that, in the circumstances of the *Chiquita* and *Volkswagen* cases, the economic crimes committed caused harm to individuals as members of a group identified on the basis of characteristics beyond their control or which contribute to determining their identity. Furthermore, in both scenarios the offences perpetrated did not undermine the economic or natural wealth of the respective countries, except indirectly. In other words, however serious they may be, the offences committed in the *Chiquita* and *Volkswagen* cases do not appear to reach the gravity threshold required to be considered 'international economic crimes'. This does not mean that terrorism financing or conspiracy to defraud a State cannot qualify as international economic crimes if committed in other contexts.

The context in which economic crimes are perpetrated thus plays a crucial role in determining their international relevance, as will be demonstrated in the next chapter. The findings of this chapter therefore pave the way for Chapters 4 and 5, which deal respectively with the definition of the constituent elements of the concept of international economic crime and its enforcement in the current international criminal justice system.

4

Definition of International Economic Crimes

IN THE PREVIOUS chapters, the term 'international economic crime' has been used to define offences of an economic nature committed in a context that means they have the potential to meet the gravity threshold of international crimes. Nonetheless, a legal definition of this concept has not yet been provided. This chapter aims to fill in this gap by discussing the most relevant issues related to a prospective definition of international economic crimes.

When defining a crime, certain guidelines must be followed to ensure that the criminalisation process is not the result of an arbitrary exercise of legislative and judicial powers.[1] Two main principles guide this process in international criminal law: the gravity principle and the legality principle. As mentioned above, the former justifies the international criminalisation of wrongful conduct by drawing a line between what should fall under the categories of international crimes and what should remain outside them. On the other hand, the latter principle places limits on the definition and interpretation of international crimes.[2]

This chapter focuses on the legality principle, which is presented as a key reference point in the attempt to provide a comprehensive definition of the concept of international economic crime. The first section explores the meaning and relevance of the principle of legality in international criminal law, with particular regard to the legal framework of the Rome Statute.[3] In the second section, the constituent elements of a potential concept of international economic crime are analysed within the limits set by the principle of legality. The third and last section outlines a tentative definition of this category of international crimes.

THE PRINCIPLE OF LEGALITY IN INTERNATIONAL CRIMINAL LAW

In 1801, Cesare Beccaria revived the Latin adage '*nullum crimen, nulla poena sine lege penale praevia*', according to which the criminalisation of wrongful

[1] L May, *Crimes against Humanity: A Normative Account* (Cambridge University Press, 2004) 66.

[2] S Starr, 'Extraordinary Crimes at Ordinary Times: International Justice Beyond Crisis Situations' (2007) 101 *Northwestern University Law Review* 1257, 1276.

[3] Rome Statute of the International Criminal Court (Rome, 17 July 1998) (also known as the ICC Statute).

conduct and the determination of the relevant penalties are subject to the adoption of criminal laws enacted prior to the commission of such conduct.[4] The principle of legality has become the foundation of modern Western criminal law, and its revolutionary essence has been reaffirmed over the years by prominent jurists and philosophers.[5] On the contrary, the affirmation of the principle of legality in international criminal law has been slower and more arduous, both because of the nature of international crimes, and because of the desire, common in the aftermath of the Second World War, to prosecute and convict criminals within a relatively short period of time.[6]

Today the legality principle is a cornerstone of both national and international criminal law, although some of its functions are more evident than others at international level.[7] A crucial function pursued by this principle is to limit the risk of arbitrary exercise of legislative powers, to preserve democracy and rule of law from any authoritarian drift and to guarantee popular sovereignty.[8] Indeed, only if criminal law is the result of a legitimate exercise of legislative powers is it possible to determine what conduct society considers wrongful and which values are worthy of protection at a given moment.[9] International criminal law provisions aim to prevent and prohibit crimes committed as a result of abuses of power. It is therefore particularly important that the international community and international tribunals respect the principle of legality both in the legislative process and in the interpretation of the law. This would make it possible to respond to abuses of power with the principles of democracy and rule of law embodied in the principle of legality, thereby preserving the legitimacy and credibility of the international criminal justice system.

A second function of the principle of legality that is particularly relevant in the context of international criminal law concerns its role as a protector of human rights.[10] On the one hand, the legality principle is itself a human right,

[4] C Beccaria, *Dei delitti e delle pene* (Mondadori, 2019), 14. See also JA Sandoval Mesa, 'Del principio de legalidad penal a la persecución de crímenes internacionales y de supralegalidad contemporánea' (2012) 2 *Revista IUSTA* 175, 179.

[5] N Barbero, 'La ¿relativa? aplicación del principio de legalidad en derecho penal internacional' (2017) 13 *Nuevo foro penal* 156, 157, citing PJA von Feuerbach. See also Sandoval Mesa, 'Del principio de legalidad' 178.

[6] H Cullen, P Kastner and S Richmond, 'Introduction: The Politics of International Criminal Law' (2018) 18 *International Criminal Law Review* 907, 907.

[7] JL Corsi, 'An Argument for Strict Legality in International Criminal Law' (2018) 49 *Georgetown Journal of International Law* 1321, 1328. See also S Braum, 'Droit pénal des risques et risques du droit pénal' in C Bourin and JL Putz, *Le risque pénal du banquier* (Anthemis, 2020) 13, 14–15.

[8] Corsi, 'An Argument' 1345. See also N Jain, 'Judicial Lawmaking and General Principles of Law in International Criminal Law' (2016) 57 *Harvard International Law Journal* 111, 116. See also A Holthoefer, 'Constructing International Crime: Lawyers, States, and the Origin of International Criminal Prosecution in the Interwar Period' (2017) 42 *Law & Social Inquiry* 711, 716.

[9] Corsi, 'An Argument' 1340.

[10] See A Doecke, 'The Principle of Legality as Protection for Human Rights' (2014) 39 *Alternative Law Journal* 249.

enshrined in the most important human rights treaties[11] and recognised by human rights courts.[12] On the other, it is a prerequisite for the respect and protection of other human rights, such as the right to life, freedom, and fair trial.[13] This clearly emerges from several decisions issued by human rights courts, including the landmark case of *Streletz, Kessler and Krenz v Germany*, brought before the European Court of Human Rights. Despite holding prominent positions in the German Democratic Republic (GDR) and in the Socialist Unity Party leadership,[14] after the reunification of Germany, Streletz, Kessler and Krenz were prosecuted and convicted for being involved in the killing of unarmed people trying to flee the GDR.[15] The applicants argued that their convictions were in breach of Article 7(1) of the ECHR, since they could not have foreseen the criminal character of their acts at the time in which these allegedly occurred.[16] On the contrary, the Government argued that the applicants, as leaders of the GDR, 'could easily [...] have foreseen that the killing of unarmed fugitives [...] might give rise to criminal prosecutions under the relevant legal provisions, notwithstanding the contrary practice followed by the GDR regime'.[17]

Besides recognising the principle of legality as a fundamental element of the rule of law[18] and providing further clarification on the interpretation of its corollaries,[19] the ECtHR also emphasised the centrality of the legality principle in international human rights law. It pointed out that the protection and respect of human rights, such as the right to life and freedom of movement, depend

[11] For instance, Art 11(2) of the Universal Declaration of Human Rights (Paris, 10 December 1948), 15 of the International Covenant on Civil and Political Rights (New York, 19 December 1966), 7 of the Convention for the Protection of Human Rights and Fundamental Freedoms (Rome, 4 November 1950) (also known as European Convention on Human Rights or ECHR), 7 of the American Convention on Human Rights, 7 of the African Charter on Human and People's Rights (Nairobi, 27 June 1981) (the 'Banjul Charter'). See H Olásolo, 'El principio nullum crimen sine iure en Derecho Internacional contemporáneo' (2013) 1 *Anuario ibero-americano de derecho internacional penal* 18, 26; Corsi, 'An Argument' 1348. See also JA Pacheco de Freitas, 'La relación entre el principio de legalidad en derecho penal internacional y la tipificación internacional de los crímenes de lesa humanidad: una perspectiva histórica' (2019) 26 *Agenda internacional* 183, 187–188.

[12] Olásolo, 'El principio nullum crimen' 26, referring to the following cases of the ECtHR that recognise the principle of legality as a human right: *Streletz et al v Germany* (Grand Chamber Judgment) Applications nos 34044/96, 35532/97 and 44801/98 (22 March 2001); *Kononov v Latvia* (Third Section Judgment) Application no 36376/04 (24 July 2008); *Korbely v Hungary* (Grand Chamber Judgment) Application no 9174/02 (19 September 2008); *Jorgić v Germany* (Grand Chamber Judgment) Application no 74613/01 (12 July 2007).

[13] Corsi, 'An Argument' 1350.

[14] *Streletz et al v Germany*, para 16.

[15] ibid para 19.

[16] ibid paras 3 and 46–47.

[17] ibid para 48.

[18] ibid para 50. The link between the principle of legality and the rule of law emerges from para 81 in which the ECtHR considers legitimate the practice of a State 'governed by the rule of law' of prosecuting individuals who have perpetrated crimes under a former regime, by adopting an interpretation of the legal provisions in force at that time that is consistent with the rule of law principles that govern the State that initiated the proceedings.

[19] ibid para 50, where the ECtHR reiterates the requirements of *lex certa* and *lex stricta*. See also para 67, where the Court interprets Art 7(1) of the ECHR as including 'unwritten law'.

on a correct interpretation of the principle of legality.[20] On these grounds, the ECtHR ultimately held that, *tempore criminis*, the criminal character of the applicants' conduct was sufficiently clear not only in the light of the GDR laws, but also according to international human rights law standards.[21]

In addition to the functions described above, the principle of legality contributes to the achievement of the main objectives of criminal law, in particular that of deterrence. Knowing in advance which conduct is wrongful and criminal and what penalties are provided for each offence, prevents individuals from 'engaging in socially undesirable conducts'.[22] Retribution is another purpose of criminal law reinforced by the principle of legality. When the criminalisation of an act or omission occurs prior to its perpetration – in full compliance with the principle of legality – the community considers the punishment of their perpetrators to be 'deserved' because they should have known the criminal nature of the behaviour and its potential consequences.[23] The principle of legality is also in line with the criminal law purpose of incapacitation, as it provides law enforcement authorities with an efficient compass to determine which conduct is prohibited and which 'wrongdoers need to be incapacitated'.[24]

The same purposes of deterrence, retribution, and incapacitation, are pursued by international criminal law, along with other objectives specific to this branch of law, including the need to ensure post-conflict reconciliation and justice.[25] In this regard, however, it has been argued that the principle of legality does not necessarily promote restorative justice goals, as it may limit the identification of perpetrators of international crimes, thus hindering the path to reconciliation.[26] Nevertheless, the principle of legality has consolidated itself as a guarantor of the rule of law in international criminal law. The decision of the drafters of the Rome Statute to include a provision on the principle of legality in the section entitled 'General principles of criminal law' is tangible proof of the importance of this concept in the current international criminal justice system.

Articles 22 and 23 of the Rome Statute respectively define the two components of legality, the principle of *nullum crimen sine lege* and the principle of *nulla poena sine lege*.[27] Several corollaries can be inferred from the first

[20] ibid paras 93 and 98.

[21] ibid para 89.

[22] T Mariniello, 'The "Nuremberg Clause" and Beyond: Legality Principle and Sources of International Criminal Law in the European Court's Jurisprudence' (2013) 82 *Nordic Journal of International Law* 221, 245.

[23] KS Gallant, *The Principle of Legality in International and Comparative Criminal Law*, Cambridge Studies in International and Comparative Law 65 (Cambridge University Press, 2009) 29.

[24] ibid 28.

[25] Corsi, 'An Argument' 1342.

[26] Gallant, *The Principle of Legality*, 31. See also KA Rodman, 'Justice as a Dialogue between Law and Politics: Embedding the International Criminal Court within Conflict Management and Peacebuilding' (2014) 12 *Journal of International Criminal Justice* 437, 465.

[27] J Nicholson, 'Strengthening the Effectiveness of International Criminal Law through the Principle of Legality' (2017) 17 *International Criminal Law Review* 656, 659.

component of the legality principle, including the fact that any criminal provision must be as specific and clear as possible in defining the objective (*actus reus*) and subjective (*mens rea*) elements of prohibited conduct (*lex certa*). This is necessary to ensure that the accused can foresee the wrongfulness of an act or omission, and to prevent the legislative and judicial powers from abusing their discretion in creating and interpreting the law. In addition to these functions, in international criminal law the *lex certa* requirement also contributes to attach the label of 'international crime' to certain behaviours, which allows perpetrators and victims to be aware of the potential consequences in terms of proceedings and to act accordingly.[28]

The corollary of non-retroactivity (*lex praevia*) prevents laws enacted after the perpetration of wrongful conduct from being applied to it. Both the corollary of the *lex certa* and *lex praevia* ensure the foreseeability of criminal law.[29] However, the requirements of the principle of legality are fulfilled when the criminal law is not only *certa* and *praevia* but also *stricta*, which means that criminal provisions must be interpreted strictly and their application cannot be extended by analogy.[30] Any uncertainty in the law should be resolved by promoting the interpretation most favourable to the defendant (*in dubio pro reo*).[31] The last corollary of the principle of legality has been the most controversial both at domestic level and, a fortiori, in international criminal law, namely whether the prohibition of wrongful conduct must necessarily be contained in written laws (*lex scripta*). In civil law countries this requirement has long been undisputed, although today it is generally accepted that the principle of legality 'does not necessarily require the law to be codified'.[32]

Over the years, a significant number of issues have emerged from the interpretation of the corollaries of the principle of legality by international tribunals, with particular regard to the requirements of *lex certa*, *stricta*, and *scripta*. First, the lack of clarity of the legal basis for international crimes has been questioned on several occasions. At Nuremberg, the Americans pointed out that the laws of humanity were too vague to serve as a legal basis for crimes against humanity,[33] while the category of 'other inhumane acts' as a crime against humanity has raised criticism at the ad hoc tribunals. In the *Kupreškić et al* case, the Trial Chamber of the ICTY raised the issue of the vagueness of the wording of this category of crimes and its potential violation of the requirement of *lex certa*, if it is not clearly established what falls within this category.[34] On the other hand, however, the judges stressed that a strict and exhaustive categorisation of crimes

[28] Corsi, 'An Argument' 1336.
[29] ibid 1334.
[30] ibid 1338.
[31] ibid 1337.
[32] Jain, 'Judicial Lawmaking' 143.
[33] Holthoefer, 'Constructing International Crime' 725.
[34] Nicholson, 'Strengthening the Effectiveness' 670, citing to *Prosecutor v Kupreškić et al* (Trial Judgment) IT-95-16-T (14 January 2000) para 563.

does not always prove useful as this could 'create opportunities for evasion of the letter of the prohibition'.[35]

The challenges posed by the alleged non-conformity of definitions of international crimes with the *lex certa* requirement have been addressed not only by international criminal law tribunals, but also by human rights tribunals, on the basis that the principle of legality is embedded in the human rights framework. In the case of *Drėlingas v Lithuania* before the ECtHR, the applicant complained of a potential collision between the definitions of international crimes, on the one hand, and the principle of specificity, on the other. After Lithuania's independence from the Soviet Union, the applicant was charged with being an accessory to genocide under Articles 24(6) and 99 of the Lithuanian Criminal Code because he had taken part in an operation during which two Lithuanian partisans had been captured. One of them was subsequently tortured, sentenced to death and executed, while the other was sentenced to deportation. The Lithuanian Prosecutor noted that both partisans were members of the 'Lithuanian armed resistance to the Soviet occupation' and of a 'separate *national-ethnic-political group*'.[36]

The applicant complained that the broad interpretation of the crime of genocide adopted by the Prosecutor and endorsed by the Lithuanian judges was not in accordance with the wording of the crime of genocide, established in the Genocide Convention – which does not mention political grounds among those on which the crime can be committed. Therefore, he argued that his conviction for genocide resulted in a violation of Article 7 of the European Convention of Human Rights.[37] The ECtHR upheld the opposite conclusion, arguing that the conviction could be foreseen *tempore criminis* by the applicant, in light of the national historical context, and the Lithuanian Constitutional Court's ruling of 18 March 2014, which 'revealed in detail the significance of the Lithuanian partisans for the entire Lithuanian *nation*'.[38]

The Strasbourg Court referred to previous case law on the matter, emphasising the function of the principle of legality as a '(safeguard) against arbitrary prosecution, conviction and punishment',[39] and reflecting upon the content of the *lex certa* requirement. The ECtHR pointed out that 'an offence must be clearly defined in the law, be it national or international',[40] which implies two main consequences: first, individuals must have access to legal sources

[35] *Prosecutor v Kupreškić et al* (Trial Judgment) para 563.

[36] ECtHR, *Drėlingas v Lithuania* (Fourth Section Judgment) Application no 28859/16 (9 September 2019) para 33 (emphasis added).

[37] ibid para 76.

[38] ibid para 86 (emphasis added) and 110.

[39] ECtHR, *Vasiliauskas v Lithuania* (Grand Chamber Judgment) Application no 35343/05 (20 October 2015) para 153, referring to *Kononov v Latvia* para 185 and to *Del Río Prada v Spain* (Grand Chamber Judgment) Application no 42750/09 (21 October 2013) para 77.

[40] *Vasiliauskas v Lithuania* para 154, referring to *Korbely v Hungary* para 70; *Kononov v Latvia* paras 185 and 196; *Del Río Prada v Spain* para 91.

(*accessibility* of the law) and, second, these sources must enable them to clearly foresee what acts and omissions may lead to their criminal liability (*foreseeability* of the law). This interpretation of the *lex certa* requirement coincides with that endorsed by the *ad hoc* tribunals[41] and the ICC.[42] In conclusion, the *lex certa* element of the principle of legality requires that the elements of an international crime be specified in its legal basis. However, this does not prevent, but rather encourages, courts to fill in any gaps in written or unwritten norms that are accessible and foreseeable.

It follows that judicial interpretation of the law is not contrary to the principle of legality, provided that such interpretation is in line with the 'essence' of the offence.[43] In other words, any norm of international criminal law must be strictly construed. This means that legal ambiguities must be interpreted in favour of the accused and 'against the legislature which has failed to explain itself'.[44] Accordingly, the principle of strict interpretation forbids any interpretation of criminal law by analogy, as expressly specified in Article 22(2) of the Rome Statute. The purpose of the *lex stricta* requirement is to prevent a court from creating new law or 'extending existing law beyond the reasonable limits of acceptable clarification'.[45] These limits correspond to the foreseeability and accessibility of the law: as far as judicial interpretation of a criminal provision does not deprive it of its predictable and accessible character, the *lex stricta* requirement is fulfilled. An additional purpose of the principle of strict interpretation is to balance the interpretative function of the courts, on the one hand, with the gradual and inevitable development of the law, on the other.[46] This is of paramount importance in international criminal law, a rather new field that has yet to be perfected.

Lastly, over the years, national jurisdictions 'have showed a significant interest in prosecuting and punishing alleged perpetrators of war crimes and crimes against humanity taking place' before the entry into force of national

[41] See, inter alia, *Prosecutor v Hadžihasanović et al* (Decision on Interlocutory Appeal Challenging Jurisdiction in Relation to Command Responsibility) IT-01-47-AR72 (16 July 2003) para 34. See also A Cassese, 'The ICTY: A Living and Vital Reality' (2004) 2 *Journal of International Criminal Justice* 585, 592 fn 22 citing relevant ICTY case law on the *lex certa* requirement.

[42] See, inter alia, *Prosecutor v Katanga* (Judgment pursuant to Article 74 of the Statute) ICC-01/04-01/07-3436-tEN (7 March 2014) para 1388; ICC, *Prosecutor v Ngudjolo Chui* (Judgment pursuant to Article 74 of the Statute – Concurring Opinion of Judge Christine Van den Wyngaert) ICC-01/04-02/12-4 (18 December 2012) para 20.

[43] *Vasiliauskas v Lithuania* para 157. See also *Streletz et al v Germany* para 50; *Jorgić v Germany* para 101; and *Kononov v Latvia* para 185.

[44] *Prosecutor v Delalić et al* (Trial Judgment) IT-96-21-T (16 November 1998) paras 412–413.

[45] M Shahabuddeen, 'Does the Principle of Legality Stand in the Way of Progressive Development of Law?' (2004) 2 *Journal of International Criminal Justice* 1007, 1013. See, inter alia, *Prosecutor v Katanga* (Judgment pursuant to Article 74 of the Statute) para 52. For further details on the concept and limits of 'judicial creativity' see S Darcy and J Powderly, *Judicial Creativity at the International Criminal Tribunals* (Oxford University Press, 2010).

[46] A Bufalini, 'The Principle of Legality and the Role of Customary International Law in the Interpretation of the ICC Statute' (2015) 14 *The Law & Practice of International Courts and Tribunals* 233, 235.

laws criminalising these offences.[47] The rationale for this lies in the gravity of these offences and in the need to provide their victims with justice. These same reasons were behind the drafting of Article 7(2) of the ECHR, also known as the 'Nuremberg clause'. This clause is believed to have removed international crimes from the scope of the principle of legality, because it allowed national courts to prosecute perpetrators of conduct that had not yet been recognised as international crime at domestic level, but that was 'unacceptable under the *general principles of law recognized by civilised countries*'.[48] This apparent deviation from the legality principle was explained at Nuremberg – hence the name Nuremberg clause – by resorting to the concept of justice, which justified ex post facto criminalisation and prosecution of wrongful conduct committed during the Second World War.[49] In this respect, Kelsen noted that 'justice required the punishment of these men, in spite of the fact that under positive law they were not punishable at the time they performed the acts made punishable with retroactive force.'[50]

Article 7(2) of the European Convention of Human Rights allows the criminal character of conduct to be inferred from general principles of law, that is, unwritten sources of law. Hence, it would not be correct to argue that the Nuremberg clause removed international crimes from the scope of the *nullum crimen sine lege* principle; rather, it encouraged a broad interpretation of this principle, according to which the term *lex* includes both written and unwritten law.

This conclusion was upheld by the ECtHR.[51] On several occasions, the Strasbourg Court has recognised that general principles of law are a valid legal basis for international crimes and for the imposition of criminal

[47] Mariniello, 'The "Nuremberg Clause"' 223.

[48] ibid 227 (emphasis added).

[49] At Nuremberg, the judges unanimously considered the principle of legality as a 'principle of justice', with the result that it could be legitimately non-applied by the Allies; see Mariniello, 'The "Nuremberg Clause"' 226–7; Olásolo, 'El principio nullum crimen' 22. In its 1946 judgment, the IMT stated that the criminal provisions contained in the Nuremberg Charter could not be deemed contrary to the maxim *nullum crimen sine lege*, since it would be unjust not to punish the acts of those who must have known that they were doing wrong and were 'acting in defiance of all international law'; see IMT, *Trial of the Major War Criminals before the International Military Tribunal*, Vol I (Judgment, 1 October 1946) 219. This position was supported by the Prosecutor before the IMTFE; see X Mao, 'Substantive or Jurisdictional? The Tokyo Charter and the Legality Challenge at the International Military Tribunal for the Far East' (2018) 11 *Journal of East Asia and International Law* 435, 438. However, the first disagreements with this interpretation of the principle of legality emerged at the IMFTE. According to three judges – Rolling, Bernard and Pal – the principle of legality was a 'subjective individual right', meaning that States were mandated to apply it; see Olásolo, 'El principio nullum crimen' 23. Since then, the principle of legality has been considered a subjective individual right in many supranational treaties, both international human rights instruments (see Art 11 of the UDHR, Art 15 of the ICCPR)and regional human rights instruments (see Art 7 of the ECHR, Art 9 of the American Convention on Human Rights; Art 7 of the ACHPR).

[50] Mariniello, 'The "Nuremberg Clause"' 228, citing H Kelsen, 'Will the Judgment in the Nuremberg Trial Constitute a Precedent in International Law?' (1947) 1 *International Law Quarterly* 153, 165.

[51] Jain, 'Judicial Lawmaking' 143.

sanctions, provided that those principles meet the criteria of accessibility and foreseeability.[52] For instance, in the abovementioned *Streletz, Kessler and Krenz* case, the ECtHR held that:

> Article 7 alludes to the very same concept as that to which the Convention refers elsewhere when using that term, a concept which comprises written as well as unwritten law and implies qualitative requirements, notably those of accessibility and foreseeability.[53]

A similar conclusion was reached by the ECtHR in the *Milanković* case, this time with reference to Article 7(1) of the European Convention of Human Rights. In this case, the judges held that customary international law constitutes an adequate legal basis for a conviction for war crimes, provided that the customary source is accessible and foreseeable.[54] In other words, the *lex scripta* requirement should not be conceived as a mandatory condition for compliance with the principle of legality, since its absence can be balanced by the requirements of accessibility and foreseeability.

This broad interpretation of the term 'law' is in line with jurisprudential developments in international criminal law.[55] Since its inception, this branch of law has experienced an 'identity crisis' due to the interaction between its international and criminal dimensions and the attempt to merge civil law and common law systems.[56] In the Nuremberg Charter, the Allies explicitly included custom among the sources of international criminal law, albeit with exclusive reference to war crimes.[57] Article 3 of the ICTY Statute reiterated the definition of war crimes as violations of the laws and 'customs' of war, and the jurisprudence of the ad hoc tribunals supported the consideration of custom as a source of international criminal law.[58]

[52] See A Cassese, 'Balancing the Prosecution of Crimes against Humanity and Non-Retroactivity of Criminal Law: The *Kolk and Kislyiy v Estonia* Case before the ECHR' (2006) 4 *Journal of International Criminal Justice* 410.

[53] *Streletz et al v Germany* para 50 (emphasis added). See also Barbero, 'La ¿relativa? aplicación' 158; Pacheco de Freitas, 'La relación' 191.

[54] See N Citeroni, 'The Milanković Case: Do Convictions Based on Rules of Customary International Law Violate Article 7 of the Convention?' (2022) 9 *Quaderni di SIDIBlog* 387.

[55] See, inter alia, *Prosecutor v Hadžihasanović et al* (Decision on Joint Challenge to Jurisdiction) IT-01-47-PT (12 November 2002) paras 93 and 179, where the ICTY stated that the doctrine of command responsibility for war crimes perpetrated in NIACs was already established as a rule of customary international law in 1991.

[56] Nicholson, 'Strengthening the Effectiveness' 656. See also Jain, 'Judicial Lawmaking' 114.

[57] Starr, 'Extraordinary Crimes' 1267. On the relevance of 'customary law' as a source of law see P Grossi, *Prima lezione di diritto* (Giuseppe Laterza & Figli 2012) 92, describing custom as 'a fact that is repeated over time, because the collective conscience finds in it a value to protect and observe'.

[58] *Prosecutor v Tadić* (Decision on the Defence Motion for Interlocutory Appeal on Jurisdiction) IT-94-1 (2 October 1995) para 143; Olásolo, 'El principio nullum crimen' 31. The same approach was reiterated at the ICTR in *Prosecutor v Akayesu* (Trial Judgment) ICTR-96-4-T (2 September 1998) para 617. The Special Tribunal for Lebanon also took a stand on this matter, see STL (Interlocutory Decision on the Applicable Law: Terrorism, Conspiracy, Homicide, Perpetration, Cumulative Charging) STL-11-01/1 (16 February 2011) para 83. See also Nicholson, 'Strengthening the Effectiveness' 666.

With respect to the Rome Statute, the drafters discussed the possibility of excluding customary international law from the range of legal sources that can be applied by the ICC.[59] Indeed, Article 21 does not contain any reference to 'customary international law'.[60] However, Article 21(1)(b) provides for the possibility of resorting to 'principles and rules of international law [...]', while Article 21(1)(c) refers to 'general principles of law derived by the Court from national laws of legal systems of the world'. This implicit and vague reference to unwritten legal bases of international crimes has been interpreted in two different ways. According to the first approach, there is no place for customary law in the Rome Statute because the level of uncertainty that characterises this source of law would inevitably conflict with the principle of legality.[61] In other words, accepting custom as a legal source would relativise the 'essence' of the principle of legality, creating a contrast between the international and criminal sides of international criminal law.[62]

Other scholars have provocatively responded to this observation by arguing that in the Rome Statute, the principle *nullum crimen sine iure* should replace the traditional principle *nullum crimen sine lege*, where the term *ius* incorporates both written and unwritten law.[63] Following this second approach, customary law is considered to be included in Article 21 of the Rome Statute under the expression 'rule of general international law'.[64] This interpretation is in line with the objective of the principle of legality to provide the defendant with fair

[59] Bufalini, 'The Principle of Legality' 236. See also UN Diplomatic Conference of Plenipotentiaries on the Establishment of an International Criminal Court, Official Records, (15 June–17 July 1998) A/CONF.183/13 (Vol II) 67 para 44; 74 para 21; 75 para 44.

[60] Bufalini, 'The Principle of Legality' 238, stating that Art 21 of the Rome Statute is one of the innovations of international criminal law and that no similar rule can be found in the statutes of the ad hoc international criminal tribunals. The only explicit reference to custom is in Art 8 of the Rome Statute concerning war crimes.

[61] Barbero, 'La ¿relativa? aplicación' 168.

[62] ibid. See also *Prosecutor v Lubanga Dyilo* (Decision on the Confirmation of the Charges) ICC-01/04-01/06-803-tEN (29 January 2007) para 303, which expressly included the *lex scripta* requirement among the corollaries of the principle of legality.

[63] Corsi, 'An Argument' 1371.

[64] For instance, in order to provide a definition of the notion of armed conflict, which is absent from both the provisions of the Rome Statute and the Elements of Crimes, the ICC referred to the jurisprudence of the ICTY, which reflects customary international law. See inter alia, *Prosecutor v Tadić* (Decision on the Defence Motion for Interlocutory Appeal on Jurisdiction), para 70; *Prosecutor v Kunarac et al* (Appeals Judgment) IT-96-23&IT-96-23/1-A (12 June 2002) para 56. Also, in the *Al Bashir* case, Pre-Trial Chamber I recalled consistent case law before the Court that accepted the possibility to apply 'customary rules and general principles of law' when the Statute, the Elements of Crimes and the Rules are deficient and their lacunae cannot be remedied by 'the criteria provided for in articles 31 and 32 of the Vienna Convention on the Law of the Treaties and article 21(3) of the Statute'. See *Prosecutor v Al Bashir* (Decision on the Prosecution's Application for a Warrant of Arrest against Omar Hassan Ahmad Al Bashir) ICC-02/05-01/09-3 (4 March 2009) para 44. In the *Ntaganda* case, the Court went further, arguing that 'the specific reference to the "established framework of international law" within article 8 (2) (b) and (e) of the Statute permits recourse to customary and conventional international law regardless of whether any lacuna exists, to ensure an interpretation of Article 8 of the Statute that is fully consistent with, in particular, international humanitarian law'. See *Prosecutor v Ntaganda* (Judgment on the appeal of Mr Ntaganda against the 'Second decision on the Defence's challenge to the jurisdiction of the Court in respect of Counts 6 and 9') ICC-01/04-02/06-1962 (15 June 2017) para 53.

notice of the wrongfulness of the conduct and the consequences thereof. This notice risks being fictitious if its effectiveness depends on a rigorous codification of criminal conduct.[65] This would not be the case if adequate notice existed whenever the defendant is aware of the heinous nature of their conduct, regardless of the written or unwritten character of the criminal law.

In sum, the *lex scripta* corollary of the principle of legality should be interpreted as a possible but not mandatory requirement in international criminal law. Furthermore, compared to the early stages, which were characterised by the need to supplement the lack of written norms with other sources of law,[66] there is now a trend in international criminal law toward the codification of international crimes.[67]

In this section, an attempt has been made to provide an overview of the most relevant literature and case law on the central role of the principle of legality in international criminal law. In the next section, the concept of international economic crime will be defined within the limits dictated by the corollaries of the *nullum crimen sine lege* principle.

CONSTITUENT ELEMENTS OF INTERNATIONAL ECONOMIC CRIMES

International crimes are two-tiered offences.[68] The first layer consists of a set of 'contextual elements' that defines the essence of each category of international crime and reflects its gravity. The second layer consists of criminal conduct – act or omission – that reaches the level of an international crime because it is committed in the scenario outlined by the contextual elements.

Regarding contextual elements, they serve multiple functions, the most important of which is to enable the distinction between domestic and international crimes by revealing the 'broad context of macro criminality'[69] of the latter. Contextual elements are the 'distinguishing' feature of international crimes,[70] due to their potential to make offences a matter of concern to the global and international community.[71]

[65] Jain, 'Judicial Lawmaking' 143–44.

[66] Since the answers to most of the issues raised by international criminal law tribunals could not be found in written legal provisions, judges were repeatedly confronted with the dilemma of whether to resort to customary international law. See Bufalini, 'The Principle of Legality' 233.

[67] See eg the efforts to codify a concept of 'ecocide'; Stop Ecocide Foundation, 'Independent Expert Panel for the Legal Definition of Ecocide: Commentary and Core Text' (*Stop Ecocide Foundation*, June 2021) www.stopecocide.earth/legal-definition.

[68] M Cupido, 'Causation in International Crimes Cases: (Re)Conceptualizing the Causal Linkage' (2021) 32 *Criminal Law Forum* 1, 3.

[69] I Marchuk, *The Fundamental Concept of Crime in International Criminal Law: A Comparative Law Analysis* (Springer, 2014) 114.

[70] ibid 70 and 92.

[71] Pacheco de Freitas, 'La relación' 195; MC Bassiouni, *Crimes against Humanity: Historical Evolution and Contemporary Application* (Cambridge University Press, 2011) 8.

Secondly, contextual elements have a jurisdictional function.[72] The only crimes that fall under the jurisdiction of supranational tribunals called upon to adjudicate international crimes, are those that occur because of and in connection with an international context, while those that occur in such a context but that have no relation to it must be excluded. For instance, the practice of reporting Jews to Nazi authorities during the Second World War was considered a crime against humanity of persecution, since the conduct was committed because of the context – the existence of a State policy of persecution directed against the Jews – and was in connection with it.[73] Thus, the contextual elements are aimed to exclude purely random or isolated offences from the material scope of jurisdiction of international courts – and consequently, from the realm of international criminal law. The only exception may be the crime of genocide, whose definition seems to contemplate the possibility of the lone genocidaire, ie an individual seeking to destroy in whole or in part a group of individuals.[74] This possibility, however, does not seem realistic but rather a *cas d'école*.[75] According to some scholars, the only realistic concept of genocidal intent implies the existence of a context.[76] An act is likely to constitute genocide only when it is committed in a context characterised by the existence of a pattern aimed at the perpetration of multiple acts against a targeted group of individuals with the intent to destroy them.[77]

The third function performed by the contextual elements of an international crime is more controversial than the previous ones. It is argued that these elements hold together crimes committed in a specific context, with the result that it would not be possible to assess one offence in isolation from the others.[78] This argument is unpersuasive. The fact that some crimes are committed under the same circumstances may imply that they are related to the context, but this

[72] M Osiel, 'Guest Post: Why the 'Contextual Element' in All ICC Crimes?' (*Opinio Juris*, 7 September 2009) https://opiniojuris.org/2009/09/07/guest-post-why-the-contextual-element-in-all-icc-crimes/.

[73] See P Akhavan, 'The Core Elements of International Crimes' in P Akhavan (ed), *Reducing Genocide to Law: Definition, Meaning, and the Ultimate Crime* (Cambridge University Press, 2012) 28.

[74] C Kress, 'The Crime of Genocide and Contextual Elements: A Comment on the ICC Pre-Trial Chamber's Decision in the Al Bashir Case' (2009) 7 *Journal of International Criminal Justice* 297, 297. See also ICTY, Appeals Chamber of the ICTY in the *Prosecutor v Jelisić* (Appeals Judgment) IT-95-10-A (5 July 2001) para 48, contending that a 'plan' or 'policy' is not an ingredient of the crime of genocide. The possibility of the lone genocidaire was not contested by the Darfur Commission, see International Commission of Inquiry on Darfur, 'Report of the International Commission of Inquiry on Darfur to the UN Secretary-General' (25 January 2005) para 520.

[75] Kress, 'The Crime of Genocide' 300. On this debate see also, Marchuk, *The Fundamental Concept of Crime* 108.

[76] Kress, 'The Crime of Genocide' 304. On the same position see WA Schabas, 'State Policy as an Element of International Crimes' (2008) 98 *Journal of Criminal Law and Criminology* 953, 966, referring to Lemkin's book 'Axis Rule in Occupied Europe', in which he conceived the existence of a plan 'as a *sine qua non* for the crime of genocide'. The same position is also in line with Art 6 of the Elements of Crimes of the ICC.

[77] Kress, 'The Crime of Genocide' 299. See also Osiel, 'Guest Post'; G Mettraux, *International Crimes and the Ad Hoc Tribunals* (Oxford University Press, 2005) 206.

[78] See Osiel, 'Guest Post'.

does not necessarily mean that they are connected to each other. Furthermore, potential links between different crimes committed in the same context can be fully 'captured by different modes of participation'.[79]

For each category of international crime, it is possible to clearly identify a material and mental contextual element that must be met in addition to the material and mental elements of the underlying criminal conduct.[80] In the provisions of the Nuremberg Charter and the statutes of the ad hoc and internationalised criminal tribunals, contextual elements were mentioned but not expressly defined. This textual gap was filled in by judicial interpretation. In contrast, the drafters of the Rome Statute not only identified the contextual elements for international crimes but also defined those elements in the Statute and the Elements of Crimes. The material and mental contextual elements of war crimes delimit the scope of this category to those offences that are grave breaches of the the Geneva Conventions or seriously violate the laws and customs of war and are committed during an international or non-international armed conflict. Likewise, the gravity of crimes against humanity does not arise from the inhumane nature of isolated and random criminal conduct, but from the existence of a widespread or systematic attack directed against a civilian population, of which such conduct is part. With respect to aggression, the context in which the act of aggression is perpetrated by State officials in a position of authority makes it a 'leadership crime'.[81] Although some contextual elements of crimes against humanity and aggression may also be relevant to defining the concept of international economic crime, it is crucial to identify and discuss the potential material and mental contextual elements specific to this concept in light of the principles of gravity and legality.

Contextual Material Elements of International Economic Crimes

In a potential concept of international economic crime, the definition of contextual elements poses major challenges in terms of compliance with the principle of legality. The contextual material elements have already been outlined in Chapter 3, where an attempt was made to distinguish ordinary economic offences from economic crimes that can justifiably be considered serious and international. It is now appropriate to elaborate on each of these elements, which include: the systemic nature of international economic crimes (i), the

[79] ibid.

[80] The only debatable exception is the crime of genocide, as discussed above.

[81] N Hajdin, 'The Nature of Leadership in the Crime of Aggression: The ICC's New Concern?' (2017) 17 *International Criminal Law Review* 543, 558–566. See also F Jessberger, 'On the Origins of Individual Criminal Responsibility under International Law for Business Activity: IG Farben on Trial' (2010) 8 *Journal of International Criminal Justice* 783, 795; M Lippman, 'War Crimes Trials of German Industrialists: The Other Schindlers' (1995) 9 *Temple International and Comparative Law Journal* 173, 182.

abuse of power by high-level state or non-state actors (ii), the existence of an attack on a country's public wealth (iii).

The Systemic Nature of International Economic Crimes and the 'Policy' Element

A systemic crime is an offence that '*serves* the system and *is caused by* the system'.[82] One of the main consequences of the systemic nature of criminal conduct is that it becomes an 'invisible' crime, consciously approved by the system that the crime feeds and blindly accepted by the (victimised) community in which the criminal system operates. In this sense, the concept of systemic crime is not foreign to international criminal law. Although this term has never been explicitly used by international criminal tribunals to qualify international crimes, during the Nuremberg trials both the Prosecutor[83] and the IMT judges[84] consistently referred to offences committed within and because of the Nazi 'system'.

Today, the notion of systemic crime is mainly used to describe offences that represent examples of 'indirect violence',[85] 'long-term abuses [of power] of the sort that cause everyday suffering',[86] seriously undermine human rights, and can constitute crimes against humanity.[87] To give a concrete example, the Commission of Inquiry on Systemic Racism has determined that this form of discrimination can constitute a crime against humanity.[88] In this respect, the numerous incidents of racism reported in the US have been qualified as systemic

[82] ND White, 'Responses of Political Organs to Crimes by States' in A Nollkaemper and H van der Wilt, *System Criminality in International Law* (Cambridge University Press, 2009) 316.

[83] IMT, *Trial of the Major War Criminals* 32: '[T]he Nazi conspirators established and extended a *system of terror* against opponents and supposed or suspected opponents of the regime' (emphasis added).

[84] IMT, *Trial of the Major War Criminals* 244: '[T]he *system of deporting labourers* to Germany was put into force' (emphasis added); 292: 'Jews, commissars, and others who were thought to be ideologically hostile to the *Nazi system* were reported to the RSHA' (emphasis added); 295: '[…] a *system of organized plunder of both public and private property* throughout the invaded countries of Europe' (emphasis added); 344: 'Schacht provided to the last detail for *the system of exploitation of the German economy* in war time, all the way from the utilization of industrial enterprises, of raw material resources and man-power down to the distribution of 80,000,000 ration cards' (emphasis added).

[85] On the concept of 'indirect' or 'invisible violence', see ML Böhm, *The Crime of Maldevelopment: Economic Deregulation and Violence in the Global South* (Routledge, 2019) 42–43, see also above, '"Extraordinary" Offenses' in ch 2.

[86] Starr, 'Extraordinary Crimes' 1257 (emphasis added).

[87] Kress, 'The Crime of Genocide' 297.

[88] MM deGuzman, 'Systemic Racist Police Brutality Shocks the Conscience of Humanity, but Is It an International Crime?' (*Just Security*, 11 July 2020) www.justsecurity.org/71255/systemic-racist-police-brutality-shocks-the-conscience-of-humanity-but-is-it-an-international-crime/. See also International Commission of Inquiry on Systemic Racist Police Violence against People of African Descent in the United States, 'Section 7: The Systemic Racism and Police Violence against People of African Descent Constitute Crimes against Humanity' (2021) https://inquirycommission.org/crimes-against-humanity/.

crimes because 'such actions are rooted in a system'[89] and contribute to the perpetuation of that same 'system of discrimination, intimidation, and coercion that prevents Black Americans from enjoying or gaining social, political and economic power'.[90]

The concepts of 'kleptocracy' or 'grand corruption' mentioned above can be equally defined as long-term abuses of power that result in daily violations of human rights and serve a deviant system on the one hand, while being caused by it on the other. They consist of the plundering of people's fundamental resources by systemic structures, ie high-level representatives of a State and private actors holding de facto power.[91] The systemic nature of these crimes is externalised through the explicit or implicit elaboration of a policy. In this regard, Schabas has correctly pointed out that 'insisting that the policy be an element of the [international] crime[s] clarifies the reality of this special form of criminality and facilitates its distinction […]'[92] from ordinary crimes that do not reach the gravity threshold of international criminal law. With the exception of the lone genocidaire, the perpetration of international crimes does not follow a random course of events.[93] To reach the threshold of gravity discussed above, systemic crimes must be committed following an agreement or plan that does not need to be formalised, but must certainly be endorsed by the members of the system in which the offences are perpetrated.[94]

The IMT's judgment emphasised the central role played by the Nazi policy in ensuring the smooth and coordinated perpetration of international crimes during the Second World War:[95] without the criminal system established in accordance with the Nazi policy, the offences committed could not have been considered 'crimes in violation of international law'.[96]

[89] deGuzman, 'Systemic Racist Police'.

[90] ibid.

[91] Starr, 'Extraordinary Crimes' 1283; N Kofele-Kale, *The International Law of Responsibility for Economic Crimes: Holding State Officials Individually Liable for Acts of Fraudulent Enrichment* (Ashgate, 2006) 15.

[92] Schabas, 'State Policy' 982.

[93] For instance, with respect to crimes against humanity, Schabas contends that the notion of 'course of conduct' is a 'systemic aspect as it describes a series or overall flow of events as opposed to a mere aggregate of random acts'. See WA Schabas, 'Part 2 Jurisdiction, Admissibility, and Applicable Law: Compétence, recevabilité, et droit applicable, Art 7 Crimes against Humanity/ Crimes contre l'humanité' in WA Schabas (ed), *The International Criminal Court: A Commentary on the Rome Statute*, 2nd edn (Oxford University Press, 2016) 145, 154.

[94] The flow of events follows a policy that does not need to involve a structured common plan – for instance, a policy of racist discrimination – but can also consist of a failure to act, which sustains the system in a country, see Art 7(2) of the Elements of Crimes. See also deGuzman, 'Systemic Racist Police'; White, 'Responses of Political Organs' 319, arguing that a '[p]lan or policy can be exteriorized through *authorization* of crimes (eg in legislation), *acquiescence* by systematically not acting, *providing material conditions* needed for the commission' (emphasis added).

[95] IMT, *Trial of the Major War Criminals*, 225: 'Indeed the threat of war – and war itself if necessary – was an integral part of the Nazi *policy*'; 248: 'the Nazi *policy* towards the Jews' (emphasis added).

[96] ibid 411, 466. This concept was further explained by Schabas, 'State Policy' 982.

The Rome Statute and the ICC have ushered in a 'revival' of the policy element, with particular regard to crimes against humanity.[97] According to the second paragraph of Article 7 of the Rome Statute, the attack directed against any civilian population must be committed 'pursuant to or in furtherance of a State or organisational *policy*'.[98] It is controversial whether 'State or organisational policy' refers exclusively to State policies or whether it also includes the policies developed and implemented by non-state actors.[99] A number of scholars support an intermediate position, which includes policies developed by state or state-like entities.[100]

In her book on the concept of 'economic crimes against humanity', Arenal Lora argued that the notion of 'organisational policy' needs to be reconceptualised to include policies elaborated by non-state actors, in particular corporations.[101] To this end, she adopted a broad interpretation of the criteria

[97] Scholars have pointed out the importance of the policy element in the definition of crimes against humanity as it emerges from Article 7 of the Rome Statute. Without the policy element, crimes against humanity would be potentially applicable to an excessively broad list of crimes, see Schabas, 'State Policy' 960.

[98] ibid 960, emphasis added.

[99] There are several theories interpreting the policy element of crimes against humanity. According to a minority view, the policy element is not seen by the tribunals as a constitutive requirement of crimes against humanity but as 'one of the factors a tribunal may take into account as a matter of evidence' see, inter alia, G Mettraux, 'The Definition of Crimes against Humanity and the Question of a "Policy" Element' in LN Sadat (ed), *Forging a Convention for Crimes against Humanity* (Cambridge University Press, 2011) 142, 175–176; see also, *Prosecutor v Kunarac et al* (Appeals Judgment) para 98, whereby fn 114 summarises the main jurisprudential debate on whether a policy or plan constitutes an element of the definition of crimes against humanity. Others argue that the policy element is a contextual element of crimes against humanity and should be interpreted strictly to include policies created by States or organisations within a State, see MC Bassiouni, 'Crimes against Humanity: The Case for a Specialized Convention' (2010) 9 *Washington University Global Studies Law Review* 575, 585; Schabas, 'State Policy' 973 referring to MC Bassiouni, *The Legislative History of the International Criminal Court*, Vol 1 (Transnational Publishers, 2005) 151–152. A third theory recognises as a contextual element of crimes against humanity any policy developed by States or state-like organisations (such as the Republika Srpska or the FARC-EP) see Schabas, 'State Policy' 972. The last theory is based on a broad interpretation of the policy element, according to which policies developed by States or any other group that possesses a structure that allows it to perpetrate international crimes, may constitute a contextual element of crimes against humanity. See, inter alia, G Werle and B Burghardt, 'Do Crimes against Humanity Require the Participation of a State or a 'State-Like' Organization?' (2012) 10 *Journal of International Criminal Justice* 1151, 1167; CC Jalloh, 'What Makes a Crime against Humanity a Crime against Humanity' (2013) 28 *American University International Law Review* 381, 429; TO Hansen, 'The Policy Requirement in Crimes against Humanity: Lessons from and for the Case of Kenya' (2011) 43 *George Washington International Law Review* 1, 15–19, referring to international law jurisprudence indicating that 'non-state actors can also commit crimes against humanity under certain circumstances'. It would be desirable that the drafters of the Convention on Crimes against Humanity clarify the notion of 'state or organizational policy', see Mettraux, 'The Definition' 176.

[100] For a definition of state-like entities see Schabas, 'State Policy' 972. See also *Prosecutor v Tadić* (Trial Opinion and Judgment) IT-94-1-T (7 May 1997) para 654–655.

[101] L Arenal Lora, *Crímenes económicos en derecho internacional: Propuesta de una nueva categoría de crímenes contra la humanidad* (Editorial Aranzadi, 2019) 124. The concepts of 'organisation' and 'non-state actors' are addressed at 127.

identified in the *Kenya* situation by the majority of judges to define the concept of 'organisation' within the meaning of Article 7(2) of the Rome Statute:[102]

> [T]he determination of whether a given group qualifies as an organization under the Statute must be made on a case-by-case basis [...] the Chamber may take into account a number of considerations, inter alia: (i) whether the group is under a responsible command, or has an established hierarchy; (ii) whether the group possesses, in fact, the means to carry out a widespread or systematic attack against a civilian population; (iii) whether the group exercises control over part of the territory of a State; (iv) whether the group has criminal activities against the civilian population as a primary purpose; (v) whether the group articulates, explicitly or implicitly, an intention to attack a civilian population; (vi) whether the group is part of a larger group, which fulfils some or all of the abovementioned criteria.[103]

Arenal Lora focused on two requirements: first, the ability of an organisation to dispose of adequate tools to provoke an attack against a civilian population; second, the ability of an organisation to control the territory where this attack is committed. With respect to the first criterion, she revitalised Habermas' pioneering argument that most multinational corporations today wield greater economic and political power than some States.[104] As the 'economic sovereigns' of the twenty-first century,[105] these non-state actors have the means to launch

[102] ibid 133–134. For further details on the concept of 'organisation' under Art 7(2)(a) of the Rome Statute see also T Rodenhäuser, 'Beyond State Crimes: Non-State Entities and Crimes against Humanity' (2014) 27 *Leiden Journal of International Law* 913.

[103] *Situation in the Republic of Kenya* (Decision Pursuant to Article 15 of the Rome Statute on the Authorization of an Investigation into the Situation in the Republic of Kenya) ICC-01/09-19-Corr (31 March 2010) para 93. As it can be inferred from the use of the term 'inter alia', the requirements listed by the Chamber (Judge Hans-Peter Kaul dissenting) 'do not constitute a rigid legal definition, and do not need to be exhaustively fulfilled'. See also Arenal Lora, *Crímenes económicos*, 133.

[104] J Habermas, *The Inclusion of the Other: Studies in Political Theory* (The MIT Press, 2018) 174, arguing that 'nongovernmental actors such as multinational corporations and internationally influential private banks undermine the formal sovereignty of nation-states. Today each of the thirty largest corporations operating on a global scale has an annual turnover greater than the gross domestic product of ninety countries represented in the UN'. See also Arenal Lora, *Crímenes económicos* 140, referring to a study conducted by Global Justice Now, according to which today most economic powers are multinational corporations and not States, including Apple, Shell and Facebook. See '10 Biggest Corporations Make More Money Than Most Countries in the World Combined' (*Global Justice Now*, 12 September 2016) www.globaljustice.org.uk/news/10-biggest-corporations-make-more-money-most-countries-world-combined/. The results of this study have been commented in M Babic, EM Heemskerk and J Fichtner, 'States Versus Corporations: Rethinking the Power of Business in International Politics' (2017) 52 *The International Spectator* 20; M Babic, EM Heemskerk and J Fichtner, 'Who Is More Powerful – States or Corporations?' (*The Conversation*, 10 July 2018) https://theconversation.com/who-is-more-powerful-states-or-corporations-99616.

[105] The term 'economic sovereignty' has been used by Arenal Lora, *Crímenes económicos* 140. This is in line with the evolution (or rather involution) of the concept of sovereignty analysed by S Braum, '"Rechtsstaat" and European Criminal Law – From the End of Sovereignty' (2021) 12 *New Journal of European Criminal Law* 14, 17. Commenting on the draft EU Regulation on the collection of digital evidence, Braum argues that nowadays 'sovereignty is no longer what it used to be' as the real sovereigns of the twenty-first century are those who have access to information, ie economic actors who are at the top of the 'cloud'.

economic attacks against any civilian population. Regarding the second criterion, it is much harder to claim that corporations, however large and powerful, have control over the territory and population of a State. Nonetheless, Arenal Lora argued that some multinational corporations may exercise indirect control over the territory and population of a State since they are able to influence vulnerable States through priming practices, such as corruption.[106]

The examples of serious economic crimes discussed in this book share some features with the concept of 'economic crimes against humanity' developed by Arenal Lora. Both may be committed pursuant to a policy elaborated by the following structures: state actors; state-like actors; non-state actors; or a combination of these entities. The State represents the systemic structure *par excellence*.[107] As the *Haarde* case shows, criminal conduct capable of generating international harm may be committed on the basis of a non-formalised policy adopted and pursued exclusively by state actors.

Although States are the collective entities most involved in the perpetration of systemic economic crimes,[108] other actors have also been involved over the years, including organised armed groups, political parties, and industrialists.[109] These actors can be divided into state-like actors and non-state actors. An example of state-like entity that meets most of these criteria detailed in the *Kenya* situation might be the AUC in Colombia.[110] The relationship between state-like groups and the victims of international crimes is based on the vulnerability of the latter and their dependence on state-like organisations.

On the other hand, despite their internal hierarchical organisation, non-state actors such as multinational corporations do not always have de jure or de facto control over the territory and population of a State. The 'indirect control' argument developed by Arenal Lora is valid, but it would exclude from the list of entities capable of creating a policy pursuant to which serious economic crimes are committed, powerful corporations operating in countries that are not weak and easily corruptible. It would therefore be appropriate to consider an alternative argument that replaces the territorial control relationship between 'victims and States' and 'victims and state-like actors', with an ad hoc relationship between 'victims and non-state economic actors'.

Corporations are endowed with duties to respect individuals' human rights.[111] This relationship of dependency between victims as human rights

[106] Arenal Lora, *Crímenes económicos* 140.

[107] White, 'Responses of Political Organs' 314 and 316.

[108] ibid 318.

[109] Sandoval Mesa, 'Del principio de legalidad' 187.

[110] See the examples of 'state-like' entities provided by Schabas, 'State Policy' 972–3. See also Arenal Lora, *Crímenes económicos*, 128–129.

[111] Although the BHR Treaty has not yet been adopted, national and regional due diligence laws and initiatives outline a legal framework for companies' human rights obligations. See, inter alia, the Modern Slavery Act 2015 (c 30) in the UK; the 'Loi no 2017-399 du 27 mars 2017 relative au devoir de vigilance des sociétés mères et des entreprises donneuses d'ordre' in France; the 'Entwurf eines

holders, on the one hand, and corporations as human rights duty bearers, on the other, would allow the latter to be included among the systemic structures capable of developing policies resulting in serious abuses of fundamental human rights that overlap with international crimes.[112]

Lastly, the above-mentioned cases show that in many situations States, state actors, and non-state entities cooperate with each other in the development and implementation of policies underlying the commission of serious economic crimes,[113] which recalls the abovementioned concepts of 'state-facilitated corporate crimes' and 'corporate-facilitated state crimes'.[114]

Therefore, both States and entities other than States with certain characteristics are capable – either individually or jointly – of devising policies aimed at perpetrating economic crimes of international significance. Hence, a generic reference to a 'State or organisational policy' should be avoided in a definition of 'international economic crimes' that reflects as closely as possible the reality in which we live and that complies with the *lex certa* requirements of the principle of legality. Instead, a more detailed qualification of the systemic structures responsible for the development of criminal policies pursuant to which international economic crimes are committed, should be provided.

The Abuse of Power by High-Level Public and Private Actors

Although globalisation has contributed significantly to technological and economic progress for humanity, it has also accelerated social inequalities and environmental degradation on planet Earth.[115] As early as the 1990s, Habermas described globalisation as one of the main causes of complexity and vulnerability of contemporary society.[116] Nonetheless, States have not been the only actors responsible for shaping a complex world. It is believed that 'globalisation

Gesetzes über die unternehmerischen (19/28649)' adopted on 19 April 2021 in Germany; and the Directive (EU) 2024/1760 of the European Parliament and of the Council of 13 June 2024 on corporate sustainability due diligence and amending Directive (EU) 2019/1937 and Regulation (EU) 2023/2859. For an updated chart on national due diligence laws and initiatives, see 'National & Regional Movements for Mandatory Human Rights & Environmental Due Diligence in Europe' (*Business & Human Rights Resource Centre*, 2022) www.business-humanrights.org/en/latest-news/national-regional-movements-for-mandatory-human-rights-environmental-due-diligence-in-europe/.

[112] The ability of a group to 'perform acts which infringe on basic human values' for it to be considered an 'organisation' within the meaning of Art 7(2) of the Rome Statute is highlighted in *Situation in the Republic of Kenya* (Decision Pursuant to Article 15 of the Rome Statute on the Authorization of an Investigation into the Situation in the Republic of Kenya) para 90.

[113] Examples of collaboration between state and non-state actors are the *Petrobras* case, the *Bolichicos* case and the *Niger Delta* situation. The *Chiquita* case is an example of cooperation between state-like and non-state actors.

[114] See above, '"Systemic" Offenses' in ch 2.

[115] See Habermas, *The Inclusion of the Other* 183, arguing that globalisation has polarised the world, dividing it in two. See also Braum, '"Rechtsstaat" and European Criminal Law' 15, challenging the idea that the financial and technological tools have positively influenced our ability to manage the 'existential shocks' of our globalised world.

[116] Habermas, *The Inclusion of the Other* 174. See also S Wharton, 'Redrawing the Line? Serious Crimes of Concern to the International Community Beyond the Rome Statute' (2015) 52 *Canadian Yearbook of International Law/Annuaire canadien de droit international* 129, 133.

has led to a global structure in which state power is not the exclusive governing principle anymore',[117] but in which the power of non-state actors also plays an increasingly important role.[118]

As can be inferred from Chapter 2, powerful companies existed and operated even before the twenty-first century,[119] but they cannot be compared to today's corporations 'in terms of sheer size and volume'.[120] In this sense, the 2008 financial crisis represented a turning point, as it highlighted the significant impact of private economic actors not only in business and finance, but also in other areas, including law and international politics.[121] According to existing international political studies on the mechanisms of power allocation among *élites*, the idea that multinational corporations are subordinate to States no longer corresponds to reality.[122] On the contrary, multinational corporations represent such a concentration of power that, according to Habermas' words, they have called into question the 'formal sovereignty of nation-States'.[123] Böhm defined the 'governments, transnational corporations, the global economy and the social structures' that are behind systemic problems of the world – including corruption, poverty, environmental damage – as 'sovereign powers'.[124]

In this regard, it is important to clarify what is meant by 'power' and 'sovereignty' for the purposes of this book. The former is a socio-political concept, which has been defined as the 'ability to get someone to do something that they would not otherwise do'.[125] This ability stems from the excessive amount of freedom, resources and control that individuals and entities may have. In this sense, therefore, both private and public individuals and entities can be powerful. When applied to criminal law, the concept of power thus creates an asymmetry between the perpetrator and the victim, ie between powerful criminals who have an excessive amount of freedom, resources and control to induce victims to perform actions that they would not otherwise do.[126]

[117] Babic, Heemskerk and Fichtner, 'Who Is More Powerful'.

[118] Babic, Heemskerk and Fichtner, 'States Versus Corporations' 21.

[119] The IMT stated that 'Hitler could not make aggressive war by himself. He had to have cooperation of statesmen, military leaders, diplomats, and businessmen', see Hajdin, 'The Nature of Leadership' 547.

[120] Habermas, *The Inclusion of the Other* 174. See also Babic, Heemskerk and Fichtner, 'Who Is More Powerful'.

[121] On the impact of the 2008 financial crisis on various sectors see A Tooze, *Crash: cómo una década de crisis financieras ha cambiado el mundo* (Crítica, 2021).

[122] Babic, Heemskerk and Fichtner, 'States Versus Corporations' 30.

[123] Habermas, *The Inclusion of the Other* 174. See also Braum, '"Rechtsstaat" and European Criminal Law' 17.

[124] Böhm, *The Crime of Maldevelopment* 180.

[125] SD Krasner, 'New Terrains: Sovereignty and Alternative Conceptions of Power' in M Finnemore and J Goldstein (eds), *Back to Basics: State Power in a Contemporary World* (Oxford University Press, 2013) 339, 339 and 346. Krasner endorses the definition of 'power' developed in RA Dahl, 'The Concept of Power' (1957) 2 *Behavioral Science* 201.

[126] V Ruggiero and M Welch, 'Power Crime' (2009) 51 *Crime, Law and Social Change* 297, 297–299.

On the other hand, sovereignty is a fundamental principle of modern international law that defines 'the supreme authority within a territory'.[127] Sovereignty thus concerns States, which are the formal and legal construct used to represent the people, who are the true sovereigns of a territory. This legal concept entails a series of consequences for States, including 'their immunity from other States' own jurisdiction, their freedom from other States' intervention on their territory, [...] their equal rank to other sovereign States'.[128]

There may be a correspondence between the concept of sovereignty and that of power, but this is not always the case. Three scenarios can be envisaged: there are States that, in addition to holding sovereignty, are particularly powerful in the sense indicated above, namely in terms of freedom, resources and control (i); there are States that, while retaining their sovereignty intact, are unable to exercise power (ii); and lastly, there are non-state actors, such as multinational corporations, which may have the material capabilities – including, in particular, capital – that make them powerful players on the international stage, but which are not and will never be sovereigns in the legal sense of the term (iii). For these reasons and for the purposes of this research, it is argued that power can be abused not only by representatives of States, but also by representatives of concentrations of power other than the State, notably large corporations.

This digression on the concept of power is not an end in itself, since international economic crimes are 'power crimes'.[129] Like the crime of aggression and unlike other international crimes that can be committed by anyone 'regardless of any hierarchical position',[130] international economic crimes are 'leadership crimes',[131] which means that these offences are perpetrated by those who have access to power and can exercise it, such as heads of States,[132] ministers and CEOs of companies. Only the acts or omissions carried out by these individuals

[127] S Besson, 'Sovereignty' (*Oxford Public International Law*, 2011) https://opil.ouplaw.com/display/10.1093/law:epil/9780199231690/law-9780199231690-e1472.

[128] ibid.

[129] On the notion of 'power crime' see V Ruggiero and M Welch, 'Power Crime'; see also, D Whyte, 'Power, Crime and Deadly Deception' in D Gordon Scott and J Sim (eds) *Demystifying Power, Crime and Social Harm: The Work and Legacy of Steven Box* (Palgrave Macmillan, 2023) 103.

[130] Mettraux, 'The Definition' 207. Nonetheless, in practice, international criminal law tribunals have focused mainly on the prosecution of high-level individuals. See UNSC Res 1534 (26 March 2004) S/RES/1534 para 5: 'Calls on each Tribunal [...] to ensure that any such indictments concentrate on the *most senior leaders* suspected of being most responsible for crimes within the jurisdiction of the relevant Tribunal [...]' (emphasis added). See also ICC-OTP, 'Paper on Some Policy Issues'; Del Ponte, 'Prosecuting the Individuals'.

[131] In the subsequent Nuremberg proceedings, the distinction between, on the one hand, politicians – 'men of leadership' – and on the other, industrialists – 'men of industry' – removed the latter from the scope of the potential perpetrators of crimes against peace. However, the case studies analysed above in Chapter 2 show that serious economic crimes are committed by individuals that occupy high-level positions in both public and private institutions. Thereby, along the lines of the crime of aggression, international economic crimes are leadership crimes, where the term 'leader' must be reconceptualised and broadly interpreted to include high-level private actors.

[132] On this see EL Lutz and C Reiger, *Prosecuting Heads of State* (Cambridge University Press, 2009).

can have a detrimental impact on the public wealth of a country and therefore on the human rights of its population. However, this would not prevent individuals who are not high-level actors from being involved in international economic crimes as accomplices or through other modes of liability.

An international economic crime is committed when high-level public or private actors abuse their power. Since the term 'abuse' means to use something improperly or excessively, when high-level public and private actors use their power to illegally divert public money or exploit natural resources, they are abusing the power conferred to them by those who recognise and legitimise it.

What has been said so far calls into question the argument that the principle of individual criminal responsibility is capable of capturing the systemic and collective nature of international crimes.[133] Over the years, international criminal courts have tended to focus on the 'big fishes' in the system.[134] It is thus inevitable to ask whether, despite the removal from conflict territories – and in some cases the prosecution – of high-level perpetrators, the intricate network of criminal acts and omissions underlying the perpetration of mass crimes will continue to provide fertile ground for new international crimes.[135] This question arises because, when prosecuting international crimes – and international economic crimes in particular – 'there is a need to address the underlying source of impunity, which lies in the power of entrenched regimes or active rebel movements relative to those that oppose them'.[136]

The principle of individual criminal responsibility has been the cornerstone of international criminal law since the Nuremberg trials, where the Allies felt the need to hold individuals, rather than abstract entities, liable for the most serious crimes committed during the Second World War.[137] One of the main advantages of the principle of individual criminal responsibility is that it allows victims to clearly identify the perpetrators of international crimes, thereby facilitating, in principle, the process of restoring justice and truth in their countries. Moreover, the principle of individual criminal responsibility is consistent with the principle of legality: it is individuals who can foresee, *tempore criminis*, the criminal nature of a wrongful behaviour and act accordingly to prevent it from being committed and avoid being held criminally responsible.

For these reasons, a dual system has been created, in which individuals may be held criminally responsible for international crimes before national courts

[133] White, 'Responses of Political Organs' 314. See also Braum, 'Droit pénal des risques', pointing out that the systemic problems of modern societies challenge the principle of individual responsibility.

[134] White, 'Responses of Political Organs' 320, arguing that in most of the cases the big fishes are 'small cogs in the system'.

[135] ibid 326.

[136] Rodman, 'Justice as a Dialogue' 442 (emphasis added).

[137] A Nieto Martín, 'Bases para un futuro derecho penal internacional del medio ambiente' (2011) 82 *Revue internationale de droit pénal* 477, 496.

and international criminal law tribunals, while the responsibility of States for the same offences may be established before the ICJ. Nonetheless, in a world dominated by powerful corporations that can seriously violate human rights, which may overlap with international crimes, the principle of corporate criminal responsibility may be considered an additional tool for preventing and suppressing systemic and collective criminal phenomena.[138]

The Attack against the Public Wealth of a Country

With a few exceptions,[139] international crimes are 'harm-type' offences, which means that the intended harm must have materialised[140] for these crimes to be committed. The harm caused by international economic crimes stems from an attack directed against the public wealth of a country, where the term 'attack' can be construed around the interpretation provided by international criminal law tribunals on crimes against humanity. This means that the attack does not necessarily have to be military or involve violence,[141] but can include any non-violent conduct of economic significance. According to Arenal Lora, any course of conduct aimed at obtaining a profit, an advantage, keeping a position or indirectly damaging an economic-political power balance can be included in the concept of 'attack' in the definition of crimes against humanity.[142] Furthermore, the attack should not necessarily consist of acts, as '[i]n exceptional circumstances, a governmental or organizational policy that deliberately fails to take actions may be considered an attack […]'.[143]

It is essential that the attack is directed against the public wealth of a country, where the concept of 'public wealth' includes both the economic wealth and the

[138] Nieto Martín argues that modern international criminal law must stand on two legs: on the one hand, individual criminal responsibility, and on the other hand, corporate criminal responsibility, see A Nieto Martín, 'Ecocidio y justicia restaurativa: el derecho penal internacional post-Nuremberg' (*Almacén de Derecho*, 26 November 2020) https://almacendederecho.org/ecocidio-y-justicia-restaurativa-el-derecho-penal-internacional-post-nuremberg. See also Arenal Lora, *Crímenes económicos* 131, referring to the UN Diplomatic Conference of Plenipotentiaries on the Establishment of an International Criminal Court that rejected France's proposal to include the criminal responsibility of legal persons under Article 23 of the Rome Statute.

[139] For instance, incitement to genocide, which is a 'conduct-type' international crime.

[140] JG Stewart, 'Overdetermined Atrocities' (2012) 10 *Journal of International Criminal Justice* 1189, 1197. Stewart presents a three-way division of crimes at 1195: 'inchoate crimes, such as attempt, where the subjective disposition is the primary ground for responsibility; conduct-type crimes, such as rape and fraud, where wrongdoing is constituted by the conduct itself; and harm-type offences, such as murder, where a potentially wide range of actions are prohibited if they lead to proscribed harm'.

[141] Arenal Lora, *Crímenes económicos* 120 and 124. See also R Cryer et al, *An Introduction to International Criminal Law and Procedure*, 1st edn (Cambridge University Press, 2010) 237: 'An attack need not involve the use of armed force, and can encompass mistreatment of the civilian population'.

[142] Arenal Lora, *Crímenes económicos* 123.

[143] Y Gottlieb, 'Attacks against Cultural Heritage as a Crime against Humanity' (2020) 52 *Case Western Reserve Journal of International Law* 287, 324. See also Elements of Crimes 3, fn 6.

natural wealth of a country.[144] When criminal acts or omissions are committed in pursuance of a systemic policy directed against the public wealth of a country, they seriously undermine its economic foundations and, consequently, the rights of its civilian population.[145] This is the main difference between the concept of international economic crimes proposed here and that of economic crimes against humanity suggested elsewhere: the former undermines the roots of a country's economic stability, thereby violating the principle of international peace and security, the principle of sovereignty over natural resources, the right to self-determination of peoples, with detrimental consequences for collective and individual human rights; the latter are ordinary economic crimes that, if committed as part of an attack targeting primarily the civilian population of a country, can rise to the level of crimes against humanity.

An economic attack can be systematic and/or widespread.[146] The 'systematic' character of an attack should be distinguished from its 'systemic' nature. While 'systemic' is used to describe what relates to or affects a system, 'systematic' defines what follows a pattern and is carried out accordingly.[147] Thus, a systemic crime can also be systematic when its perpetration reaches a certain degree of organisation.[148] By way of example, the multiple crimes committed over more than a decade on the basis of a state-corporate policy directed against Venezuelan public wealth constitute an example of systemic crimes perpetrated in a systematic manner.

In light of the above, the question arises whether an economic attack occurs not only when harm is caused to the public wealth of a country, but also when

[144] The UN Convention against Corruption (New York, 9 December 2003) (UNCAC) uses the term 'national wealth' to refer to the economic wealth of a country. See also Kofele-Kale, *The International Law of Responsibility for Economic Crimes* 107, stating that 'it is therefore something of an irony that countries that championed this form of indigenous control over *national wealth and resources* would turn out to be the victims of perhaps the most systematic spoliation of this wealth by their own rulers' (emphasis added). See also UNGA Res 1803(XVII) (14 December 1962) A/RES/1803(XVII) using the term 'natural wealth and resources'.

[145] On the concept of 'economic foundations', see Kofele-Kale, *The International Law of Responsibility for Economic Crimes* 12.

[146] For more details on how to interpret the concept of 'widespread attack' see, inter alia, *Prosecutor v Kunarac et al* (Appeals Judgment) para 94, defining 'widespread' as 'the large-scale nature of the attack and the number of victims, [...]'; *Prosecutor v Akayesu* (Trial Judgment), para 580, defining 'widespread' 'as massive, frequent, large-scale action, carried out collectively with considerable seriousness and directed against a multiplicity of victims'; see also, *Prosecutor v Kayishema and Ruzindana* (Trial Judgment) ICTR-95-1-T (21 May 1999) para 123. The ICC judges reiterated this interpretation of 'widespread' in, inter alia, *Prosecutor v Ntaganda* (Trial Judgment) ICC-01/04-02/06-2359 (8 July 2019) para 691: 'massive, frequent, carried out collectively with considerable seriousness and directed against a multiplicity of victims'. It is well-established that the number of victims that allows qualifying an attack as widespread should be decided on a case-by-case basis.

[147] '"Systematic" or "Systemic"? Methodically Explaining a Pervasive Question' (Merriam-Webster) www.merriam-webster.com/words-at-play/systematic-vs-systemic.

[148] This is in line with the school of thought whereby the policy element cannot be inferred from the systematic nature of the attack committed against a civilian population in crimes against humanity, as these elements are distinct; see D Robinson, 'Defining "Crimes against Humanity" at the Rome Conference' (1999) 93 *American Journal of International Law* 43, 50–51.

there is a real danger that such an attack will occur. On the one hand, this broad approach – which should be limited to real and concrete dangers, excluding abstract ones – would strengthen the goal of international criminal law to prevent international crimes. On the other hand, however, this approach risks being hampered by the shortcomings of the international criminal justice enforcement system and by criticism of the attempt to over-anticipate the criminal response by creating a 'danger-type' category of international crimes. Therefore, it would be preferable for a definition of international economic crimes to cover economic attacks that cause harm to the public wealth of a country, while addressing the possibility of a concrete danger to it by resorting to alternative modes of liability, such as attempt to commit international economic crimes.[149]

Contextual Mental Elements of International Economic Crimes

The *mens rea* required for the crime of genocide is *dolus specialis*, ie the perpetrator's intention to pursue a specific objective, namely the total or partial destruction of a targeted group of individuals.[150] This high mental threshold cannot be used as a contextual mental element for international economic crimes, since the perpetration of these offences is not aimed at a specific purpose. In contrast, it is possible to resort to a lower *mens rea* standard, which is 'knowledge'. The drafters explicitly referred to 'knowledge' as a mental element for crimes against humanity in Article 7 of the Rome Statute, and for war crimes in the Elements of Crimes.[151] The rationale for this explicit provision lies in the fact that contextual material elements relate 'to the broader context that renders the crime an international crime'.[152] This means that the default *mens rea* under Article 30, which covers the material elements of the underlying offences, does not also cover the contextual material elements of international crimes; hence

[149] Art 25(3)(f) of the Rome Statute includes 'attempt' among the listed modes of liability.

[150] Considering the *mens rea* standard for genocide, this turns out to be an extreme and inhumane form of persecution. See *Prosecutor v Kupreškić et al* (Trial Judgment) para 636; see also, *Prosecutor v Brđjanin* (Trial Judgment) IT-99-36-T (1 September 2004) para 699, contending that '[genocide is] a denial of the right of existence of entire human groups, as homicide is the denial of the right to live of individual human beings'. It is this *mens rea* that 'gives genocide its speciality and distinguishes it from an ordinary crime and other [international crimes]', see *Prosecutor v Jelisić* (Trial Judgment) IT-95-10-T (14 December 1999) para 66. See also Schabas, 'State Policy' 971, suggesting a 'radical rethinking of the definition of genocide' in which it would be crucial to establish the existence of a state policy pursuant to which genocide is committed and the perpetrator's knowledge of such a policy.

[151] See Art 7(1) of the Rome Statute, Art 7, Introduction, para 2 of the Elements of Crimes, and Art 8, Introduction, para 3 of the Elements of Crimes.

[152] ME Badar, 'The Mental Element in the Rome Statute of the International Criminal Court: A Commentary from a Comparative Criminal Law Perspective' (2008) 19 *Criminal Law Forum* 473, 478. The same position is supported by H Von Hebel and M Kelt, 'What Are the Elements of Crimes?' in RS Lee (ed), *The International Criminal Court: Elements of Crimes and Rules of Procedure and Evidence* (Transnational Publishers, 2001) 13.

the need to provide an appropriate contextual mental element for each category of international crimes.

The *mens rea* standard of 'knowledge' is a gradation of intent characterised by a high cognitive component accompanied by a low volitional component, which allows criminal liability to be reasonably extended to individuals who did not necessarily intend to create the criminal context but were aware of its existence and carried out their acts or omissions accordingly. In relation to crimes against humanity and war crimes, international criminal law tribunals have interpreted the perpetrators' 'knowledge' as encompassing both the broader context in which their conduct occurred – namely, the attack against a civilian population or the factual circumstances that established the existence of an armed conflict – and the existence of a link between their conduct and the broader context.[153] This does not mean that the perpetrators must know the details of the attack against a civilian population or the legal assessment of the armed conflict,[154] as it is sufficient that they are aware of the circumstances under which their conduct takes place and the fact that such conduct fosters that criminal context.

For the purposes of defining international economic crimes, it is reasonable to require that perpetrators be aware of the context – a systemic attack directed against the public wealth of a country – and of the connection between that context and their criminal conduct. Due to their prominent position, perpetrators of international economic crimes can easily acquire knowledge of the context in which such crimes take place. Indeed, it is unlikely that cases of grand corruption escape the scrutiny of high-level public officials, whether through personal supervision or tacit acquiescence.[155]

However, the question arises whether a less stringent mental threshold might be equally appropriate to cover the contextual material elements of international economic crimes. In the *Haarde* case, the special tribunal set up to try the

[153] See inter alia, *Prosecutor v Tadić* (Appeals Judgment) IT-94-1-A (15 July 1999) para 248.

[154] With respect to crimes against humanity, see inter alia, Introduction, para 2 of the Elements of Crimes: '[it is not required that the perpetrator] had knowledge of all characteristics of the attack or the precise details of the plan or policy of the State or organization'; *Prosecutor v Blaškić* (Trial Judgment) IT-95-14-T (3 March 2000) para 251; *Prosecutor v Kunarac et al* (Appeals Judgment) para 102; *Prosecutor v Katanga* (Judgment pursuant to Article 74 of the Statute), para 1125: '[…] that stipulation should not be interpreted as a requirement of proof that the perpetrator had knowledge of all of the characteristics of the attack or the precise details of the plan or policy of the State or organisation. Nor is it required that the perpetrator of the act subscribed to the State or the organisation's criminal design, any more than it must be shown that the perpetrator deliberately intended his or her act to form part of the attack against the civilian population […]'. With respect to war crimes, see inter alia, *Prosecutor v Lubanga Dyilo* (Decision on the Confirmation of the Charges) para 360: '[t]he perpetrator was aware of factual circumstances that established the existence of an armed conflict', without going as far as to require that he or she conclude, on the basis of a legal assessment of the said circumstances, that there was an armed conflict'.

[155] Kofele-Kale, *The International Law of Responsibility for Economic Crimes* 18.

offences allegedly committed by the Prime Minister of Iceland recognised the existence of a constitutional duty to tackle the economic crisis and qualified the breach of this duty as gross negligence. This is an overt form of negligence, which lacks both the volitional and cognitive components of 'knowledge' but consists of a conscious choice on the part of the person under a legal duty of care to deviate from it.[156] There is no consensus in the literature on whether this concept can be applied to serious economic crimes. Starr correctly observed that '[b]ecause international law does not impose a general affirmative duty to assist those in need throughout the world, mere failure to give such assistance will not be a basis for international criminal prosecution'.[157] On the contrary, Davidsson recognised that '[...] failing by gross negligence to ensure basic necessities to a dependent person may also give rise to criminal penalties'.[158] While the question remains open as to whether the conscious choice to deviate from the duties of assistance can be qualified as gross negligence, it seems peaceful to recognise that the conscious choice to deviate from legal or customary duties inherent in the functions performed by public or private economic actors, on whom the respect and protection of collective and individual human rights depends, can be classified as gross negligence. Therefore, for the purposes of defining international economic crimes, consideration could be given to broadening the contextual mental element of 'knowledge' to include 'gross negligence', namely those circumstances in which the existence of an economic attack directed against the public wealth of a country is consciously disregarded by those who have a legal or customary duty to prevent such circumstances from occurring.[159]

Offences Underlying the Concept of International Economic Crimes

This subsection examines the second layer of the concept of international economic crimes, namely those acts or omissions which, when committed in the context outlined by the contextual elements, can be prosecuted as international economic crimes. This analysis does not aim to provide an exhaustive list of crimes, but rather to identify and discuss the most critical issues that would arise in attempting to compile a potential list of crimes in compliance with the standards of the Rome Statute, both in terms of material and mental elements.

[156] S Finnin, 'Mental Elements under Article 30 of the Rome Statute of the International Criminal Court: A Comparative Analysis' (2012) 61 *International & Comparative Law Quarterly* 325, 328, citing GP Fletcher, *Rethinking Criminal Law* (Oxford University Press, 2000) 508–510.

[157] Starr, 'Extraordinary Crimes' 1300.

[158] Davidsson defines these duties of assistance 'good faith obligations'; see E Davidsson, 'Economic Oppression as an International Wrong or as Crime against Humanity' (2005) 23 *Netherlands Quarterly of Human Rights* 173, 173 and 179.

[159] Crosby qualifies this conscious disregard as 'incompetence causing serious economic damage', see S Crosby, 'Brexit: Lessons from Different Quarters' (2019) 10 *New Journal of European Criminal Law* 205, 208.

Critical Issues Related to the Actus Reus *Element*

The principle that there is no crime without conduct is fundamental to the imperative need for criminal law to regulate the behaviour of members of society.[160] However, it is not always easy to define the main characteristics of criminal conduct, or its connection to other elements of a crime, in particular the harm that it might cause. These critical issues and the theories that have been developed to address them will be discussed within the parameters established by the Rome Statute and the jurisprudence of the ICC, with a view to provide a solid standard for the *actus reus* of crimes that might constitute international economic crimes.

Defining 'Conduct'

The word 'conduct' is mentioned on several occasions throughout the Rome Statute to refer to the behaviour underlying an international crime.[161] However, Article 12(2)(a) of the Statute, which defines the preconditions for the exercise of the ICC's jurisdiction, refers to 'conduct' as a synonym for 'crime'.[162] This inaccuracy was the result of debates on the meaning of 'conduct', during which criticism was levelled at the overlapping of the concept of 'conduct' with that of 'crime' on the ground that conduct is an element of crime and therefore cannot be equated with it.[163] On the other hand, it was observed that a broad interpretation of the term 'conduct' would allow the ICC to exercise its jurisdiction over crimes committed not only in the State – a State Party or a State that has temporarily accepted the ICC jurisdiction – in which the conduct took place but also in the State where the effects of the conduct occurred.[164]

A related issue that was intensively discussed by the drafters during their negotiations was how to define the concept of 'conduct'. It is clear from the Report of the Preparatory Committee on the Establishment of an International Criminal Court that this term was intended to refer to the 'act or omission' of a crime.[165]

[160] This principle is also known as the *nullum crimen sine actione* principle. See F Palazzo, *Corso di diritto penale. Parte generale*, 5th edn (G. Giappichelli Editore, 2013) 217.

[161] For instance, it is used in the following articles of the Rome Statute: Art 7(2) ('course of *conduct*'); Art 17 ('The person concerned has already been tried for *conduct* which is the subject of the complaint […]'); Art 20 ('[…] no person shall be tried before the Court with respect to *conduct* which […]') (emphasis added).

[162] Art 12(2)(a) of the Rome Statute: 'The State on the territory of which the *conduct* in question occurred or, if the *crime* was committed on board a vessel or aircraft, the State of registration of that vessel or aircraft' (emphasis added).

[163] See J Maillart, 'Article 12(2)(a) Rome Statute: The Missing Piece of the Jurisdictional Puzzle' (*EJIL:Talk!*, 7 August 2014) www.ejiltalk.org/article-122a-rome-statute-the-missing-piece-of-the-jurisdictional-puzzle/.

[164] ibid.

[165] 'UN Diplomatic Conference of Plenipotentiaries on the Establishment of an International Criminal Court' (Vol III) 23, Art 7; 25, Art 11; 26, Art 7. See also M Vagias, *The Territorial Jurisdiction of the International Criminal Court* (Cambridge University Press, 2014) 95.

The Preparatory Committee drafted an article aimed at defining the *actus reus* of a crime, in which it proposed to include not only acts, but also omissions and mixed conduct offences. The first paragraph of draft Article 28 stated that 'conduct for which a person may be criminally responsible and liable for punishment as a crime can constitute either an act or an omission, or a combination thereof'.[166]

The second paragraph of draft Article 28 further elaborated on the concept of omission, specifying that

> [...] a person may be criminally responsible and liable for punishment for an omission where [...] (a) The omission is specified in the definition of the crime under this Statute; or (b) [...] the person is [either] under a pre-existing [legal] obligation under this Statute to avoid the result of such crime [or creates a particular risk or danger that subsequently leads to the commission of such crime].[167]

The vagueness of this definition was further complicated by footnotes 82 and 83 to draft Article 28. In the former, some delegations questioned whether the Rome Statute should be the only source of legal obligations to prevent harmful results. In the latter footnote, some delegations expressed concerns about the reference to omissions creating the risk of the commission of a crime, while others simply considered this clause unnecessary, since the existence of a violation of a legal obligation is already sufficient to define an omission.

In the Report of the Committee of the Whole, the term 'acts or omissions' was again used as a synonym for 'conduct' and the Committee envisaged the option 'to have no article dealing with omission'.[168] Eventually, the Committee of the Whole instructed the Working Group on General Principles of Criminal Law to review some draft articles, including Article 28.[169] The Working Group decided to delete this provision, leaving open the possibility for further discussion at the appropriate time.[170] As a result, no provision defining an '*actus reus* standard' was included in the Report of the Drafting Committee and, ultimately, in the Rome Statute.[171]

Despite the lack of unanimity on the definition of 'omission' and the consequent decision not to include any statutory provision on *actus reus*, this brief historical overview shows that the term 'conduct' was understood by the drafters to refer to both acts and omissions, the latter generally regarded as failures to act.[172] This

[166] 'UN Diplomatic Conference of Plenipotentiaries on the Establishment of an International Criminal Court' (Vol III) 33.

[167] ibid.

[168] ibid 251.

[169] ibid 253.

[170] ibid 255, Art 28 Actus reus (act and/or omission) (Deleted), fn 60.

[171] See 'UN Diplomatic Conference of Plenipotentiaries on the Establishment of an International Criminal Court' (Vol III) 151, Art 28 (Deleted). However, a reference to 'acts or omissions' can be found at page 173 of the report, 'Art 90 Other forms of cooperation'.

[172] E Mayr, 'International Criminal Law, Causation, and Responsibility' (2014) 14 *International Criminal Law Review* 855, 859.

approach is confirmed by some provisions of the Rome Statute.[173] Therefore, the list of offences that could amount to international economic crimes may include both acts and omissions.

The Causal Link between Conduct and Harm

The Preparatory Committee inserted a third paragraph into draft Article 28 requiring a causal link between conduct and harm and stating that 'a person is only criminally responsible under this Statute for committing a crime if the harm required for the commission of the crime is caused by and [accountable] [attributable] to his or her act or omission'.[174]

The delegations could not agree on this third paragraph either.[175] The idea that a provision on causation was unnecessary was supported by the Committee of the Whole, and this issue was no longer raised in the subsequent negotiations of the Rome Statute.[176] Nonetheless, since the purpose of causation is to attribute criminal liability for the harm produced by a conduct to its perpetrator,[177] it is necessary to establish causation only in 'harm-type crimes'[178] and not in mere 'conduct crimes'.[179] As for how the causation is to be established with respect to 'harm-type' crimes, this varies according to the theories of causation that are applied. Although several theories of causation have been developed at national

[173] For instance, Art 93 of the Rome Statute, listing forms of cooperation between the States Parties and the Court; and Art 28, describing a peculiar form of omission, namely the superior's failure to exercise control over the crimes of his or her subordinates. On the definition of the term 'conduct' as including 'acts and omissions' see Finnin, 'Mental Elements' 338 fn 64, citing A Cassese, *International Criminal Law*, 2nd edn (Oxford University Press, 2008) 55: '[t]he conduct is described by the international rule that imposes a certain behavior [...] and therefore criminalizes any act or omission contrary to such a rule'. See also Von Hebel and Kelt, 'What Are the Elements of Crimes?' 14.

[174] 'UN Diplomatic Conference of Plenipotentiaries on the Establishment of an International Criminal Court' (Vol III) 33, Art 28 para 3.

[175] ibid fn 84, noting that some delegations believed a provision on causation was not necessary.

[176] 'UN Diplomatic Conference of Plenipotentiaries on the Establishment of an International Criminal Court' (Vol III) 251, Art 28.

[177] Mayr, 'International Criminal Law' 856. See also J Gadirov, 'Causal Responsibility in International Criminal Law' (2015) 15 *International Criminal Law Review* 970, 971; Cupido, 'Causation in International Crimes Cases' 2.

[178] Examples of 'harm-type crimes' are the acts of genocide of 'killing' and 'causing serious bodily or mental harm to members of the group', as well as the crime against humanity of 'murder'. On the need to establish causation in 'harm-type' crimes see S Mir Puig, *Derecho penal. Parte general*, 10th edn (Reppertor, 2016) 246. It is worth noting that it is controversial whether it is possible to establish a causality link between an omission and the harm.

[179] Not only acts but also some types of omissions can constitute 'conduct crimes'. According to some scholars, even 'abstract risk crimes' (*abstrakte Gefährdungsdelikte*) do not require the causation of harm; see PK Ryu, 'Causation in Criminal Law' (1958) 106 *University of Pennsylvania Law Review* 773, 802. An example of 'conduct crime' in the Rome Statute is the act of genocide of 'imposing measures intended to prevent births within the group', where the mere imposition of such measures constitutes a crime, regardless of the harm caused to the members of the targeted group. On the non-relevance of causation for conduct crimes see GP Fletcher, *Basic Concepts of Criminal Law* (Oxford University Press, 1998) 60–61. On the concerns raised by the category of 'conduct crimes' see Mayr, 'International Criminal Law' 860–861.

level, only a few of them have been imported into international criminal law.[180] Despite the lack of a comprehensive jurisprudential debate on causation in international criminal law,[181] some scholars have reflected on the most challenging questions that arise in this field.[182]

Cupido identified three characteristics of international crimes that can make it difficult to establish a causal link between an act or omission and its harmful consequences: first, the context in which international crimes are perpetrated, characterised by widespread and systematic violence;[183] secondly, the collective nature of international crimes and the fact that they committed at different levels; and thirdly, the remoteness of the masterminds, who are usually political and military leaders, physically distant from the crime scene.[184] These features constitute a first filter for selecting theories of causation applicable to international crimes.

A second filter is provided by the ad hoc circumstances of each case, which means that a flexible and tailored approach to causation should prevail in international criminal law.[185] Although consistency is essential, it should be possible to differentiate legal responses when necessary. In this sense, international criminal law has been the perfect scapegoat for testing the transition from a unified approach to a diversified and more flexible approach to causation.

Over the years, international criminal law tribunals have gradually moved away from a strict application of empirical causation theories, which allows determining whether the defendant's conduct caused harm in factual terms, toward the safer ground of theories of normative causation and objective imputation.[186] This does not mean that empirical theories have become irrelevant and inapplicable in international criminal law. In cases of liability for direct perpetration and co-perpetration, the so-called theory of the equivalence (*Äquivalenztheorie*) allows a clear connection to be established between the harm and all its *sine qua non* conditions.[187] However, as has been correctly argued, the focus on

[180] In international criminal law, the terms 'causation' and 'causality' are used interchangeably, see Cupido, 'Causation in International Crimes Cases' 2, fn 2. For an overview of traditional causation theories developed in the US and German criminal law and influential in international criminal law see Cupido, 'Causation in International Crimes Cases' 9–14, 24–31.

[181] Cupido concludes that the ICC jurisprudence has not yet formulated a theory of causation, nor a definition of what causality means; see Cupido, 'Causation in International Crimes Cases' 6.

[182] Among them are Cupido, 'Causation in International Crimes Cases'; Stewart, 'Overdetermined Atrocities'; Gadirov, 'Causal Responsibility'.

[183] The difficulty of establishing a link between the crimes charged and the context in which they were committed is evident in the US Military Tribunal, 'The Flick case', Vol VI, Trials of War Criminals before the Nuremberg Military Tribunals under Control Council Law No. 10 (October 1946–April 1949) 1207, referring to Count 2, plunder as a war crime.

[184] Cupido, 'Causation in International Crimes Cases' 3–4. See, for instance, 'The Flick Case' 1199, referring to Count 1, slave labour as war crime and crime against humanity.

[185] This tailored approach was already used at Nuremberg; see 'The Flick Case' 1208 and 1212.

[186] Cupido, 'Causation in International Crimes Cases' 31.

[187] ibid 26; Mir Puig, *Derecho penal* 248.

empirical causality in international criminal law raises challenges.[188] These challenges stem both from the complexity of the aforementioned characteristics of international crimes and from a problem of overdetermination inherent in the theory of the equivalence: the principle that any conduct necessary to cause harm should be considered a *conditio sine qua non* could lead to overdetermination or over-selection of the number of causal contributions.[189] The difficulties raised by the theory of the equivalence are evident in the above-mentioned subsequent Nuremberg proceedings, where the judges ultimately excluded the sale and supply of chemicals, weapons, and ovens, from the list of *sine qua non* conditions that caused harm, thereby restricting the scope of such conditions to acts carried out by direct material perpetrators.

Therefore, in many cases involving international crimes, normative theories of causation have been used to limit the scope of the empirical chain to legally relevant causal contributions.[190] These theories appraise only those facts that contribute to the commission of a crime according to the purposes of criminal law – hence the name 'normative' theories. This allows the weak empirical link between the harm caused and the accused's conduct to be compensated by strong normative arguments in favor of attribution.[191] In other words, what matters is the accused's normative criminal involvement[192] in the context in which the crimes charged were committed. This approach was adopted in the *Auschwitz* cases against Nazi concentration camps guards, where the German judges emphasised the institutional role of the accused, who were part of 'an organised bureaucratic system (a concentration camp) that was specifically designed for exterminating Jews. Anyone who worked within this system, facilitated the mass extermination, and can therefore be considered an aider of all crimes committed within the system'.[193] The judges thus found that there was a link, not factual but normative, between the conduct attributed to the

[188] Cupido, 'Causation in International Crimes Cases' 5.

[189] ibid. On the problem of overdetermination in the theory of the equivalence see also Mir Puig, *Derecho penal*, 248, 254. As an alternative to solve the problem of overdetermination inherent in the theory of the equivalence, the NESS-test (acronym for 'necessary element of a sufficient set' of conditions) is a theory according to which a causal contribution is a necessary element because it is essential to complete a set of conditions that are 'jointly sufficient' to produce the consequence, see Cupido, 'Causation in International Crimes Cases' 9.

[190] According to the 'relevance' theory, the conduct that constitutes the cause of the harm can be determined by looking at the relevant norm designed to prevent the type of harm that occurred. In contrast, the '*causa proxima*' theory considers the causal contribution closest to the harm as the cause of harm. The theory of 'adequate causation' is another normative theory that allows the conduct that appears adequate or suitable to produce harm to be qualified as the cause of harm, based on general human experience. See Mir Puig, *Derecho penal*, 255 and 257; Cupido, 'Causation in International Crimes Cases' 36.

[191] Cupido, 'Causation in International Crimes Cases' 22–23.

[192] ibid.

[193] ibid 14.

guards and the international crimes perpetrated within and because of the 'system'.[194]

Another attractive way to narrow down the almost endless list of empirical causal contributions has been to develop the notion of risk-taking. From the Greek word *rhizikon*, over the years this term has taken on the meaning of 'hazard', understood as the possibility of suffering harm depending on a series of circumstances that may or may not be foreseeable.[195] In our postmodern globalised society, risks are an integral part of life as they are taken on a daily basis in various of areas, although only some of them lead to harmful consequences.[196]

The notion of 'risk' underlies the criminal theory of objective imputation, which consists of a two-step test: first, the assessment of whether a conduct created or increased an unlawful risk; second, the assessment of whether the harm caused is the realisation of the unlawful risk created or increased by that conduct. Thus, what really matters for the purposes of this theory is to clearly distinguish between socially acceptable risks and unlawful risks that may give rise to criminal liability. The concept of 'unlawful risk' excludes risks that are perceived as the negative side of a lawful conduct, such as risks that are socially and generally accepted in sport, transportation, and business. Similarly, risks arising from circumstances that could not have been objectively foreseen by the person engaging in the conduct and over which that person could not exercise any control or influence, are not unlawful.

As far as financial and business risks are concerned, it is commonly acknowledged that these are socially acceptable risks because they are inherent in the hardly predictable course of economic activities. Nonetheless, there has been an increasing proliferation of economic risks that can have a global negative impact. The main trend in response to this, both within and outside the financial and business sector, has been to trivialise the very concept of risk and regard it as *le mal necessaire* to achieve certain benefits. However, a fundamental principle of risk management is that while risks cannot be eliminated, they can be controlled, that is, there should always be a threshold above which even financial and business risks are to be considered excessive, socially undesirable, and unlawful.[197] Today, it is essential that this threshold protects

[194] See L Schuldt, 'Decision Review: German Federal Court of Justice Approves Conviction of Ex- Auschwitz Officer' German-Southeast Asian Center of Excellence for Public Policy and Good Governance (*CPG*, 1 November 2016) https://cpg-online.de/decision-review-german-federal-court-of-justice-approves-conviction-of-ex-auschwitz-officer/.

[195] Dizionario Treccani, 'Rìschio' www.treccani.it/vocabolario/rischio/.

[196] On the significance of risk in contemporary society see U Beck, *La société du risque. Sur la voie d'une autre modernité* (Éditions Flammarion, 2008). See also M Delmas-Marty, *Libertés et sûreté dans un monde dangereux*, (Édition du Seuil, 2010).

[197] X Heude, 'La notion de risque dans une approche éthique de la finance. Conditions et implications' (2006) 1 *Finance Bien Commun* 47, 52. See also KJ Engemann, 'Developments in Risk Security' in KJ Engemann (ed), *The Routledge Companion to Risk, Crisis and Security in Business* (Routledge, 2018) 1, 11.

fundamental human rights. The advantage of a human rights-sensitive standard of 'risk unlawfulness' is that it would be globally applicable: instead of relying solely on national laws, which may be absent or circumvented, economic actors might rely on international human rights laws and principles to assess the lawfulness of economic and financial risks.[198]

In some of the cases discussed in this book, the acts and omissions allegedly committed by the perpetrators created or increased financial risks – for instance, the *Haarde* case – or business risks – for instance, the *Volkswagen* and the *Chiquita* case – which led to significant human rights violations.[199] The application of the theory of objective imputation to situations in which a conduct created or increased an economic risk that entails a violation of fundamental human rights could be particularly useful in attributing international criminal responsibility to public or private economic actors, without running into the difficulties posed by the *conditio sine qua non* theory.

Critical Issues Related to the Mens Rea *Element*

There is not a single, generally accepted doctrine on *mens rea* in international criminal law.[200] It was Article 29 of the Statute drafted by the Preparatory Committee – which corresponds to the current Article 30 – that established for the first time in the history of international criminal law a standard of subjective element for crimes within the jurisdiction of the ICC.[201] The first paragraph of Article 29 poses a rule and an exception. According to the rule, the material elements of a crime, which represent the 'external side of criminal conduct',[202] need to be covered by 'intent and knowledge' in order for them to be fully internalised by the perpetrator. However, this rule applies 'unless otherwise provided'. The Preparatory Committee did not clarify the meaning of this exception, nor whether its source should be limited to the Rome Statute or extend to other legislative instruments.[203]

[198] The United Nations Environment Programme (UNEP) Finance Initiative has highlighted the main human rights risks and issues that can be faced by the financial sector and provided some guidelines to control them. See 'Human Rights Guidance Tool for the Financial Sector' (*UNEP Finance Initiative*, 24 January 2025) https://www.unepfi.org/themes/social-issues/unep-fis-human-rights-toolkit-a-game-changer-for-financial-institutions/.

[199] The industrialists prosecuted at Nuremberg had also taken unlawful business risks involving serious human rights violations. An example of unlawful economic risk can be found in 'The Flick Case' 101, referring to Flick's act of financing the Himmler's Circle of Friends.

[200] Marchuk, *The Fundamental Concept of Crime* 113.

[201] Finnin, 'Mental Elements' 325.

[202] ibid 337.

[203] Regarding the determination of the source of the exception posed by Art 30 of the Rome Statute, different approaches have been elaborated and endorsed in the literature. For a comprehensive overview of this doctrinal debate see Finnin, 'Mental Elements' 351–355; see also G Werle and F Jessberger, '"Unless Otherwise Provided": Article 30 of the ICC Statute and the Mental Element of Crimes under International Criminal Law' (2005) 3 *Journal of International Criminal Justice* 35, 45.

The second and third paragraphs of draft Article 29 describe the concepts of 'intent' and 'knowledge' respectively, and their text was translated with minor amendments into the current Article 30 of the Rome Statute. This provision still contains some grey areas that have posed interpretative difficulties for both judges and scholars, since the drafters tried to condense into a single article various notions of *mens rea* from different legal systems.[204] Among the main peculiarities of Article 30 are, first, the narrow scope of the *mens rea* standard and, second, the complexity of the 'element analysis' approach underlying its application.[205] Regarding the first peculiarity, the term 'intent and knowledge' indicates that, by definition, only crimes that reach a high *mens rea* threshold are eligible as international crimes. The apparent clarity of this rule is complicated by the conjunction 'and', which the Preparatory Committee justified by arguing that it is necessary to show that some degree of both cognitive and volitional components are present in the minds of the perpetrators.[206] However, this does not mean that every material element of a crime must be committed with both intent and knowledge.[207]

As regards the second peculiarity of Article 30, the second and third paragraphs of that provision suggest that the drafters opted for an 'element analysis' approach instead of a 'crime analysis' approach to determine the *mens rea* required for the offences underlying international crimes.[208] In other words, for each of the three types of material elements identified in Article 30 – conduct (*i*), consequence (*ii*), and circumstance (*iii*)[209] – a specific mental element is required:

(*i*) The second paragraph specifies that the material element of conduct and consequence must be committed with *dolus directus in the first degree* or, in common law terms, with *direct intent*.[210]

[204] H Von Hebel and M Kelt, 'General Principles of Criminal Law and the Elements of Crimes' in RS Lee (ed), *The International Criminal Court: Elements of Crimes and Rules of Procedure and Evidence* (Transnational Publishers, 2001) cited in Finnin, 'Mental Elements' 327.

[205] CF Stuckenberg, 'Problems of "Subjective Imputation" in Domestic and International Criminal Law' (2014) 12 *Journal of International Criminal Justice* 311, 316.

[206] 'UN Diplomatic Conference of Plenipotentiaries on the Establishment of an International Criminal Court' (Vol III) 33, Art 29. See Finnin, 'Mental Elements' 328 and 336, stating that each gradation of *mens rea* has two components: a cognitive component (the element of awareness) and a volitional component (the element of desire), and what distinguishes different *mens rea* standards is the level of each component. See also *Prosecutor v Bemba Gombo* (Decision pursuant to Article 61(7)(a) and (b) of the Rome Statute on the Charges of the Prosecutor Against Jean-Pierre Bemba Gombo) ICC-01/05-01/08-424 (15 June 2009) para 357.

[207] Finnin, 'Mental Elements' 337.

[208] ibid. See also Von Hebel and Kelt, 'What Are the Elements of Crimes?' 14; Badar, 'The Mental Element' 476; GP Fletcher, *The Grammar of Criminal Law: American, Comparative, and International,* Vol 1: Foundations (Oxford University Press, 2007) 43. The 'element analysis' approach is also mentioned in the General Introduction, point 2 of the Elements of Crimes.

[209] For a comprehensive definition of the three types of material elements, see Finnin, 'Mental Elements' 338.

[210] 'In relation to conduct, that person *means to engage in the conduct*'; 'in relation to a consequence, that person *means to cause that consequence*' (emphasis added). For a comprehensive comparison between civil law and common law *mens rea* standards see Finnin, 'Mental Elements' 328–336.

(*ii*) However, a consequence can also be committed with 'awareness that it will occur in the ordinary course of events', that is, with some certainty or high probability that consequences will result from a conduct. This *mens rea* corresponds to the civil law notion of *dolus directus in the second degree*, or *oblique intent* in common law terms.[211]

(*iii*) Lastly, the third paragraph of Article 30 provides another gradation of intent for the circumstance element. In this respect, knowledge or 'awareness that a circumstance exists' is required. This *mens rea* standard is characterised by a high cognitive component that compensates for the lower volitional component.[212]

Delimiting the Scope of 'Intent and Knowledge'

There is no consensus in the literature and case law on the question of whether the concepts of 'intent and knowledge' can be interpreted broadly to include lower categories of *mens rea*. First, the phrase '[…] will occur in the ordinary course of events', used to establish one of the two *mens rea* standards for consequences, has prompted scholars and judges to wonder whether this also encompasses the concept of *dolus eventualis*. This type of intent is used in civil law systems to define a mental element that 'exists when a person is aware that a material element included in the definition of a crime may result from his conduct and "reconciles himself" or "makes peace" with this fact'.[213] In other words, the person knows that their conduct may lead to a harmful consequence and, nonetheless, accepts this result. The ICTY recognised this mental element as an appropriate *mens rea* standard for international crimes.[214] On the other hand, the ICC has not adopted a clear position on this matter.[215]

A second interpretive challenge stems from the *mens rea* standard of 'awareness that a circumstance exists', which raises the question of whether the common law notion of wilful blindness is included. A person is wilfully blind when he or she senses that a circumstance exists but deliberately closes his or her eyes to avoid any actual knowledge.[216] It has been generally accepted

[211] 'In relation to a consequence, that person […] is *aware that it will occur in the ordinary course of events*', see Finnin, 'Mental Elements' 344.

[212] ibid 340, specifically, see Table 2 at 341.

[213] ibid 334. See also Werle and Jessberger, '"Unless Otherwise Provided"' 51–52. See RS Aitala, *Diritto Internazionale Penale* (Le Monnier Università, 2021) 71.

[214] See eg *Prosecutor v Stakić* (Trial Judgment) IT-97-24-T (31 July 2003) paras 587, 616, 642; *Prosecutor v Blaškić* (Appeals Judgment) IT-95-14-A (29 July 2004) para 42. See also Stuckenberg, 'Problems of "Subjective Imputation"' 315.

[215] On the ICC jurisprudential debate on the matter, see Finnin, 'Mental Elements' 348. Pre-Trial Chamber I interpreted 'intent' as encompassing the concept of *dolus eventualis* in *Prosecutor v Lubanga Dyilo* (Decision on the Confirmation of the Charges) para 352. However, in the *Bemba* case, Pre-Trial Chamber II took the opposite position, holding that *dolus eventualis* is not covered by Article 30, see *Prosecutor v Bemba Gombo* (Decision pursuant to Article 61(7)(a) and (b) of the Rome Statute on the Charges of the Prosecutor Against Jean-Pierre Bemba Gombo) paras 362–363.

[216] Finnin, 'Mental Elements' 350.

that knowledge under Article 30 can be interpreted to include not only actual knowledge but also wilful blindness, strictly meant as a virtual certainty or high probability that a circumstance exists.[217] This approach is also in line with the jurisprudence of the ad hoc criminal tribunals[218] and the military criminal tribunals.[219]

The third challenging issue arising from the default rule in Article 30, concerns the question of whether recklessness is an appropriate mental element to cover 'consequences' and 'circumstances' of an offence. This issue was extensively debated by the Preparatory Committee, which included a fourth paragraph on recklessness in the draft Article 29. However, the Working Group, instructed by the Committee of the Whole to review some provisions, decided to delete this paragraph. The deletion was approved by the Committee of the Whole on the ground that the concept of 'recklessness did not appear in the provisions defining crimes in the final text of the Statute; thus, adopting a definition of recklessness would have made no sense'.[220]

The most thought-provoking part of the deleted paragraph concerned the definition of recklessness, according to which a reckless person is aware 'of a risk that the circumstance exists or that the consequence will occur' (i) and 'of the highly unreasonable nature of the risk' (ii); moreover, the person is indifferent to the possibility that the circumstance exists or the consequence will occur (iii). This description reflected the common law definition of subjective recklessness as 'conscious risk-taking'[221] and it would have helped to distinguish this mental element from *dolus eventualis*. Although both *mens rea* elements are based on the defendant's ability to foresee a circumstance or consequence of an offence,[222] the person acting with *dolus eventualis* accepts the possibility of this prediction coming true and acts consciously despite this prediction, regardless of the collateral result, whereas a reckless person is indifferent to both the prediction and the result. Yet, the lack of any volitional component in the concept of recklessness was emphasised by the ICTY Trial Chamber[223] and, to date, the ICC has not interpreted Article 30 to include recklessness.[224]

[217] ibid 351; Badar, 'The Mental Element' 496.

[218] See Marchuk, *The Fundamental Concept of Crime* 123.

[219] See the 'Funk case', IMT, *Trial of the Major War Criminals* 306. As already mentioned in Chapter 2, the IMT held that the accused 'either knew what was being received or was *deliberately closing his eyes* to what was being done' (emphasis added).

[220] Werle and Jessberger, '"Unless Otherwise Provided"' 52.

[221] Finnin, 'Mental Elements' 334.

[222] Marchuk, *The Fundamental Concept of Crime* 119.

[223] ME Badar, 'Drawing the Boundaries of Mens Rea in the Jurisprudence of the International Criminal Tribunal for the Former Yugoslavia' (2006) 6 *International Criminal Law Review* 313, 332, citing *Prosecutor v Stakić* (Trial Judgment) para 642. Some scholars disagreed with the position endorsed by the Trial Chamber in the *Stakić* case, pointing out that the volitional component in recklessness is not completely absent but only lower than that of *dolus eventualis*, see Finnin, 'Mental Elements' 335 fn 52.

[224] This was the position adopted by the Pre-Trial Chamber I in the *Prosecutor v Lubanga Dyilo* (Decision on the Confirmation of the Charges) para 355 fn 438: 'The concept of recklessness

The last aspect to consider in relation to the definition of 'intent and knowledge' within the meaning of Article 30 of the Statute concerns the *mens rea* standard of 'negligence'. In a footnote to the fourth paragraph of draft Article 29, the Preparatory Committee briefly mentioned that 'there is no reason for rejecting the concept of commission of an offence also through negligence, in which case the offender shall be liable only when so prescribed by the Statute'.[225] The debate was not resumed by the Committee of the Whole as a logical consequence of the decision to delete the paragraph on recklessness. However, it would have been interesting to understand the position of the drafters in this respect, considering that the ICTY had rejected negligence as a sufficient mental element,[226] but the ICTR had made a distinction between ordinary and gross negligence, accepting the latter as an adequate standard of *mens rea*.[227]

The 'Unless Otherwise Provided' Exception

The previous section has shown that the adoption of a broad interpretation of 'intent and knowledge' raises a series of debatable issues, which would risk undermining the principle of strict construction.[228] On the other hand, excluding standards of *mens rea* that do not fall within the parameters of 'intent and knowledge' could be problematic with respect to certain forms of economic crimes. Although many international definitions of economic crimes identify 'intent' as the requisite mental element,[229] other crimes may require a different standard of *mens rea* that includes recklessness and gross negligence. For instance, some definitions of offences of economic significance committed

requires only that the perpetrator be aware of the existence of a risk that the objective elements of the crime may result from his or her actions or omissions, but does not require that he or she reconcile himself or herself with the result [...] it is not part of the concept of intention'. These arguments were concluded citing GP Fletcher, *Rethinking Criminal Law*, 443, whereby recklessness is a form of *culpa* and not intention. The same opinion was reiterated in *Prosecutor v Bemba Gombo* (Decision pursuant to Article 61(7)(a) and (b) of the Rome Statute on the Charges of the Prosecutor Against Jean-Pierre Bemba Gombo) para 360.

[225] 'UN Diplomatic Conference of Plenipotentiaries on the Establishment of an International Criminal Court' (Vol III) 33, Art 29 fn 87.

[226] Werle and Jessberger, '"Unless Otherwise Provided"' 54, noting that the Trial Chamber in *Prosecutor v Stakić* (Trial Judgment) para 642, 'emphasised that negligence on the part of the perpetrator does not suffice to meet the requirements of the mental element of the war crime of murder. The Chamber set the same standard – *dolus eventualis* as a minimum requirement – for the crime against humanity of extermination'.

[227] *Prosecutor v Kayishema and Ruzindana* (Trial Judgment) para 146; Werle and Jessberger, '"Unless Otherwise Provided"' 54.

[228] ibid 42; Finnin, 'Mental Elements' 346.

[229] See, for instance, the UNCAC, where the crimes defined from Art 15 to Art 25 must be 'committed intentionally'. The same applies to the criminal offences defined in Art 3 of the UN Convention against Illicit Traffic in Narcotic Drugs and Psychotropic Substances Financing Terrorism (Vienna, 19 December 1988) and for the criminal offences defined in Arts 6 and 8 of the UN Convention against Transnational Organised Crime and the Protocols (Palermo, 15 November 2000) (Palermo Convention).

against natural resources require a standard of *mens rea* that is lower than 'intent and knowledge'.[230]

The 'unless otherwise provided' clause in Article 30 would allow such offenses to be prosecuted as international crimes. The only requirement for this to be possible is that the provisions of the Rome Statute, the Elements of Crimes or customary international law explicitly provide for these crimes a type of *mens rea* that is different from 'intent and knowledge'.[231] This approach would be consistent with the requirements of *lex certa* and *lex stricta* of the principle of legality as interpreted above.[232]

DRAFTING A DEFINITION OF INTERNATIONAL ECONOMIC CRIMES

At this point, the coordinates have been drawn up for a provisional definition of international economic crimes that complies with the limits set by the principle of legality in international criminal law. An international economic crime can be defined as 'any act or omission committed as part of a systemic attack directed against the public wealth of a country by state, state-like or non-state actors with knowledge of the attack or gross negligence'. According to this definition, the gravity of international economic crimes is reflected in the following four contextual elements:

(i) *First*, there must be an attack directed against the public wealth of a country: this means that a single crime is not sufficient, but it is essential for multiple acts or omissions to be committed primarily against the economic or natural wealth of a country, so as to threaten fundamental international values such as international peace and security, the right to self-determination, and individual human rights and fundamental freedoms.
(ii) *Second*, the attack against the public wealth of a country must be systemic, which means that it must be conducted in accordance with a policy rooted in the system and which, as in a vicious circle, perpetuates the system.
(iii) *Third*, the structures behind the development and implementation of the policy underlying the systemic attack may include state, state-like, and non-state actors, ie all those actors who have access to power and can abuse it.
(iv) *Fourth*, knowledge of the context and of the existence of a link between it and the acts or omissions perpetrated is required; alternatively, gross negligence regarding the existence of the attack is required.

[230] Art 3 of the Directive 2008/99/EC of the European Parliament and of the Council of 19 November 2008 on the Protection of the Environment through Criminal Law provides examples of environmental offences committed 'intentionally or with at least serious negligence'.

[231] This solution is supported by Werle and Jessberger, '"Unless Otherwise Provided"'54–55. On the need to adopt a holistic interpretation of Art 30 of the Rome Statute, see Aitala, *Diritto Internazionale Penale* 73–74.

[232] On customary international law as a legal basis for the crime of indigenous spoliation, see Kofele-Kale, *The International Law of Responsibility for Economic Crimes* 9, 79 et seq. and 113.

These *chapeau* elements would serve multiple purposes, the main one being the need to clearly distinguish ordinary economic crimes from international economic crimes. They would also serve a jurisdictional purpose, namely, to exclude purely accidental or isolated economic offences, however serious they may be, from the material scope of jurisdiction of supranational and national courts called upon to adjudicate those responsible for international economic crimes. Lastly, these elements partially overlap with the *chapeau* elements of crimes against humanity. Their similarity remains important in determining whether international economic crimes can be considered a subcategory of crimes against humanity or whether they should constitute a separate category of international crimes.[233]

With respect to the offences that can rise to the status of international economic crimes, compiling an exhaustive list of crimes of economic significance is beyond the scope of this investigation, the main purpose of which was to outline the general standards of *actus reus* and *mens rea* required by the most recent written expression of international criminal law, that is the Rome Statute. Based on these considerations, it can be concluded that:

(i) The offences underlying international economic crimes should be prohibited by international conventions or customary international law.[234] In other words, they should be crimes whose prohibition is subject to general agreement by the international community.

(ii) They should be crimes of economic significance. This means that the list of offences is not limited to traditional economic offences committed against the economic wealth of a country but may also include environmental crimes perpetrated against the natural wealth of a country.

(iii) Regarding the *actus reus* standard, the conduct of these offences can be an act, an omission, or a combination of both. Furthermore, both 'conduct crimes' and 'harm-type crimes' may be included in the list of offences. With respect to the latter category, theories of empirical causation may help establish a link between the conduct of direct perpetrators or co-perpetrators and the harm. However, when this is not possible or recommended, judges should not refrain from applying normative causation theories, as well as the theory of objective imputation. As mentioned above, this would be in line with the established practice of international criminal law courts and tribunals and would not encroach upon the respect of the principle of strict construction of criminal law or the principle of foreseeability. In particular, the theory of objective imputation could make it possible to establish a link between the acts and omissions of high-level economic actors, on the one hand, and the creation or increase of unlawful economic or financial risks involving violations of human rights, on the other hand.

(iv) The default standard of *mens rea* for these offences would be 'intent and knowledge', which can be legitimately interpreted as including *dolus eventualis*

[233] This issue will be further developed below in ch 5.

[234] For instance, corruption, financing of terrorism, money-laundering, fraud, environmental crimes are prohibited at international and regional level and criminalised at national level.

with respect to the consequences of conduct and wilful blindness with respect to circumstances. However, according to some scholars, lower *mens rea* standards, such as recklessness and negligence, should be considered appropriate only if expressly provided for in the Rome Statute, the Elements of Crimes, or any other treaty criminalising international economic crimes, or if they can be inferred from customary international norms.

As regards the name of the category of crimes in question, over the last years, several terms have been used in the literature to refer to serious economic crimes deserving of international classification. The term 'patrimonicide' coined by Kofele-Kale or the term 'economicide' coined by Zaffaroni are particularly attractive because of their symbolic and etymological reference to genocide, the 'crime of the crimes'.[235] Nonetheless, these terms could be subject to the same criticism levelled at the term 'ecocide' with respect to the lack of specific intent that characterises genocide.[236] Another term used as a synonym for patrimonicide is 'indigenous spoliation'. Yet, the word 'spoliation' can be confusing because its common meaning does not encompass the wide range of offences of economic significance that may constitute international economic crimes, nor does it adequately emphasise the international nature of such crimes. Lastly, Arenal Lora's use of the term 'economic crimes against humanity' refers only to economic crimes committed in the specific context of crimes against humanity – an attack primarily directed against a civilian population. Thus, at present, the term 'international economic crime' seems the most appropriate to define the main characteristics of the category of crimes discussed so far: *crimes* of *economic* significance that reach the gravity threshold of *international* crimes.

CONCLUDING REMARKS

This chapter has described the principle of legality as a necessary and indispensable tool for establishing the boundaries of the process of creation and interpretation of international criminal law. This principle is supposed to guide both the international community, in defining the concept of international economic crimes, and judges – whether in national courts, the ICC or other tribunals established for this purpose – in interpreting the rules that criminalise such offences.

This chapter goes on to suggest that the constituent elements of a concept of international economic crime can be defined in a manner consistent with the principle of legality and its corollaries. In line with the research findings outlined

[235] N Kofele-Kale, 'Patrimonicide: The International Economic Crime of Indigenous Spoliation' (1995) 28 *Vanderbilt Journal of Transnational Law* 45; ER Zaffaroni, '¿Por qué no un delito de economicidio?' (*La Tecla Eñe*, 2021) https://lateclaenerevista.com/por-que-no-un-delito-de-economicidio-por-e-raul-zaffaroni/.

[236] This criticism was levelled at the crime of 'ecocide', but could equally apply to 'patrimonicide', see M Karnavas, 'Ecocide: Environmental Crime of Crimes or Ill-Conceived Concept?' (*Opinio Juris*, 29 July 2021) http://opiniojuris.org/2021/07/29/ecocide-environmental-crime-of-crimes-or-ill-conceived-concept.

above, an accurate definition of the elements of this crime would allow respecting the *lex certa* corollary of the legality principle as well as the requirements of accessibility and foreseeability. Moreover, the idea of introducing a provision defining international economic crimes in the Rome Statute or in another treaty would be in line with the *lex scripta* corollary. However, this would not prevent judges from resorting to unwritten sources of law, such as general principles of law and customary international law,[237] to clarify the elements of the crime in accordance with the established practice of international criminal law courts and tribunals.[238] In sum, there is no reason to believe that the development of a concept of international economic crime would not be consistent with the most recent interpretation of the principle of legality provided by international criminal law courts and tribunals, in particular by the ICC.

A concept of international economic crime that respects the parameters of the principle of legality would also make it possible to overcome the criticism of 'over-criminalisation' often levelled when proposing to use (international) criminal law as a means of preventing unlawful conduct. In this case, the criticism of over-criminalisation would not stem from the fact of criminalising conduct that should not be considered a crime, considering that the concept of international economic crime would encompass wrongful conduct that causes international harm, but rather from the fact of over-broadly defining the concept of 'international crime'.[239] Thus, adhering to the principle of legality in creating and interpreting the concept of international economic crime could avoid any risk of over-criminalisation.

The time is ripe to take this step forward in international criminal law. In this sense, the provisional definition of international economic crimes set out above has symbolic significance. It should stimulate actors in the international community to reflect on the unjustified lack of international norms criminalising systemic economic crimes as international crimes. The non-violent nature of these offences should not discourage the international community from recognising their high criminal and criminogenic potential. As a matter of fact, these are among the most serious forms of international crime in contemporary society, in terms of their negative long-term impact on collective and individual values, including human rights and fundamental freedoms. Accordingly, the following chapter reflects on the possibility of including international economic crimes among the existing categories of international crimes so that their perpetrators can be held accountable in the international criminal justice system.

[237] Starr, 'Extraordinary Crimes'1306.
[238] Nicholson, 'Strengthening the Effectiveness' 672.
[239] See RA Duff, *The Realm of Criminal Law* (Oxford University Press, 2018) 1.

5

The Prosecution of International Economic Crimes in the Multilevel System of International Criminal Justice

THIS CHAPTER ADDRESSES the question of how the concept of international economic crime defined above can be prosecuted in the system of international criminal justice, which is an illustrative example of multilevel regulatory system that has progressively relied on interactions among national and international jurisdictions. Although national courts remain the core of this system, the ICC has played a key role in complementing the inertia of domestic authorities.

Therefore, the following section examines the role that the ICC could play in prosecuting serious economic crimes if domestic courts are unable or unwilling to do so, while the second section sheds light on additional or alternative solutions to the prosecution of international economic crimes before the ICC, which could be implemented at national, regional, and international levels.

THE ICC: A QUASI-DIRECT ENFORCEMENT SYSTEM FOR PROSECUTING INTERNATIONAL ECONOMIC CRIMES?

This section addresses the question of how crimes of economic significance committed in the context of a systemic attack directed against the public wealth of a country can be included among the categories of international crimes mentioned in Article 5 of the Rome Statute. Two potential ways of including international economic crimes in the Rome Statute are outlined, before discussing the main obstacles and opportunities that such inclusion may entail.

Possible Avenues for Prosecuting International Economic Crimes before the ICC

A limited debate on the possibility of introducing certain economically relevant conduct into the Rome Statute was conducted before and during the negotiations of the Rome Statute, but economic crimes were never considered.[1] In recent years, the ICC has had the opportunity to fill in this gap by expressing its position on the prosecution of crimes committed in Ecuador, where the representatives of the Texaco-Chevron company were allegedly involved in the perpetration of serious crimes of economic significance – through the harmful exploitation of oil exploration and extraction – and, as accessories, in murder, extermination and forced displacement as crimes against humanity. However, the OTP decided not to open any investigation into this situation on the grounds that the crimes allegedly committed did not fall under the jurisdiction of the ICC.[2] Another opportunity missed by the Court was the *Chiquita* case, in relation to which a communication was submitted to the OTP in 2015, alleging that officials working for Chiquita – found guilty of funding the AUC for almost a decade – should be held accountable under Article 25(3)(d)(ii) of the Rome Statute for their contribution to the commission of crimes against humanity committed by a paramilitary and terrorist organisation.[3] No investigation was launched in this regard either.

The general lack of interest in the international prosecution of serious economic offences is the result of both the decision of the drafters not to include any serious economic crimes in the Rome Statute and the decision of the OTP not to open any investigations in situations where such crimes are allegedly committed alongside other international crimes, such as crimes against humanity and war crimes. Nonetheless, there are three possible ways out of this impasse. The first option put forward by most scholars is to interpret existing categories of international crimes broadly to include international economic offences. An additional or alternative option would be to explicitly introduce international economic crimes as a separate category of international crimes. Lastly, the creation of a hybrid chamber within the ICC, dedicated exclusively to the prosecution of new contemporary threats to peace and security, has also been explored in the literature.

[1] See UN Diplomatic Conference of Plenipotentiaries on the Establishment of an International Criminal Court, Official Records, (15 June-17 July 1998) A/CONF.183/13 (Vol III) 240. Cuba proposed to refer to economic measures under the paragraph of 'other inhumane acts' as crimes against humanity: 'Crimes against humanity. Paragraph 1 (j). Other inhumane acts, such as *economic, financial and commercial blockades* intentionally causing great suffering or seriously injuring physical integrity or mental or physical health' (emphasis added).

[2] E Bernabé Toledo and P Fajardo Mendoza, 'Ecuadorian Claim before the International Criminal Court to Investigate Chevron's CEO' (*Business and Human Rights Resource Centre*, 23 October 2014) www.business-humanrights.org/en/latest-news/pdf-ecuadorian-claim-before-the-international-criminal-court-to-investigate-chevrons-ceo/; see also L Arenal Lora, *Crímenes económicos en derecho internacional: Propuesta de una nueva categoría de crímenes contra la humanidad* (Editorial Aranzadi, 2019) 116. For an analysis of the Texaco-Chevron case through the lens of the concept of the 'crime of maldevelopment', see ML Böhm, *The Crime of Maldevelopment: Economic Deregulation and Violence in the Global South* (Routledge, 2019) 78–87.

[3] See Colectivo de Abogados José Alvear Restrepo, Fédération Internationale des Ligues des Droits de l'Hommes (FIDH), and International Human Rights Clinic at Harvard Law School, 'The Contribution of Chiquita Corporate Officials to Crimes against Humanity in Colombia – Article 15 Communication to the International Criminal Court' (18 May 2017) https://www.refworld.org/reference/countryrep/ifhr/2017/en/116811.

Prosecuting International Economic Crimes under the Current Provisions of the Rome Statute

From the outset, the ICC judges were faced with the dual difficulty of interpreting a new legal instrument, the Rome Statute, and creating jurisprudence from scratch. Their role was facilitated by the existence of previous jurisprudence on international criminal law, stemming from the judgments of the Nuremberg and ad hoc criminal tribunals. However, although the Rome Statute was more innovative and detailed than the Nuremberg Charter and the statutes of the ad hoc tribunals, it was necessary for the judges to clarify certain issues and fill in its gaps, such as the use of generic terms in the provisions defining international crimes. Some scholars have called for an inclusive approach to legitimise an interpretation of international crimes that includes serious forms of economic crimes.

International Economic Crimes as Crimes against Humanity?

Arenal Lora stated that the importance of crimes against humanity 'is unquestionable to deal with the major challenges that, under international law, represent new threats for humanity'.[4] This statement can be supported by at least three reasons. First, crimes against humanity are the category that has undergone the most significant evolution over the years since the Nuremberg trials. Secondly, the list of offences that may constitute crimes against humanity – if their contextual elements are fulfilled – is not exhaustive as Article 7(1)(k) of the Rome Statute leaves open the possibility of including 'other inhumane acts'. Lastly, unlike other international crimes, crimes against humanity are the only category that allows for the punishment of acts that violate human rights of civilians in peacetime and not necessarily in a violent manner. For these reasons, scholars have seen in the concept of crimes against humanity an appropriate and valid legal basis for prosecuting international economic crimes before the ICC.[5]

Most arguments in favour of including serious economic crimes within the material jurisdiction of the ICC are based on Article 7(1)(k) of the Rome Statute. This provision has often been seen as a catch-all clause as it does not refer to a specific crime but outlines the category of 'other inhumane acts' that should be similar in character to other offences explicitly listed in Article 7. The attempt to extend the concept of 'other inhumane acts' to classify new threats to peace and security as crimes against humanity, thus avoiding amending the Rome Statute, is not a novelty. It has recently been proposed for environmental crimes on the

[4] Arenal Lora, *Crímenes económicos* 88.

[5] Similar proposals have been made with respect to environmental crimes, see inter alia, J Durney, 'Crafting a Standard: Environmental Crimes as Crimes against Humanity under the International Criminal Court' (2018) 24 *Hastings Environmental Law Journal* 413.

grounds that they are similar in character to other crimes against humanity and they meet the requirements set forth in Article 7(1)(k).[6]

Along these lines, Starr claimed that the crime of grand corruption, defined as 'the large-scale ransacking of public treasuries and resources by heads of States and their families and associates,'[7] can be likely prosecuted as a crime against humanity under the category of 'other inhumane acts' as it satisfies each of the elements listed in the Elements of Crimes.[8] In particular, she argued that a causal link can be established between acts of grand corruption and the suffering or serious injury caused to the civilian population, as it is not necessary for such suffering or injury to be the immediate consequence of criminal conduct.[9] Similarly, Bloom argued that 'deep-rooted corruption at high levels of government'[10] must be considered and punished under the heading of 'other inhumane acts' since it is capable of 'inflicting severe deprivation, impacting the fundamental necessities of life in a manner comparable to deportation, forcible transfer, and economic persecution'.[11] Bloom reported a case study involving the governor of Rivers State, Peter Odili, to demonstrate the inherent inhumanity of grand corruption in Nigeria.[12] This analysis was further developed by Roksandić Vidlička, who argued that Article 7(1)(k) of the Rome Statute is the 'most plausible solution for prosecuting serious economic crimes'.[13] However, unlike Starr, Roksandić Vidlička considers grand corruption (or kleptocracy) to be one of the most serious economic crimes, along with money-laundering, economic oppression, famine, and illegal enrichment, that can be implicitly inferred from 'other inhumane acts'.[14]

A more elaborate approach has been proposed by Arenal Lora, who recommended resorting to 'other inhumane acts' to prosecute economic crimes and argued that the benchmark the ICC should use to define their inhumanity includes international human rights law.[15] It is well established that international

[6] The conduct must 'intentionally' cause 'great suffering, or serious injury to body or to mental or physical health'.

[7] S Starr, 'Extraordinary Crimes at Ordinary Times: International Justice Beyond Crisis Situations' (2007) 101 *Northwestern University Law Review* 1257, 1281.

[8] ibid 1299–1300.

[9] ibid 1301.

[10] B Bloom, 'Criminalizing Kleptocracy: The ICC as a Viable Tool in the Fight against Grand Corruption' (2014) 29 *American University International Law Review* 627, 633.

[11] ibid 656.

[12] ibid 659.

[13] S Roksandić Vidlička, *Prosecuting Serious Economic Crimes as International Crimes – a New Mandate for the ICC?*, Research Series of the Max Planck Institute for Foreign and International Criminal Law Series BC: Publications of the Max Planck Partner Group for Balkan Criminology 2 (Duncker & Humblot, 2017) 427.

[14] ibid.

[15] Arenal Lora, *Crímenes económicos* 20, 148, 150–151. To elaborate her approach, Arenal Lora referred to L Benería and C Sarasúa, 'Delitos y crímenes económicos contra la humanidad' (2011) 12 *Revista de economía crítica* 156 and by J Torres in 'Crímenes económicos contra la humanidad' (*Sistema Digital*, 27 May 2013). In *Prosecutor v Katanga and Chui* (Decision on the Confirmation of Charges) ICC-01/04-01/07-717 (30 September 2008) para 448, Pre-trial Chamber I of the ICC

crimes, including 'other inhumane acts', can overlap not only with violations of civil and political human rights but also with violations of economic, social and cultural human rights.[16] Considering that systemic economic crimes affect the vital foundations of society and undermine the standard of living and other economic, social and cultural rights of people, these crimes can be classified as inhuman acts.

Arenal Lora further argues that not only grand corruption and financial speculation, but also environmental crimes and policies that have an impact on the economy of a country, can fall under the definition of 'other inhumane acts'.[17] Although, from a moral standpoint, this position is undoubtedly understandable, it is less convincing from a legal point of view. Elevating the policies of States and financial institutions to the level of crimes would be problematic for at least two reasons: on the one hand, it would mean making demagogic use of criminal law; on the other, it would not be in line with the principle of legality, according to which the list of 'crimes against humanity' includes 'crimes'. Moreover, criminalising public and private financial policies would likely have a considerable chilling effect on the exercise of fundamental public and private prerogatives, which in some cases could be arguably seen as illegitimate from a constitutional law perspective.

International crimes can be committed pursuant to or in furtherance of a policy, but policies are not crimes in themselves, unless the elements of a 'policy-crime' have been previously and clearly specified in such a way as to meet the requirements of accessibility and foreseeability of the law. An illustrative example is the crime of genocide, which contains two 'policy-crimes', namely the act of inflicting on the targeted group conditions of life calculated to bring about its physical destruction in whole or in part, and the imposition of measures intended to prevent births within the group. In both cases, the components of these offences are clearly defined in the Elements of Crime and are foreseeable. Thus, if economic and financial policies adopted by States or financial institutions were to be criminalised, a similar approach should be adopted. This

considered that 'in accordance with article 7(1)(k) of the Statute and the principle of nullum crimen sine lege pursuant to article 22 of the Statute, *inhumane acts are to be considered as serious violations of international customary law and the basic rights pertaining to human beings, drawn from the norms of international human rights law*, which are of a similar nature and gravity to the acts referred to in article 7(1) of the Statute' (emphasis added). For the list of international human rights law instruments that can serve as a parameter, see *Prosecutor v Kupreškić et al* (Trial Judgment) IT-95-16-T (14 January 2000) para 566.

[16] On the relevance of economic, social, and cultural human rights in international criminal law see E Schmid, *Taking Economic, Social and Cultural Rights Seriously in International Criminal Law* (Cambridge University Press, 2015) and SI Skogly, 'Crimes against Humanity-Revisited: Is There a Role for Economic and Social Rights?' (2001) 5 *The International Journal of Human Rights* 58.

[17] Arenal Lora, *Crímenes económicos* 111–113, 125. Among the conduct that constitute economic crimes against humanity, Arenal Lora includes the policies – eg economic programs, price changes – adopted by the International Military Fund. A similar proposal was elaborated by ER Zaffaroni, '¿Por qué no un delito de economicidio?' (*La Tecla Eñe*, 2021) https://lateclaenerevista.com/por-que-no-un-delito-de-economicidio-por-e-raul-zaffaroni/.

approach was considered in the drafting of the crime of 'economic oppression', which was clearly defined in its elements and classified as an 'other inhumane act'.[18]

In conclusion, Article 7(1)(k) of the Rome Statute can no longer be conceived as a catch all provision, since the Statute, the Elements of Crimes and the jurisprudence of the ICC have defined the constituent elements of this subcategory of crimes against humanity.[19] This has limited the margin of interpretation available to the judges. Nevertheless, this provision still raises interpretative and conceptual questions. First, the term 'act' would seem to exclude economic crimes committed through omissions by high-level actors having a legal duty to act. However, on this point, there is consistent case law interpreting the term 'act' as including 'omission'.[20]

Secondly, the question arises as to whether the adjective 'inhumane' can be used to describe not only the suffering inflicted by psycho-physical harm but also socio-economic harm. Although the literature advocates a broad interpretation of this term, the practice of international criminal law tribunals has mainly considered serious physical and mental harm to civilians as inhumane,[21] taking a position on the inhumanity of acts causing socio-economic harm and suffering only with regard to the crime of forced marriage.[22] This may be related to the strict interpretation of the concept of 'crisis' that has prevailed in international

[18] Davidsson defines economic oppression as those 'deliberate measures adopted with the intent or knowledge that they will subject a civilian population to inhumane conditions of existence of perpetuate such conditions', see E Davidsson, 'Economic Oppression as an International Wrong or as Crime against Humanity' (2005) 23 *Netherlands Quarterly of Human Rights* 173, 185.

[19] See *Prosecutor v Katanga and Chui* (Decision on the Confirmation of Charges) ICC-01/04-01/07-717 (30 September 2008) para 450, where the Chamber noted that 'the Statute has given to 'other inhumane acts' a different scope than its antecedents like the Nuremberg Charter and the ICTR and ICTY Statutes. *The latter conceived 'other inhumane acts' as a 'catch all provision'*, leaving a broad margin for the jurisprudence to determine its limits. In contrast, *the Rome Statute contains certain limitations*, as regards to the action constituting an inhumane act and the consequence required as a result of that action' (emphasis added).

[20] See, inter alia, *Prosecutor v Kordić and Čerkez* (Appeals Judgment) IT-95-1472-A (17 December 2004) para 117: '[…] the suffering must be the result of an act or omission of the accused or his subordinate […]'.

[21] This is due to the explicit reference to 'serious injury to body or to mental or physical health' in Art 7(1)(k) of the Rome Statute of the International Criminal Court (Rome, 17 July 1998) (also known as the ICC Statute).

[22] The crime of forced marriage qualifies as a crime against humanity of 'other inhumane acts', according to the jurisprudence of the SCSL, ECCC and ICC. It consists of the imposition on the victim of a social status that generates suffering, including social stigma. See *Prosecutor v Ongwen* (Decision on the Confirmation of Charges against Dominic Ongwen) ICC-02/04-01/15-422-Red (23 March 2016) para 93, contending that '[t]he central element of forced marriage is the imposition of 'marriage' on the victim, ie the imposition, regardless of the will of the victim, of duties that are associated with marriage, as well as of a social status of the perpetrator's wife'. See also *Prosecutor v Sesay, Kallon and Gbao* (Appeals Judgment) SCSL-04-15-A (26 October 2009) para 253; *Prosecutor v Brima, Kamara and Kanu* (Appeals Judgment) SCSL-2004-16-A (22 February 2008) para 199; *Prosecutor v Chea and Samphan* (Closing Order) 002/19-09-2007-ECCC-OCIJ (15 September 2010) paras 1443–1447.

(criminal) law to date. As mentioned in Chapter 1, today the 'crisis focus' of international criminal law should be viewed through a different lens, so as to include offences that cause socio-economic harm.

Lastly, the context in which 'other inhumane acts' should be committed in order to qualify as crimes against humanity implies the existence of a widespread or systematic attack directed against any civilian population. Systemic economic crimes are perpetrated with the primary objective of carrying out an attack against the public wealth of a country, whether economic or natural, and consequently against the fundamental human rights of the civilian population suffering the consequences of that attack. This means that, in order to include international economic crimes in the category of crimes against humanity as 'other inhumane acts', the contextual elements of 'attack' and 'policy' should be interpreted as outlined in Chapter 4.[23]

In addition to 'other inhumane acts', other crimes listed in Article 7(1) of the Rome Statute could be interpreted in such a way as to also prosecute serious economic crimes. Arenal Lora conducted an in-depth analysis of the crime of 'murder' to determine whether deaths caused by insufficient access to food, medicines, and health services due to systemic political corruption in a country could fall under the concept of murder.[24] This proposal raises some concerns regarding the definition of the *actus reus*, considering that the crime of murder requires the act or omission of killing to 'result into the death' of one or more persons.[25] This might be difficult to prove in the case of an economic crime, such as grand corruption, if the equivalence theory were applied. Instead, normative theories of causation or the theory of objective imputation could make it possible to establish a link between systemic economic conduct that creates life-threatening conditions and the death of civilians.

The crime of economic oppression, as defined by Davidsson, is even more likely than corruption to be equated with murder when the act or omission committed consists of 'depriving human beings of something needed by the victim's organism for survival'.[26] On closer examination, it appears that economic oppression may even constitute the crime of 'extermination', since footnote 8 of Article 7(1)(d) of the Elements of Crimes expressly states that 'the conduct [of extermination] could be committed by various methods of killing, either *directly or indirectly*'.[27] As Castillo-Monterrey correctly argued, acts of grand corruption and plundering of public wealth do not kill

[23] See above, 'Abuse of Power' and 'Attack against Public Wealth' in ch 4.

[24] Arenal Lora, *Crímenes económicos* 170.

[25] See Art 7(1)(a), fn 7 of the Elements of Crimes. On the other hand, the difficulties raised by the *mens rea* element of 'murder' could be overcome by adopting a broad interpretation of 'intent', which encompasses *dolus eventualis*. See Arenal Lora, *Crímenes económicos* 173.

[26] Davidsson, 'Economic Oppression' 193, citing HLA Hart and T Honoré, *Causation in the Law*, 2nd edn (Clarendon Press, 1998) 240.

[27] Emphasis added.

immediately but may in the long run result in the death of members of the victim population.[28]

Another crime against humanity that may accommodate international economic crimes is 'persecution on economic grounds', which is not expressly provided for in Article 7(1)(h) of the Rome Statute and must be distinguished from the crime of economic oppression, as the latter lacks the discriminatory intent that characterises persecution.[29] In a footnote to the draft provision defining persecution, the Preparatory Committee pointed out that this crime can be perpetrated not only on political, racial, national, ethnic, and cultural grounds, but also on social and economic grounds, as well as mental or physical disability grounds.[30] This approach was in line with the jurisprudence of the international military tribunals, in particular with the position upheld by the IMT in the *Funk* case, which had convicted Walter Funk for approving, in his capacity as Minister of Economics, discriminatory measures aimed at preventing Jews from playing any role in German economic life.[31]

The definition of persecution, which derives from a combined reading of Article 7(1)(h) of the Rome Statute and Article 7(1)(h)(3) of the Elements of Crimes, provides that acts of persecution may be committed on the basis of 'other grounds that are universally recognized as impermissible under international law'. It might be plausible to interpret the notion of 'other grounds' so as to include persecution on economic grounds, considering that this is already recognised as a form of persecution in several countries.[32]

An alternative or additional solution to the theories discussed so far is to add the concept of 'economic crimes against humanity' to the crimes listed in Article 7(1) of the Statute.[33] In this respect, it would be worth considering Castillo-Monterrey's

[28] MA Castillo-Monterrey, 'Contornos de un "modelo tipo" de expolio de las riquezas de las naciones como crimen de Derecho Internacional' (2017) 1 *Revista de derecho de la facultad de ciencias jurídicas y sociales UNAN-Léon*, 203, 205.

[29] Davidsson, 'Economic Oppression' 184.

[30] See 'UN Diplomatic Conference of Plenipotentiaries on the Establishment of an International Criminal Court' (Vol III) 21, fn 22.

[31] See the 'Funk case' IMT, *Trial of the Major War Criminals before the International Military Tribunal*, Vol I (Judgment, 1 October 1946) 305. Additionally, in US Military Tribunal, 'The Flick case', Vol VI, Trials of War Criminals before the Nuremberg Military Tribunals under Control Council Law No. 10 (October 1946–April 1949) 1212, the US military tribunal stated that '[…] the defendants […] participated in the Nazi *persecution of Jews* [by] taking advantage of the so-called Aryanization program by *seeking and using State economic pressure to obtain from the owners*, not all of whom were Jewish, the four properties in question' (emphasis added).

[32] For a comparative analysis of 'economic persecution' in the context of international refugee law, see See K Jastram, 'Economic Harm as a Basis for Refugee Status and the Application of Human Rights Law to the Interpretation of Economic Persecution' in JC Simeon (ed), *Critical Issues in International Refugee Law: Strategies toward Interpretative Harmony* (Cambridge University Press, 2010) 143, 147–159, arguing that economic persecution encompasses 'various types of socio-economic harm'. Among these, economic mistreatment has been recognised as a form of persecution and an independent ground for asylum, see JL Falkler, 'Economic Mistreatment as Persecution in Asylum Claims: Towards a Consistent Standard' (2007) 1 *University of Chicago Legal Forum* 471.

[33] A similar solution has been proposed with respect to a potential new crime against humanity of 'causing severe damage to cultural heritage', which is a crime against property and persons. See

proposal to outline the contours of the crime that he calls '*expolio de riquezas*' – ie plundering of public wealth – and that, in his view, should be prosecuted as a new crime against humanity.[34] This would mean revitalising the position adopted by the IMT in the *Funk* case, according to which crimes against persons and crimes against property can both fall within the concept of crimes against humanity.[35] However, following this approach would also mean that the contextual elements of crimes against humanity, as defined in the Rome Statute and the Elements of Crimes, would have to be expressly modified or interpreted by judges to take into account the peculiarities of the concept of international economic crimes described in Chapter 4, in particular the concepts of 'attack' and 'policy'.[36]

Economic Crimes in the Context of Armed Conflict

Serious economic crimes are systematically committed not only in peacetime, but also during war. This scenario is partially regulated by the provisions of the Rome Statute that criminalise war crimes resulting in an economic advantage for their perpetrators. This is the case with 'pillage', which is criminalised both when committed in IACs and in NIACs and whose constituent elements are defined by the Elements of Crimes as including the appropriation of certain property without consent of the owner for personal and not for military use.[37] The object of the war crime of pillage is limited to a 'town or place', which may correspond to a part of the public wealth of a country.

War crimes with an economic dimension also include the 'seizing of the enemy's property' protected under international law of armed conflict, which can be committed in both IACs and NIACs,[38] and the 'extensive appropriation of property' protected under the Geneva Conventions of 1949, which can

Y Gottlieb, 'Attacks against Cultural Heritage as a Crime against Humanity' (2020) 52 *Case Western Reserve Journal of International Law* 287, 319.

[34] Castillo-Monterrey, 'Contornos de un "modelo tipo"' 204, defining the 'expolio de riquezas' as, 'un saqueo sistemático o a gran escala de las riquezas y recursos de una nación por parte de los jefes de Estado, funcionarios de mayor nivel y los grandes agentes económicos, que según la magnitud del daño causado puede lesionar las bases económicas de una sociedad y poner en peligro la paz, la seguridad y bienestar de la humanidad' (trans: 'the systematic or large-scale plundering of a nation's wealth and resources by heads of state, senior officials and major economic actors, which, depending on the extent of the damage caused, can undermine the economic foundations of a society and endanger the peace, security and well-being of humanity').

[35] IMT, *Trial of the Major War Criminals* 74. This position is different from the one held by the judges at the subsequent Nuremberg proceedings, whereby crimes against humanity are limited to 'offences against persons', see 'The Flick Case' 1215.

[36] Castillo-Monterrey, 'Contornos de un "modelo tipo"' 214–218, arguing that the context in which the '*expolio de riquezas*' is committed corresponds to the contextual elements of crimes against humanity, but that these elements must be interpreted in accordance with the specific nature of this offence, taking into account in particular the fact that this widespread or systematic attack is directed primarily against the public wealth of a population, and secondarily against its individuals.

[37] Article 8(2)(b)(xvi) and Article 8(2)(e)(v) of the Statute and the Elements of Crimes. On pillage as a war crime with an economic dimension, see Starr, 'Extraordinary Crimes'1305.

[38] Article 8(2)(b)(xiii) and Article 8(2)(e)(xii) of the Statute and the Elements of Crimes.

be committed in IACs.[39] Furthermore Article 8(2)(b)(iv) of the Rome Statute provides for the possibility to prosecute the crime of 'intentionally launching an attack in the knowledge that such attack will cause [...] widespread, long-term, and severe damage to the natural environment which would be clearly excessive in relation to the concrete and direct overall military advantage anticipated'. This crime would allow protecting the country's natural wealth from conduct that occurred in the context of an international armed conflict and was associated with that conflict.

Despite their economic dimension, the above-mentioned offences are war crimes and not 'economic crimes'. Nevertheless, the report issued by the Truth and Reconciliation Commission for Liberia shows that economic crimes can also be committed during armed conflict. The TRC included the following crimes among those subject to its investigation:

> (1) Mercenarism; (2) Official Oppression; (3) Murder; (4) Kidnapping; (5) Rape; (6) Sexual Assault; (7) Fraud on the Internal Revenue of Liberia; (8) Theft and/or Illegal Disbursement and Expenditure of Public Money; and (9) Possession, Distribution, Transportation and/or use of Tools and Materials for Counterfeiting Purposes; and (10) Misuse of Public Money, Property or Record.[40]

In the report, these economic offences are qualified as 'egregious domestic crimes', which are usually related to armed conflict but, with a few exceptions,[41] do not constitute war crimes and cannot be prosecuted as such because the list of war crimes in IACs and NIACs contained in the Rome Statute is exhaustive – as evidenced by the adverb 'namely', instead of the preposition 'including', used in Article 8(2)(b), (c) and (e).

Therefore, the protection of the public wealth of a country in times of war is only partially regulated by the Rome Statute and by the laws and customs of war. To increase this protection, the only solution would be to include in the Rome Statute a category of international economic crimes applicable both in times of peace and in times of war, without prejudice to the rules of humanitarian law. This would make it possible to prosecute as international crimes those 'egregious economic crimes' listed in the report of the Truth and Reconciliation Commission in Liberia, which are committed in times of armed conflict but cannot be prosecuted as war crimes.

Is there Room for a Crime of Economic Aggression?

The crime of aggression was introduced into the Rome Statute following an amendment adopted at the Review Conference held in Kampala in 2010.

[39] Article 8(2)(a)(iv) of the Statute and the Elements of Crimes.

[40] TRC, 'Final Report, Vol I: Preliminary Findings and Determinations' (1 December 2009) 22.

[41] Only some of these crimes are officially recognised by the Rome Statute as war crimes: the crime of murder (or wilful killing), rape, and sexual slavery and violence.

Article 8bis(2) of the Rome Statute defines aggression as 'the use of armed force by a State against the sovereignty, territorial integrity or political independence of another State, or in any other manner inconsistent with the Charter of the United Nations', before listing the acts of aggression classified as such by Resolution 3314 (XXIX) of the General Assembly.[42]

From this list of acts and their definition, it is clear that the drafters in Rome and the delegations in Kampala adopted an interpretation of the term 'aggression' that corresponds primarily to 'military' aggression. However, it is worth mentioning that during the drafting of the Code of Crimes against the Peace and Security of Mankind, some delegations proposed that 'economic' aggression should be considered an international crime. As stated in the conclusions of the Second Report on the Draft Code of Crimes against the Peace and Security of Mankind prepared by the then Special Rapporteur, Doudou Thiam, the proposal of these delegations was based on the need to protect the independence of States, which must necessarily include their economic independence.[43] The question then arose as to 'whether the meaning of the term 'aggression' is not traditionally so linked to the use of armed force that it cannot safely be extended to cover other coercive measures of a different character',[44] for example, coercive economic measures such as the imposition of embargoes and the freezing of funds.

Doudou Thiam did not answer this question and shifted the focus to the fact that the concept of economic aggression is a political rather than a legal concept, as its constituent elements are unclear. However, he ultimately identified the real problem with the issue of economic aggression, which is not so much the lack of a definition of economic aggression as the lack of a thorough debate on the definition of aggression itself.[45] Since then, there has been no institutional debate on whether economic aggression can be considered a form of aggression under international law and within the meaning of Article 8bis of the Statute, although academic debate on this issue has continued.[46] Should it become necessary to revise the general content of the Rome Statute to make it a legal instrument more in line with today's realities and to fill in the gaps relating to the prosecution of serious crimes of economic significance, such a debate will become unavoidable.

[42] UNGA Res 3314(XXIX) (14 December 1974) A/RES/3314.

[43] ILC, 'Second Report on the Draft Code of Offences against the Peace and Security of Mankind, by Mr Doudou Thiam, Special Rapporteur' (1 February 1984) A/CN.4/377 and Corr.1, 100 para 80.

[44] ibid.

[45] ibid.

[46] See M Domb, 'Defining Economic Aggression in International Law: The Possibility of Regional Action by the Organization of American States' (1978) 11 *Cornell International Law Journal* 85; PS Dempsey, 'Economic Aggression & Self-Defense in International Law: The Arab Oil Weapon and Alternative American Responses Thereto' (1977) 9 *Case Western Reserve Journal of International Law* 253.

Prosecuting International Economic Crimes as an Autonomous Category of International Crimes

A more innovative and challenging option to be added to the previous solutions or to consider as an alternative would be to include 'international economic crimes' as a separate category in the Rome Statute. The rationale behind this option is to expressly punish systemic criminal conduct aimed at directly damaging the public wealth of a country and indirectly affecting its civilian population, whether committed in times of peace or conflict. The concept of 'international economic crime' defined above provides a model for such an autonomous category of international crimes. A provision defining such offences would include a *chapeau* section identifying the contextual elements, followed by a non-exhaustive list of crimes with an economic dimension. Furthermore, the meaning of the most controversial contextual elements – for instance, the terms 'attack' and 'public wealth', as well as the state, state-like and non-state character of the entities behind the attack – and the meaning of the constituent elements of each underlying offence would be specified in the Rome Statute and in the Elements of Crimes.

Nonetheless, other definitions of crimes of economic significance that reach the gravity threshold of international crimes have been proposed in the literature and deserve consideration as models of an autonomous category of international crimes. These include Kofele-Kale's concept of 'patrimonicide',[47] Jodoin and Saito's concept of 'crimes against future generations',[48] and Anderson's concept of 'international money-laundering' as an international crime.[49]

In each of these crimes, the wrongful conduct involves the unlawful appropriation and diversion of economic or natural resources without the consent of their owner, namely the civilian population of the victim State. Another common element is the deprivation of human rights of individuals resulting from the commission of the crime. However, while the concepts of patrimonicide and international money-laundering are defined in general terms, Jodoin and Saito accurately describe the constitutive elements of 'crimes against future generations', which consist of a list of offences committed with 'knowledge of the substantial likelihood of their severe consequences on the long-term health, safety, or means of survival of any identifiable group or collectivity'.[50]

[47] N Kofele-Kale, 'Patrimonicide: The International Economic Crime of Indigenous Spoliation' (1995) 28 *Vanderbilt Journal of Transnational Law* 45.

[48] S Jodoin and Y Saito, 'Crimes Against Future Generations: Harnessing the Potential of Individual Criminal Accountability for Global Sustainability' (2012) 7 *McGill International Journal of Sustainable Development Law & Policy* 115, 127–128.

[49] M Anderson, 'International Money Laundering: The Need for ICC Investigative and Adjudicative Jurisdiction' (2013) 53 *Virginia Journal of International Law* 762.

[50] One of the offences listed is the unlawful appropriation of public or private resources and property belonging to the members of a group or collectivity, which includes the 'large scale embezzlement, misappropriation or other diversion of such resources or property by a public official'; see Jodoin and Saito, 'Crimes Against Future Generations' 127.

The scope of application of the three categories of crimes is also different. International money-laundering is an act through which patrimonicide can be committed, since the latter is not confined to the unlawful appropriation of public wealth but also includes the diversion or stashing in foreign banks of the financial resources of a State.[51] As for patrimonicide, it is one of the ten offences that Jodoin and Saito qualify as 'crimes against future generations'. These also include other serious offences that have an economic dimension, for instance the deliberate deprivation of objects indispensable to the survival of members of any identifiable group or collectivity; forced labour, enforced prostitution and human trafficking; and serious environmental crimes, causing widespread, long-term and severe damage to the natural environment and to the health, safety or means of survival of members of any identifiable group or collectivity.

Thus, the three concepts fit perfectly into each other and fall under the macro concept of 'crimes against future generations'. The question that arises at this point is whether crimes against future generations are not already included in crimes against humanity. According to Jodoin and Saito, the difference between these categories lies in fact that the criminal policy under which crimes against future generations are carried out is not directed towards the civilian population of a State but any kind of group or collectivity, regardless of the affiliation, nationality or location of the group or collectivity.[52]

The Creation of a Hybrid Chamber within the ICC

A proposal has been suggested by Parliamentarians for Global Action to address new contemporary threats to peace and security – such as environmental crimes – and could also be considered for the category of international economic crimes. The proposal suggests amending the Rome Statute in accordance with Articles 39 and 122, in order to create a hybrid chamber within the ICC. This chamber would be composed of two international judges appointed from amongst the permanent judges at the ICC and one ad hoc judge.[53]

Like all the solutions discussed so far, the creation of a hybrid chamber has advantages and disadvantages. For example, amending the Rome Statute

[51] Anderson, 'International Money Laundering' 768.

[52] Jodoin and Saito, 'Crimes Against Future Generations' 148.

[53] Parliamentarians for Global Action, 'Modernising the International Criminal Court: Crimes against the Environment, Trafficking in Human Beings, Hybrid Justice and Corporate Accountability' (2022) https://www.pgaction.org/resources/modernising-the-international-criminal-court.html 3–16, highlighting that the appointment of ad hoc judges is an option provided by the statutes of many supranational courts, such as Art 31 of the Statute of the International Court of Justice (San Francisco, 26 June 1945), Art 10 of the Convention for the Protection of Human Rights and Fundamental Freedoms (Rome, 4 November 1950) (also known as European Convention on Human Rights or ECHR) and Art 10 of the Inter-American Court of Human Rights Statute.

would be a challenging task,[54] as will be explained below. On the other hand, appointing an ad hoc judge from the country where international economic crimes were allegedly committed would likely 'increase the perceived legitimacy of the ICC',[55] as it would bring the Court much closer to the context and people affected by the crimes and would provide the Court with 'all know-how and ability to interact with domestic authorities'.[56] In other words, this hybrid solution would allow international economic crimes to be prosecuted before an international, independent and impartial court, but with greater proximity to the national context concerned.

Challenges and Advantages of Prosecuting International Economic Crimes before the ICC

The proposal to include international economic crimes among the most serious offences of concern to the international community is legally justified because of their gravity and the possibility of developing a definition that complies with the principle of legality. The concept of international economic crime could fall within existing categories of international crimes listed in the Rome Statute or in a new separate category of international crimes, and therefore also be prosecutable by the International Criminal Court.

There would be considerable challenges, including the difficulty of reconciling the principle of state sovereignty with the possible interference of the Court. There are also practical arguments relating both to the process of amending the Rome Statute and to the challenges that the Rome Statute enforcement system would pose in relation to the prosecution of international economic crimes. Nevertheless, this would offer two main advantages: on the one hand, it would foster the development of the international criminal law, while on the other hand, it would benefit victims of international crimes by combating impunity for serious crimes of economic significance that are not prosecuted at national level, and by recognising their right to adequate reparation.

Balancing State Sovereignty and Global Justice: The Role of Complementarity in International Criminal Law

Unlike previous international criminal law tribunals, which had primacy over national jurisdictions, the Rome Statute system is based on the complementary role of the ICC in relation to domestic jurisdictions. The drafters resorted to the

[54] Parliamentarians for Global Action, 'Modernising the International Criminal Court' 16.
[55] ibid.
[56] ibid 15, highlighting the advantages of creating a hybrid chamber within the ICC, which include respect for sovereignty; knowledge-transfer; increase of States willing to bring international justice at domestic level; increase of the use of the language of the incident State.

principle of complementarity to strike a balance between the need to preserve state sovereignty and jurisdiction, on the one hand, and the desire to ensure international criminal justice through the creation of the first permanent international criminal court, on the other.[57] In light of its crucial role, the principle of complementarity was included at the beginning of the Rome Statute, in the preamble and in Article 1.[58]

The reconciliation between state sovereignty and global justice achieved through this principle has taken shape in two ways. First, the principle of complementarity has triggered a process of decentralisation of the international criminal justice system, whose centre has been placed at the periphery, ie in the hands of sovereign States, despite the existence of an international criminal court.[59] This system is reminiscent of Kant's idea of a 'permanent congress of States', defined as a 'federation of nations' (*Völkerbund*) in which these are not subordinate to the 'public coercive laws of a superordinate power but retain their independence'.[60] The main difference between Kant's permanent and voluntary coalition, on the one hand, and the decision by a group of States to criminalise and prosecute crimes that threaten international peace by creating a permanent international criminal court, on the other, lies in the very existence of the Rome Statute, which makes voluntary accession by States Parties binding. On the contrary, in Kant's proposal, the permanent and lasting nature of the union of States depends on the fact that they feel morally obliged to be part of the federation and to respect it, without being formally bound to it.[61]

[57] On the need to balance state sovereignty and global justice see S Wharton, 'Redrawing the Line? Serious Crimes of Concern to the International Community Beyond the Rome Statute' (2015) 52 *Canadian Yearbook of International Law/Annuaire canadien de droit international* 129,167, arguing that one of the main obstacles to attempts to expand the macro-category of international crimes is the risk of violating the principle of state sovereignty. See also *Prosecutor v Kony and Otti* (Decision on the Admissibility of the Case under Article 19(1) of the Statute) ICC-02/04-01/05-377 (11 March 2009) para 34, describing complementarity as the 'principle reconciling the States' persisting duty to exercise jurisdiction over international crimes with the establishment of a permanent international criminal court having competence over the same crimes'. See also *Prosecutor v Kenyatta* (Judgment on the Appeal of the Republic of Kenya against the Decision of Pre-Trial Chamber II of 30 May 2011 entitled 'Decision on the Application by the Government of Kenya Challenging the Admissibility of the Case Pursuant to Article 19(2)(b)' – Dissenting Opinion of Judge Ušacka) ICC-01/09-02/11-342 (20 September 2011) para 19, describing complementarity as '[…] a core guiding principle for the relationship between States and the Court is confirmed by its prominent place in the Statute (article 1 and Preamble) […] Complementarity reinforces the principle of international law that it is the sovereign right of every State to exercise its criminal jurisdiction; but it also ensures that the Court can step in to give effect to the goals of international criminal justice'.

[58] See para 10 of the Preamble of the Rome Statute: '[…] the International Criminal Court established under this Statute shall be complementary to national criminal jurisdictions'; Article 1 of the Rome Statute: 'An International Criminal Court […] shall be complementary to national criminal jurisdiction'.

[59] N Roht-Arriaza, 'Just a "Bubble"? Perspectives on the Enforcement of International Criminal Law by National Courts' (2013) 11 *Journal of International Criminal Justice* 537, 537.

[60] J Habermas, *The Inclusion of the Other: Studies in Political Theory* (The MIT Press, 2018) 168 (emphasis added).

[61] ibid 169.

Secondly, the principle of complementarity reconciles States sovereignty and global justice by bridging the gap between, on the one hand, the permanent nature and the broad scope of the Court's jurisdiction and, on the other, the limited resources of time and personnel at its disposal. This means that, since the Court is practically incapable of dealing with all situations in which serious crimes of international concern are perpetrated, the ICC acts only as a court of last resort, allowing States affected by the commission of international crimes to exercise their jurisdiction in the first instance.[62] This aims to preserve States sovereignty and ensure more efficient management of the international criminal justice system, while countering the risk of impunity for international crimes.[63]

In sum, the mechanism of complementarity can help counter arguments against prosecuting international economic crimes before the ICC based on fears that States will lose their jurisdiction over such crimes and that their sovereignty will thus be compromised. The latter scenario is neither desirable nor possible. States would be the architects of their own destiny: they would retain jurisdiction if they demonstrated that they were genuinely able and willing to prosecute international economic crimes; otherwise, they would lose jurisdiction and be forced to accept the intervention of the ICC.

It could also be contended that the principle of complementarity is likely to encourage the prosecution of international economic crimes for three reasons. First, States involved in international economic crimes or victims of such crimes are generally reluctant to initiate investigations or proceedings against their public leaders or private actors who still hold power.[64] Furthermore, if these States were to initiate such proceedings, their impartiality and fairness could reasonably be called into question.[65] Lastly, a prospective intervention by the ICC would likely encourage the States concerned to prosecute international economic criminals.[66] In other words, the complementary role of the ICC

[62] On the definition of the ICC as a court of last resort see *Prosecutor v Ruto and Sang* (Decision on Defence Applications for Judgments of Acquittal) ICC-01/09-01/11-2027-Red-Corr (5 April 2016) para 453. On the concept of 'positive complementarity', see KA Rodman, 'Justice as a Dialogue between Law and Politics: Embedding the International Criminal Court within Conflict Management and Peacebuilding' (2014) 12 *Journal of International Criminal Justice* 437, 441, whereby through this concept 'the Court combines the threat of asserting jurisdiction with efforts to assist national systems of justice to prosecute those complicit in Rome Statute crimes'.

[63] F Jr Sullivan, 'The Rome Statute: Opportunities and Challenges in Enforcement' (2016) 26 *Indiana International & Comparative Law Review* 1, 5.

[64] Kofele-Kale, 'Patrimonicide' 107. The *Bolichicos* case highlights the reluctant approach taken by Venezuelan justice in prosecuting high-level economic criminal offenders.

[65] M Arruda de Almeida and B Zagaris, 'Political Capture in the Petrobras Corruption Scandal: The Sad Tale of an Oil Giant' (2015) 39 *Fletcher Forum of World Affairs* 87, 91, 92 and 97, raises the issue of the impartiality and unfairness of the proceedings in the *Petrobras* case.

[66] P Kirsch, 'The International Criminal Court: From Rome to Kampala' (2010) 43 *The John Marshall Law Review* 515, 532; Starr, 'Extraordinary Crimes' 1288; CJM Safferling, 'Can Criminal Prosecution be the Answer to Massive Human Rights Violations' (2004) 5 *German Law Journal* 1469, 1478.

should be welcomed as an instrument of last resort to ensure international criminal justice, including in relation to systemic economic crimes of international significance.

Difficulties Underlying the Process of Amending the Rome Statute

Various ways of prosecuting international economic crimes before the ICC have been outlined above. The proposal to expressly add economic crimes to the list of crimes against humanity, as well as the idea of including a separate category of international economic crimes, are undoubtedly consistent with the principle of legality. However, they are more challenging than the proposal to interpret existing international crimes, such as the crime against humanity of 'other inhuman acts', to encompass serious economic crimes, as they would require explicit codification through an amendment of the Rome Statute.

According to some scholars, 'an express codification [of serious economic crimes] is extremely unlikely for the indefinite future' due to the complexity of the process of amending the Rome Statute.[67] This process is regulated by Article 121 of the Rome Statute, which makes the amendment conditional on the fact that seven years must have elapsed since the entry into force of the Rome Statute (i), that the amendment must be proposed by a State Party (ii), and that the amendment on which there is no consensus is adopted only if a two-thirds majority of the States Parties agree with its adoption (iii). While the first two conditions are likely to be met, the last one is a particularly difficult hurdle to overcome. It is not unlikely that some States would oppose the amendment of the Statute for various reasons, including the alleged non-violent nature of international economic crimes, which makes them – without any real reason – less serious than traditional categories of international crimes.

Moreover, some States Parties might resort to the same arguments put forward against the proposal to include international drug trafficking and international terrorism within the subject-matter jurisdiction of the ICC. In particular, the argument developed during the Eight Assembly of the States Parties that these crimes raise political sensitivities is not different from the observation that international economic crimes are necessarily intertwined with sensitive political issues, which could prevent States Parties involved in these contemporary forms of crimes from signing a potential amendment to the Rome Statute aimed to redraw its material boundaries.[68] In response to these arguments, though, it should be noted that every international crime has a 'highly political nature'.[69] Moreover, the choice of the global community to qualify certain offences as international crimes, the States

[67] Starr, 'Extraordinary Crimes' 1297.

[68] ICC-ASP, 'Report of the Bureau on the Review Conference' (15 November 2009) ICC-ASP/8/43, para 17. See also Starr, 'Extraordinary Crimes' 1297.

[69] MM deGuzman, 'How Serious Are International Crimes-the Gravity Problem in International Criminal Law' (2012) 51 *Columbia Journal of Transnational Law* 18, 27.

Parties' self-referrals, the Security Council's decisions to refer a case to the ICC, and the decisions of the Prosecutor to initiate proceedings against crimes committed in one situation rather than another, are influenced by global geopolitical balances and have a significant impact on them. In other words, the international criminal justice system of the Rome Statute cannot ignore politics,[70] which is an integral part of it. Nonetheless, this element must be balanced with the law, just as the goal of ensuring justice must be balanced with that of achieving peace.[71]

This forced combination of international criminal justice and politics has fuelled accusations of political bias against the ICC's alleged regional focus, to the extent that some have spoken of the Court's participation in 'neo-colonialism in Africa'.[72] The idea of a politically biased and illegitimate ICC could be mitigated by considering – among other things – the attention that the ICC has paid to other situations not involving African countries and that could send 'a strong signal that the application of international criminal law is potentially universal'[73] and does not occur on a regional basis.[74]

It might be argued that the idea of a politically biased Court could be strengthened by including international economic crimes within the ICC's jurisdiction, due to the political nature of such crimes. However, this is a rather unfounded generalisation since, as shown by the cases mentioned in this book, international economic crimes are not necessarily committed in situations of conflict and mass violence, which generally affect developing countries in the Global South, but are also committed in some of the most developed and powerful countries of the Global North.

Anticipating the difficulty of reaching the two-thirds threshold of Article 121 of the Rome Statute, on the basis of these and other arguments that may be put forward by States to keep the ICC's scope of substantive jurisdiction intact, the drafters provided for a loophole in paragraph 5 of Article 121, whereby States may decide whether or not to accept an amendment to one of the articles defining the material jurisdiction of the ICC,[75] and may even withdraw from the Rome Statute with immediate effect if the amendment is accepted by seven-eighths

[70] Rodman, 'Justice as a Dialogue' 440. See also H Cullen, P Kastner and S Richmond, 'Introduction: The Politics of International Criminal Law' (2018) 18 *International Criminal Law Review* 907, 913.

[71] Cullen et al, 'Introduction: The Politics' 920. For instance, it is important that the ICC takes part in a political process of consultation with donor States, international institutions, non-governmental organisations, and local stakeholders. See also Rodman, 'Justice as a Dialogue' 463; JN Clark, 'International Criminal Courts and Normative Legitimacy: An Achievable Goal?' (2015) 15 *International Criminal Law Review* 763, 783.

[72] Cullen et al, 'Introduction: The Politics' 925.

[73] ibid. 914, referring to the Situation in the Islamic Republic of Afghanistan.

[74] MM deGuzman and T Lockwood Kelly, 'The International Criminal Court Is Legitimate Enough to Deserve Support' (2019) 33 *Temple International & Comparative Law Journal* 397, 401.

[75] Art 121(5) of the Rome Statute: 'Any amendment to articles 5, 6, 7 and 8 of this Statute shall enter into force for those States Parties which have accepted the amendment […]'.

of the States Parties. The non-acceptance of an amendment by a State Party prevents the Court from exercising its jurisdiction over crimes covered by the amendment and committed on the territory of that State or by its nationals.

This mechanism raises the question of whether it is worth considering the incorporation of international economic crimes into the Rome Statute, knowing that States Parties would have more than one means of evading the inclusion of such crimes and the resulting obligations to prosecute them at national level or to assist the Court in doing so.[76]

The work carried out so far by the ICC and the growing doctrinal interest in resolving the controversial legal issues raised by the legal framework of the Rome Statute have sought to create an increasingly cohesive and comprehensive system of international criminal justice. Any scenario or mechanism that could fragment this system is undesirable. Therefore, emphasis should first be placed on the need to change the perceptions of States both with regard to the 'crisis focus' of international criminal law and with regard to the alleged lesser gravity of international economic crimes. Only in this way would an amendment of the Rome Statute aimed at prosecuting such crimes before the ICC not create a rift between States Parties willing to accede to the amendment and States Parties using the mechanism referred to in paragraph 5 as a shield to protect themselves from international investigations into international economic crimes.

Enforcement Challenges in the Prosecution of International Economic Crimes

In his commentary on Kant's 'Perpetual Peace', Habermas emphasises the importance of the binding and enforceable nature of 'cosmopolitan law', that is, the law that underpins the association of free and equal world citizens and that differs from international law in that the latter struggles to be enforced.[77] Habermas provides concrete examples of the enforcement challenges that plague institutions of international law, such as the UN, which he criticises for not having military forces to 'deploy under its own command' and, thus, for relying on the cooperation of its members to implement its resolutions.[78] Another international institution accused of being more symbolic than effective is the ICJ, whose judgments, according to the German philosopher, have proven to be de facto non-binding.[79] Similarly, Habermas criticises the lack of executive power to enforce the human rights declarations that have been adopted over the years.[80] Had he written his commentary

[76] N Citeroni, 'International Economic Crimes in the Rome Statute? Reflections on Multilevel Enforcement of International Criminal Law' in K Ligeti and KH Brodersen (eds), *Studies on Enforcement in Multilevel Regulatory Systems* (Nomos, 2022) 255.

[77] Habermas, *The Inclusion of the Other*, 179–181.

[78] ibid 180.

[79] ibid.

[80] ibid 182. Habermas wrote his commentary at the end of the 1990s, when several human rights committees had been set up to supervise the respective conventions. See also Safferling, 'Can Criminal

after the Rome Statute came into force, he would have also noted the enforcement difficulties that the ICC faces.

The ability to enforce the provisions of the Rome Statute is essential to ensure the effectiveness of the international criminal justice system and the legitimacy of the ICC.[81] As already mentioned, the decentralisation process triggered by the principle of complementarity has reversed the trend from a direct to a quasi-direct enforcement mechanism of international criminal law. Indeed, the first generation of international criminal law tribunals set up in the aftermath of the Second World War embodied an unprecedented direct system of enforcement of international criminal law,[82] which was 'a vertically integrated and comprehensive international criminal justice system consisting of all the components found in national criminal justice systems, namely: investigation, prosecution, adjudication, sanctions, and enforcement'.[83]

In such a system, the direct application of the provisions of the Nuremberg and Tokyo Charters and the CCL no 10 was accompanied by the indirect application by domestic courts of international criminal law enshrined in national laws.[84] On the contrary, the statutes of the ICTR and ICTY provided for a quasi-direct system of enforcement,[85] as both tribunals significantly depended on the assistance of States for the performance of crucial enforcement tasks.[86] States were required to cooperate at different stages of the proceedings, including in establishing the jurisdiction of the ad hoc tribunal during an investigation (i),[87] after the indictment had been confirmed (ii),[88] as well as in the enforcement of sentences (iii).[89] This multilevel system of enforcement was also endorsed by the hybrid or internationalised courts and tribunals.[90]

Prosecution be the Answer' 1471, pointing out that 'the adherence [of states to human rights obligations] would remain unsupervised unless the national state subdued itself under a specific regime of control'.

[81] N Kofele-Kale, *The International Law of Responsibility for Economic Crimes: Holding State Officials Individually Liable for Acts of Fraudulent Enrichment* (Ashgate, 2006) 41.

[82] MC Bassiouni, 'The "Direct Enforcement System:" History of International Criminal Investigations and Prosecutions' in MC Bassiouni (ed), *Introduction to International Criminal Law*, 2nd edn (Brill, 2012) 535, 536.

[83] ibid 535. See also Citeroni, 'International Economic Crimes in the Rome Statute?' 242.

[84] See, inter alia, the abovementioned 'Barbie case', Cour de Cassation, Chambre criminelle, 85–95.166 (20 December 1985) www.legifrance.gouv.fr/juri/id/JURITEXT000007064048.

[85] Bassiouni, 'The "Direct Enforcement System:"' 539.

[86] In line with a consolidated interpretation of the statutory provisions of the ad hoc tribunals and their Rules of Procedure and Evidence (RPE), both individual States and collective enterprises of States were called to assist the ad hoc tribunals in their enforcement functions. See HR Zhou, 'The Enforcement of Arrest Warrants by International Forces: From the ICTY to the ICC' (2006) 4 *Journal of International Criminal Justice* 202, 207–208 and 215.

[87] Art 18(2) of the ICTY Statute; Rules 8, 9, 10 and 11, 40 of the ICTY and ICTR RPE. See Citeroni, 'International economic crimes in the Rome Statute?' 243.

[88] Rules 11*bis* of the ICTY and ICTR RPE. See Citeroni, 'International Economic Crimes in the Rome Statute?' 244.

[89] Art 27 of the ICTY Statute and Art 26 of the ICTR Statute. See Citeroni, 'International Economic Crimes in the Rome Statute?' 244.

[90] See for instance, Art 8(2) of the SCSL Statute and Part two of the SCSL RPE.

Like the second-generation of international criminal law tribunals, the Rome Statute was endowed with a quasi-direct enforcement system,[91] according to which the ICC can directly intervene to enforce statutory provisions – when States Parties are unwilling or unable to proceed – but in so doing the Court must rely on the cooperation of States and may avail itself of the cooperation of international organisations.[92] The first ICC prosecutor, Luis Moreno Ocampo, noted that 'the ICC is independent and interdependent at the same time. It cannot act alone. It will achieve efficiency only if it works closely with other members of the international community'.[93]

The advantage of this multilevel regulatory system is that it avoids overloading the system itself and allows for a more efficient distribution of tasks among the various levels of enforcement. The cooperation between the ICC and the States Parties is governed by the Rome Statute and is subject to the incorporation of the statutory provisions into national law.[94]

From what has been said so far, the more international criminal law has evolved and expanded, the more international criminal law tribunals have relied on States for enforcement purposes. Thus, the question arises whether the multilevel mechanism of enforcement of the Rome Statute risks being short-circuited, should the ICC's material jurisdiction be further expanded with the introduction of new forms of serious crimes in the coming years.

It is undeniable that the ICC faces enforcement challenges that may hinder the prosecution of international economic crimes. First, the ICC does not have unlimited resources – financial, human and time resources – but rather resources commensurate with the number and complexity of the cases it has to deal with. Furthermore, unlike ad hoc and internationalised tribunals, the ICC is a permanent court with broader personal, territorial and temporal scope of jurisdiction.[95] This implies that the 'ICC's broad mandate and limited resources make hard choices

[91] YM Dutton, 'Enforcing the Rome Statute: Evidence of (Non) Compliance from Kenya' (2016) 26 *Indiana International & Comparative Law Review* 7, 8.

[92] Art 86 of the Rome Statute envisages a general obligation of States Parties to cooperate with the Court. The scope of this obligation includes the arrest and surrender of suspects (Arts 89, 90, 91, 92 of the Rome Statute), the taking of evidence, and the identification, tracing and freezing or seizure of proceeds, property and assets (Art 93 of the Rome Statute). See also Art 87(6) of the Rome Statute, stating that the Court 'may ask' intergovernmental organisations to cooperate.

[93] See ICC-OTP, 'Second Assembly of States Parties to the Rome Statute of the International Criminal Court', cited in also Citeroni, 'International Economic Crimes in the Rome Statute?' 247. On the existence of a correspondence between increased cooperation between States and the efficiency of international criminal law, see Safferling, 'Can Criminal Prosecution be the Answer' 1487, arguing that the metaphor of the 'giant without arms and legs' that Judge Cassese used to describe the dependence of the ICTY on state authorities can be extended to the ICC. See also A Cassese, 'On the Current Trends towards Criminal Prosecution and Punishment of Breaches of International Humanitarian Law' (1998) 9 *European Journal of International Law* 2, 13.

[94] Bassiouni, 'The "Direct Enforcement System"' 623. See Part nine of the Rome Statute.

[95] WA Schabas, 'State Policy as an Element of International Crimes' (2008) 98 *Journal of Criminal Law and Criminology* 953, 980. See also Citeroni, 'International Economic Crimes in the Rome Statute?' 254.

inevitable'.[96] For this reason, the inclusion of new crimes may be perceived as an unnecessary burden, which could push the OTP to make biased choices, favouring investigations in situations of mass violence and conflict at the expense of those in which systemic crimes of economic significance have been committed.

Secondly, the ICC is deemed to lack adequate investigative powers and expertise to prosecute economic crimes. This, too, could lead the OTP to skew the selection of situations and focus on crimes it is accustomed to investigating, in order to better ensure that suspects are brought to justice and prosecuted.

A third challenge for the enforcement of the provisions of the Rome Statute lies in the cooperation between the ICC and the States Parties, which is also a double-edged sword.[97] On the one hand, it preserves the sovereignty of States, thus ensuring a more effective and timely prosecution of international crimes; on the other hand, it risks subordinating law and justice to politics. Both sides of the coin are visible when the relationship between the Court and the States is adversarial but also when it is cooperative.[98] In the first scenario, the ICC deals with recalcitrant States that are unwilling to pursue the aims of international criminal justice.[99] In such situations, it is necessary that other actors – external States, international organisations, the Security Council or the Assembly of States Parties – intervene 'to deploy coercive political instruments to change the balance of forces against the government'[100] that is uncooperative. On the contrary, when States adopt a cooperative approach – usually in cases of self-referrals – there are fewer obstacles to enforcement. However, even in such circumstances, there is a risk of instrumentalisation of the Court to prosecute 'political adversaries [...] rebels, the political opposition or leaders from a prior regime',[101] without allowing it to investigate the criminal conduct in which the cooperative government is allegedly involved. In other words, cooperation is likely to be partial and oriented towards pursuing the interests of the State involved rather than the collective interests of ensuring impartial justice.[102]

In both scenarios, the ICC has the authority to issue orders to States Parties, which are required to cooperate in a wide range of enforcement activities, including the seizure of defendants' economic assets. When States Parties are reluctant to cooperate,[103] the Court may refer the matter to the Assembly of States Parties

[96] Starr, 'Extraordinary Crimes' 1258. On the risk of overloading the ICC by adding new crimes to its jurisdiction see Wharton, 'Redrawing the Line?' 181, calling for the need to strike a balance between 'the needs of the international community to address serious crimes with the ability of the ICC to function effectively'.

[97] See Citeroni, 'International Economic Crimes in the Rome Statute?' 255.

[98] Rodman, 'Justice as a Dialogue' 437.

[99] ibid 443.

[100] ibid 437.

[101] ibid 450.

[102] deGuzman and Lockwood Kelly, 'The International Criminal Court' 400.

[103] See eg *Prosecutor v Al Bashir* (Decision under article 87(7) of the Rome Statute on the non-compliance by Jordan with the request by the Court for the arrest and surrender or Omar Al-Bashir) ICC-02/05-01/09 (11 December 2017), in which the Court addressed the failure of Jordan to comply with requests for the arrest and surrender of Mr Al Bashir.

or to the Security Council.[104] Hence, law meets politics once again: political considerations could have an impact on the resolution of issues relating to the enforcement of international criminal law.

Overall, the quasi-direct enforcement system of the Rome Statute would enable the ICC to ensure the enforcement of orders or judgments issued against the perpetrators of international economic crimes.[105] Should these be convicted by the ICC, the Court could issue an order of forfeiture of their assets and funds, thereby guaranteeing compensation for the victims.[106] Nonetheless, bank secrecy laws may hinder, and even prevent, the tracing of assets.[107]

The Rome Statute as a 'Living Treaty'

In less than a century, international criminal law has almost completely changed its physiognomy: the macro-category of international crimes has been expanded; the definitions of international crimes have undergone changes; enforcement mechanisms have become more complex; and the protection of fair trial rights during international criminal proceedings has been strengthened. In short, the international criminal justice system has developed dynamically to respond to the changing needs of society.[108]

Since the entry into force of the Rome Statute, this evolutionary process intensified. The fact that the content of this treaty is not 'set in stone'[109] has been demonstrated on several occasions, through a more inclusive interpretation

[104] Art 87(7) of the Rome Statute. See Rodman, 'Justice as a Dialogue' 441.

[105] At the investigation and trial stages of the proceedings, States Parties can be requested to cooperate with the Court to identify, trace, and freeze the proceeds, property, and instrumentalities of crimes; see Arts 57(3)(e) and Art 93(1)(k) of the Rome Statute.

[106] After trial, the Court may issue executing orders for fines and confiscation of proceeds, property and assets derived directly or indirectly from the crime (Art 109 of the Rome Statute) and use them for reparative purposes (Arts 75 and 79 of the Rome Statute). Moreover, the accused may voluntarily assist the Court by 'providing assistance in locating assets subject to orders of fine, forfeiture or reparation which may be used for the benefit of victims' (Art 110(4)(b) of the Rome Statute).

[107] Starr, 'Extraordinary Crimes' 1288. See also O Sillitti and MP López Velásquez, 'El proyecto COPLA para el establecimiento de una corte penal latinoamericana y del caribe contra el crimen organizado transnacional' in Olásolo Alonso H et al (eds), *Respuestas nacionales e internacionales al fenómeno de la corrupción: particular atención al ámbito iberoamericano*, Perspectivas iberoamericanas sobre la justicia 12 (Tirant lo Blanch, 2021) 767, arguing that the identification and tracing of funds of those who commit the most serious crimes against the international community is the Achilles heel of the existing system of international criminal justice.

[108] See I Marchuk, *The Fundamental Concept of Crime in International Criminal Law: A Comparative Law Analysis* (Springer, 2014) 70, highlighting the existence of a 'dynamic development of international criminal law'.

[109] HL Kiefer, 'Just Say No: The Case against Expanding the International Criminal Court's Jurisdiction to Include Drug Trafficking' (2009) 31 *Loyola of Los Angeles International and Comparative Law Review* 157, 157. The macro category of international crimes has undergone some adjustments over the years, which proves that it is not and should not be conceived as an 'immutable core'. This position is supported by NM Rajkovic, 'What Is a "Grave" International Crime? The Rome Statute, Durkheim and the Sociology of Ruling Outrages' (2020) 16 *Loyola University Chicago International Law Review* 65, 82 and by Wharton, 'Redrawing the Line?' 129 and 133.

of its provisions and, above all, with the introduction of the crime of aggression in 2010. The ICC can therefore be described as a 'living and vital reality', in the words used by Cassese with reference to the ICTY.[110] Nonetheless, it is crucial that such an evolution of the Statute takes place within the limits of its fundamental principles, namely the principle of gravity and legality. Compliance with these principles constitutes a *passe-partout* for the inclusion of other serious and contemporary threats to individual and collective interests, including international economic crimes, within the jurisdiction of the ICC.[111]

Extending the material scope of jurisdiction of the ICC would also help counter the perception of the Court as a hostile institution, encouraging its positive re-evaluation as a truly international and legitimate court. Although major economic powers – eg United States, China and Russia – are not parties to the Rome Statute,[112] the international dimension of the Court rests on its institutional mission to adjudicate crimes that qualify as extremely serious violations of international law and fundamental human rights and that are of concern to the international community. Therefore, not including the most serious economic crimes in the Court's jurisdiction could undermine its truly international character.

Regarding the legitimacy of the ICC, the States Parties to the Rome Statute have amended – or are in the process of amending[113] – their national laws to bring them into line with the provisions of the Statute.[114] This means that the inclusion of serious crimes of economic significance among the categories of international crimes listed in the Rome Statute would imply a commitment on the part of States Parties to codify these crimes at national level, thereby recognising the normative legitimacy of the ICC and capacity of the Rome Statute to

[110] See A Cassese, 'The ICTY: A Living and Vital Reality' (2004) 2 *Journal of International Criminal Justice* 585.

[111] For instance, see Parliamentarians for Global Action, 'Modernising the International Criminal Court' which suggests 'modernising' the ICC by expanding its subject-matter jurisdiction and including other serious contemporary threats to individual and collective interests, such as crimes against the environment. The inclusion of economic crimes in the Statute was discussed during the side event 'The Prosecution of Economic and Financial Crimes: Towards an Extension of the ICC's Jurisdiction?' hosted by the *Association Française pour la promotion de la compétence universelle*, at the Assembly of States Parties in December 2019. See Public International Law and Policy Group, 'ASP 18 Side Event: The Prosecution of Economic and Financial Crimes: Towards an Extension of the ICC's Jurisdiction?' (*PILPG*, 3 December 2019) https://www.publicinternationallawandpolicygroup.org/lawyering-justice-blog/2019/12/4/asp18-side-event-the-prosecution-of-economic-and-financial-crimes-towards-an-extension-of-the-iccs-jurisdiction.

[112] deGuzman and Lockwood Kelly, 'The International Criminal Court' 401.

[113] In March 2022, the Italian Ministry of Justice Marta Cartabia set up a committee for drafting a Code of international crimes. See 'Decreto 22 Marzo 2022 – Commissione per l'elaborazione di un progetto di Codice dei Crimini internazionali' (Ministero della Giustizia, 22 March 2022) www.giustizia.it/giustizia/it/mg_1_8_1.page?contentId=SDC372746&previsiousPage=mg_1_8. See also M Crippa, 'Codice dei Crimini internazionali: pubblicata la relazione della commissione Palazzo-Pocar' (*Sistema Penale*, 24 Giugno 2022) https://www.sistemapenale.it/it/documenti/codice-dei-crimini-internazionali-pubblicata-la-relazione-della-commissione-palazzo-pocar.

[114] deGuzman and Lockwood Kelly, 'The International Criminal Court' 402.

'express global norms in the hopes that over time those norms will permeate the fabric of global society'.[115]

An International Court of Last Resort to Prevent Impunity for International Economic Criminals

The risk of impunity for perpetrators of international economic crimes poses an even greater challenge than that posed for perpetrators of existing categories of international crimes. First, evidence relating to the commission of international economic crimes emerges more slowly and with greater difficulty; it is no coincidence that these crimes are considered externalisations of 'structural' or 'indirect' violence.[116] As such, 'indirect violence' generates invisible consequences on the part of invisible actors, hidden by the system. This façade of invisibility allows offenders to remain shielded from national criminal justice and unpunished for a long time. However, even when serious forms of economic crimes come to light, it is likely that the alleged perpetrators will not be prosecuted: either high-ranking individuals allegedly guilty of international economic crimes flee to other countries with their accumulated wealth,[117] or the State competent to adjudicate their conduct protects them de facto by not initiating proceedings or by conducting them in a partial and unfair manner.[118] It is unlikely that a corrupt State will investigate its own representatives for war crimes, genocide, aggression or crimes against humanity: a fortiori, it is practically impossible that it will decide to investigate precisely those serious economic crimes that make it a corrupt State.[119]

The second reason underlying the high risk of impunity for international economic criminal offenders lies in the fact that in certain circumstances – for instance, in cases of grand corruption associated with international laundering of money or criminal proceeds – the perpetrators spend or hide their illicit assets in other countries, which are usually financial havens with banking secrecy laws that are particularly difficult for national courts to overcome.[120] Another ground of impunity concerns cases in which serious economic crimes are committed by

[115] ibid 398.

[116] On the concept of 'indirect' or 'invisible violence', see Böhm, *The Crime of Maldevelopment* 42–43; see also '"Extraordinary" Offences' in ch 2.

[117] Starr, 'Extraordinary Crimes' 1291.

[118] ibid; Kofele-Kale, *The International Law of Responsibility for Economic Crimes* 19.

[119] See Castillo-Monterrey, 'Contornos de un "modelo tipo"' 206, emphasising the unlikelihood of crimes involving state structures being prosecuted by the victim State, as this would mean putting the prosecution of the perpetrators in the hands of the perpetrators themselves. It is precisely in these circumstances that criminal prosecutions before an international criminal court of last resort will help to 'canvass the rule of law' and control 'the powerful despite their power and control over national institutions', see Safferling, 'Can Criminal Prosecution be the Answer' 1475.

[120] On the difficulties posed by bank secrecy laws for criminal proceedings, see, inter alia, S Booysen and D Neo, *Can Banks Still Keep a Secret? Bank Secrecy in Financial Centres around the World* (Cambridge University Press, 2017).

high-ranking public officials, who can thus escape domestic criminal proceedings in other countries thanks to immunity doctrines.

In light of the above, potential intervention by the ICC in the prosecution of international economic crimes could help counter impunity for their perpetrators. Starr provided a broad overview of the reasons in favour of the Court's intervention, to which further considerations may be added. Starting from the issue of immunity doctrines, this limitation could be overcome by considering that Article 27 of the Rome Statute expressly declares both functional and personal immunity of heads of State, government and other high-ranking officials allegedly involved in international crimes to be irrelevant.

With regard to the failure of some States to prosecute international economic criminals, it should be noted that in the cases covered in this book, most of the States involved in the commission of serious economic crimes – on the basis of territoriality or nationality principles of jurisdiction – are States Parties to the Rome Statute. This would trigger the ICC's jurisdiction whenever the States in question are unable or unwilling to proceed with the investigation or prosecution of the case. Moreover, unlike existing categories of international crimes, which are typically committed in one or two States, the perpetration of international economic crimes usually involves more than two States – for instance, the State where the proceeds are stolen, the State where the proceeds are laundered, and the State of nationality of the defendant.[121] This means that the chances increase that an international economic crime is either committed in the territory of a State Party to the Rome Statute or a State that has accepted the jurisdiction of the Court, or that one of the accused is a national of these States.[122]

On the issue of banking secrecy laws, the same difficulties faced by domestic jurisdictions in prosecuting transnational economic crimes would likely be faced by the ICC in prosecuting international economic crimes. However, the Court has the authority to issue orders to States Parties, which have a general obligation to cooperate.[123] If international economic crimes were included in the Rome Statute, States Parties would be required to adapt their national laws to comply with the new statutory provisions and to cooperate with the Court. This would make it easier for the ICC to seize large sums of money embezzled from the coffers of a State or a state-owned enterprise, thereby bringing justice to the people of that State.[124] Furthermore, Starr emphasises that labelling serious forms of economic crimes as international crimes would bring these 'invisible offences' under the spotlight of international justice, not only for deterrence purposes but also to shape an international or global norm in this respect.[125]

[121] Starr, 'Extraordinary Crimes' 1289.

[122] See Art 12 of the Rome Statute on the preconditions to the exercise of jurisdiction of the ICC.

[123] Art 86 and 87 of the Rome Statute.

[124] Starr, 'Extraordinary Crimes' 1279, 1288 and 1296. See also Citeroni, 'International Economic Crimes in the Rome Statute?' 257.

[125] Starr, 'Extraordinary Crimes' 1290. See also deGuzman and Lockwood Kelly, 'The International Criminal Court' 398. On the limits of the deterrent effect of international criminal law see Safferling, 'Can Criminal Prosecution be the Answer' 1484.

There is also a pragmatic reason for the intervention of an international court of last resort in prosecuting international economic crimes. If an international court such as the ICC were not called upon to adjudicate these crimes, the alternative would be to resort to a pure system of indirect enforcement of international criminal law. The national courts of the State in whose territory international economic crimes were allegedly committed, or the courts of the State of which the defendants were nationals would be the most appropriate *fora* as they would be easily accessible to victims and closer to the crime scenes for the collection of evidence.[126] However, as explained above, these same courts may not be willing to investigate and prosecute their own representatives for perpetrating systemic economic crimes.[127] In addition, those courts may lack adequate investigative powers.[128] Therefore, providing an international court such as the ICC with the possibility to intervene in these cases would at least ensure that impunity for international economic crimes could be reduced, that justice could be done and that the truth could be established.[129]

The Right to Reparation for Victims of International Economic Crimes

Compared to the charters and statutes underlying the first and second generation of international criminal law courts and tribunals,[130] the Rome Statute revolutionised the role of victims in international criminal proceedings. One of the most significant innovations of the Rome Statute was the recognition of victims' right to reparations.[131] Pursuant to Rule 85 of the Rules of Procedure and Evidence (RPE), a victim is any natural person who has suffered a harm as a result of the commission of a crime that falls under the jurisdiction of the ICC. The concept of 'victim' was extended in the second paragraph of the same Rule to include organisations or institutions that suffered a direct harm to their property having a religious, educational, artistic, scientific or charitable purpose, and to their historic monuments, hospitals and other places or objects

[126] Starr, 'Extraordinary Crimes' 1279.

[127] ibid 1272. See also Roksandić Vidlička, *Prosecuting Serious Economic Crimes*, 334 and JI Turner, 'Nationalizing International Criminal Law' (2005) 41 *Stanford Journal of International Law* 1, 30.

[128] Anderson, 'International Money Laundering' 765. See also Kofele-Kale, *The International Law of Responsibility for Economic Crimes* 260.

[129] deGuzman and Lockwood Kelly, 'The International Criminal Court' 401.

[130] At the IMT and the IMTFE, victims' rights and participation in the trials were limited, which had a considerable impact on the length of the proceedings. On the evolution of the role of victims in international criminal law proceedings see L Moffett, 'The Role of Victims in the International Criminal Tribunals of the Second World War' (2012) 12 *International Criminal Law Review* 245; S Karstedt, 'From Absence to Presence, from Silence to Voice: Victims in International and Transitional Justice since the Nuremberg Trials' (2010) 17 *International Review of Victimology* 9; CH Wheeler, 'Justice in the Absence of the Accused. Can the Rights of Victims be Fully Vindicated without the Participation of the Accused?' (2019) 17 *Journal of International Criminal Justice* 413.

[131] The victims' right to reparations has been recognised since the *Lubanga* case, where judges affirmed for the first time that this right is well-established in global and regional human rights treaties and in IHL instruments. See *Prosecutor v Lubanga Dyilo* (Decision Establishing the Principles and Procedures to be Applied to Reparations) ICC-01/04-01/06-2904 (7 August 2012) para 23.

protected under humanitarian law.[132] According to case law, the harm can be both direct – physical, psychological or material harm suffered by the victims themselves – and indirect, when it is sustained by a 'third person who may have a close relationship with the victim'.[133]

Article 75(1) lists three forms of reparations for victims of international crimes, namely restitution, compensation and rehabilitation, which are in addition to the forms of symbolic reparation that may be ordered by the Court.[134] It has been pointed out that symbolic reparations play an important role when they complement other forms of reparation, otherwise they would be inadequate 'because "the crimes were not symbolic"'.[135]

The drafters did not specify the principles that should guide the choice of the most appropriate type of reparation or other aspects of the reparation process, including the determination of the scope and extent of harm. It can be inferred from the wording of Article 75 that these aspects may be determined by the Court on a case-by-case basis. In fact, since the *Lubanga* case, the ICC has relied on the UN Basic Principles of Justice for Victims of Crime and Abuse of Power and the UN Basic Principles on Reparations for Victims to establish its own guiding principles for the reparation process.[136]

In addition to recognising the existence of a right to reparation for victims of international crimes, in the *Lubanga* case, the ICC clarified the main objectives of reparations, which include 'healing' the harm suffered by victims.[137] Nonetheless, this objective cannot fully meet the needs of victims of international crimes, given their high number in cases of mass violence.[138] It is therefore important that the function of reparations be complemented by other purposes, including a retributive purpose that allows for expressing the 'outrage by the international community against the intolerable and heinous acts of individuals who have violated societal norms and who, as a result, are deemed deserving

[132] For a comprehensive definition of the concept and status of victims under the Rome Statute see MJ Kelly, 'The Status of Victims Under the Rome Statute of the International Criminal Court' in T Bonacker and C Safferling (eds), *Victims of International Crimes: An Interdisciplinary Discourse* (Springer, 2013) 47.

[133] A Wiersing, 'Lubanga and Its Implications for Victims Seeking Reparations at the International Criminal Court' (2012) 4 *Amsterdam Law Forum* 21, 24. See, inter alia, *Prosecutor v Lubanga Dyilo* (Judgment on the Appeals of The Prosecutor and The Defence against Trial Chamber I's Decision on Victims' Participation of 18 January 2008) ICC-01/04-01/06-1432 (11 July 2008) para 31.

[134] See *Prosecutor v Lubanga Dyilo* (Decision Establishing the Principles and Procedures to be Applied to Reparations) para 107.

[135] Wiersing, 'Lubanga and Its Implications' 28. In general, every form of reparation should be complementary to each other in order to be adequate. See UNSC, 'The Rule of Law and Transitional Justice in Conflict and Post-Conflict Societies, Report of the Secretary-General' (23 August 2004) S/2004/616, para 55: 'No single form of reparation is likely to be satisfactory to victims. Instead, appropriately conceived combinations of reparation measures will usually be required, as a complement to the proceedings of criminal tribunals and truth commissions'.

[136] See eg *Prosecutor v Al Mahdi* (Reparations Order) ICC-01/12-01/15-236 (17 August 2017) para 24.

[137] See *Prosecutor v Lubanga Dyilo* (Decision Establishing the Principles and Procedures to be Applied to Reparations) para 179.

[138] Wiersing, 'Lubanga and Its Implications' 24.

of punishment in the form of "punitive measures" […]'.[139] These aims are accompanied by longer-term and broader objectives, including the promotion of reconciliation between victims, communities and perpetrators.[140] The application of these and other principles of reparation established in the *Lubanga* case must be based on the principles of dignity, non-discrimination, and non-stigmatisation.[141]

One last aspect remains to be examined in order to understand the relevance of the reparation system provided for in Rome Statute for victims of international economic crimes. The drafters envisaged a hybrid system of reparations, including a case-based reparation scheme and the Trust Fund for Victims (TFV), which collects private donations, voluntary contributions from States, and fines and forfeitures ordered by the Court.[142] To secure fines and forfeitures 'for the ultimate benefit of victims',[143] the Pre-trial Chamber may request States Parties to identify, trace and freeze or seize proceeds, property and assets and instrumentalities of crimes.[144] In addition to this reparatory function, the TFV also performs a function of general assistance to the victims.

The reparation system just described could benefit victims of international economic crimes in several ways. First, restitution and compensation are forms of reparation that may be particularly satisfactory for victims of international economic crimes, who wish to obtain financial compensation for the losses suffered and the return of economic or natural wealth to their country, in order to restore the *status quo ante*.[145] This does not mean that these measures will totally repair the harm suffered by the victims of international economic crimes. They too may need rehabilitation, considering that systemic economic attacks on the foundations of society can permanently damage a country's essential services, including hospitals and schools, causing psychological and physical harm to victims. Furthermore, since international economic crimes often overlap with human rights and environmental violations, their inclusion in the Rome Statute should encourage the exploration of restorative justice solutions that actively involve international economic criminals in reparations that go beyond mere compensation, including measures aimed at improving human rights compliance programmes.[146] This would be in line with the nature of the harm caused by such crimes.

[139] ibid 23–24.

[140] See ICC, *Prosecutor v Lubanga Dyilo* (Decision Establishing the Principles and Procedures to be Applied to Reparations) para 244.

[141] ibid para 243.

[142] Art 79 of the Rome Statute.

[143] Art 57(3)(e) of the Rome Statute.

[144] Art 93(1)(k) of the Rome Statute. On the application of Arts 57(3)(e) and 93(1)(k) see eg *Prosecutor v Lubanga Dyilo* (Decision on the Prosecutor's Application for a Warrant of Arrest. Article 58) ICC-01/04-01/06-1-Corr-Red (10 February 2006) paras 130–141.

[145] Wiersing, 'Lubanga and Its Implications' 27.

[146] See A Nieto Martín, 'Ecocidio y justicia restaurativa: el derecho penal internacional post-Nuremberg' (*Almacén de Derecho*, 26 November 2020) https://almacendederecho.org/ecocidio-y-justicia-restaurativa-el-derecho-penal-internacional-post-nuremberg.

A second way in which the reparation system provided for in the Rome Statute can benefit victims of international economic crimes relates to the existence of the TFV. Although perpetrators of such crimes are not typically indigent, they may seek to conceal their assets as soon as they become aware of the possibility of international criminal proceedings against them. In such cases, the principle whereby the convicted person should compensate the victims for the harm suffered may not be effective. Although Rule 218(1) of the RPE provides that when a State Party is unable to enforce an order for forfeiture in relation to the specified proceeds, property or assets, the same State should take measures to recover their value, this does not mean that the recovery would be easy and successful. This is what happened in the *Lubanga* case, where the defendant was declared indigent because no assets could be identified for reparation purposes,[147] and the only alternative left to secure reparations for the victims was the TFV.[148] Should international economic crimes be included in the Rome Statute, this collective fund could be seen as a valuable instrument to guarantee victims' right to reparation.

ADDITIONAL OR ALTERNATIVE SOLUTIONS TO THE PROSECUTION OF INTERNATIONAL ECONOMIC CRIMES BEFORE THE ICC

There exist additional or alternative solutions to the potential prosecution of international economic crimes before the ICC. On the one hand, it would be possible to rely exclusively on national courts, namely the courts of the State of which the perpetrator is a national, or the courts of the States in whose territory the alleged international economic crime was committed. Although this choice undoubtedly has advantages, it entails difficulties that make it necessary to consider the possibility that other national courts may intervene on the basis of the principle of universal jurisdiction. On the other hand, the ICC is not the only supranational body that could fill in the gaps left by national jurisdictions in the prevention and prosecution international economic crimes; other solutions have been proposed at regional and international level that deserve consideration.

[147] See *Prosecutor v Lubanga Dyilo* (Decision Establishing the Principles and Procedures to be Applied to Reparations) para 269.

[148] It was also suggested that an international civil tribunal be created, to which victims of international crimes can claim reparations for their harm, and which would be 'dependent neither on political will, nor on the will of the prosecutor'. However, so far, no proposal has been developed in this respect. See Wiersing, 'Lubanga and Its Implications' 38, citing B Evans-Pritchard and M Gouby, 'Lubanga Verdict Prompts Debate on Reparations. Following International Court's Conviction of First War Crimes Suspect, Will Proposed Reparations Process Heal or Divide Communities?' (*Institute for War & Peace Reporting*, 30 April 2012) https://iwpr.net/global-voices/lubanga-verdict-prompts-debate-reparations.

National Solutions to Prevent and Prosecute International Economic Crimes

Relying on the Territoriality and Nationality Principles of Jurisdiction

The fact that national courts are located in the countries where the alleged crimes were committed facilitates access to evidence and allows victims and witnesses to follow the proceedings easily. For example, in July 2008, a special division of the High Court of Uganda, known as the International Crimes Division (ICD), was established to prosecute perpetrators of international crimes committed during the internal conflict in Uganda, which include both rebels and commanders of the Lord Resistance Army (LRA). Nonetheless, with the surrender and transfer to The Hague of one of the LRA commanders indicted by the ICC, Dominic Ongwen, 'Uganda became one of the few countries to conduct parallel criminal proceedings at both the national and international levels for crimes committed during the same armed conflict'.[149] These parallel proceedings have inevitably stimulated comparison between the ICD and the ICC. According to those who have been involved in the implementation of the ICD, the benefits of administering international criminal justice at domestic level are numerous: in addition to its proximity to victims and witnesses, who welcomed the creation of the ICD and were eager to collaborate with the investigators, the ICD could easily cooperate with local police and detention centre and was able to gain a greater understanding of the culture and history surrounding the events under investigation.[150] On the other hand, criticism has been levelled at the lack of resources and a solid legal framework governing reparations.[151]

In Colombia, the *Jurisdicción Especial para la Paz* (JEP or Special Jurisdiction for Peace) was set up in 2016 as part of the *Sistema Integral de Verdad, Justicia, Reparación y No Repetición* established by the Peace Agreement signed by the Colombian National Government and the Revolutionary Armed Forces of Colombia (FARC-EP). Since its creation, this special national court has actively investigated crimes committed during the armed conflict that has ravaged the country for more than fifty years. The reactivity with which Colombian ordinary and special courts responded to the call of international criminal justice prompted the OTP of the ICC to close its preliminary examinations on the Situation of

[149] S Kihika Kasande, 'Uganda's Long Road to Accountability: The Kwoyelo Verdict and Lessons for Future International Crimes Prosecutions' (*ICTJ*, 21 August 2024) https://www.ictj.org/latest-news/uganda%E2%80%99s-long-road-accountability-kwoyelo-verdict-and-lessons-future-international.

[150] The advantages of applying international criminal justice at national level, including at the ICD, were discussed during the conference entitled 'War Crimes Committee Conference – Session 4: The Challenges to Undertaking Domestic and Hybrid Trials for Atrocity Crimes' (*IBA*, 12 May 2022) www.ibanet.org/session-details/se_112117.

[151] See Kihika Kasande, 'Uganda's Long Road'.

Colombia in October 2021, on the basis that 'there was not a reasonable basis to believe that potential cases arising from an investigation of the situation would be admissible' before the Court.[152] Nonetheless, this decision was considered premature by some, given the challenges the JEP is facing in its mandate.[153]

From a financial point of view, the government of Iván Duque decided to significantly cut the budget allocated to the JEP for 2020.[154] Furthermore, his government allegedly tried to undermine the functioning of the JEP with two proposals launched in 2018. On the one hand, Duque's parliamentary group sought to prevent all transitional justice bodies from accessing 'confidential information affecting national security'.[155] On the other hand, it proposed creating special chambers within the JEP with the limited competence to prosecute members of the Colombian Armed Forces, which would have undermined the JEP's function 'to bring *all parties of the conflict to justice*' without privileging one party over another.[156] The JEP's legitimacy and independence were further threatened by Duque's objection that this special court should not have exclusive jurisdiction over crimes committed during Colombia's internal armed conflict, to the detriment of ordinary courts. In this respect, Ambos and Aboueldahab pointed out that one of the reasons behind the establishment of the JEP was precisely the need to remedy the burden and lack of diligence of the ordinary courts.[157]

In light of these attempts to interfere with the proper functioning of the JEP and other challenges it faces,[158] some have questioned Colombia's genuine willingness and ability to investigate and prosecute international crimes and,

[152] The preliminary examinations in the Situation of Colombia were concluded with the signature of a Cooperation Agreement between the OTP and the government of Colombia in October 2021. See ICC-OTP, 'ICC Prosecutor, Mr Karim A. A. Khan QC, concludes the preliminary examination of the Situation in Colombia with a Cooperation Agreement with the Government charting the next stage in support of domestic efforts to advance transitional justice Cooperation Agreement' (28 October 2021) www.legal-tools.org/doc/uozzd2/. Overall, the JEP is considered an example of positive complementarity, see K Ambos, 'The Return of 'Positive Complementarity'' (*EJIL:Talk!*, 3 November 2021) www.ejiltalk.org/the-return-of-positive-complementarity/.

[153] For a critical approach to the prosecutor's position, see J Peppier and L Evenson, 'ICC Starts Next Chapter in Colombia, but Will It Lead to Justice?' (*EJIL:Talk!* 15 December 2021) https://www.ejiltalk.org/icc-starts-next-chapter-in-colombia-but-will-it-lead-to-justice/. See also 'Colombia: Letter to the Prosecutor of the International Criminal Court' (*Human Rights Watch*, 2021) https://www.hrw.org/news/2021/10/14/colombia-letter-prosecutor-international-criminal-court.

[154] See R Quintero M, 'Three Major Challenges the Special Jurisdiction for Peace in Colombia Faces' (*OpinioJuris*, 30 July 2019) http://opiniojuris.org/2019/07/30/three-major-challenges-the-special-jurisdiction-for-peace-in-colombia-faces/; and A Morales, 'The Rocky Road to Peace: Current Challenges at the Special Jurisdiction for Peace in Colombia' (*EJIL:Talk!*, 3 May 2021) https://www.ejiltalk.org/the-rocky-road-to-peace-current-challenges-at-the-special-jurisdiction-for-peace-in-colombia/.

[155] K Ambos and S Aboueldahab, 'Colombia: Time for the ICC Prosecutor to Act?' (*EJIL:Talk!*, 2 April 2019) www.ejiltalk.org/colombia-time-for-the-icc-prosecutor-to-act/.

[156] ibid (emphasis added).

[157] ibid.

[158] On the structural challenges facing the JEP, see A Morales, 'The Rocky Road to Peace II: Additional Challenges at the Special Jurisdiction for Peace in Colombia' (*EJIL:Talk!*, 12 May 2022) www.ejiltalk.org/the-rocky-road-to-peace-ii-additional-challenges-at-the-special-jurisdiction-for-peace-in-colombia/.

thus, the OTP's decision to close the preliminary examinations on the Situation in Colombia.[159] However, immediately after his election in 2022, the President of the Republic of Colombia, Gustavo Petro, expressed his appreciation for the work carried out by the JEP in the peace-building process in Colombia,[160] and has since engaged in critical dialogue with it, while continuing to support its work.[161]

The problems encountered by the ICD and the JEP could also arise for national courts responsible for prosecuting international economic crimes. Two scenarios can be envisaged: one in which national courts strive to prosecute economic criminals as effectively as possible, and succeed in doing so;[162] and one in which national courts political power obstructs justice, interferes with it and sometimes nullifies it. In other words, national courts that can exercise jurisdiction over international (economic) crimes according to the territoriality or nationality principles are not always genuinely able or willing to ensure international criminal justice. There may be practical challenges, such as logistical problems, financial constraints, and the security level of national detention facilities, which may affect a country's ability to prosecute international economic crimes. Furthermore, political difficulties may arise, such as the involvement of judges and law enforcement authorities with perpetrators of international economic crimes, which could affect a country's genuine willingness to conduct investigations and prosecutions. Since the risk of impunity or partial and unfair justice is high, the need to resort to complementary justice systems should be considered as a viable alternative.

Domestic Courts Exercising Universal Jurisdiction

The concept of universal jurisdiction dates back to the 1600s, when Hugo Grotius and other international lawyers began to advocate that there are crimes that can be subject to the 'jurisdiction of any court in the world, no matter where they [are] committed or by whom'.[163] This idea was met with resistance from a group of sceptics who, while not denying the existence of

[159] ibid.

[160] See Redacción Política, 'Gustavo Petro le pidió a la JEP maximizar la verdad en el país' (*El Tiempo*, 30 July 2022) https://www.eltiempo.com/politica/proceso-de-paz/gustavo-petro-le-solicitamos-a-la-jep-maximizar-la-verdad-en-el-pais-691295; JP Cuellar Torres, 'Gustavo Petro le solicitó a la JEP maximizar la verdad en Colombia durante una reunión' (*El país*, 30 July 2022) https://www.elpais.com.co/politica/gustavo-petro-le-solicito-a-la-jep-maximizar-la-verdad-en-colombia-durante-una-reunion.html.

[161] See Redacción Política, 'Petro volvió a lanzarle pullas a la JEP por su operatividad interna' (*El Espectador*, 31 March 2025) www.elespectador.com/politica/petro-critica-de-nuevo-a-la-jep-por-su-operatividad-interna-noticias-hoy; JS Lombo Delgado, 'Presidente Petro anuncia que Gobierno pondrá los recursos que deje de recibir la JEP por congelamiento de ayudas de EE. UU.' (*El Tiempo*, 29 January 2025) www.eltiempo.com/politica/gobierno/presidente-petro-anuncia-que-gobierno-pondra-los-recursos-que-deje-de-recibir-la-jep-por-congelamiento-de-ayudas-de-ee-uu-3421994.

[162] For instance, the *Volkswagen* case discussed above in 'Defrauding the US' in ch 3.

[163] D Hawkins, 'Universal Jurisdiction for Human Rights: From Legal Principle to Limited Reality' (2003) 9 *Global Governance* 347, 347.

universal jurisdiction, criticised the possibility of applying this principle to a wide range of crimes, arguing that universal jurisdiction could only be invoked to prosecute piracy on the high seas and other similar crimes committed outside the territorial jurisdiction of any State.[164] In contrast, proponents of a broader application of universal jurisdiction initially included 'piracy, slavery, war crimes, crimes against peace, crimes against humanity, genocide, and torture'[165] among the crimes that can be tried before any court in the world. While the application of the principle of universal jurisdiction to some of these crimes has been provided for in international instruments,[166] this is not the case for others. This gap has been filled by separating the application of the principle of universal jurisdiction from its express provision in international instruments and linking it instead to the nature of the offences.[167] This was expressly stated in Principle 1 of the Princeton Principles on Universal Jurisdiction, according to which

> [...] universal jurisdiction is criminal jurisdiction based solely on the nature of the crime, without regard to where the crime was committed, the nationality of the alleged or convicted perpetrator, the nationality of the victim, or any other connection to the state exercising such jurisdiction.[168]

The Princeton Principles formed the starting point for a more comprehensive definition of the concept of universal jurisdiction, which has continued to evolve. In 2002, the Cairo-Arusha Principles on Universal Jurisdiction expanded the category of crimes subject to universal jurisdiction to include offences of economic significance that have an impact on economic, social, or cultural rights, such as 'acts of plunder and gross misappropriation of public resources'.[169] More recently, a further step forward was taken by the International Congress on Universal Jurisdiction, which drafted and disseminated the Madrid-Buenos Aires Principles on Universal Jurisdiction. In the Preamble, the drafters reiterated that the application of the principle of universal jurisdiction depends on 'the nature and seriousness of certain crimes' since

[164] ibid 348.

[165] Principle 2 of The Princeton Principles on Universal Jurisdiction. See Princeton University Program in Law and Public Affairs, 'The Princeton Principles on Universal Jurisdiction' (2001) http://hrlibrary.umn.edu/instree/princeton.html.

[166] See inter alia Art 5 of the Convention against Torture, and Other Cruel, Inhuman or Degrading Treatment or Punishment (New York, 10 December 1984), for the crime of torture.

[167] This occurred at Nuremberg and Tokyo, where the tribunals were assigned the power to try 'war criminals whose offenses have no particular geographical location' without referring to the principle of universal jurisdiction. In addition, the nature of the crimes committed in the former Yugoslavia and Rwanda prompted the Security Council to set up ad hoc criminal tribunals on the basis of the UN Charter and not on the basis of the principle of universal jurisdiction. See Hawkins, 'Universal Jurisdiction' 352.

[168] Emphasis added.

[169] Starr, 'Extraordinary Crimes' 1279. See also EA Ankumah, 'The Cairo-Arusha Principles on Universal Jurisdiction in Respect of Gross Human Rights Offenses: An African Perspective' (2004) 98 *Proceedings of the ASIL Annual Meeting* 238, 238.

these features transcend 'the responsibility of a particular Sovereign State and affects humanity as a whole',[170] and emphasised the role of universal jurisdiction as a mechanism to prevent the scourge of impunity for the most serious crimes.

The Madrid-Buenos Aires Principles are based on the legacy of the Princeton and Cairo-Arusha Principles on Universal Jurisdiction, which have been expanded and developed in light of today's social threats, including 'major economic, financial and environmental aggressions'.[171] One of the innovations of the Madrid-Buenos Aires Principles is precisely the extension of universal jurisdiction to international crimes other than those identified by the Princeton Principles. Human trafficking, enforced disappearance and extrajudicial executions were added to other international crimes in Principle 2, which notes that '[s]uch [international] crimes may be committed in many ways, including through economic activities and those that affect the environment'. This observation lays the foundation for Principle 3, according to which economic and environmental crimes that 'seriously affect group or collective human rights or cause the irreversible destruction of ecosystem' also fall within the category of crimes subject to universal jurisdiction.[172] This is in line with the idea advocated in this book of considering the most serious forms of economic offences as crimes that affect humanity as a whole and that can thus be prosecuted by any State in the world, regardless of the territory in which 'those crimes were committed, the nationality of the alleged perpetrator and the victims, or any other connection to the State exercising the jurisdiction'.[173]

Lastly, it is important to mention Principle 12, which recalls the need for cooperation both among States and between States and other international criminal justice institutions, such as the ICC, to ensure the effective exercise of universal jurisdiction. As in the case of the Rome Statute, cooperation is the Achilles heel of the international criminal justice system based on the principle of universal jurisdiction. Indeed, investigations are complicated by the fact that both the crime scenes and witnesses are far from the courts where universal jurisdiction is exercised and are sometimes located on the other side of the world.[174]

[170] See Preamble of the 'Madrid-Buenos Aires Principles of Universal Jurisdiction' available at 'II International Congress on Universal Jurisdiction' (FIBGAR) https://fibgar.es/en/portfolio-item-en/ii-international-congress-on-universal-jurisdiction/.

[171] ibid, see Preamble.

[172] ibid, see Principle 3. Economic crimes that may fall within this category of offences, when they reach the required threshold of gravity, are listed in the Annex to the Madrid-Buenos Aires Principles of Universal Jurisdiction and include: 'Food fraud; Price speculation on essential goods on which the survival or health of a large number of people depends […]; Illicit use of the property of the victims of the crimes set out in these Principles […]; Illicit exploitation of natural resources seriously affecting the health, life or the peaceful co-existence of humans with their natural habitat in the area where the exploitation takes place'.

[173] ibid, see Principle 1.

[174] Trial International, 'Evidentiary Challenges in Universal Jurisdiction Cases' (2019) *Universal Jurisdiction Annual Review* 1, 9.

These evidentiary difficulties can only be overcome by relying on cooperation with local authorities, which 'is as necessary as it is tricky'.[175]

Other issues relating to cooperation may be raised by States seeking to protect alleged perpetrators of international crimes. This is the case of Hissène Habré, former President of Chad, against whom Belgium had issued an arrest warrant for international crimes allegedly perpetrated during his regime from 1982 to 1990. On-site investigations were carried out by Belgium with cooperation of the government of Chad; however, the extradition of the suspect was prevented by the reluctance of Senegal, the country where the suspect lived, to cooperate with Belgium.[176] This impasse was eventually resolved thanks to the intervention of the African Union, which instructed Senegal to hand Habré over to justice. After years of impunity, the former President of Chad was tried before the Extraordinary African Chambers established in 2012 within the Senegalese courts, following an agreement between the African Union and the government of Senegal.[177]

This case offers a twofold lesson. On the one hand, it shows that, despite certain difficulties, the principle of universal jurisdiction can be an effective response to the inertia of national courts in exercising their jurisdiction according to the territoriality or nationality principles of jurisdiction. On the other hand, this case illustrates that when national courts – regardless of whether they have jurisdiction based on the principle of territoriality, nationality, or universal jurisdiction – are unable or unwilling to provide justice for particularly serious crimes, the intervention of supranational judicial mechanisms may prove useful, if not indispensable.

Supranational Solutions to Prevent and Prosecute International Economic Crimes

Regional Criminal Courts and Other Initiatives

Several initiatives have been launched and developed in different regions of the world that could help prevent and prosecute international economic crimes. On the one hand, regional complaint and cooperation mechanisms have been suggested or implemented with the main objective of preventing the commission of serious economic crimes. On the other hand, over the years, various proposals have been put forward regarding the creation of regional criminal courts.[178]

[175] ibid.

[176] 'Senegal: Stop Stalling with Habré Extradition' (*Human Rights Watch*, 12 January 2012) www.hrw.org/news/2012/01/12/senegal-stop-stalling-habre-extradition.

[177] On the Extraordinary African Chambers see Hybrid Justice, 'Chambres Africaines Extraordinaires/Extraordinary African Chambers' https://hybridjustice.com/extraordinary-african-chambers/.

[178] Among the scholars suggesting the creation of alternative mechanisms for addressing international crimes other than core crimes is N Boister, 'Treaty Crimes, International Criminal Court?' (2009) 12 *New Criminal Law Review* 341, 359–364, exploring the possibility to create regional treaty-based criminal courts or an international court of last resort.

The idea of entrusting certain areas of criminal justice to regional courts has been widely accepted as a viable alternative to national courts that fail to address impunity for criminals in their countries.[179] The material scope of jurisdiction of the regional criminal courts established or proposed to date mainly covers ordinary forms of economic crime, although in some cases it has been suggested that they should focus on the most serious economic crimes. In Africa, the so-called Malabo Protocol is aimed at providing the African Court of Justice and Human Rights (ACtJHR) with jurisdiction over cases of grand corruption and money-laundering, while in South America some NGOs have proposed the creation of a Latin-American and Caribbean Criminal Court against transnational organised crime, including economic crimes. These regional courts are designed to complement national courts, in line with the principle of complementarity governing relations between the ICC and the States Parties to the Rome Statute.

The Malabo Protocol and the ACtJHR

Since 2002, the African Union has reversed the approach adopted until then by the Organisation of African Unity and embraced a policy of 'non-indifference' towards the humanitarian and security situation in the African region.[180] This policy is reflected in the Constitutive Act of the African Union, which gives this regional body the right to intervene in the internal affairs of any African State when there are grave circumstances, including international crimes, and where it is necessary to restore peace and security.[181] The other side of the coin is the duty of the African Union to ensure that every State respects 'democratic principles, human rights, the rule of law and good governance'.[182]

As a result of the African Union's commitment to greater protection of human rights, the Protocol to the African Charter on Human and Peoples' Rights on the Establishment of an African Court on Human and Peoples' Rights entered into force in 2004.[183] Article 3 of the Protocol gives this court jurisdiction to hear cases concerning the interpretation and application

[179] Wharton, 'Redrawing the Line?' 177, according to whom 'national responses are insufficient to tackle' transnational organised crimes and economic crimes.

[180] L Bergholm, 'The African Union (AU) and Its Commitment to Non-Indifference: Can the AU Be an Actor for the Promotion of Human Security?' in A Swain et al (eds), *Globalization and Challenges to Building Peace* (Anthem Press, 2012) 181, 186.

[181] Art 4(h) and (j) of the Constitutive Act of the African Union (Lomé, 11 July 2000). See also Bergholm, 'The African Union' 187.

[182] Art 4(m) of the Constitutive Act of the African Union. On the interrelation and interdependence between these concepts, see W Zhang, 'The Relationship between Rule of Law, Human Rights, Good Governance and Democracy' in W Zhang et al (eds), *Human Rights and Good Governance* (Brill, 2016) 1, 1–8. See also HRC Res 45/9 (6 October 2020) A/HRC/RES/45/9, entitled 'The Role of Good Governance in the Promotion and Protection of Human Rights' and HRC Res 47/7 (12 July 2021) A/HRC/RES/47/7, entitled 'The Negative Impact of Corruption on the Enjoyment of Human Rights'.

[183] Bergholm, 'The African Union' 189. See Protocol to the African Charter on Human and Peoples' Rights on the Establishment of an African Court on Human and Peoples' Rights (Ouagadougou, 10 June 1988).

not only of the Protocol and the African Charter on Human and Peoples' Rights,[184] but also of other human rights instruments ratified by the concerned States. Another significant development in the field of human rights protection in Africa was the adoption of the Malabo Protocol,[185] aimed to amend the Protocol on the Statute of the ACtJHR.[186] Article 14 of the Malabo Protocol suggests extending the international criminal jurisdiction of the ACtJHR to include crimes of economic significance, such as corruption, money-laundering, trafficking in hazardous waste, and illicit exploitation of natural resources, in addition to core crimes – genocide, crimes against humanity, war crimes, aggression – and other crimes traditionally subject to universal jurisdiction – such as piracy.

The Malabo Protocol suggests including Article 28I in the Protocol on the Statute of the African Court of Justice and Human Rights, which provides no definition of corruption but specifies that acts and omissions of corruption that are relevant 'for the purposes of [the] Statute' are those that affect 'the stability of a state, a region, or the Union'. In other words, due the 'prevalence of grand corruption [in the African region] and the need to prevent a flood of cases',[187] this provision introduces a threshold of gravity according to which corruption offences falling within the jurisdiction of the ACtJHR must be serious, which excludes cases of petty corruption. Nevertheless, the threshold of gravity required by the provision has been criticised for its vagueness, in particular with regard to the question of whether the destabilisation caused by grand corruption should constitute an actual or potential threat.[188] A literal interpretation of the wording of this provision suggests that both options should be considered.[189]

On the other hand, the new Article 46Abis of the Protocol on the Statute of the African Court of Justice and Human Rights would impose a second restriction on the jurisdiction of the ACtJHR in cases of grand corruption, introducing a general immunity provision for acts of corruption committed by senior state officials during their office.[190] This immunity clause would de facto shield perpetrators of grand corruption from being prosecuted before the ACtJHR, thus strengthening the culture of impunity that is 'entrenched in most African countries'.[191]

[184] African Charter on Human and People's Rights (Nairobi, 27 June 1981) (the 'Banjul Charter').

[185] Protocol on Amendments to the Protocol on the Statute of the African Court of Justice and Human Rights (Malabo, 27 June 2014) (the Malabo Protocol).

[186] Sharm El-Sheikh, 1 July 2008.

[187] J Hatchard, *Combating Corruption: Legal Approaches to Supporting Good Governance and Integrity in Africa* (Edward Elgar Publishing, 2014) 492.

[188] ibid.

[189] The use of the present tense, 'affects', may refer to both actual and potential acts of destabilisation.

[190] Hatchard, *Combating Corruption* 494.

[191] ibid 502. On the concerns raised by the immunity clause, see, 'Malabo Protocol. Legal and Institutional Implications of the Merged and Expanded African Court' (*Amnesty International*, 22 January 2016) www.amnesty.org/en/documents/afr01/3063/2016/en/, 26–27.

Corruption is only one of the economic crimes over which the ACtJHR would exercise jurisdiction – albeit within the significant limits mentioned above. The Malabo Protocol also suggests including Article 28Ibis in the Protocol on the Statute of the African Court of Justice and Human Rights, which would refer to ordinary acts of money-laundering without setting any threshold of gravity. This would be provided in Article 28Lbis, which would criminalise serious acts of illicit exploitation of natural resources that affect the stability of a State, a region or the Union.

The choice of the drafters of the Malabo Protocol to grant a regional court jurisdiction over serious economic crimes is commendable, both because crimes that are a common problem for a region of the world can best be addressed by that same region, taking into account cultural, historical and political factors, and because no other supranational court could currently exercise this type of jurisdiction.[192] Furthermore, compared to the ICC, the ACtJHR would have the advantage of being able to prosecute not only individuals but also companies,[193] which in most cases are actively involved in the perpetration of serious economic crimes – as demonstrated by the cases explored in this book.

However, there would be important limitations to the ACtJHR's exercise of jurisdiction over serious economic crimes that are worth mentioning. First, it is reasonable to question the entry into force of the Malabo Protocol – or at least its timing – given that since its adoption in 2014, fifteen out of fifty-five States have signed the protocol, while none have ratified it.[194] Furthermore, even assuming it enters into force, the aforementioned immunity clause would have to be revised to ensure effective criminal prosecution of all perpetrators of serious economic crimes. Another limitation to be addressed concerns the possible lack of cooperation with the ACtJHR by the country where serious economic crimes are committed or by other African States. To this end, Article 22 of the Malabo Protocol envisages the inclusion of new Article 46L in the Protocol on the Statute of the African Court of Justice and Human Rights, providing for a general obligation for Member States to cooperate with the ACtJHR,[195] which, however, is not accompanied by any enforcement mechanism in the event that States do not comply with the ACtJHR's order. This could undermine the credibility of the ACtJHR in prosecuting those responsible for international economic crimes.

Lastly, the effectiveness of criminal proceedings before the ACtJHR could be undermined by its power to order the confiscation of criminal proceeds

[192] Hatchard, *Combating Corruption* 500–503.

[193] See Art 22 of the Malabo Protocol referring to new Arts 46B and 46C of the Protocol on the Statute of the African Court of Justice and Human Rights.

[194] See the Status List at African Union, 'Protocol on Amendments to the Protocol on the Statute of the African Court of Justice and Human Rights' available at https://au.int/en/treaties/protocol-amendments-protocol-statute-african-court-justice-and-human-rights.

[195] On concerns about the African Court's ability to deliver justice on the expanded mandate redefined by the Malabo Protocol and to cooperate with the ICC, see 'Malabo Protocol. Legal and Institutional Implications' 24–29.

or illicit assets and their return to their rightful owners and to an appropriate Member State.[196] It has been noted that the main problem underlying the ACtJHR's confiscation system is that it is contingent on criminal convictions.[197] Thus, it has been suggested that entering into reparation agreements with alleged perpetrators in exchange for the withdrawal of criminal charges would incentivise them to collaborate and return the proceeds of crimes to the population of the victim State.[198] In this way, reparation purposes would certainly be pursued, but at the expense of other functions of criminal law, including general prevention. It would therefore be appropriate to reflect on how to ensure a more balanced approach between these functions.

The COPLA Project

The creation of the Latin-American and Caribbean Criminal Court against transnational organised crime (*Corte Penal Latinoamericana y del Caribe contra el crimen transnacional organizado*; 'COPLA') was promoted by *Democracia Global*, an Argentinian non-governmental organisation, and by other NGOs, gaining the support of prominent scholars, jurists, and politicians.[199] The COPLA was presented as a viable alternative to national courts that are unwilling or unable to initiate criminal proceedings against leaders of organised groups – '*cúpulas, jefes u organizadores criminales*' – involved in the perpetration of transnational crimes in the South American region.[200] As provided for in Article 1 of the COPLA Statute, the role played by this regional court would be complementary to that of national courts in the fight against transnational crimes that have reached regional proportions and escaped the control of national institutions.[201]

However, at present, COPLA remains a project that is slowly taking shape. For this Court to become a reality, ten of the thirty-two countries that could potentially be parties to the COPLA Statute, must deposit their instruments

[196] See Art 19 of the Malabo Protocol referring to new Art 43A(5) of the Protocol on the Statute of the African Court of Justice and Human Rights.

[197] Hatchard, *Combating Corruption* 491.

[198] ibid 503.

[199] 'Corte penal latinoamericana y del caribe contra el crimen transnacional organizado' (COPLA) www.coalicioncopla.org/single-post/2019/11/26/proyecto-corte-penal-latinoamericana-y-del-caribe-contra-el-crimen-transnacional-organiza. See also Sillitti and López Velásquez, 'El proyecto COPLA' 763.

[200] The organised crimes over which COPLA would have jurisdiction are those expressly listed in the COPLA Statute – see Art 5 of the COPLA Statute, referring to a series of crimes including transnational corruption, transnational money-laundering – and in the Palermo Convention – see Art 6 of the COPLA Statute, which provides definitions of offences modelled on the Palermo Convention. On the substantive jurisdiction of this Court and the qualification of the crimes within its scope as 'leadership crimes', see RJ Currie and J Leon, 'COPLA: A Transnational Criminal Court for Latin America and the Caribbean' (2019) 88 *Nordic Journal of International Law* 587, 598 et seq.

[201] Sillitti and López Velásquez, 'El proyecto COPLA' 764 and 767, arguing that complementarity represents a fundamental pillar of the COPLA Statute and reflects its purpose of strenghtening, rather than replacing, national jurisdictions.

of ratification, acceptance, approval or accession.[202] This threshold has not yet been reached. On the other hand, as already noted in relation to the ICC and the ACtJHR, what could really prevent the COPLA from being an effective court not only de jure but also de facto, are enforcement obstacles that could arise following its entry into force. A first obstacle may be the failure of States Parties to comply with the general obligation to cooperate with COPLA, laid down in Article 35 of its Statute. In the absence of a cooperative relationship between the States Parties and COPLA, the complexity of the investigations would pose serious enforcement challenges that would undermine COPLA's goals.[203] The lack of cooperation would be mainly due to political reasons: States in which the highest authorities representing democracy and the rule of law are involved in transnational crimes are unlikely to fully cooperate with a regional body investigating precisely those crimes.[204]

Despite their shortcomings, regional initiatives such as the Malabo Protocol and the COPLA project should not be underestimated, for a number of reasons. First, both initiatives seek to draw collective attention to the need to tackle impunity for transnational (economic) crimes, which represent a systemic and widespread problem for many States in the Global South. Secondly, these initiatives embody the collective awareness of the importance of preventing and tackling such crimes at regional level.[205] Lastly, both initiatives are projects and, as such, are perfectible, which means that they can be improved by reflecting, inter alia, on the challenges mentioned above.

Since the entry into force of the Malabo Protocol and the COPLA Statute would mean that regional criminal courts would play a complementary role to that played by States in exercising jurisdiction over ordinary economic crimes, it cannot be ruled out that these regional bodies may also prove to be an effective tool for assisting national courts in the prevention and prosecution of the most serious economic crimes, should the concept of 'international economic crime' crystallise in the coming years. One criticism that could be levelled at the adoption of a regional approach to prevent and punish international economic crimes is that this 'may ignore the truly global nature of some of these crimes'.[206] However, just as international crimes can fall within the jurisdiction of a national court without losing their 'global nature', the same applies to regional criminal courts. This is because the international relevance of a crime does not depend on the nature of the institution that can prosecute it but, as discussed above, on several parameters that determine its gravity.

[202] Art 46 of the COPLA Statute.
[203] Sillitti and López Velásquez, 'El proyecto COPLA' 767.
[204] ibid 768.
[205] Wharton, 'Redrawing the Line?' 182.
[206] ibid.

Other Initiatives: Regional Complaint and Cooperation Mechanisms

In other regions of the world, economic crimes have been tackled through initiatives that do not involve the creation of regional criminal courts, but regional complaint or cooperation mechanisms. An example of a regional cooperative mechanism aimed at preventing the commission of ordinary economic crimes is the Economic Crime and Cooperation Division, which is responsible for the Council of Europe's cooperation and assistance to its Member States in taking measures against corruption, money laundering and terrorist financing.[207]

On the other hand, an example of a regional complaint mechanism – limited to the prosecution of corruption – has been proposed for ASEAN, the Association of Southeast Asian Nations, established on 8 August 1967 in Bangkok. Since its entry into force, the ASEAN Charter has been signed by ten countries,[208] which have pledged to promoting economic growth, social and cultural development in the region, and cooperating mutually in the pursuit of peace, regional stability and respect for justice and the rule of law. With these objectives in mind, ASEAN identified its three main pillars, namely the political-security community, the socio-cultural community and the economic community (AEC).

The latter community was established on the basis of guidelines outlined in the AEC Blueprint 2015, followed by the most recent AEC Blueprint 2025, which emphasises the importance of promoting good governance in the Southeast Asian region.[209] This objective is even more important when considering reports presented by Transparency International according to which countries in the Asia-Pacific region – including the Southeast Asian States bordering the Mekong River, ie Laos, Thailand, Cambodia, and Vietnam – must make greater efforts to resolve corruption issues in their region.[210] Transparency International highlighted that many of these countries are plagued by grand corruption, which can 'destroy entire sectors, create recessions and put an end to democracies',[211] and which can exacerbate climate change.[212] Thus, for these States, adopting policies that prioritise good governance should be imperative.

[207] See 'Economic Crime and Cooperation Division' (Council of Europe) https://www.coe.int/en/web/corruption.

[208] See 'Asean – Association of Southeast Asian Nations' (ASEAN) https://asean.org.

[209] See ASEAN Economic Community, 'Asean Economic Community Blueprint 2025' (Jakarta, November 2015) paras 5 and 6.

[210] The call for action arises from most of the last Transparency International's Corruption Perceptions Index (CPI), see Transparency International, 'CPI 2021 for Asia Pacific: Grand Corruption and Lack of Freedoms Holding Back Progress' (2022) www.transparency.org/en/news/cpi-2021-for-asia-pacific-grand-corruption-holding-back-progress; Transparency International, 'CPI 2024 for Asia Pacific: Leaders Failing to Stop Corruption Amid an Escalating Climate Crisis' (2025) https://www.transparency.org/en/news/cpi-2024-asia-pacific-leaders-failing-to-stop-corruption-amid-escalating-climate-crisis.

[211] Transparency International, 'CPI 2021 for Asia Pacific: Grand Corruption and Lack of Freedoms Holding Back Progress'.

[212] Transparency International, 'CPI 2024 for Asia Pacific: Leaders Failing to Stop Corruption Amid an Escalating Climate Crisis'.

During the regional conference held in Bangkok in 2017 on 'Fast-tracking Implementation of UNCAC for Economic and Social Development in Southeast Asia', Civil Society Organisations (CSO) developed a set of recommendations and urged ASEAN States to implement them at national and regional levels. These recommendations include a call to recognise grand corruption as 'a cause of human rights violations and as an international crime requiring criminal sanctions and civil remedies',[213] and to join forces to establish a regional 'commission to receive and review complaints about cross-border corruption and, where appropriate, issue recommendations'.[214] This regional complaint mechanism is not yet operational in any ASEAN States, but could be considered an appropriate tool to help prevent the most serious systemic economic crimes, such as grand corruption, from spreading in the region.

International Alternatives to the ICC

Although the ICC is the only permanent judicial mechanism of last resort that exists to prosecute the most serious crimes of concern to the international community, alternative mechanisms of an international nature have been discussed and proposed to prevent international economic crimes from going unpunished. These include the creation of international tribunals with exclusive jurisdiction to prosecute serious economic crimes, such as grand corruption, and the drafting of treaties defining the concept of international economic crimes and prohibiting it as an international crime.

International Courts for the Prosecution of International Economic Crimes

The creation of an International Anti-Corruption Court (IACC) was proposed in 2014 by Mark Wolf, a Senior Judge of the United States District Court for the District of Massachusetts and Chair of Integrity Initiatives International,[215] who reiterated his position a few years later in a journal article entitled 'The World Needs an International Anti-Corruption Court'.[216] By corruption, Wolf means the 'abuse of public office for private gain by a nation's leaders',[217] which includes the most serious and high forms of corruption committed by high-level public officials.

[213] See Civil Society Organisations, 'Statement to the Regional Conference on Fast-Tracking UNCAC Implementation for Economic and Social Development in Southeast Asia' available at UNODC, 'CSOs Call for Action in Implementing UNCAC in the ASEAN' (3 February 2017) www.unodc.org/unodc/en/ngos/cn24_-csos-call-for-action-in-implementing-uncac-in-the-asean.html, 1.

[214] ibid 2.

[215] ML Wolf, 'We Need an International Court to Stamp out Corruption' (*The Washington Post*, 2014) www.washingtonpost.com/opinions/mark-l-wolf-we-need-an-international-court-to-stamp-out-corruption/2014/07/22/a15ecc38-10ff-11e4-9285-4243a40ddc97_story.html. See also Wolf, 'The Case'.

[216] ML Wolf, 'The World Needs an International Anti-Corruption Court' (2018) 147 *Daedalus* 144.

[217] ibid.

Wolf cites a number of reasons that justify the need to create a new international judicial mechanism, primarily to prevent corruption from going unpunished. Since the proliferation of corruption and the impunity of its perpetrators are not due to the lack of national and supranational laws prohibiting this crime,[218] but rather to the failure of national authorities to enforce them, Wolf believes that the creation of an ad hoc international court could prompt States to strengthen the enforcement of existing anti-corruption laws. Another reason behind the establishment of the IACC would be the need to revitalise democracy and the rule of law in States affected by grand corruption.[219] Lastly, effectively prosecuting kleptocrats would also prevent human rights abuses and incentivise States to adopt a human rights-oriented culture and policy.[220]

In terms of content, Wolf suggests creating a court similar to the ICC, which would complement national jurisdictions and be able to prosecute kleptocrats who are nationals of or operate in countries that are unwilling or unable to genuinely 'enforce their own laws against powerful offenders'.[221] However, Wolf also believes that the IACC must remain to some extent distinct from the ICC, as the latter's jurisdiction could arguably not extend to economic crimes, either by adopting a broad interpretation of the Rome Statute or by amending it.[222]

With regard to the composition of the court, the IACC would be composed of impartial judges and prosecutors who have national experience and expertise in grand corruption cases and who are able, in accordance with the principle of positive complementarity, to collaborate with and offer their assistance to their counterparts in countries seeking to prosecute such cases.[223] The IACC would investigate and try crimes committed by 'any head of state or of government, anyone appointed by a head of state or government, and anyone who conspires with one of those officials'.[224] The procedures described for triggering the IACC's jurisdiction over crimes committed by these individuals would mirror those mentioned in the Rome Statute: States Parties' referrals, investigations

[218] ibid 147. See above, 'Fragmentation to Alignment' in ch 2.

[219] ibid. See also Wolf, 'We Need an International Court', arguing that 'the most serious consequence of grand corruption is that it destroys democracy'.

[220] Wolf, 'The World Needs an International Anti-Corruption Court' 147. On this point, Wolf cites the former UN High Commissioner for Human Rights, Navi Pillay, who stated that '[…] the money stolen through corruption every year is enough to feed the world's hungry 80 times over […]' and that '[…] corruption denies people their right to food, and, in some cases, their right to life.' See High Commissioner for Human Rights Navi Pillay, 'Opening Statement: Panel on 'the Negative Impact of Corruption on Human Rights'' (13 March 2013) https://www.ohchr.org/en/statements-and-speeches/2013/03/opening-statement-navi-pillay-high-commissioner-human-rights-panel.

[221] Wolf, 'The World Needs an International Anti-Corruption Court' 145 and 149.

[222] ibid 149.

[223] ibid. See also Wolf, 'We Need an International Court', arguing that '[…] an IACC would employ an elite corps of investigators expert at unraveling complex financial transactions and prosecutors experienced in preparing and presenting complicated cases. It would also include experienced, impartial international judges'.

[224] Wolf, 'The World Needs an International Anti-Corruption Court' 150.

initiated *proprio motu* by the OTP, and Security Council's referrals.[225] This last trigger of jurisdiction is relevant not only from a procedural point of view, as it would allow the IACC to exercise its jurisdiction over crimes committed in the territory or by nationals of non-State Parties, but also from a substantive point of view, as it would automatically include grand corruption among threats to international peace and security of the world, which the Security Council may refer to the OTP acting under Chapter VII of the Charter of the UN.

The proposal elaborated by Wolf was welcomed by organisations, politicians, businessmen and scholars, to the extent that a 'Declaration in Support of the Creation of an International Anti-Corruption Court' was drafted and signed by 'individuals, former officials, business leaders, representatives of civil society and of government'.[226] After recalling the reasons why grand corruption cannot be fought by States alone, the Declaration lists the main characteristics that the IACC should have, specifying that one of its main priorities would be to guarantee the right to reparation for victims.[227]

Several scholars and politicians emphasised the advantages related to the creation of an international anti-corruption court, including Roksandić Vidlička who referred to the IACC as a secondary valid alternative to the primary possibility of prosecuting serious economic crimes before the ICC.[228] Similarly, Danilo Türk, former president of Slovenia and current president of the Club de Madrid, wrote an article in favour of the creation of the IACC,[229] in which he argued that one of its merits would be to finally recognise that grand corruption is not a local but an international crime, because it violates universal and borderless values, such as human rights, democracy, and the rule of law. However, Türk's enthusiasm for the proposal at hand was tempered by the realistic consideration that the creation of a new international court would be a 'long-term endeavour'.[230]

This is precisely the main weakness of Wolf's proposal, according to his opponents. Among them, Whiting went further, stating that the IACC is not simply a long-term commitment but a 'dream or a distraction'.[231] He noted that despite the massive support of some States for the IACC, it is very unlikely that this court will achieve global reach. In this respect, Whiting challenged the argument that the Security Council could refer to the IACC situations involving the commission of grand corruption in the territory or by nationals of non-State

[225] ibid.

[226] Integrity Initiatives International, 'Declaration in Support of the Creation of an International Anti-Corruption Court' http://integrityinitiatives.org/declaration.

[227] ibid: '[…] the IACC should have, in civil as well as criminal cases, the authority to recover, repatriate, and repurpose illicit assets for the victims of Grand Corruption'.

[228] Roksandić Vidlička, *Prosecuting Serious Economic Crimes* 411.

[229] D Türk, 'We Need an International Anti-Corruption Court' (*Politico*, 24 June 2022) https://www.politico.eu/article/need-international-anti-corruption-court/.

[230] ibid.

[231] A Whiting, 'Guest Post: Is an International Anti-Corruption Court a Dream or a Distraction?' (*The Global Anticorruption Blog*, 4 October 2018) https://globalanticorruptionblog.com/2018/10/04/guest-post-is-an-international-anti-corruption-court-a-dream-or-a-distraction/.

parties, on the ground that corruption cannot be considered a threat to peace under Chapter VII of the UN Charter. Although this is true for ordinary corruption offences that do not reach a high gravity threshold, it is debatable whether the same can be said for grand corruption, based on the above considerations regarding the capacity of international economic crimes to violate collective values, including international peace and security.

On the other hand, Withing argued that, as with the ICC, the effectiveness of anti-corruption investigations and the overall functioning of the IACC would depend entirely on the cooperation of countries, which are unlikely to grant the IACC adequate enforcement tools, and on substantial financial contributions.[232]

In sum, the creation of an international criminal court specifically dedicated to prosecuting grand corruption is undoubtedly a good intention, but some aspects of Wolf's proposal could be revised so that the IACC can represent a viable alternative to the ICC. For example, consideration could be given to redefining the IACC's subject-matter jurisdiction to include other serious economic crimes, leaving the prosecution of ordinary economic crimes to States and regional mechanisms. As the establishment of a new court would be a long-term commitment, it is not clear why the effort to create it should be limited to grand corruption cases, given that other economic crimes often reach similar levels of gravity. Extending the jurisdiction of the IACC to serious economic crimes other than grand corruption would also be justified by the fact that they are often interrelated, as demonstrated by the cases analysed in this book. This means that investigations into one crime may contribute to investigations into other crimes, and vice versa.

Furthermore, if agreement could be reached on the content of the concept of international economic crime, this category of international crimes would be an ideal candidate for inclusion in the jurisdiction of a new international court. This would also imply a rethinking of the name of the court in question, which should better reflect its broader scope of jurisdiction. For the purposes of this book, the term 'International Economic Crimes Court' (IECC) will be used. The material jurisdiction of the new court would 'assure that cases of grand corruption [and of international economic crimes, in general] are given priority',[233] which would not be the case if these crimes were prosecuted by the ICC without the initiation of thematic prosecutions on serious economic crimes and

[232] Wolf himself acknowledges that 'creating another court comparable to the ICC, which costs about $160 million a year, would be too expensive', see Wolf, 'The World Needs an International Anti-Corruption Court' 150.

[233] R Goldstone and R Rotberg, 'Guest Post: An International Anticorruption Court Is Not a Utopian Dream or a Distraction' (*The Global Anticorruption Blog*, 18 October 2018) https://globalanticorruptionblog.com/2018/10/18/guest-post-an-international-anticorruption-court-is-not-a-utopian-dream-or-a-distraction/. In this post, Goldstone and Rotberg replied to Whiting's argument that the IACC would be a 'utopian' dream. On similar arguments see also *R Goldstone and R Rotberg*, 'The Argument for an Int'l Anti-Corruption Court' (*Corruption Watch*, 19 October 2018) https://www.corruptionwatch.org.za/the-argument-for-an-international-anti-corruption-court/.

without the adoption of a broader conception of the 'crisis-focus' of international criminal law.

Another aspect that could be reconsidered concerns the scope of personal jurisdiction of the new court, which should be able to exercise its jurisdiction over crimes committed not only by natural persons but also by legal persons, thus filling a gap in the Rome Statute. In 2010, *Enlazando Alternativas*, a network of civil society organisations, proposed the drafting an international legal code of a coercive, sanctioning and binding nature, aimed at defining the legal responsibilities of corporations for the consequences of their activities,[234] and the creation an International Economic Tribunal with jurisdiction over natural and legal persons. Despite its merits, this proposal has remained on paper.[235]

In terms of weaknesses, the IECC risks facing challenges similar to those faced by the IACC. The entry into force of the IECC would require the support of a substantial number of States. It would be possible to count on the cooperation of States that voluntarily and consciously decide to join the Court, starting with the countries that have given their support to the IACC. On the other hand, it might prove more problematic to obtain the cooperation of States that are not parties but could facilitate investigations into international economic crimes committed on their territory or by their nationals. In this respect, the advantage of the IECC over the IACC is that the former would prosecute international economic crimes, which as such should be considered threats to international peace and security for which the Security Council could resort to Chapter VII of the United Nations Charter to trigger the IECC's jurisdiction. This would not completely overcome the risk of non-cooperation by non-State Parties – a utopian goal nowadays for any international criminal court – but it would at least represent a legally justified solution to limit it.

Lastly, the issue of costs cannot be underestimated. A new international court would entail a cost similar to that incurred for maintaining the ICC, amounting to approximately €195 million per year.[236] However, the right question to ask in this case is not whether this cost is high or not, but whether, given the enforcement and cost challenges that a new court would entail, the benefits outweigh the obstacles. Wolf's response regarding the IACC can also be applied to the IECC, namely that this new judicial body should be inherently cost-efficient.

[234] MC Olivet, 'Towards an International Tribunal on Economic Crimes' (*Global Policy Forum*, 20 July 2010) https://archive.globalpolicy.org/social-and-economic-policy/international-trade-and-development-1-57/transnational-corporations/49433-towards-an-international-tribunal-on-economic-crimes.html.

[235] Some UN rapporteurs proposed the creation of an International Human Rights Tribunal with the power to try multinational corporations. See M Scheinin, 'Towards a World Court of Human Rights, Anniversary of the Universal Declaration of Human Rights' (2009) https://cadmus.eui.eu/entities/publication/b3ac0ab9-0945-520e-9548-2fb254afb319.

[236] See ICC-ASP, 'Resolution of the Assembly of States Parties on the Proposed Programme Budget for 2025 and Related Policy and Administrative Matters' (6 December 2024) ICC-ASP/23/Res.6. See also Whiting, 'Guest Post'; also Wolf, 'The World Needs an International Anti-Corruption Court' 150.

This can be explained by looking again at the specific material scope of the new court's jurisdiction: the goal of preventing grand corruption – and potentially other types of international economic crimes – that threaten public wealth would enable many States to save huge sums of money. Furthermore, a conviction by the new court would result not only in a prison sentence, but also in an order to return the misappropriated public assets to the people of the victim country.[237]

Treaties and Statutes Prohibiting International Economic Crimes

Whether one considers the creation of a new court to prosecute international economic crimes, the possibility of bringing them under the jurisdiction of the ICC, or simply the need to reflect on their gravity, an important first step would be to put the definition of these crimes on paper. To this end, in 2013 Anderson proposed drafting an ad hoc statute to be included in the Rome Statute to prosecute international money laundering before the ICC, on the grounds that this crime constitutes 'a widespread international problem'.[238] Despite the innovative nature of his proposal, at least two aspects are unconvincing. The first concerns the fact that, like other academic theories, Anderson's proposal focuses on a single economic crime, excluding other economic crimes of similar gravity that might equally deserve international criminal recognition and prosecution.

Secondly, it should not be the fact that international money-laundering is a 'widespread international problem' that makes it prosecutable by international judicial bodies, but rather that this crime reaches the threshold of gravity of international crimes. This is only possible when the offence of money-laundering is committed in the context of crimes against humanity described in Article 7 of the Rome Statute[239] or in the context of international economic crimes, should this category be included as an autonomous crime in the Rome Statute.

Another initiative that could be taken outside the legal framework of the Rome Statute and with a view to the creation of an international criminal court for economic crimes could be the drafting of a multilateral treaty codifying international economic crimes, along the lines of the Genocide Convention or the draft treaty on crimes against humanity. Unlike the former, the latter has not yet been adopted, although some crimes against humanity are already prohibited by ad hoc international treaties.[240] However, as Juan Méndez, the former UN Special Rapporteur on torture, noted that

[237] Wolf, 'The World Needs an International Anti-Corruption Court' 150.

[238] Anderson, 'International Money Laundering' 772.

[239] Roksandić Vidlička, *Prosecuting Serious Economic Crimes* 417.

[240] For instance, the crime of torture and apartheid. See LN Sadat, 'Towards a New Treaty on Crimes against Humanity: Next Steps' (*Just Security*, 13 September 2021) https://www.justsecurity.org/78063/towards-a-new-treaty-on-crimes-against-humanity-next-steps/.

> there's still a need for a treaty that establishes state responsibility for crimes against humanity. It's also important to establish the kind of obligations for mutual assistance between states that are characteristic of both genocide and war crimes. There's currently nothing mandating it for crimes against humanity.[241]

In other words, the adoption of a treaty on crimes against humanity would help define the role of States in preventing and punishing such egregious crimes. However, the advantages of a treaty on crimes against humanity are offset by several problems relating to its drafting. First, the proposal for a Convention was put forward thirteen years ago by the Crimes Against Humanity Initiative,[242] before being included in the work program of the ILC. In 2019, the ILC adopted the Draft Articles on Prevention and Punishment of Crimes Against Humanity (Draft Articles) and transmitted them to the UN General Assembly. Since then, the General Assembly has discussed the Draft Articles for years and has taken note of them in several resolutions, without achieving any positive outcome,[243] to the point that a group of States felt compelled to draw attention to the 'the risk – as it has been the case with other ILC products in the past – of getting caught in a cycle of consideration and postponement of the articles without concrete action'.[244] Sadat, who followed the drafting process from the outset, described the debate that took place at the Sixth Committee of the General Assembly in 2021 as 'heated', pointing out that at the end of a '"fierce" and "difficult" negotiation' only a few States – including China and the Russian Federation – opposed the establishment of a new treaty on crimes against humanity and the resumption of the ILC's work.[245]

The turning point came in November 2024, when the Sixth Committee recommended to the General Assembly the adoption of a resolution convening the UN Conference of Plenipotentiaries on Prevention and Punishment of Crimes against Humanity that will be held in New York in 2028 and 2029 to 'elaborate and conclude a legally binding instrument on prevention and punishment of crimes against humanity'.[246] The resolution was adopted by the General Assembly on 4 December 2024,[247] setting a path for the preparatory sessions

[241] R Green, 'Draft Global Treaty on Crimes against Humanity Reaches Critical Juncture' (*IBA*, 29 September 2021) www.ibanet.org/draft-global-treaty-on-crimes-against-humanity.

[242] See Washington University in St Louis, 'Crimes Against Humanity Initiative' available at https://sites.wustl.edu/crimesagainsthumanity/.

[243] UNGA Res 74/187 (18 December 2019) A/RES/74/187; UNGA Draft Res (12 November 2020) A/C.6/75/L.20; UNGA Res 75/136 (15 December 2020) A/RES/75/136; UNGA Res 76/114 (9 December 2021) A/RES/76/114. For a brief and comprehensive summary of the steps taken so far by the General Assembly, see UNGA, 'Sixth Committee (Legal) – 77th Session' available at www.un.org/en/ga/sixth/77/cah.shtml.

[244] For a commentary of this risk, see also Sadat, 'Towards a New Treaty'.

[245] LN Sadat, 'Little Progress in the Sixth Committee on Crimes against Humanity' (2022) 54 *Case Western Reserve Journal of International Law* 89, 96.

[246] UNGA, 'Report of the Sixth Committee' (25 November 2024) A/79/470.

[247] UNGA Res 79/122 (4 December 2024) A/RES/79/122. See also R Dicker, 'Moving Ahead to Crimes Against Humanity Treaty' (OpinioJuris, 19 December 2024) https://opiniojuris.org/2024/12/19/moving-ahead-to-a-crimes-against-humanity-treaty/.

to the conference that will be held in 2026 and 2027. While not explicitly listed in the Draft Articles, which reiterate the definition of crimes against humanity contained in the Rome Statute, should certain economic crimes be recognised as crimes against humanity, the upcoming drafting of a treaty on crimes against humanity could provide a valuable opportunity to discuss their prosecution at national level.

It is plausible to assume that the same problems encountered so far by the attempt to draft a treaty on crimes against humanity will hinder the attempt to draft a multilateral international treaty on international economic crimes, especially considering that the adoption of measures directing States on how to prevent and punish these offences could strike at the heart of many States' interests.[248] Therefore, although negotiating a treaty to define the category of international economic crimes would risk being a symbolic step, it is important that the international community commits to debating issues such as the prevention of economic crimes that threaten international peace and security, without waiting for crises to catalyse attention on these issues.[249]

CONCLUDING REMARKS

This chapter has sought to answer the sub-question of how the concept of international economic crime can be integrated into the multilevel system of international criminal justice. Three solutions for including the concept in the legal framework of the Rome Statute can be envisaged, each of which involves a different degree of desirability and feasibility.

The first option is the most desirable in terms of compliance with the principle of legality, but also the most difficult to implement, as it requires a significant amendment of the Rome Statute to include the concept of 'international economic crimes' – eg grand corruption, international money laundering, plunder of natural resources – as an autonomous category of international crimes. However, this solution would only be successful if accompanied by an investigative policy on the part of the OTP that does not always prioritise the prosecution of violent crimes over non-violent economic offences. Perhaps, resorting to the practice of thematic prosecutions would help draw attention to international

[248] Starr, 'Extraordinary Crimes' 1294, stating that '[n]egotiating and obtaining widespread ratification of a new treaty [is] a process likely to run up against political obstacles. The States that have declined to join the existing anti-corruption treaties (especially the money-laundering havens and the kleptocracies themselves) may be unlikely to join any future treaty specifically and vigorously targeting corruption'.

[249] RA Denemark and MJ Hoffmann, 'Just Scraps of Paper? The Dynamics of Multilateral Treaty-Making' (2008) 43 *Cooperation and Conflict* 185, 188, arguing that '[t]here is no evidence that multilateral treaty-making is a crisis-driven activity or that as crises fade into historical memory our propensity to make treaties declines', although it is true that treaty making increased following the two world wars.

economic crimes as a matter of international concern.[250] Already adopted at the subsequent Nuremberg trials,[251] this practice has recently allowed the OTP to emphasise the importance of prosecuting certain particularly reprehensible criminal phenomena, such as the use of sexual violence in conflict.[252]

The second option can be considered a 'compromise solution' as it would allow prosecuting international economic crimes without amending the Rome Statute. This solution implies the adoption of a broad interpretation of the concept of crimes against humanity to include serious economic crimes. However, such a broad interpretation should be supplemented with clarifications relating to Article 7(2) of the Rome Statute and to the Elements of the Crimes.[253] In particular, these clarifications should provide a more inclusive interpretation of the following concepts: (i) the concept of an 'attack' directed against any civilian population, which should be interpreted as including economic attacks against the public wealth of the State in which the targeted civilian population lives; (ii) the term 'State and organizational policy', which should be interpreted as referring to policies developed by states, state-like and non-state actors, including non-state economic actors; (iii) the 'inhumanity' of the harm caused by 'other inhumane acts', which should be interpreted as also referring to socio-economic harm.

The third option can be regarded as a purely façade solution, as it would have no real impact on the prosecution of international economic crimes. This consists of prosecuting international economic crimes by adopting a broad interpretation of Article 7(1)(k) of the Rome Statute, without making the adjustments or clarifications mentioned above. Although this option would not require any amendment to the Rome Statute, it is unlikely that the OTP and the judges would implement it, as they could more easily resort to 'aiding and abetting' and other modes of liability to prosecute economic actors involved in war crimes, genocide and crimes against humanity. Although this approach would be a step forward in punishing the perpetrators of ordinary economic crimes as accomplices to international crimes, it would fail to convey the message that there are economic crimes of international significance and that individuals can be held accountable for such crimes both before national courts and before the ICC.

Even if none of these three avenues open up in the near future and the attempt to extend the jurisdiction of the ICC to international economic crimes fails, there are other *fora* available to compensate for the inability or unwillingness of States

[250] Kyriakakis, 'Developments in International Criminal Law and the Case of Business Involvement in International Crimes' (2012) 94 *International Review of the Red Cross* 981, 1001.

[251] ibid. As explained above, the Prosecution had divided the subsequent Nuremberg proceedings according to the 'area of expertise' of the perpetrators, namely industry, the medical sector, and the judiciary.

[252] ibid. See, inter alia, *Prosecutor v Kunarac et al* (Trial Judgment) IT-96-23-T & IT-96-23/1-T (22 February 2001). See also MM deGuzman, 'An Expressive Rationale for the Thematic Prosecution of Sex Crimes' in M Bergsmo (ed), *Thematic Prosecution of International Sex Crimes*, 1st edn (Torkel Opsahl Academic EPublisher, 2012) 13.

[253] Arenal Lora, *Crímenes económicos* 23.

to prosecute international economic crimes. The second section of this chapter has shown that States can play a role through the mechanism of universal jurisdiction, which, according to the Madrid-Buenos Aires Principles, can also be applied to economic and environmental offences that 'seriously affect group or collective human rights or cause the irreversible destruction of ecosystem'. In addition, various initiatives have been proposed or implemented at regional and international level to tackle ordinary and transnational forms of economic crimes and could be used as models to prevent and punish crimes falling within the category of international economic crimes.

In presenting these initiatives, a bottom-up analysis of potential additional or alternative solutions to the ICC to fill in the current accountability gap for international economic crimes was favoured. Furthermore, this chapter did not intend to establish a rigid hierarchy of mutually exclusive solutions: on the contrary, to the extent that one or more of these solutions prove effective, they can be implemented at different levels, provided that certain limits are respected.[254] For instance, the principle of complementarity may apply in determining the allocation of jurisdiction over international crimes between national and supranational courts, whereas if both regional and international courts had jurisdiction over international economic crimes, then it would be necessary to envisage principles that regulate 'issues of overlapping jurisdiction and competing obligations' that States owe to these courts.[255] One option could be to give priority to regional courts based on the principle of proximity to the place where the crime was committed, while maintaining international courts as courts of last resort.

[254] Wharton, 'Redrawing the Line?' 182, stating that '[d]omestic capacity building and the possible expansion of the ICC's jurisdiction or creation of other international institutions should not be considered mutually exclusive options'.

[255] See 'Malabo Protocol. Legal and Institutional Implications' 28.

6

Conclusion

International criminal law and justice can no longer ignore that certain economic crimes are committed in contexts that make them reach a threshold of gravity, for which no accountability vacuum is permissible. This implies the need to rethink the concept of 'international crime' from a contemporary perspective, one that conceives the possibility of discussing new paradigms of mass criminality.

Based on existing literature, this book has helped shed light on the question of whether, and if so to what extent, the concept of international economic crime can be classified as an international crime and prosecuted as such. To this end, it was necessary to investigate the origins of the concept of international economic crime, on what grounds it can be argued that certain economic crimes are sufficiently serious to reach the gravity threshold of an international crime, which elements of the concept of international economic crime reflect its gravity, and how such a crime can be prosecuted in the current multilevel system of international criminal justice. In addition to summarising the main findings of this book, an overview of their significance, limitations, and implications for the field of international criminal law will be provided, with a view to formulating recommendations for future research and legal practice.

RESEARCH FINDINGS

This book argues that considering international economic crimes as a new paradigm of international crime and prosecuting them as such would not represent an unexpected and undesirable revolution of the scope of international criminal law but rather its most natural and predictable evolution: systemic crimes that affect the economic and social foundations of countries are the missing piece that completes the current set of international crimes.

Chapter 2 demonstrated that the premises for a primordial concept of international economic crime were already present in post-war international military trials. The Nuremberg trial and the subsequent proceedings against industrialists were pioneers in recognising that economic crimes committed in a certain context – characterised, at the time, by the existence of a deviant state-corporate system – deserve the attention of international criminal law. However, the historical context in which international criminal law originated and developed justifies why first-, second- and third-generation international criminal tribunals have focused on prosecuting crimes related to war and mass violence, rather than on crimes of an economic nature.

Yet, in light of the 2008 economic and financial crisis that marked the twenty-first century and whose consequences are still evident in most countries and regions of the world, it is worth asking whether the current system of international criminal law should broaden its horizons towards new paradigms of mass criminality in order to better reflect modern criminal dynamics. For this reason, the chapter proposes a review of the 'crisis focus' of international criminal law: in addition to crimes committed in extraordinary critical situations of armed conflicts and mass violence, systemic offences perpetrated in peacetime can also seriously jeopardise collective and individual legal goods, including peace and security of the world.

In Chapter 3, the main rationales of international criminality were applied to six cases involving economic crimes committed in different contexts and regions of the world, in order to identify a series of elements that would allow drawing a line between ordinary economic offences, on the one hand, and crimes of economic significance that could justifiably be considered international crimes, on the other. The chapter concludes that the context in which economic crimes are committed plays a crucial role in determining their international relevance, since only economic crimes that violate collective and individual legal goods and create international harm can be considered international.

Building on the foundations laid in previous chapters, Chapter 4 examined the potential constituent elements of a legal concept of international economic crime, in a manner consistent with the principle of legality and its corollaries. First, the chapter focused on defining the contextual elements that reflect its peculiar gravity, thus finding that an international economic crime can be defined as 'any act or omission committed as part of a systemic attack directed against the public wealth of a country by state, state-like or non-state actors with knowledge of the attack or gross negligence'. Secondly, the chapter provided guidance on the requirements that must be met by the material and mental elements of the potential offences listed as international economic crimes.

Chapter 5 proposed three options for including international economic crimes in the Rome Statute, either as an autonomous category of international crimes or as a subcategory of crimes against humanity – which would entail a revision of its contextual elements. However, extending or broadly interpreting the material scope of jurisdiction of the ICC is not the only possible solution to prevent this criminal phenomenon and counter the impunity that international economic criminals often enjoy in their own countries. Regional complaint or cooperation mechanisms, as well as the drafting of a multilateral treaty codifying the legal concept of international economic crimes can play a key deterrent role. Furthermore, if the interpretation of the principle of universal jurisdiction according to the Madrid-Buenos Aires principles were to prevail, domestic courts could intervene to overcome the inability or unwillingness of national jurisdictions competent to adjudicate international economic crimes on the basis of the territoriality and nationality principles of jurisdiction. Some regional courts, such as the ACtJHR or the COPLA, could also prove to be useful mechanisms for prosecuting international economic crimes. Another solution would be to establish an international court to adjudicate the most serious economic crimes. Although this solution seems premature and complex at this stage, in the long term it could also lead to the creation of a fourth generation of international criminal courts with jurisdiction to prosecute new categories of international crimes, such as ecocide and international economic crimes.

There is at least one element common to all the solutions examined as possible ways of preventing and prosecuting international economic crimes, namely the need for cooperation, both among States and between States and supranational institutions, which is essential for reaching agreements and ensuring the proper enforcement of international criminal law. This finding confirms that any proposal for reform of international criminal law must take into account the multilevel nature of the international criminal justice system in order to be effective.

In conclusion, this book argues that the concept of international economic crime can be qualified as an international crime and prosecuted as such, provided that a definition of international economic crime is elaborated following the parameters of the principle of legality and that existing or emerging accountability mechanisms within the multilevel system of international criminal justice take action to investigate and prosecute these offences.

This conclusion complements the findings of previous studies in at least three respects. First, it sheds new light on the role that public and private economic actors play as perpetrators of systemic economic crimes that reach a high gravity threshold. Secondly, it refers to concrete cases, applying theoretical considerations to the analysis of the facts. Lastly, it is one of the first attempts to examine in depth the constituent elements of a potential legal concept of international economic crime. In this way, the book aims to contribute to the ongoing debate stimulated by legal scholars to promote the study of the concept of political-economic crime, which has been at the centre of important criminological studies.[1]

Overall, the book helps raise awareness of the seriousness of economic offences resulting from systemic abuses of power by high-level individuals in the public and private sectors. Although these crimes have been neglected by international criminal law, they silently erode the economic, political, social, and cultural development of countries, depriving them of economic and

[1] See inter alia RJ Michalowski and RC Kramer, *State-Corporate Crime: Wrongdoing at the Intersection of Business and Government* (Rutgers University Press, 2006); V Ruggiero and M Welch, 'Power Crime' (2009) 51 *Crime, Law and Social Change* 297; ML Böhm, *The Crime of Maldevelopment: Economic Deregulation and Violence in the Global South* (Routledge, 2019).

natural wealth while undermining human rights and fundamental freedoms to the detriment of present and future generations.

THE WAY FORWARD: RECOMMENDATIONS FOR FUTURE RESEARCH AND LEGAL PRACTICE

To provide as comprehensive an overview as possible of the proposal to recognise international economic crimes as international crimes, this book has raised a number of questions in need of further investigation. The issue of revising the 'crisis focus' of international criminal law could be explored in further research, for example by examining in greater detail both the concept of international economic crime and that of ecocide as new paradigms of international criminality. To advance the debate on this issue, a better understanding of the constituent elements of the concept of international economic crimes needs to be developed. Although the above definition outlines the crime and provides food for thought, it would be interesting to carry out more in-depth examination on each of the contextual elements identified or to attempt to compile a list of offences which, if committed in the required context, may constitute international economic crimes.

The methodology and findings of this book could also be applied to study new cases of economic crimes committed in regions that have not been considered in this book, including Asia, the Middle East and Oceania. Lastly, there are issues that have not been addressed in this book due to time constraints or lack of expertise, but which deserve constant attention, despite having already been extensively covered in the literature. These include the recognition of the principle of corporate criminal responsibility in international criminal law and the study of accountability mechanisms for international economic crimes in areas of law other than criminal law, such as civil and administrative law.

In addition to theoretical insights for further research, the findings of this book may have a number of practical implications. The critical views expressed on the gravity of international economic crimes, on the need to tackle the impunity of their perpetrators and on the benefits of relying on a multilevel enforcement system, are intended to stimulate public opinion as well as political and legal actors to continue discussing these issues and to consider viable solutions to prevent such crimes from recurring in the future. The initiatives presented in Chapter 5 can help develop targeted measures at national, regional, and international level. For instance, should the inclusion of a new category of international economic crimes in the Rome Statute be prevented or prove too complex for the reasons outlined above, consideration may be given to the 'compromise solution', which would at least allow serious economic crimes to be classified and prosecuted as crimes against humanity, interpreting the contextual elements of this category in a manner consistent with the observations made regarding the contextual elements of international economic crimes.

Any additional or alternative solutions deemed appropriate and feasible must be discussed by the international community or, at least initially, by the regional communities that have shown themselves to be most sensitive to the issue.

The time is ripe to bring justice to the victims of crimes that stem from systemic abuses of power, which silently undermine the axiological and practical foundations of countries. The means to achieve this goal are available, but every member of the international community must feel the need and duty to activate them efficiently, favouring a cooperative approach over the pursuit of individual interests. After all, the crimes under scrutiny can lead to the collapse of entire countries, destroy their economic and natural resources, and undermine human rights and fundamental freedoms. If there is no willingness to cooperate to avoid these scenarios, then we should rethink and perhaps rewrite the meaning of global community and public conscience.

Bibliography

Abthai, H and Webb, P, *The Genocide Convention: The Travaux Préparatoires*, The Travaux Préparatoires of Multilateral Treaties Vol 2 (Brill, 2008).

Aitala, RS, *Diritto Internazionale Penale* (Le Monnier Università, 2021).

Akhavan, P, 'The Core Elements of International Crimes' in P Akhavan (ed), *Reducing Genocide to Law: Definition, Meaning, and the Ultimate Crime* (Cambridge University Press, 2012).

Akpomera, E, 'International Crude Oil Theft: Elite Predatory Tendencies in Nigeria' (2015) 42 *Review of African Political Economy* 156.

Alford, KD, *Hermann Goring and the Nazi Art Collection: The Looting of Europe's Art Treasures and Their Dispersal After World War II* (McFarland & Co, 2014).

Allen, MT, *The Business of Genocide: The SS, Slave Labor, and the Concentration Camps* (The University of North Carolina Press, 2005).

Alonso, W, 'Citizenship, Nationality and Other Identities' (1995) 48 *Journal of International Affairs* 585.

Ambos, K, 'Bien jurídico y harm principle: bases teóricas para determinar la "función global" del derecho penal internacional: una segunda contribución para una teoría coherente del derecho penal internacional' (2013) 10 *Revista de derecho penal y criminología* 343.

Ambos, K, 'International Economic Criminal Law. The Foundations of Companies' Criminal Responsibility under International Law' (2018) 29 *Criminal Law Forum* 499.

Amjad, RM, et al, 'Non-Linear Impact of Globalization on Financial Crimes: A Case of Developing Economies' (2021) 25 *Journal of Money Laundering Control* 360.

Anderson, M, 'International Money Laundering: The Need for ICC Investigative and Adjudicative Jurisdiction' (2013) 53 *Virginia Journal of International Law* 762.

Andreski, S, 'Kleptocracy or Corruption as a System of Government' in S Andreski (ed), *The African Predicament: A Study in the Pathology of Modernisation* (Atherton Press, 1968).

Ankumah, EA, 'The Cairo-Arusha Principles on Universal Jurisdiction in Respect of Gross Human Rights Offenses: An African Perspective' (2004) 98 *Proceedings of the ASIL Annual Meeting* 238.

Arenal Lora, L, *Crímenes económicos en derecho internacional: Propuesta de una nueva categoría de crímenes contra la humanidad* (Editorial Aranzadi, 2019).

Arruda de Almeida, M, and Zagaris, B, 'Political Capture in the Petrobras Corruption Scandal: The Sad Tale of an Oil Giant' (2015) 39 *Fletcher Forum of World Affairs* 87.

Baars, G, 'Capitalism's Victor's Justice? The Hidden Stories Behind the Prosecution of Industrialists Post-WWII' in KJ Heller and G Simpson (eds), *The Hidden Histories of War Crimes Trials* (Oxford University Press, 2013).

Baars, G, *The Corporation, Law and Capitalism: A Radical Perspective on the Role of Law in The Global Political Economy*, Historical Materialism Book Series 188 (Brill, 2019).

Babic, M, Heemskerk, EM and Fichtner, J, 'States Versus Corporations: Rethinking the Power of Business in International Politics' (2017) 52 *The International Spectator* 20.

Badar, ME, 'Drawing the Boundaries of Mens Rea in the Jurisprudence of the International Criminal Tribunal for the Former Yugoslavia' (2006) 6 *International Criminal Law Review* 313.

Badar, ME, 'The Mental Element in the Rome Statute of the International Criminal Court: A Commentary from a Comparative Criminal Law Perspective' (2008) 19 *Criminal Law Forum* 473.

Barbero, N, 'La ¿relativa? aplicación del principio de legalidad en derecho penal internacional' (2017) 13 *Nuevo foro penal* 156.

Bassiouni, MC, *The Legislative History of the International Criminal Court*, Vol 1 (Transnational Publishers, 2005).
Bassiouni, MC, 'Crimes against Humanity: The Case for a Specialized Convention' (2010) 9 *Washington University Global Studies Law Review* 575.
Bassiouni, MC, *Crimes against Humanity: Historical Evolution and Contemporary Application* (Cambridge University Press, 2011).
Bassiouni, MC, 'International Crimes: Ratione Materiae' in MC Bassiouni (ed), *Introduction to International Criminal Law*, 2nd edn (Brill, 2012).
Bassiouni, MC, 'The "Direct Enforcement System:" History of International Criminal Investigations and Prosecutions' in MC Bassiouni (ed), *Introduction to International Criminal Law*, 2nd edn (Brill, 2012).
Beccaria, C, *Dei delitti e delle pene* (Mondadori, 2019).
Beck, U, *La société du risque. Sur la voie d'une autre modernité* (Éditions Flammarion, 2008).
Benería, L, and Sarasúa, C, 'Delitos y crímenes económicos contra la humanidad' (2011) 12 Revista de economía crítica 156.
Berghoff, H, and Spiekermann, U, 'Shady Business: On the History of White-Collar Crime' (2018) 60 *Business History* 289.
Bergholm, L, 'The African Union (AU) and Its Commitment to Non-Indifference: Can the AU Be an Actor for the Promotion of Human Security?' in A Swain et al (eds), *Globalization and Challenges to Building Peace* (Anthem Press, 2012).
Binding, K, *Handbuch Des Strafrechts*, Vol 1 (Duncker & Humblot, 1885).
Black, E, *IBM and the Holocaust: The Strategic Alliance between Nazi Germany and America's Most Powerful Corporation* (Time Warner Paperbacks, 2002).
Bloom, B, 'Criminalizing Kleptocracy: The ICC as a Viable Tool in the Fight against Grand Corruption' (2014) 29 *American University International Law Review* 627.
Bloxham, D, 'A Survey of Jewish Slave Labour in the Nazi System' (2001) 10 *Journal of Holocaust Education* 25.
Böhm, ML, *The Crime of Maldevelopment: Economic Deregulation and Violence in the Global South* (Routledge, 2019).
Boister, N, 'The Exclusion of Treaty Crimes from the Jurisdiction of the Proposed International Criminal Court: Law, Pragmatism, Politics' (1998) 3 *Journal of Armed Conflict Law* 27.
Boister, N, 'Treaty Crimes, International Criminal Court?' (2009) 12 *New Criminal Law Review* 341.
Booysen, S, and Neo, D, *Can Banks Still Keep a Secret? Bank Secrecy in Financial Centres around the World* (Cambridge University Press, 2017).
Bovens, L, 'The Ethics of Dieselgate' (2016) 40 *Midwest Studies in Philosophy* 262.
Bragadóttir, R, 'Criminal Law and the Financial Crisis: The Proceedings against Iceland's Former Prime Minister Geir H. Haarde' in F Zimmermann (ed), *Criminal Liability of Political Decision-Makers. A Comparative Perspective* (Springer, 2017).
Braum, S, 'Droit pénal des risques et risques du droit pénal' in C Bourin and JL Putz, *Le risque pénal du banquier* (Anthemis, 2020).
Braum, S, '"Rechtsstaat" and European Criminal Law – From the End of Sovereignty' (2021) 12 *New Journal of European Criminal Law* 14.
Broomhall, B, *International Justice and the International Criminal Court: Between Sovereignty and the Rule of Law*, Vol 1 (Oxford University Press, 2003).
Bufalini, A, 'The Principle of Legality and the Role of Customary International Law in the Interpretation of the ICC Statute' (2015) 14 *The Law & Practice of International Courts and Tribunals* 233.
Burchard, C, 'Ancillary and Neutral Business Contributions to "Corporate–Political Core Crime": Initial Enquiries Concerning the Rome Statute' (2010) 8 *Journal of International Criminal Justice* 919.
Burns, T, 'Aristotle and Natural Law' (1998) 19 *History of Political Thought* 142.

Bush, JA, 'The Prehistory of Corporations and Conspiracy in International Criminal Law: What Nuremberg Really Said' (2009) 109 *Columbia Law Review* 1094.

Button, M, Hock, B and Shepherd, D, *Economic Crime: From Conception to Response* (Routledge, 2022).

Carrillo Santarelli, N 'The Protection of Global Legal Goods' (2013) 13 *Anuario mexicano de derecho internacional* 405.

Cassese, A, 'On the Current Trends towards Criminal Prosecution and Punishment of Breaches of International Humanitarian Law' (1998) 9 *European Journal of International Law* 2.

Cassese, A, 'The ICTY: A Living and Vital Reality'(2004) 2 *Journal of International Criminal Justice* 585.

Cassese, A, 'Balancing the Prosecution of Crimes against Humanity and Non-Retroactivity of Criminal Law: The Kolk and Kislyiy v. Estonia Case before the ECHR' (2006) 4 *Journal of International Criminal Justice* 410.

Cassese, A, *International Criminal Law*, 2nd edn (Oxford University Press, 2008).

Castillo-Monterrey, MA, 'Contornos de un "modelo tipo" de expolio de las riquezas de las naciones como crimen de Derecho Internacional' (2017) 1 *Revista de derecho de la facultad de ciencias jurídicas y sociales UNAN-Léon*, 203.

Citeroni, N, 'International economic crimes in the Rome Statute? Reflections on multilevel enforcement of international criminal law' in K Ligeti and KH Brodersen (eds), *Studies on Enforcement in Multilevel Regulatory Systems* (Nomos, 2022).

Citeroni, N, 'The Milanković Case: Do Convictions Based on Rules of Customary International Law Violate Article 7 of the Convention?' (2022) 9 *Quaderni di SIDIBlog* 387.

Clark, JN, 'International Criminal Courts and Normative Legitimacy: An Achievable Goal?' (2015) 15 *International Criminal Law Review* 763.

Coleman, W, 'Toward an Integrated Theory of White-Collar Crime' (1987) 93 American Journal of Sociology 406.

Consciência Silvestre, H, et al, 'Implementation of Brazil's Energy Policy through the National Oil Company: From Institutional Chaos to Strategic Order' (2018) 119 *Energy policy* 87.

Corsi, JL, 'An Argument for Strict Legality in International Criminal Law' (2018) 49 *Georgetown Journal of International Law* 1321.

Crosby, S, 'Brexit: Lessons from Different Quarters' (2019) 10 *New Journal of European Criminal Law* 205.

Cryer, R, et al, *An Introduction to International Criminal Law and Procedure*, 1st edn (Cambridge University Press, 2010).

Cryer, R, et al, *An Introduction to International Criminal Law and Procedure*, 3rd edn (Cambridge University Press, 2014).

Cullen H, Kastner P and Richmond S 'Introduction: The Politics of International Criminal Law' (2018) 18 *International Criminal Law Review* 907.

Currie, RJ, and Leon, J, 'COPLA: A Transnational Criminal Court for Latin America and the Caribbean' (2019) 88 *Nordic Journal of International Law* 587.

Cupido, M, 'Causation in International Crimes Cases:(Re)Concenptualizing the Causal Linkage' (2021) 32 *Criminal Law Forum* 1.

Dahl, RA, 'The Concept of Power' (1957) 2 *Behavioral Science* 201.

Darcy, S, and Powderly, J, *Judicial Creativity at the International Criminal Tribunals* (Oxford University Press, 2010).

Davidsson, E, 'Economic Oppression as an International Wrong or as Crime against Humanity' (2005) 23 *Netherlands Quarterly of Human Rights* 173.

deGuzman, MM, 'Gravity and the Legitimacy of the International Criminal Court' (2009) 32 *Fordham International Law Journal* 1400.

deGuzman, MM, 'An Expressive Rationale for the Thematic Prosecution of Sex Crimes' in M Bergsmo (ed), *Thematic Prosecution of International Sex Crimes*, 1st edn (Torkel Opsahl Academic EPublisher, 2012).

deGuzman, MM, 'How Serious Are International Crimes-the Gravity Problem in International Criminal Law' (2012) 51 *Columbia Journal of Transnational Law* 18.

deGuzman, MM, and Lockwood Kelly, T, 'The International Criminal Court Is Legitimate Enough to Deserve Support' (2019) 33 *Temple International & Comparative Law Journal* 397.

deGuzman, MM, *Shocking the Conscience of Humanity: Gravity and the Legitimacy of International Criminal Law* (Oxford University Press, 2020).

Del Ponte, C, 'Prosecuting the Individuals Bearing the Highest Level of Responsibility' (2004) 2 *Journal of International Criminal Justice* 516.

Delmas-Marty, M, *Libertés et sûreté dans un monde dangereux* (Édition du Seuil, 2010).

Dempsey, PS, 'Economic Aggression & Self-Defense in International Law: The Arab Oil Weapon and Alternative American Responses Thereto' (1977) 9 *Case Western Reserve Journal of International Law* 253.

Denemark, RA, and Hoffmann, MJ, 'Just Scraps of Paper? The Dynamics of Multilateral Treaty-Making' (2008) 43 *Cooperation and Conflict* 185.

Doecke, A, 'The Principle of Legality as Protection for Human Rights' (2014) 39 *Alternative Law Journal* 249.

Domb, M, 'Defining Economic Aggression in International Law: The Possibility of Regional Action by the Organization of American States' (1978) 11 *Cornell International Law Journal* 85.

Du Bois, JE, *Generals in Grey Suits: The Directors of the International 'IG Farben' Cartel, Their Conspiracy and Trial at Nuremberg* (Bodley Head, 1953).

Dubber, MD, 'Theories of Crime and Punishment in German Criminal Law' (2005) 53 *The American Journal of Comparative Law* 679.

Duff, RA, *The Realm of Criminal* Law (Oxford University Press, 2018).

Durney, J, 'Crafting a Standard: Environmental Crimes as Crimes against Humanity under the International Criminal Court' (2018) 24 *Hastings Environmental Law Journal* 413.

Dutton, YM, 'Enforcing the Rome Statute: Evidence of (Non) Compliance from Kenya' (2016) 26 *Indiana International & Comparative Law Review* 7.

El Zeidy, MM, 'The Gravity Threshold under the Statute of the International Criminal Court' (2008) 19 *Criminal Law Forum* 35.

Ellis, M, 'Breaking the Silence: Rape as an International Crime' (2006) 38 *Case Western Reserve Journal of International Law* 225.

Engemann, KJ, 'Developments in Risk Security' in Engemann KJ (ed), *The Routledge Companion to Risk, Crisis and Security in Business* (Routledge, 2018).

Enneking, L, et al, *Accountability, International Business Operations and the Law: Providing Justice for Corporate Human Rights Violations in Global Value Chains* (Routledge, 2019).

Falkler, JL, 'Economic Mistreatment as Persecution in Asylum Claims: Towards a Consistent Standard' (2007) 1 *University of Chicago Legal Forum* 471.

Feinberg, J, *The Moral Limits of the Criminal Law Volume 1: Harm to Others* (Oxford University Press, 1987).

Feldman, GD, 'Financial Institutions in Nazi Germany. Reluctant or Willing Collaborators?' in FR Nicosia and J Huener (eds) *Business and Industry in Nazi Germany* (Berghahn Books, 2004).

Ferencz, BB, *Less Than Slaves: Jewish Forced Labor and the Quest for Compensation* (Indiana University Press, 2002).

Finch, GA, 'The Nuremberg Trial and International Law' (1947) 41 *American Journal of International Law* 20.

Finnin, S, 'Mental Elements under Article 30 of the Rome Statute of the International Criminal Court: A Comparative Analysis' (2012) 61 *International & Comparative Law Quarterly* 325.

Fisse, B, and Braithwaite, J, *Corporations, Crime, and Accountability* (Cambridge University Press, 1993)

Fletcher, GP, *Basic Concepts of Criminal Law* (Oxford University Press, 1998).

Fletcher, GP, *Rethinking Criminal Law* (Oxford University Press, 2000).

Fletcher, GP, *The Grammar of Criminal Law: American, Comparative, and International,* Vol 1: Foundations (Oxford University Press, 2007).

Fourez, G, 'Victimes et terrorisme au XXIe siècle: une production spécifique' (2018) 4 *Revue de droit pénal et de criminologie* 414.

Fox, GH, et al, 'The Contributions of United Nations Security Council Resolutions to the Law of Non-International Armed Conflict: New Evidence of Customary International Law' (2018) 67 *American University Law Review* 649.

Gadirov, J, 'Causal Responsibility in International Criminal Law' (2015) 15 *International Criminal Law Review* 970.

Gallant, KS, *The Principle of Legality in International and Comparative Criminal Law*, Cambridge Studies in International and Comparative Law 65 (Cambridge University Press, 2009).

Galliher, JF, and Guess, TJ, 'Two Generations of Sutherland's White-Collar War Crime Data and Beyond' (2009) 51 *Crime, Law and Social Change* 163.

Geis, G, 'Toward a Delineation of White-Collar Offenses' (1962) 32 *Sociological Inquiry* 160.

Gilbert, GM, *Nuremberg Diary* (Da Capo Press, 1995).

Goldensohn, L, *The Nuremberg Interviews: An American Psychiatrist's Conversations with the Defendants and Witnesses* (Alfred A Knopf, 2004).

Goldman, SA, 'A Fuhrer of Industry: Krupp before, during and after Nuremberg' (2017) 39 *Loyola of Los Angeles International and Comparative Law Review* 187.

Goldstein, DM, 'Already Innocent: Radioactive Bribes, White-Collar Corruption and Nuclear Expertise in Brazil' (2018) 59 *Culture, Theory and Critique* 354.

Gordon, GS, 'The Propaganda Prosecutions at Nuremberg: The Origin of Atrocity Speech Law and the Touchstone for Normative Evolution' (2017) 39 *Loyola of Los Angeles International and Comparative Law Review* 209

Gottlieb, Y, 'Attacks against Cultural Heritage as a Crime against Humanity' (2020) 52 *Case Western Reserve Journal of International Law* 287.

Grossi, P, *Prima lezione di diritto* (Giuseppe Laterza & Figli, 2012).

Guariglia, F, 'The Selection of Cases by the Office of the Prosecutor of the International Criminal Court' in C Stahn and G Sluiter (eds), *The Emerging Practice of the International Criminal Court* (Brill, 2009).

Habermas, J, 'The Concept of Human Dignity and the Realistic Utopia of Human Rights' (2010) 41 *Metaphilosophy* 464.

Habermas, J, *The Inclusion of the Other: Studies in Political Theory* (The MIT Press, 2018).

Hajdin, N, 'The Nature of Leadership in the Crime of Aggression: The ICC's New Concern?' (2017) 17 *International Criminal Law Review* 543.

Hansen, TO, 'The Policy Requirement in Crimes against Humanity: Lessons from and for the Case of Kenya' (2011) 43 *George Washington International Law Review* 1.

Happold, M, 'Security Council Resolution 1373 and the Constitution of the United Nations' (2003) 16 *Leiden Journal of International Law* 593.

Hart, HLA, and Honoré, T, *Causation in the Law*, 2nd edn (Clarendon Press, 1998).

Hartman, JM, 'Government by Thieves: Revealing the Monsters Behind the Kleptocratic Masks' (1997) 24 *Syracuse Journal of International Law and Commerce* 157.

Hatchard, J, *Combating Corruption: Legal Approaches to Supporting Good Governance and Integrity in Africa* (Edward Elgar Publishing, 2014).

Hawkins, D, 'Universal Jurisdiction for Human Rights: From Legal Principle to Limited Reality' (2003) 9 *Global Governance* 347.

Hayes, P, 'The Chemistry of Business-State Relations in the Third Reich' in FR Nicosia and J Huener (eds), *Business and Industry* (Berghahn Books, 2004).

Hernham, R, and Findlay, M, (eds) *Exploring the Boundaries of International Criminal Justice* (Ashgate Publishing, 2011).

Heude, X, 'La notion de risque dans une approche éthique de la finance. Conditions et implications' (2006) 1 *Finance Bien Commun* 47.

Holthoefer, A, 'Constructing International Crime: Lawyers, States, and the Origin of International Criminal Prosecution in the Interwar Period' (2017) 42 *Law & Social Inquiry* 711.

Hotz, D, 'Ecocide as the Missing Fifth Crime under International Criminal Law?' (2021) 133 *Zeitschrift für die gesamte Strafrechtswissenschaft* 861.

Igbinovia, PE, *Oil Thefts and Pipeline Vandalization in Nigeria* (Safari Books, 2014).

Jacobson, KR, 'Doing Business with the Devil: The Challenges of Prosecuting Corporate Officials Whose Business Transactions Facilitate War Crimes and Crimes against Humanity' (2005) 56 *Air Force Law Review* 167.

Jain, N, 'Judicial Lawmaking and General Principles of Law in International Criminal Law' (2016) 57 *Harvard International Law Journal* 111.

Jalloh, CC, 'What Makes a Crime against Humanity a Crime against Humanity' (2013) 28 *American University International Law Review* 381.

Jastram, K, 'Economic Harm as a Basis for Refugee Status and the Application of Human Rights Law to the Interpretation of Economic Persecution' in JC Simeon (ed), *Critical Issues in International Refugee Law: Strategies toward Interpretative Harmony* (Cambridge University Press, 2010).

Jescheck, H, and Weigend, T, *Lehrbuch des Strafrechts: Allgemeiner Teil*, 5th edn (Duncker & Humblot, 1996).

Jessberger, F, 'On the Origins of Individual Criminal Responsibility under International Law for Business Activity: IG Farben on Trial' (2010) 8 *Journal of International Criminal Justice* 783.

Jodoin, S, and Saito, Y, 'Crimes Against Future Generations: Harnessing the Potential of Individual Criminal Accountability for Global Sustainability' (2012) 7 *McGill International Journal of Sustainable Development Law & Policy* 115.

Jung, JC, and 'Alison' Park, SB, 'Volkswagen's Diesel Emissions Scandal' (2017) 59 *Thunderbird International Business Review* 127.

Kaleck, W, and Saage-Maaß, M, 'Corporate Accountability for Human Rights Violations Amounting to International Crimes: The Status Quo and Its Challenges' (2019) 8 Journal of International Criminal Justice 699.

Karstedt, S, 'From Absence to Presence, from Silence to Voice: Victims in International and Transitional Justice since the Nuremberg Trials' (2010) 17 *International Review of Victimology* 9.

Kelly, MJ, 'The Status of Victims Under the Rome Statute of the International Criminal Court' in T Bonacker and C Safferling (eds), *Victims of International Crimes: An Interdisciplinary Discourse* (Springer, 2013).

Kelsen, H, 'Will the Judgment in the Nuremberg Trial Constitute a Precedent in International Law?' (1947) 1 *International Law Quarterly* 153.

Kiefer, HL, 'Just Say No: The Case against Expanding the International Criminal Court's Jurisdiction to Include Drug Trafficking' (2009) 31 *Loyola of Los Angeles International and Comparative Law Review* 157.

Kirsch, P, 'The International Criminal Court: From Rome to Kampala' (2010) 43 *The John Marshall Law Review* 515.

Kofele-Kale, N, 'Patrimonicide: The International Economic Crime of Indigenous Spoliation' (1995) 28 *Vanderbilt Journal of Transnational Law* 45.

Kofele-Kale, N, 'The Right to a Corruption-Free Society as an Individual and Collective Human Right: Elevating Official Corruption to a Crime under International Law' (2000) 34 *The International Lawyer* 149.

Kofele-Kale, N, 'Only Fools Who Send Hyenas to Roast Meat for Them: In Search of the Doctrinal Foundations of the Not-So-Ordinary Crime of Patrimonicide' (2013) 9 *Florida A&M University Law Review* 1.

Kofele-Kale, N, *The International Law of Responsibility for Economic Crimes: Holding State Officials Individually Liable for Acts of Fraudulent Enrichment*, (Ashgate, 2006).

Kohalmi, L, and Mezei, K, 'The Concept and Typical Forms of Economic Crime' (2015) 2 *Journal of Eastern-European Criminal Law* 33.

Kontorovich, E, 'When Gravity Fails: Israeli Settlements and Admissibility at the ICC' (2014) 47 *Israel Law Review* 379.

Krall, JR, and Peng, RD, 'The Volkswagen Scandal: Deception, Driving and Deaths' (2015) 12 *Significance* 12.

Krambia-Kapardis, M, *Corporate Fraud and Corruption: A Holistic Approach to Preventing Financial Crises* (Springer, 2016).

Krasner, SD, 'New Terrains: Sovereignty and Alternative Conceptions of Power' in M Finnemore and J Goldstein (eds), *Back to Basics: State Power in a Contemporary World* (Oxford University Press, 2013).

Kress, C, 'The Crime of Genocide and Contextual Elements: A Comment on the ICC Pre-Trial Chamber's Decision in the Al Bashir Case' (2009) 7 *Journal of International Criminal Justice* 297.

Kyriakakis, J, 'Developments in International Criminal Law and the Case of Business Involvement in International Crimes' (2012) 94 *International Review of the Red Cross* 981.

Kyriakakis, J, *Corporations, Accountability and International Criminal Law: Industry and Atrocity* (Edward Elgar Publishing, 2021).

Lauterpacht, H, 'The Law of Nations, the Law of Nature and the Rights of Man' (1943) 29 *Transactions Grotius Society* 1.

Leckie, S, 'Another Step Towards Indivisibility: Identifying the Key Features of Violations of Economic, Social and Cultural Rights' (1998) 20 *Human Rights Quarterly* 81.

Lemkin, R, *Axis Rule in Occupied Europe: Laws of Occupation, Analysis of Government, Proposals for Redress* (Carnegie Endowment for International Peace, 1944).

Levi, P, *If This Is a Man* (The Orion Press, 1959).

Lippman, M, 'War Crimes Trials of German Industrialists: The Other Schindlers' (1995) 9 *Temple International and Comparative Law Journal* 173.

Llano Alonso, FH, 'Cicero and Natural Law' (2012) 98 *Archives for Philosophy of Law and Social Philosophy* 157.

Lynch, MJ, Stretesky, PB, and Long, MA, *Defining Crime: A Critique of the Concept and Its Implications* (Palgrave Macmillan, 2015).

Lutz, EL, and Reiger, C, *Prosecuting Heads of State* (Cambridge University Press, 2009).

Manacorda, S, Marletta, A, and Vanacore, G, (eds) 'Individual Liability for Business Involvement in International Crimes', (2017) 1 *Revue Internationale de Droit Pénal.*

Mansouri, N, 'A Case Study of Volkswagen Unethical Practice in Diesel Emission Test' (2016) 5 *International Journal of Science and Engineering Applications* 211.

Mao, X, 'Substantive or Jurisdictional? The Tokyo Charter and the Legality Challenge at the International Military Tribunal for the Far East' (2018) 11 *Journal of East Asia and International Law* 435.

Marchuk, I, *The Fundamental Concept of Crime in International Criminal Law: A Comparative Law Analysis* (Springer, 2014).

Mariniello, T, 'The "Nuremberg Clause" and Beyond: Legality Principle and Sources of International Criminal Law in the European Court's Jurisprudence' (2013) 82 *Nordic Journal of International Law* 221.

Max-Neef, M, 'The Good Is the Bad That We Don't Do: Economic Crimes against Humanity: A Proposal' (2014) 104 *Ecological Economics* 152.

May, L, *Crimes against Humanity: A Normative Account* (Cambridge University Press, 2004).

Mayr, E, 'International Criminal Law, Causation, and Responsibility' (2014) 14 *International Criminal Law Review* 855.

McCormack, TLH, 'From Sun Tzu to the Sixth Committee: The Evolution of an International Criminal Law Regime' in TLH McCormack and GJ Simpson (eds), *The Law of War Crimes: National and International Approaches* (Martinus Nijhoff Publishers, 1997).

McHenry, J, 'Justice for Foca: The International Criminal Tribunal for Yugoslavia's Prosecution of Rape and Enslavement as Crimes against Humanity' (2002) 10 *Tulsa Journal of Comparative and International Law* 183.
Megret, F, 'Bring Forth the Accused: Defendant Attitudes and the Intimate Legitimacy of the International Criminal Trial' (2019) 36 *Arizona Journal of International and Comparative Law* 397.
Mettraux, G, *International Crimes and the Ad Hoc Tribunals* (Oxford University Press, 2005).
Mettraux, G, 'The Definition of Crimes against Humanity and the Question of a "Policy" Element' in LN Sadat (ed), *Forging a Convention for Crimes against Humanity* (Cambridge University Press, 2011).
Michalowski, RJ, and Kramer, RC, *State-Corporate Crime: Wrongdoing at the Intersection of Business and Government* (Rutgers University Press, 2006).
Michalowski, S, 'Doing Business with a Bad Actor: How to Draw the Line between Legitimate Commercial Activities and Those That Trigger Corporate Complicity Liability' (2015) 50 *Texas International Law Journal* 403.
Mill, JS, *On Liberty* (Cambridge University Press, 2011).
Mir Puig, S, *Derecho penal. Parte general*, 10th edn (Reppertor, 2016).
Moffett, L, 'The Role of Victims in the International Criminal Tribunals of the Second World War' (2012) 12 *International Criminal Law Review* 245.
Moore, MS, *Placing Blame: A Theory of Criminal Law* (Oxford University Press, 1997).
Morris, PS, 'Economic Genocide under International Law' (2018) 82 *The Journal of Criminal Law* 18.
Murphy, R, 'Gravity Issues and the International Criminal Court' (2006) 17 Criminal Law Forum 281.
Nevitt, M, 'Is Climate Change a Threat to International Peace & Security?' (2021) 42 *Michigan Journal of International Law* 527.
Nicholson, J, 'Strengthening the Effectiveness of International Criminal Law through the Principle of Legality' (2017) 17 *International Criminal Law Review* 656.
Nicosia, FR, and Huener, J, *Business and Industry in Nazi Germany* (Berghahn Books, 2004).
Nieto Martín, A, 'Bases para un futuro derecho penal internacional del medio ambiente' (2011) 82 *Revue internationale de droit pénal* 477.
Nieto Martín, A, 'Cambio climático y derecho penal internacional del medio ambiente' (2020) 98 *Jueces para la democracia* 61.
Nystrand, MJ, 'Petty and Grand Corruption and the Conflict Dynamics in Northern Uganda' (2014) 35 *Third World Quarterly* 821.
Olásolo, H, 'El principio nullum crimen sine iure en Derecho Internacional contemporáneo' (2013) 1 *Anuario ibero-americano de derecho internacional penal* 18.
Oluwakayode, OB, 'Analysing Economic Crimes in Nigeria: The Political Economy Approach' (2017) 5 *Journal of Law and Criminal Justice* 65.
Osiel, MJ, 'Why Prosecute? Critics of Punishment for Mass Atrocity' (2000) 22 *Human Rights Quarterly* 118.
Pacheco de Freitas, JA, 'La relación entre el principio de legalidad en derecho penal internacional y la tipificación internacional de los crímenes de lesa humanidad: una perspectiva histórica' (2019) 26 *Agenda internacional* 183.
Palazzo, F, *Corso di diritto penale. Parte generale*, 5th edn (G. Giappichelli Editore, 2013).
Paraschiv, G, 'On the Gravity of the Offence in International Criminal Law' (2013) 5 *Geopolitics, History, and International Relations* 136.
Penny, CK, 'Greening the Security Council: Climate Change as an Emerging "Threat to International Peace and Security"' (2007) 7 *International Environmental Agreements: Politics, Law and Economics* 35.
Peters, A, 'Corruption as a Violation of International Human Rights' (2018) 29 European Journal of International Law 1251.

Pinotti, MC, 'Lava Jato, Mani Pulite, and the Role of Institutions' in A Spilimbergo and K Srinivasan (eds), *Brazil: Boom, Bust, and the Road to Recovery* (International Monetary Fund, 2019).

Raday, F, 'Privatising Human Rights and the Abuse of Power' (2000) 13 *Canadian Journal of Law and Jurisprudence* 103.

Rajkovic, NM, 'What Is a "Grave" International Crime? The Rome Statute, Durkheim and the Sociology of Ruling Outrages' (2020) 16 *Loyola University Chicago International Law Review* 65.

Ramasastry, A, 'Corporate Complicity: From Nuremberg to Rangoon-an Examination of Forced Labor Cases and Their Impact on the Liability of Multinational Corporations' (2002) 20 *Berkeley Journal of International Law* 91.

Robinson, D, 'Defining "Crimes against Humanity" at the Rome Conference' (1999) 93 American Journal of International Law 43.

Robinson, P, 'The Missing Crimes' in A Cassese, P Gaeta and JRWD Jones (eds), *The Rome Statute of the International Criminal Court: A Commentary*, Vol 1 (Oxford University Press, 2002).

Rodenhäuser, T, 'Beyond State Crimes: Non-State Entities and Crimes against Humanity' (2014) 27 *Leiden Journal of International Law* 913.

Rodman, KA, 'Justice as a Dialogue between Law and Politics: Embedding the International Criminal Court within Conflict Management and Peacebuilding' (2014) 12 Journal of International Criminal Justice 437.

Roht-Arriaza, N, 'Just a "Bubble"? Perspectives on the Enforcement of International Criminal Law by National Courts' (2013) 11 *Journal of International Criminal Justice* 537.

Roksandić Vidlička, S, *Prosecuting Serious Economic Crimes as International Crimes – a New Mandate for the ICC?*, Research Series of the Max Planck Institute for Foreign and International Criminal Law Series BC: Publications of the Max Planck Partner Group for Balkan Criminology 2 (Duncker & Humblot, 2017).

Roscini, M, 'Gravity in the Statute of the International Criminal Court and Cyber Conduct That Constitutes, Instigates or Facilitates International Crimes' (2019) 30 *Criminal Law Forum* 247.

Rose-Ackerman, S, 'Democracy and "Grand" Corruption' (1996) 48 *International Social Science Journal* 365.

Rossi, F, *Il contrasto al terrorismo internazionale nelle fonti penali multilivello* (Jovene Editore, 2022).

Roxin, C, *Strafrecht Allgemeiner Teil*, Vol 1, 3rd edn (CH Beck, 1997).

Ruggiero, V, and Welch, M, 'Power Crime' (2009) 51 *Crime, Law and Social Change* 297.

Ryu, PK, 'Causation in Criminal Law' (1958) 106 *University of Pennsylvania Law Review* 773.

Sadat, LN, 'Little Progress in the Sixth Committee on Crimes against Humanity' (2022) 54 *Case Western Reserve Journal of International Law* 89.

Safferling, CJM, 'Can Criminal Prosecution be the Answer to Massive Human Rights Violations' (2004) 5 German Law Journal 1469.

Sandoval Mesa, JA, 'Del principio de legalidad penal a la persecución de crímenes internacionales y de supralegalidad contemporánea' (2012) 2 Revista IUSTA 175.

Saul, M, 'The Normative Status of Self-Determination in International Law: A Formula for Uncertainty in the Scope and Content of the Right?' (2011) 11 *Human Rights Law Review* 609.

Schabas, WA, 'War Economies, Economic Actors, and International Criminal Law' in K Ballentine and H Nitzschke (eds), *Profiting from Peace: Managing the Resource Dimensions of Civil War* (Lynne Rienner Publishers, 2005).

Schabas, WA, 'State Policy as an Element of International Crimes' (2008) 98 *Journal of Criminal Law and Criminology* 953.

Schabas, WA, *Genocide in International Law: The Crime of Crimes*, 2nd edn (Cambridge University Press, 2009).
Schabas, WA, 'International Crimes' in JD Armstrong and J Brunée (eds), *Routledge Handbook of International Law* (Routledge, 2009).
Schabas, WA, McDermott, Y, Hayes, N (eds), *The Ashgate Research Companion to International Criminal Law: Critical Perspectives* (Routledge, 2013).
Schabas, WA, 'Part 2 Jurisdiction, Admissibility, and Applicable Law: Compétence, recevabilité, et droit applicable, Art. 7 Crimes against Humanity/Crimes contre l'humanité' in WA Schabas (ed), *The International Criminal Court: A Commentary on the Rome Statute*, 2nd edn (Oxford University Press, 2016).
Schmid, E, *Taking Economic, Social and Cultural Rights Seriously in International Criminal Law* (Cambridge University Press, 2015).
Schmitt, C, *The Nomos of the Earth in the International Law of the Jus Publicum Europaeum* (Telos Press, 2006).
Schrijver, N, 'Self-Determination of Peoples and Sovereignty over Natural Wealth and Resources' in UN Office of the High Commissioner for Human Rights (ed) *Realizing the Right to Development: Essays in Commemoration of 25 Years of the United Nations Declaration on the Right to Development* (2013).
Schrijver, N, 'Fifty Years International Human Rights Covenants: Improving the Global Protection of Human Rights by Bridging the Gap between the Two Covenants' (2016) 41 *Nederlands Tijdschrift voor de Mensenrechten* 457.
SESA-SESPAS, 'La salud pública ante el caso Volkswagen' (2015) 15 *Revista de salud ambiental* 148.
Shahabuddeen, M, 'Does the Principle of Legality Stand in the Way of Progressive Development of Law?' (2004) 2 *Journal of International Criminal Justice* 1007.
Sillitti, O, and López Velásquez, MP, 'El proyecto COPLA para el establecimiento de una corte penal latinoamericana y del caribe contra el crimen organizado transnacional' in Olásolo H et al (eds), *Respuestas nacionales e internacionales al fenómeno de la corrupción: particular atención al ámbito iberoamericano*, Perspectivas iberoamericanas sobre la justicia 12 (Tirant lo Blanch, 2021).
Simester, AP, and von Hirsch, A, *Crimes, Harms and Wrongs: On the Principles of Criminalisation* (Hart Publishing, 2011).
Simma, B, et al, *The Charter of the UN – A Commentary*, Vol I, 3rd edn (Oxford University Press, 2012).
Skogly, SI, 'Crimes against Humanity-Revisited: Is There a Role for Economic and Social Rights?' (2001) 5 *The International Journal of Human Rights* 58.
Smith, SE, 'Inventing the Laws of Gravity: The ICC's Initial Lubanga Decision and Its Regressive Consequences' (2008) 8 *International Criminal Law Review* 331.
Smith, W, 'The Nuremberg Trials' (1946) 32 *American Bar Association Journal* 390.
Starr, S, 'Extraordinary Crimes at Ordinary Times: International Justice Beyond Crisis Situations' (2007) 101 *Northwestern University Law Review* 1257.
Stewart, JG, 'Overdetermined Atrocities' (2012) 10 *Journal of International Criminal Justice* 1189.
Stuckenberg, CF, 'Problems of "Subjective Imputation" in Domestic and International Criminal Law' (2014) 12 *Journal of International Criminal Justice* 311.
Sullivan, F Jr, 'The Rome Statute: Opportunities and Challenges in Enforcement' (2016) 26 *Indiana International & Comparative Law Review* 1.
Sutherland, EH, 'White-Collar Criminality' (1940) 5 *American Sociological Review* 1.
Sutherland, EH, Geis, G, and Goff, C, *White Collar Crime: The Uncut Version* (Yale University Press, 1983).
Sutton, AC, *Wall Street and the Rise of Hitler: The Astonishing True Story of the American Financiers Who Bankrolled the Nazis* (Clairview Books, 2010).
Taylor, MB, *War Economies and International Law: Regulating the Economic Activities of Violent Conflict* (Cambridge University Press, 2021).
Tooze, A, *Crash: cómo una década de crisis financieras ha cambiado el mundo* (Crítica, 2021).

Trial International, 'Evidentiary Challenges in Universal Jurisdiction Cases' (2019) *Universal Jurisdiction Annual Review* 1.

Turner, JI, 'Nationalizing International Criminal Law' (2005) 41 *Stanford Journal of International Law* 1.

Ufuoma, OK, and Omoruyi, O, 'Political Economy Diagnosis of Crude Oil Theft in Nigeria: The Way Forward' (2014) 5 *Mediterranean Journal of Social Sciences* 297.

Urs, P, *Gravity at the International Criminal Court: Admissibility and Prosecutorial Discretion* (Oxford University Press, 2024).

Vagias, M, *The Territorial Jurisdiction of the International Criminal Court* (Cambridge University Press, 2014).

Valarini, E, and Pohlmann, M, 'Organizational Crime and Corruption in Brazil a Case Study of the "Operation Carwash" Court Records' (2019) 59 *International Journal of Law, Crime and Justice* 1.

van den Herik, L, and Dam-de Jong, D, 'Revitalizing the Antique War Crime of Pillage: The Potential and Pitfalls of Using International Criminal Law to Address Illegal Resource Exploitation' (2011) 22 *Criminal Law Forum* 237.

Vest, H, 'Business Leaders and the Modes of Individual Criminal Responsibility under International Law' (2010) 8 *Journal of International Criminal Justice* 851.

Von Hebel, H, and Kelt, M, 'General Principles of Criminal Law and the Elements of Crimes' in RS Lee (ed), *The International Criminal Court: Elements of Crimes and Rules of Procedure and Evidence* (Transnational Publishers, 2001).

Von Hebel, H, and Kelt, M, 'What Are the Elements of Crimes?' in RS Lee (ed), *The International Criminal Court: Elements of Crimes and Rules of Procedure and Evidence* (Transnational Publishers, 2001).

Von Liszt, F, 'Der Zweckgedanke Im Strafrecht' (1883) 3 *Zeitschrift für die gesamte Strafrechtswissenschaft* 1

Walasek, H, *Bosnia and the Destruction of Cultural Heritage* (Routledge, 2016).

Weigend, T, 'Societas Delinquere Non Potest? A German Perspective' (2008) 6 *Journal of International Criminal Justice* 927.

Werle, G, and Burghardt, B, 'Do Crimes against Humanity Require the Participation of a State or a 'State-Like' Organization?' (2012) 10 *Journal of International Criminal Justice* 1151.

Werle, G, and Jessberger, F, '"Unless Otherwise Provided": Article 30 of the ICC Statute and the Mental Element of Crimes under International Criminal Law' (2005) 3 Journal of International Criminal Justice 35.

Wharton, S, 'Redrawing the Line? Serious Crimes of Concern to the International Community Beyond the Rome Statute' (2015) 52 *Canadian Yearbook of International Law/Annuaire canadien de droit international* 129.

Wheeler, CH, 'Justice in the Absence of the Accused. Can the Rights of Victims be Fully Vindicated without the Participation of the Accused?' (2019) 17 *Journal of International Criminal Justice* 413.

White, ND, 'Responses of Political Organs to Crimes by States' in A Nollkaemper and H van der Wilt, *System Criminality in International Law* (Cambridge University Press, 2009).

Whyte, D, 'Power, Crime and Deadly Deception' in D Gordon Scott and J Sim (eds) *Demystifying Power, Crime and Social Harm: The Work and Legacy of Steven Box* (Palgrave Macmillan, 2023).

Wiersing, A, 'Lubanga and Its Implications for Victims Seeking Reparations at the International Criminal Court' (2012) 4 *Amsterdam Law Forum* 21.

Wolf, ML, 'The World Needs an International Anti-Corruption Court' (2018) 147 *Daedalus* 144.

Zhang, W, 'The Relationship between Rule of Law, Human Rights, Good Governance and Democracy' in W Zhang et al (eds), *Human Rights and Good Governance* (Brill, 2016).

Zhou, HR, 'The Enforcement of Arrest Warrants by International Forces: From the ICTY to the ICC' (2006) 4 *Journal of International Criminal Justice* 202.

Index

www.ingramcontent.com/pod-product-compliance
Ingram Content Group UK Ltd.
Pitfield, Milton Keynes, MK11 3LW, UK
UKHW020844290926
15470UKWH00004B/1547

9 781509 986590